Evangelicals and Catholics in Nineteenth-Century Ireland

In this series

Evangelicals and Catholics in Nineteenth-Century Ireland

James H. Murphy

EDITOR

FOUR COURTS PRESS

Set in 10.5 on 12 point Bembo for
FOUR COURTS PRESS
7 Malpas Street, Dublin 8, Ireland
e-mail: info@four-courts-press.ie
http://www.four-courts-press.ie
and in North America by
FOUR COURTS PRESS
c/o ISBS, 920 N.E. 58th Avenue, Suite 300, Portland, OR 97213.

A catalogue record for this title
is available from the British Library.

ISBN 1–85182–917–2

Printed in England
by Antony Rowe Ltd, Chippenham, Wilts.

Contents

Contributors

WALTER L. ARNSTEIN is professor of history emeritus at the University of Illinois at Urbana-Champaign. His books include *The Bradlaugh case* (1984), *Britain yesterday and today: 1830 to the present* (2001) and *Queen Victoria* (2003).

MATTHEW BROWN is a graduate student at the University of Wisconsin-Madison, working on the topic of violence and nationalism in contemporary Irish and British fiction.

MARTIN DOHERTY is senior lecturer in history at the University of Westminster, London. Author of *Nazi wireless propaganda: Lord Haw-Haw and British public opinion in the Second World War* (2000) he is currently investigating sectarian disturbances and evangelical activity in late nineteenth-century Ireland.

TADHG FOLEY is professor of English at the National University of Ireland, Galway. He has recently published, both with Tom Boylan, a four-volume anthology, *Irish political economy* (2003) and *John Elliot Cairnes: collected works* (2004), in six volumes.

LOUISE FULLER is IRCHSS Government of Ireland post-doctoral fellow in the Department of Modern History at the National University of Ireland, Maynooth. She is the author of *Irish Catholicism since 1950: the undoing of a culture* (2004).

JILL BRADY HAMPTON is assistant professor of English at the University of South Carolina, Aiken. Her doctoral dissertation at the University of Southern Illinois-Carbondale was entitled, 'Voices outside the Irish Renaissance.'

JANCIE HOLMES is lecturer in Irish History at the University of Ulster, Coleraine. Author of *Religious revivals in Britain and Ireland, 1859–1905* (2000), she specializes in evangelicalism in nineteenth-century Ireland.

MARJORIE HOWES is associate professor of English and co-director of Irish Studies at Boston College. She is author of *Yeats's nations* (1996) and contributed to *The Field Day anthology of Irish writing*, volume iv.

EMMET LARKIN is professor of British and Irish history at the University of Chicago. Seven of the twelve volumes of his history of the Catholic Church in Ireland between 1780 and 1918 have now been published.

DAVID E. LATANÉ, JR is associate professor of English at Virginia Commonwealth University, Richmond. He is editor of the *Victorians Institute Journal*. His current research interest is William Maginn, on whom he recently contributed an entry to the *Dictionary of National Biography* (2004).

AMY E. MARTIN is assistant professor of English at Mount Holyoke College. She is working on a book entitled *Alter-nations: representing nationalisms, the state, and national identities in nineteenth-century Britain and Ireland*.

SHIRLEY MATTHEWS is a graduate student at Southampton University, working on the topic of public opinion and the campaign for Catholic emancipation.

JAMES H. MURPHY is associate professor of English and director of Irish Studies at dePaul University, Chicago. Among his recent books are *Ireland, a social, cultural and literary history, 1791–1891* (2003) and *Abject loyalty: nationalism and monarchy in Ireland during the reign of Queen Victoria* (2001).

PATRICK MAUME is a researcher with the *Dictionary of Irish biography*. He is author of *The long gestation: Irish nationalist life, 1891–1918* (1999) and, more recently, co-author of *Controversial issues in Anglo-Irish relations* (2004) and co-editor of *The Galtee boy: a Fenian prison narrative* (2004).

DAVID W. MILLER is professor of history at Carnegie Mellon University and author of *Queen's rebels: Ulster Loyalism in historical perspective* (1978).

MAUREEN O'CONNOR teaches in the Department of English at the National University of Ireland, Galway. She is co-editor of the forthcoming *Wild colonial girl: essays on Edna O'Brien*.

KATHERINE PARR is assistant professor of English at North Central College, Illinois. She has written on Mary 'Eva' Kelly and Lady Wilde and about the *caoineadh* in famine poetry.

G.K. PEATLING is a post-doctoral fellow at the University of Guelph, Canada. He is the author of *British opinion and Irish self-government, 1865–1925* (2001).

KARA M. RYAN is a graduate student at the University of Tulsa, working on the topic of nineteenth-century British and Irish women writers and the historical novel.

Introduction

JAMES H. MURPHY

Evangelicals and Catholics in nineteenth-century Ireland addresses a period of dynamic change in Irish society when a variety of often antagonistic religious movements had a profound effect on the shaping of Irish culture. At the end of the eighteenth century Wolfe Tone had famously expressed the desire to unite Protestant, Catholic and dissenter in Ireland. However, the nineteenth century saw the solidifying of more pronounced religious identities than ever. Just as the days of the Protestant Church of Ireland as the legally established church seemed threatened, both it and the dissenting Presbyterian Church were overcome with a tidal wave of evangelical enthusiasm, which led in many parts of Ireland to a zeal for the conversion of Catholics. Meanwhile, the Catholic Church was itself undergoing a devotional revolution and attaining new institutional strength. Assailed by the evangelical campaigning, the Catholic Church sought to strengthen its position through institutional support, especially in the area of education. In spite of a British distaste for what happened, the Catholic Church and, indeed, its rivals secured state backing for a system of denomination education.

These religious and educational changes were also mapped onto hardening political positions, with Church of Ireland members and Presbyterians forgetting their former differences and embracing a new common Protestant religious identity, a political commitment to the union of Ireland and Great Britain, and an Irish cultural identity which, inasmuch as it was distinctive, was also compatible with an allegiance to Britishness and the British empire. Equally, the equation of Irish nationalism with Catholicism seemed to grow inexorable through the century, though its initial formation, in the campaigns of Daniel O'Connell, was certainly at least in part the fault of Britain for denying what was rather grandly called Catholic emancipation and thus allowing a political nation to grow around the node of religious grievance.

The collection opens with a reconsideration of the concept of the devotional revolution. This term was coined by Emmet Larkin in 1972 to explain what he had identified as the sudden change in Irish Catholic religious practice in the third quarter of the nineteenth century, by which the majority Irish population became practicing Catholics, after the canons of the Council of Trent, in a manner in which they had not hitherto been. In the thirty or so years since then various scholars have argued that the change was a much less abrupt and a much more evolutionary one. Larkin's essay in this volume, 'Before the devotional revolution,' is nothing less than a magisterial analysis of the period before

9

the middle of the nineteenth century that comprehensively answers the critics of his devotional revolution theory. Combining empirical data with narrative history, in the manner so characteristic of his work, he shows 'that the level of Tridentine achievement in pre-famine Ireland was not sufficient because the social and economic resources necessary to such an achievement were not available to the Irish Church' until the famine had reversed the demographic trend. Further, he paints a fascinating picture of the Irish Catholic Church between 1750 and 1847 which he sees as *sui generis* in its reliance on the station mass as an instrument of pastoral outreach. The entire period is one, he argues, that 'deserves a better historical fate than being reduced to a mere Tridentine precursor or prolegomenon to the devotional revolution.'

In 1859, almost in the middle of the Catholic devotional revolution, the Presbyterians of Ulster experienced an extraordinary evangelical revival. Placing this event in the context of the growing search for self-identity of the Presbyterian Chuch in Ireland, David W. Miller considers the question which is posed in the title of his essay 'Did Ulster Presbyterians have a devotional revolution?' His answer is that the 1859 revival was a short-lived affair and did not substantially halt the move of the Presbyterian Church away from its communal roots towards middle-class respectability, with an attendant loss of working-class allegiance. The final examination of the concept of devotional revolution is my own, 'Unremembering the devotional revolution,' which tries to account for the loss of historical memory of the changes of the mid-nineteenth century, such that it came to be believed that Irish Catholics had always been adherents to Tridentine practice. In my reading of Charles J. Kickham's *Knocknagow* (1870) I argue that the description of the station mass in the novel is framed in terms that implicitly acknowledge the abuses, from a Tridentine perspective, which were present in the practice of station masses before the devotional revolution. What I suggest is 'that the unreformed practices of the station mass are not simply absent, they are demonstratively absent in Kickham's account. In other words, Kickham's description, in its keenness to forget the past, draws attention to it by highlighting the absence of abuses […] The memory of the older pattern of religious practice is thus paradoxically present through its pronounced absence.'

The second section of this collection takes us back to the period of Catholic emancipation and to the anxieties it caused both in Britain and in the Established Church in Ireland (the Church of Ireland). Fear of the growth of Catholic power was certainly one of the prime causes of the upsurge in the evangelical movement within the Established Church. The case of William Maginn, as described by David E. Latané, Jr, is typical of a pro-Establishment figure fighting a rear-guard action. He confronts change 'with rhetorical fireworks, mixed with an ironic appraisal of the chances of success,' while having little sympathy for the evangelical alternative. Charlotte Elizabeth Tonna was one who did embrace that option. Kara M. Ryan writes that her 'remedy for the Irish question is that disaffected Irish Catholics must be converted by a revitalized evangelical Protestantism.' This was a perspective that deeply influenced the writing of her novels, *The Rockite* (1823) and *Derry, a tale of revolution* (1833). Shirley Matthews, in '"Second spring" and "precious prejudices": Catholicism and anti-Catholicism in Hampshire in the era of emancipation', explores anti-Catholicism within British culture and tries to determine the extent to which it was a function of the rising tide of Catholic immigration. Her conclusion, at least as far as her local study of Hampshire is concerned, is 'that anti-Catholicism was not necessarily a reaction to a large Catholic or Irish presence, but was often a fear of the unknown.' Finally, Katherine Parr explores reactions to the famine through the prism of the work of two Young Ireland poets, the Anglo-Irish Jane Francesca Elgee (later Lady Wilde), and the Catholic Richard D'Alton Williams. Though employing similar religious imagery, Parr discerns the presence of a very different outlook and tone between the two poets.

'Configuring Catholicism' explores some of the ways in which Catholicism interacted with Irish culture. Marjorie Howes, in 'William Carleton's literary religion', challenges the concern which critics have traditionally had, when viewing William Carleton as an ethnographer of Irish peasant society, to establish his authority and authenticity on the basis of a supposed continuing loyalty to the Catholicism, which he had formally rejected. She refocuses the debate about Carleton away from speculation on interior states and onto religion as lived practice. She focuses on bodies and rituals. Carleton rewrites 'Catholic ritual and the sacred in sentimental and domestic terms.' And in his religio-literary imagination 'bodies figure in several ways: as the deceptive exteriors of Catholicism, as the natural, god-given foundation of rational Protestantism, and as objects that demand interpretation and therefore provide indexes that separate the discerning from the credulous viewer or reader.' In 'Nationalism as blasphemy: negotiating belief and institutionality in the genre of Fenian recollections,' Amy E. Martin notes the ways in which Fenians, such as John O'Leary, have been castigated for their apparent inadequacy as they fail to provide comprehensive histories of the Fenian movement in their published writings. She also draws attention to the ways in which they embraced the designation of Fenians as blasphemers and even heretics by the Catholic Church, which opposed them, as a clue to the real agenda of such recollections. 'By speaking from the position of blasphemer and heretic, Fenians articulate a nationalist politics that reckons with the problems of state formation, the sociopolitical role of the Catholic Church in Ireland, and the imbrication of Church and state in the 1860s, problems that were imminent and urgent as the process of decolonization approached at the end of the nineteenth century.' Jill Brady Hampton seeks to locate the perspective on both Catholicism and Protestantism of May Laffan, a novelist whose background and attitudes straddled the denominational divide. 'Throughout her fiction, Laffan's examination of social and religious conflict is directed toward portraying a pluralistic rather than a dichotomous Irish culture and society desperately in need of increased social activism and educational reform. Her work mediates rather than perpetuates conflicts in late nineteenth-century Ireland.' Finally, Louise Fuller outlines the career of Walter McDonald, professor of theology at St Patrick's College, Maynooth, who also ventured into the borders of what could be tolerated by Church authority, in his championing of the *Irish Ecclesiastical Record* and his writings on science and religion and on social questions such as peace and war. He managed to avoid being labeled a heretic but was subjected to a perhaps even more debilitating fate: 'The tragedy for McDonald, and perhaps for the Church of his day, was that because some of his ideas were seen as a threat to theological orthodoxy, and because he pursued them so doggedly, he came to be seen as somewhat of an eccentric genius, which meant that many of his ideas never received the hearing that they may have deserved.'

The fourth section of the book looks at various individuals whose careers intersect both with Ireland and other countries and in whose experience religion was an important element. Catholic or evangelical influences are strong in the stories of most, though not all, of them. G.K. Peatling looks at the writings of William Warren Baldwin, who had been born into an Irish Protestant gentry background, on the issue of the native population of Canada. He sees his legacy as a mixed one. Though his 'contribution to bi-sectarian amity in Ireland was […] limited, broadly it is true that evangelical religious impulses did the most to underpin the more humane dimensions of William Baldwin's thought, and ironically more so than the influences upon him of the secular humanism of the Enlightenment.' John Boyce, the Catholic priest and novelist, of whom Patrick Maume writes, resided in the United States but was preoccupied by Ireland in his fiction, to the extent that his reviewers accused him of subordinating Catholicism to Irishness. Indeed, he did insist 'that the lived faith of the Irish people represented an argument for Catholicism more formidable than any intellectual treatise,' and in so doing, argues Maume, prefigured the work of later priest-novelists such as Canon Sheehan, 'who blended devotional Catholicism with nostalgic images of a pious rural Ireland for emigré audiences and worried about the role of the priest amid the breakdown of older social hierarchies.'

The polarities of the influence of Ireland are reversed in Walter L. Arnstein's essay which retraces the interrelationship between Charles Bradlaugh, the radical English, Victorian atheist and parliamentarian, and Ireland. Bradlaugh's sympathies for Ireland and for the home rule movement of the 1880s were clear, but it was a sympathy which was not always reciprocated. Initially, many Irish MPs voted against attempts to allow Bradlaugh to remain in parliament without having to take an oath which compromised his atheism, a stand which was praised by the English Catholic hierarchy. By 1888, however, Irish MPs acquiesced in the measure which finally resolved the issue. Maureen O'Connor's subject is a person caught between even more Victorian dilemmas than Bradlaugh: Dublin-born, Frances Power Cobbe, who was variously a 'progressive reformer, iconoclastic theologian, lecturer, abolitionist, woman's advocate, and defender of animals.' Though she distanced herself from the formal institutions of Christianity, she paradoxically held to the superiority of Protestantism. 'There is an abundance of evidence for Cobbe's anti-Irish sentiments and repulsion towards Catholicism, no doubt deeply ingrained by the anti-papist siege mentality that was her cultural inheritance'. A progressive in so many ways, 'Cobbe's various modes of patriarchal resistance are at once stimulated and undermined by her experience as an Anglo-Irish woman, including a strain of unregenerate Protestant conservatism, which often erupts in inconvenient contradictions.'

Max Arthur Macauliffe, who is Tadhg Foley's subject, escaped from the force field of Irish and British Catholicism and Protestantism into the Sikh religion only to reproduce the patterns of the original dichotomy in the colonial context. A convert to the Sikh religion and an acclaimed translator of its religious texts into English, nonetheless, 'Macauliffe saw the Sikhs as India's indigenous "English".' Indeed, the Sikhs were the reformed Anglicans of the orient when compared with the Hindus. 'Like Matthew Arnold's flattering representations of the Irish, Macauliffe's magnificent contribution to Sikhism was also, and ultimately, in the interests of empire.'

The final section of the collection looks at the evangelical movement from a number of angles. Janice Holmes places the Irish movement in the context of its relationship with British evangelicals. She distinguishes between two types of networking, the unproblematic 'co-ordinative', and the much more problematic 'conversionist'. Because Irish evangelicals were surrounded by a largely Catholic population, conversion had distinctively political implications which British evangelicals found hard to fathom. 'Irish evangelicals may have wanted to eschew their ethnic and geographic origins, but the evangelical emphasis on conversion meant that they were never entirely successful in doing so.' The notion that the Church of Ireland retreated into a siege mentality after the 1869 measure to bring about its disestablishment is questioned in Martin Doherty's essay on the Arklow disturbances of 1890–92. He argues that in the late nineteenth century, 'the combination of reinvigorated Catholicism and politicized evangelicalism was both an engine and an indictor of the gradual worsening of sectarian relationships in many parts of the island.' His essay recounts the animosities caused by evangelical street preaching, initiated by the local Church of Ireland clergyman, in Arklow in the early 1890s and the difficulties it posed to the authorities at Dublin Castle who were anxious not to fan the flames of sectarian tension. Finally, Matthew Brown focuses on the controversy surrounding the famous address on evolution by John Tyndall to the meeting of the British Association for the Advancement of Science, held in Belfast in 1874. Yet this is only the starting point for an essay which explores the tension between models of cultural experience which contended with each other in nineteenth century society and which derived from the Darwinian conflict between science and religion. Brown contrasts a gradualist approach to cultural change, associated with the theory of evolution, with the notion of instant conversion, inherent in the evangelical experience, though he also notes that Tynall himself sought to accommodate the two. He further points out that, ironically, though the grad-ualist model seemed to prevail in the scientific realm, the notion of instanta-neous insight and change gained currency later on in the cultural and literary spheres, especially with modernist and Irish writers. Thus 'Yeats finds in Celticism, with its high degree of mysticism and pantheism, a profound narra-tive emphasis on instantaneous change.' Similarly, though less optimistically, the moments of insight or 'epiphany' in the works of Joyce also find their cultural antecedent in instantaneous conversion.

Evangelicals and Catholics in nineteenth-century Ireland is the product a confer-ence entitled, 'Structures of belief in nineteenth-century Ireland,' a joint inter-national conference of the Society for the Study of Nineteenth-Century Ireland and the Midwest Victorian Studies Association, which was held at DePaul University, Chicago, 16–18 April 2004. The running of the conference was gen-erously supported by the University Research Council and the College of Liberal Arts and Sciences and its dean, Dr Michael L. Mezey.

Before the devotional revolution

EMMET LARKIN

The purpose of this essay is to revisit the notion of the devotional revolution that I first advanced in an article in 1972 in the *American Historical Review*.[1] In this visit I propose to accomplish two things. First I shall attempt to settle the vexed question that has emerged about the timing of the devotional revolution, and second, which the first has, in fact, made mandatory, to examine more closely the question of the much-neglected pastoral role of the Irish Church in pre-famine Ireland. In regard to the timing of the devotional revolution, it will be recalled that in 1972 I argued that the Irish people *as a people* became, in the generation after the great famine of 1847, the pious and practicing Catholics they had remained down until that day. Since then, the main thrust of the criticism levelled at that notion has been to deny that the devotional revolution was really a revolution, but rather that it was a long-term, incremental, and evolutionary process. According to this historical scenario, the evolutionary process had been initiated at the Council of Trent in the sixteenth century, but the enactment of the Tridentine canons in Ireland was delayed by two centuries of Protestant persecution. With the relaxation, however, of the celebrated penal laws in Ireland about 1775, Tridentine reform began to emerge and gathered strength over the next one hundred years, when it finally achieved its full-flowering in the consolidation that took place between 1875 at the first Synod of Maynooth and 1962 at the Second Vatican Council. The historical validity of this evolutionary process obviously rests on what the Irish Church was able to achieve in regard to Tridentine pastoral and administrative reform in pre-famine Ireland, and whether that achievement was really sufficient to provide for a continuous evolutionary Tridentine transformation in post-famine Ireland.

I propose to demonstrate that the level of Tridentine achievement in pre-famine Ireland was not sufficient because the social and economic resources necessary to such an achievement were not available to the Irish Church. The pre-famine Irish Church was, in fact, frustrated in its pastoral efforts by a chronic shortage of clergy and an inadequate supply of space for worship, both of which were crucial to any

---

1 Since the system of quoting from the evidence in this essay is not quite orthodox, a word of explanation to the reader is in order. The problem of indicating a break or omission in a letter or document quoted in the text has been resolved by using the word 'then' in parenthetical interpolation. For example, '[T]he Roman authorities,' Curtis informed Murray on 8 May , 'have of late been very slow in responding to our expressed needs.' 'I am therefore,' he *then* observed, 'in not a very great hurry to reply to their request', indicates that between the last quotation and the previous one there has been a break in the original text.

effective concept of Tridentine reform. In an effort to compensate for this insufficiency of clergy and sacred space, the Irish Church introduced the unique Irish religious custom of stations. The custom involved transforming the Irish secular clergy into a part-time itinerant ministry in a circuit of their parishes for four months of the year at Christmas and Easter, when they collected their dues and provided their congregations with catechesis and the sacraments of confession and communion in the designated houses of their more substantial parishioners. While the custom of stations certainly had the pastoral advantage of rationalizing and alleviating the difficulties in regard to clergy and space, it also had the effect of further rooting religious practice in the home rather than in the church, which was totally at variance with the Tridentine norm of church-centered practice.

Before the uniqueness of the pre-famine Church can be truly appreciated, however, it is first necessary to understand that the society of which the Church was a social and institutional product was itself *sui generis*. About 1750 profound changes began to take place in the social and economic structure of Irish society because of the extraordinary growth in population and the adoption of the potato as the people's staple. This new and novel combination of blind social and economic forces resulted in an increase of the Catholic population by some five millions, or 270 per cent, between 1750 and 1847. This enormous increase in population had the effect, in turn, of creating a class society where the divide was drawn between those who had more than a potato patch and those who did not. The social impact of both this population growth and the creation of a very large subsistence economy obviously presented a massive challenge to the Irish Church in its efforts to respond to the pastoral needs of the Catholic community in pre-famine Ireland. How the Irish Church met this challenge and was uniquely shaped by it, therefore, is the crucial question to be resolved.

The most serious problem faced by the Church in pre-famine Ireland, and what finally determined the shape and structure of that Church, was the chronic shortage of priests in relation to the increase in the Catholic population. Just how serious the problem of the number of priests relative to the Catholic population had become in Ireland by 1840 is made clear by the following estimates of priests to people between 1770 and 1840 (see table one).

Table one: National ratios of priests to people, 1770–1840[2]

Year	Priests	Population	Ratio
1770	1,600	2,650,000	1,660
1800	1,860	4,200,000	2,260
1840	2,400	6,600,000	2,750

2 For the Catholic population in Ireland in 1770 and 1800 see the estimates of Stuart Daultrey et al., in Joel Mokyr and Cormac Ó Gráda, 'New developments in Irish popula-

While the Catholic population increased, therefore, by nearly 150 per cent between 1770 and 1840, the number of priests increased by only 50 per cent over the same period. The crucial point to be made in regard to these figures, however, is that a ratio of one priest to 1,660 people in 1770 already represented a heavy pastoral load, and the increase of that load by 66 per cent to 2,750 in 1840, simply turned a very difficult situation into a virtually impossible one. In comparing the ratios, for example, of priests to Catholic population, in a number of European countries in 1839, the *Irish Catholic Directory* noted that the ratio in France was about one to 800, in Austria one to 750, and in Prussia one to 900.[3] The *Directory* also pointed out that the French bishops thought the ratio of one to 800 in France too high, and would have preferred it to be about one to 650.[4] What must be made clear, however, is that these ratios of priests to people in the various continental Churches were based on the long-established Tridentine model for pastoral care. Because the reforms enjoined by the Council of Trent in the sixteenth century for the universal Church could not be generally applied or rigorously enforced in Ireland, given the state of the country in the seventeenth and eighteenth centuries, the Tridentine norm should be viewed more perhaps as an ideal upper limit than as a practical goal when discussing pre-famine Ireland. A more realistic ratio for providing adequate pastoral care for the Catholic community in pre-famine Ireland, especially given the more modest pastoral expectations of that community, would be about one priest to 1,700 people.

Because the ratios in table one represent only a national average, however, they actually mask some very considerable regional differences in the worsening ratios of priests to people over time in pre-famine Ireland. If the figures for 1800 and 1840, for example, are broken down into those which represent the four ecclesiastical provinces that then constituted the Irish Church, the regional differences are both interesting and revealing (see table two).

tion history, 1770–1850', *Economic History Review*, second series, 37:4 (1984), p. 475. Daultrey's estimates of the total Irish population have been reduced by twenty per cent to arrive at the Catholic population. For the total population in 1840 see the *Census of Ireland, 1841* (Dublin: HMSO, 1843). The census figure of 8,200,000 has also been reduced by 20% to arrive at the Catholic population. See also the appendix to this chapter for the Catholic population in 1840. For the number of clergy in Ireland in 1770 see Hugh Fenning, *The undoing of the friars in Ireland* (Louvain: Publications universitaires de Louvain, 1972), pp 278–85, 333–38. Fenning estimates the regulars at something more than 500, and the seculars at about 1,000, which would appear to be a little low. For the number of clergy in 1800 see the Charles Vane (ed.), *Memoirs and correspondence of Viscount Castlereagh, second marquess of Londonderry*, 12 vols (London, 1848–53), iv (1849), pp 97–173. For the number of Irish clergy in 1840 see the appendix. **3** *Irish Catholic Directory, 1839*, p. 154. The figure for Austria was given at 923, but this would seem to be incorrect, because the *Irish Catholic Directory's* own figures for the number of priests and Catholics in Austria work out at a ratio of one to 764. **4** Ibid., p. 145.

	Table two: Provincial ratios of priests to people, 1800–40[5]					
	Number of priests			*Ratio of priests to people*		
Province	1800	1840	%	1800	1840	%
Armagh	529	727	37	2,400	2,760	15
Cashel	543	758	40	2,640	2,970	13
Dublin	407	508	25	1,710	2,150	26
Tuam	381	407	7	2,100	3,080	47
Ireland	1,860	2,400	29	2,260	2,750	22

Positive percentage ratios represent a worsening of the ratio.

If these provincial ratios in table two are tabulated for 1800 and 1840 in four categories – less than 2,000; 2,000 to 2,400; 2,400 to 2,800; and more than 2,800 – and they are then represented on provincial maps (see maps one and two), the pastoral situation within and across the provinces becomes a good deal more intelligible. Everywhere the ratio changes for the worse between 1800 and 1840, and in the western province of Tuam the change is nothing less than calamitous.

The most obvious thing about the figures in table two is that although the ratio of priests to people worsened everywhere between 1800 and 1840, it did not worsen everywhere at the same rate. In 1800, for example, the ratio was worst in the provinces of Armagh and Cashel, but by 1840 it had only worsened in those provinces respectively by some 15 and 13 per cent because the number of priests had been increased by 37 and 40 per cent. On the other hand the ratio of priests to people in the province of Tuam, which in 1800 was second only to that of Dublin, had declined by some 47 per cent by 1840 because the number of priests there had only been increased by 4 per cent. Indeed, given the overall growth of population by some 57 per cent between 1800 and 1840, both Armagh and Cashel did relatively well in keeping pace with what was already in 1800 a patently impossible situation, while Dublin, surprisingly, did less well, and Tuam very poorly, in the light of their initially and relatively more favorable ratios in 1800. What is also interesting about these figures is that they do not reflect any necessary correlation to Catholic wealth. Dublin was reputed to be the wealthiest of the four ecclesiastical provinces with Cashel, Armagh, and Tuam ranking in that order after Dublin. It might have been expected, if Catholic wealth was the main determinant, therefore, that Dublin would have done better in maintaining its ratio of priests to people than either Cashel, or more especially, Armagh.

But perhaps the provincial figures in table two, like the national figures in table one, also serve to mask an even more complex situation both within and

5 See appendix for the number of priests and Catholics respectively for 1800 and 1840 on the provincial level.

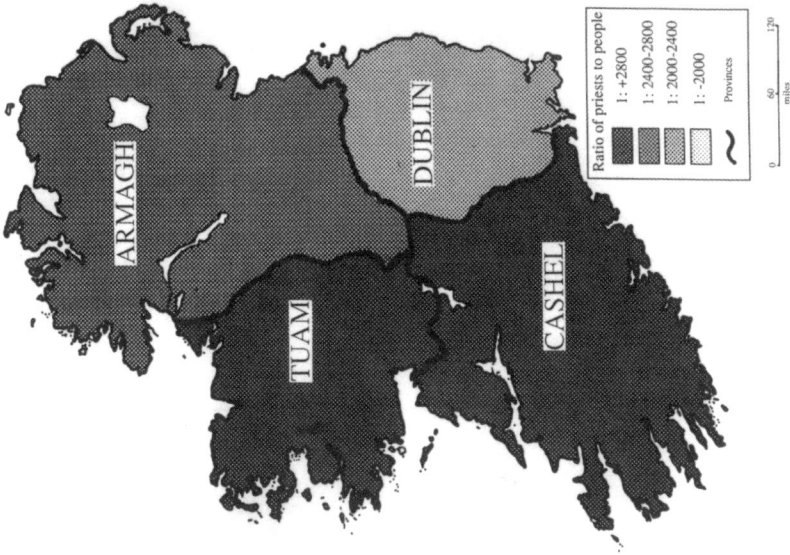

Map 2 Ecclesiastical provinces of Ireland, 1840

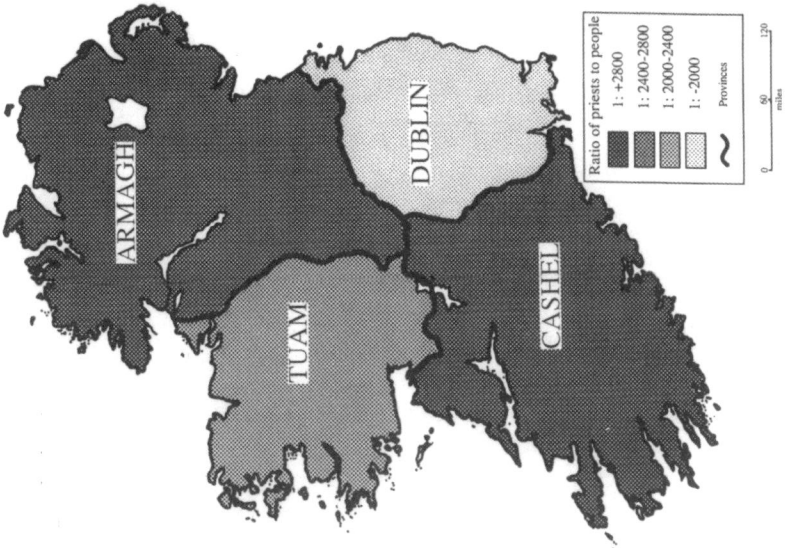

Map 1 Ecclesiastical provinces of Ireland, 1800

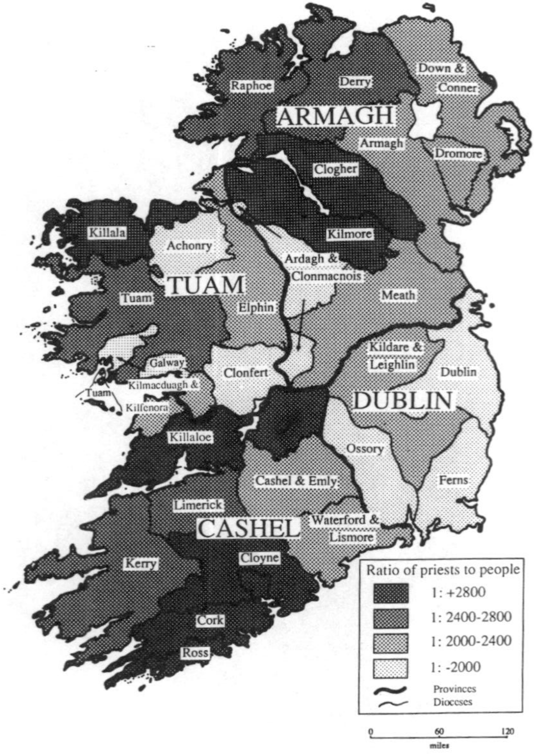

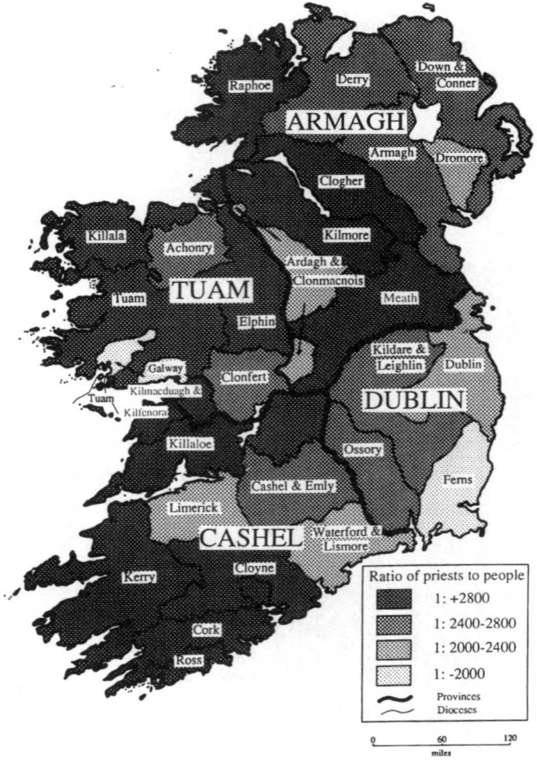

Map 4   Provinces and dioceses of Ireland, 1840

Map 3   Provinces and dioceses of Ireland, 1800

Map 5 Provinces and dioceses in pre-famine Ireland

across provincial boundaries. If the provincial ratios, for example, are further broken down for 1800 and 1840 into those for the twenty-seven dioceses that comprised the four ecclesiastical provinces (see table three and maps three and four), it becomes clear that even in those areas that made up the Catholic economic heartland (see maps five and six) in the east and south in pre-famine Ireland, the ability of the Church to provide an adequate number of priests had deteriorated to an alarming extent.

If these diocesan ratios in table three are tabulated for 1800 and 1840 in the four numerical categories that were used in the provincial maps, and they are then represented on diocesan maps, the pastoral situation within the dioceses and across the provinces becomes very graphic indeed. In 1800, 10 of the 27 dioceses in Ireland had a ratio of priests to people that was more than 2,400, and 6 of those 10 had a ratio of more than one to 2,800. By 1840, 20 of the 27 dio-

Dioceses	Ratios of priests to people		
	1800	1840	%[a]
ARMAGH	2,380	2,520	6
Ardagh	1,900	2,300	21
Clogher	3,200	3,100	−3
Derry	2,470	2,760	12
Down & Connor	2,090	2,630	26
Dromore	2,260	2,230	−1
Kilmore	2,960	3,010	2
Meath	2,160	2,890	34
Raphoe	2,710	3,390	25
TOTAL	2,410	2,760	15
CASHEL	2,280	2,650	16
Cloyne & Ross	3,350	3,420	2
Cork	2,830	3,500	24
Kerry	2,590	3,720	44
Killaloe	2,830	3,100	10
Limerick	2,360	2,340	−1
Waterford & Lismore	2,140	2,280	7
TOTAL	2,640	2,970	13
DUBLIN	1,510	2,060	36
Ferns	1,480	1,690	14
Kildare & Leighlin	2,130	2,480	16
Ossory	1,900	2,450	29
TOTAL	1,710	2,150	26
TUAM	2,410	3,460	44
Achonry	1,870	2,790	49
Clonfert	1,690	2,540	50
Elphin	2,150	3,530	64
Galway[b]	1,170	1,610	38
Killala	2,970	3,680	24
Kilmacduagh & Kilfenora	2,320	2,890	25
TOTAL	2,100	3,080	47
IRELAND	2,260	2,750	22

Table three: Diocesan ratios of priests to people, 1800–40[6]

a Positive percentages changes represent a worsening in the ratio of priests to people.
b Technically Galway did not become a diocese until 1831 when its first bishop was provided. Up until that time it was a wardenship.

6 See ibid. for the number of priests and Catholics respectively on the diocesan level.

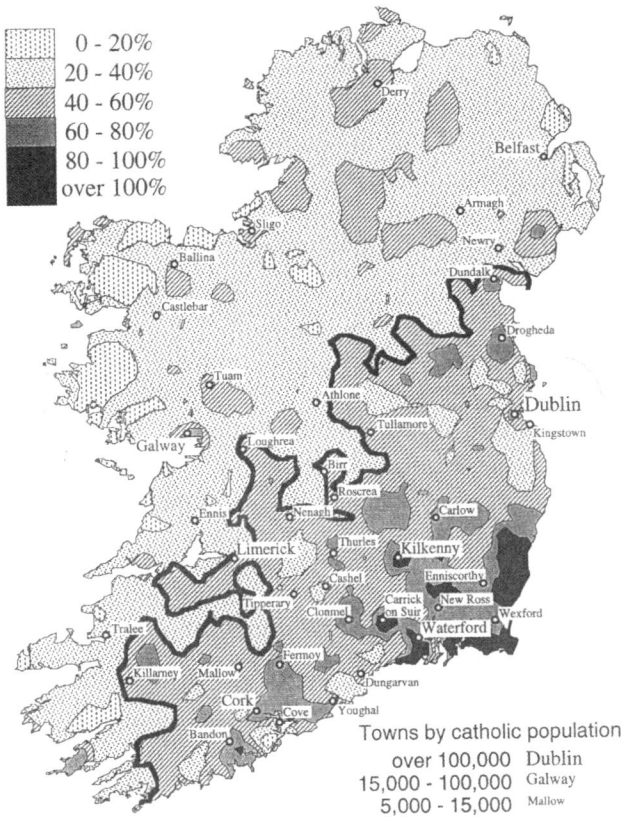

Map 6 Contour map of estimated mass attendance as percent of
Catholic population, 1834

ceses had a ratio of more than 2,400, and 12 of those 20 had a ratio of more
than 2,800. As critical as the situation had become in the north and west by
1840, however, that was not perhaps the most threatening aspect of the problem. What really proved most alarming was that the ratios of priests to people
in the Catholic economic heartland in the east and south, which was dominated
by the more than thirty-acre Catholic tenant-farming class, now also appeared
to be approaching the point of no return as far as their ratios were concerned.
This economic heartland (see map five), which may be roughly defined by
drawing a line from Galway city on the west coast to the town of Dundalk on
the east coast, and another line from Galway city to Clonakilty on the south
coast, and which was easily discernible on the diocesan map in 1800, had been
virtually obliterated by 1840. Though the decline in ratios was particularly pre-
cipitous in the dioceses of Dublin (36 per cent), Ossory (29 per cent), Meath

(34 per cent), and Clonfert (50 per cent), it was in fact general everywhere in this most prosperous part of Catholic Ireland.

If all the dioceses in Ireland, moreover, are ordered from the best to the worst in terms of the percentage improvement or decline in their ratios between 1800 and 1840, no diocese showed any improvement. The small improvement in the diocese of Clogher (−3 per cent) was not only marginal, but the ratio for that diocese since 1800 had been one of the worst in Ireland. Even the ratios for the only two remaining bright spots in Ireland in 1840, the dioceses of Ferns and Galway, had worsened by 14 per cent and 37 per cent respectively between 1800 and 1840. Indeed, on more careful analysis, the case of Galway proves to be a very special one. The reason for the more favorable ratio there in 1840 was really the result of a fortuitous combination of circumstances that did not obtain elsewhere. Galway not only had a very large number of regular clergy (17) in relation to the total number of priests (40) in the diocese, but the diocese was virtually confined to the city of Galway and its environs, and it was not therefore burdened with a large rural hinterland, which had a tendency, as in the dioceses of Cork, Limerick, and Dublin, where there were also significant numbers of regular clergy, to worsen the priest to people ratio.

At whatever level, national, provincial, or diocesan, therefore, the ratios of priests to people are examined, they clearly demonstrate not only that the ratios had worsened virtually everywhere in Ireland between 1800 and 1840, but that since 1770, at least, they had never been really satisfactory with regard to providing for the pastoral needs of the Catholic population. By the 1820s this was also certainly very clear to the Irish bishops and clergy. When, for example, the very able and articulate parish priest of Skibbereen in the diocese of Cloyne and Ross, and later bishop of that diocese (1827–1832), Michael Collins, gave evidence before a select committee of the House of Commons in London on 11 June 1824, on the state of Ireland, he was asked by a member of the committee 'whether you consider that the number of the Catholic clergy has increased in the same proportion with the population of their respective parishes?'[7] 'There has been,' Collins replied, 'an increase in the number of the Catholic clergy, but I do not think the number has increased in proportion to the population.' The member then asked, 'do you conceive that the duties cast upon each Catholic clergyman have considerably augmented of late years?' 'I do not believe,' Collins explained, 'that at any time there were an adequate number of clergymen for the performance of the duties, and they are still less adequate in proportion now than ever, in consequence of the increase in population.' 'Do you consider,' Collins was then asked, 'that the number of persons that attend to their religious duties diminishes or increases?' 'They diminish,' Collins responded, 'in consequence of the inability of the priests to attend them all.' 'What number of coad-

7 *Parliamentary papers*, 'Second report of the select committee of the House of Commons appointed to inquire into the state of Ireland,' minutes of evidence, sessional papers 1825, viii (129) (hereafter 'State of Ireland, 1825'), pp 356–7.

jutors,' the member then finally asked, 'do you employ in that district?' 'Only one,' he replied, 'I have not the means of supporting more.'

Several days later, when Collins was recalled as a witness on 14 June, the subject of his pastoral load was again brought up. 'Have you and your assistant in your parish,' he was asked, 'sufficient opportunities of attending to all the religious duties of the numerous people living in it?'[8] 'We endeavor to instruct them,' Collins explained, 'but many of them cannot hear our instructions from the smallness of the places of worship; and then our duties are very laborious, our numbers being small. We have two chapels to attend to, and each of us celebrates two masses on Sundays and holidays, in each of those chapels.' 'What other laborious duties,' the member further inquired, 'have you to perform in the course of a week?' 'The sick are very numerous,' Collins replied, referring to the administration of last rites, 'and they must be attended.' 'Do you,' the member asked, somewhat incredulously, 'attend all the sick that apply?' 'Certainly;' Collins replied, adding that 'the confessional is a labour that must be likewise attended to, though from the fewness of our numbers we are not able to hear the whole of those who apply; and in a wide district of country, the priest on horseback loses a great deal of time going from place to place.' In the course of his evidence, Collins had also explained that he and his curate were responsible for the care of nearly 10,000 souls in the parish of Skibbereen, and that as recently as 1822, when the potato crop failed in their part of the country, more than 6,000 of his parishioners had to be classified as paupers and were only saved from starvation by private charity. On the parish level, Skibbereen undoubtedly represented the lower limit in the ability of the Irish Church to provide enough priests for the pastoral needs of its people in pre-famine Ireland.

When the select committee reconvened in London the following year in February 1825, a representative number of the Irish Catholic bishops were also summoned to give evidence before it. Among those who testified was the celebrated bishop of Kildare and Leighlin, James Warren Doyle (1819–1834), who was certainly among the most zealous and successful pastoral reformers of his day in the Irish Church. During the course of his very able testimony on 25 March 1825, Doyle was asked by a member of the committee, 'Do you consider the number of priests in your diocese to be adequate to the full performance of their religious duties?'[9] 'The priests in my diocese,' Doyle explained, 'are perhaps somewhat more numerous in proportion to the number of people to be served, than in most others in Ireland; the reason is that I have a college at Carlow, to which a lay school is attached, and from the profits of that lay school we have been enabled to put together a very considerable sum of money; and by the interest of this money we are enabled to support a president and vice-president, and a competent number of professors; and hence we are, in my diocese, enabled to educate at Carlow such a number of priests as are wanted

---

8 Ibid., pp 364–5. **9** Ibid., pp 198–9.

immediately in the diocese itself.' 'But I will state,' Doyle added, by way of qual-
ification, 'that not withstanding this supply of ours, which is greater than can be
found in any other diocese perhaps in Ireland, we have not yet employed upon
the mission, more than two-thirds of the number which would be necessary for
the due discharge of the priestly functions amongst the people; the reason however is, not that I could not furnish a sufficient number of priests, because I have
at my disposal the college to which I have just alluded, but I do not like to
burden the people who are too much weighed down with other claims, by
sending amongst them an additional number of priests, who of course should
be supported by their contributions.'

In considering Doyle's reply to the select committee, a number of important and significant points emerge. First, in spite of all his pastoral zeal and
energy, as well as his being very advantageously placed with Carlow College as
a seminary to train his clergy, it should be noted that Doyle had still not been
able by the time of his death in 1834 to improve on what the ratio of priests to
people had been in Kildare and Leighlin in 1800. In 1800 there had been 88
priests in the diocese for a ratio of 2,150 and in 1835, there were 131 priests for
a ratio of 2,210.[10] There is little doubt that the significant increase of 49 per cent
in the number of priests between 1800 and 1835 was largely the result of
Doyle's own heroic efforts from 1819 to 1834 because his immediate predecessors had been notoriously lax in fulfilling their pastoral duties as bishops.[11]
Under the leadership of Doyle, in fact, the diocese of Kildare and Leighlin was
a good example of the upper limit in what could be achieved in terms of providing priests for the people, and it is worth noting that by 1840, only six years
after the death of Doyle, the number of priests serving in the diocese had fallen
from 131 to 120, and the ratio of priests to people had worsened by more than
12 per cent, or from one to 2,210 to 2,480.[12] The second important point to

---

10 'First report of the commissioners of public instruction, Ireland,' *Parliamentary papers*, sessional papers 1835, xxxiii (45), appendix two, p. 52. This list of 45 parish priests, one admin-
istrator, and 62 curates for Kildare and Leighlin does not include the bishop, the 3 curates in
his mensal parish of Carlow, and 19 regulars. For the number of priests in Kildare and
Leighlin in 1800 see appendix. 11 W.J. Fitzpatrick, *The life, times and correspondence of the Right
Rev. Dr Doyle, Bishop of Kildare and Leighlin*, 2 vols (Dublin: James Duffy, 1880), i, pp 126–8.
12 For the number of priests in Kildare and Leighlin in 1840 see appendix. In the early
spring of 1843, the bishop of Kildare and Leighlin, Francis Haly, wrote Paul Cullen, rector of
the Irish College in Rome, explaining that the very serious down-turn in the Irish economy,
consequent on three successive bad harvests and a deepening depression in trade, had also
resulted in very hard times for his clergy. 'So diminished have been the incomes of the
parochial Clergy,' Haly reported, 'as a necessary and inevitable consequence of this depression
that I am seriously apprehensive for some time that I shall be under the necessity of withdrawing from some parishes portions of the younger Clergy, the means of supporting them
having suffered so great and so alarming a diminution. If that should be the case – which
Heaven Avert – I shall be able to assist your foreign missions with an active, pious, and zealous Clergy', Cullen Papers (C), archives of the Irish College, Rome, 8 April 1843.

emerge from Doyle's evidence before the select committee was that he did not believe the number of priests was two-thirds of what was necessary to provide adequate pastoral care for his flock.

In other words, the number of priests in Kildare and Leighlin would have to be increased by about 50 per cent, and in 1825, at the time of his evidence, that would have resulted in a ratio of about one priest to 1,700 people. Finally, the third important point to emerge from Doyle's testimony was that, in the last analysis, the real problem in providing enough priests for the adequate pastoral care of his people was not either in finding suitable candidates with vocations for the priesthood, nor even in securing the means to pay for the training of those candidates, but rather in acquiring the necessary financial resources from the Catholic community at large to support a greater number of priests. Indeed, the parish priest of poverty-stricken Skibbereen in west Cork, and the bishop of Kildare and Leighlin in the more affluent Catholic economic heartland both faced the same fundamental problem – how to find the necessary resources to support an increase in the number of clergy. In whatever way, therefore, quantitatively or qualitatively, the evidence regarding the ratios of priests to people down to 1840, is examined, the ineluctable fact that emerges from its consideration is that the economic resources available were not adequate to provide the number of priests necessary to meet the basic pastoral needs of an ever-burgeoning Catholic population, let alone provide pastoral care on a Tridentine model.

The second most serious problem faced by the Irish Church in its efforts to meet the pastoral needs of its people between 1770 and 1847 was the acute shortage of church and chapel accommodation. This problem of providing suitable space for Catholic worship, like that of the shortage of clergy, was also initially rooted in the chronic lack of resources of the Catholic community and greatly exacerbated by the enormous growth in the Catholic population after 1750. From about 1790 until 1847 there was inaugurated in Ireland a significant period of new chapel building. The first stage of this boom, which was to continue until 1815, was initially based on the agricultural prosperity induced by the great increase in British demand caused by both the large growth in population and improved standard of living that was the result of the industrial revolution that was taking place in Britain. This phenomenon, which had begun in the 1760s, was greatly accelerated during the wars of the French revolution and the imperium between 1793 and 1815. During that period, agricultural prices doubled in Britain and Ireland, and in the wake of the increased prosperity for the Catholic-farming class many of the old chapels and 'mass houses' were leveled, and new 'barn chapels' were built in their stead.

This gradual replacement of the older 'mass houses' by the larger and more permanent 'barn chapels' was a very slow and uneven process.[13] The pattern of

13 Kevin Whelan, 'The Catholic parish, the Catholic chapel and village development in Ireland', *Irish Geography*, 16 (1983), p. 8. See for the classical example of chapel

improvement between 1790 and the great famine in 1847 was markedly a regional phenomenon. The most rapid progress was made in the east and south, in the Catholic economic heartland and in the cities and the towns, while the slowest improvement was in the far west and north. The chief exception to the pattern was in north-east Ulster where a developing industrial revolution, especially after 1820, was beginning to increase the general level of prosperity, even for Catholics, in this Protestant economic heartland, While the new chapel building boom began nearly everywhere in the Catholic economic heartland in the 1790s, it peaked in the various dioceses in different decades before the famine. In 1835, in fact, the very remarkable religious census published for Ireland in that year made it patently clear what the achievement in chapel building had been and where over the previous forty years (see table four).

The census reported that in 1834 there were some 2,109 chapels in Ireland.[14] Given the fact that there were 1,029 parishes in Ireland in 1835, the average number of chapels per parish was about 2.0. If this national average is broken down in terms of ecclesiastical provinces and dioceses, both the regional and local pictures become a good deal clearer.

Table four: Diocesan ratios of chapels to parishes and people to chapels, 1834[15]

Dioceses	Chapels	Parishes to parish	Chapels	Population to Chapel	People
ARMAGH	120	51	2.4	309,564	2,580
Ardagh	60	43	1.4	195,056	3,251
Clogher	81	37	2.2	260,241	3,213
Derry	70	37	1.9	196,614	2,809
D & C[a]	82	39	2.1	154,029	1,878
Dromore	34	17	2.0	76,275	2,243
Kilmore	76	45	1.7	240,593	3,166
Meath	156	66	2.4	377,562	2,420
Raphoe	36	29	1.2	145,385	4,038
TOTAL	715	364	2.0	1,955,319	2,735
CASHEL	88	46	1.9	296,667	3,371
C & R[b]	119	52	2.3	436,627	3,669
Cork	73	35	2.1	303,984	4,164

metamorphosis, the transformation over time of River chapel, near Courtown, in north Wexford from an early eighteenth-century mass house to a Victorian Gothic church in the late nineteenth century. **14** 'First report,' appendix three, p. 74. **15** See 'First report', for numbers of chapels in Ireland, 'Summary', pp 9–45, and 'Corrected summary', appendix III, pp 68–74. For numbers of parishes, see *Irish Catholic Directory, 1836*, passim, supplemented by the lists of parish priests in 'First report', appendix two, pp 38–66. For population figures, see 'First report', appendix III, pp 68–74.

Kerry	76	45	1.7	297,131	3,910
Killaloe	111	49	2.3	359,585	3,240
Limerick	78	40	2.0	246,302	3,158
W & L^c	78	37	2.1	253,091	3,245
TOTAL	623	304	2.0	2,193,387	3,521
DUBLIN	121	48	2.5	391,006	3,231
Ferns	91	37	2.5	172,789	1,899
K & L^d	110	46	2.4	290,038	2,637
Ossory	94	32	2.9	209,848	2,232
TOTAL	416	163	2.6	1,063,681	2,557
TUAM	118	50	2.4	405,306	3,435
Achonry	33	25	1.3	108,835	3,298
Clonfert	44	23	1.9	119,082	2,706
Elphin	80	43	1.9	309,761	3,872
Galway	16	12	1.3	62,664	3,917
Killala	30	24	1.3	136,383	4,546
K & K^e	34	21	1.6	81,642	2,401
TOTAL	355	198	1.8	1,223,673	3,447
IRELAND	2,109	1,029	2.0	6,436,060	3,052

a Down and Connor; **b** Cloyne and Ross; **c** Waterford and Lismore; **d** Kildare and Leighlin; **e** Kilfenora and Kilmacduagh.

Table four indicates that the provinces of Armagh and Cashel approximated the national average with 2.0 chapels per parish, while the province of Dublin was significantly above the national average with 2.6, and the province of Tuam lagged behind with 1.8. When the figures for Armagh and Cashel are broken down into dioceses, they reveal that the worst ratios for chapels to parishes were in the far west, namely Raphoe and Kerry respectively. The buoyancy of the figures for the four dioceses in the province of Dublin speak for themselves, while those for the province of Tuam confirm as they did in Armagh and Cashel that the problem of the lack of chapels was again largely confined to the far west, namely Achonry, Galway, and Killala.

When all the counting and estimating is done, it appears that in 1834 there was enough chapel accomodation for almost 3,400,000, or nearly 52 per cent of the Catholic population, but the census had reported that only 2,700,000 faithful attended mass.[16] In 1834, therefore, the Irish Church was able to meet the

16 The figure of 3,400,000 for the chapel accommodation available in 1834 was arrived at by multiplying the 2,109 chapels in Ireland by the estimated of 800 places for each chapel, which comes to 1,687,000, and then doubling that figure for the two masses each priest was permitted by his bishop to celebrate on Sundays, and holy days, for a grand total of 3,374,000. Miller estimates mass attendance at about 42% of the total Catholic population of 6,436,000

demand for space for worship, but why did the demand only involve about half the Catholic population, and who were those 2,700,000 that attended mass in 1834? The evidence appears to indicate that they were, for the most part, essentially those 500,000 Catholic tenant farmers who held more than three acres, and who numbered with their families and shopkeeper cousinhood in the towns, something more than 3,000,000, or nearly half of the total Catholic population of 6,436,000 in 1834.[17] This class had been in the making and increasing slowly with the growth in population since 1750 while a corresponding class, rooted in the subsistence economy based on the potato, had been increasing at a more rapid and accelerating rate during the same period, until by 1834 the two classes were about numerically equal. The two classes, though very distinct from each other, were not in themselves homogeneous. In the tenant-farmer class there was an obvious gradation, or hierarchy, since there was a considerable difference between the three-acre tenant and the more than thirty-acre farmer, while in the subsistence class, there was a real distinction between the poor, who depended on their labor for survival, and the very poor, or paupers, who were the objects of charity and immiserated in a culture of poverty.

The system of stations, which emerged concurrently with this evolving class society in pre-famine Ireland, was, of course, the Irish Church's response to a unique and extraordinary pastoral challenge.[18] By 1800 the system had become vital to sustaining Catholic religious practice The system of stations contributed in two very significant ways. The first was economic and the second was pastoral. Economically, stations provided for the greater part of the annual income of the Irish clergy right up to the advent of the famine. Pastorally, stations allowed the crucial tenant farming class to practice, however attenuated in its form, their religion, and thus retain their identity as Catholics.

In regard to the first of these achievements, the stabilizing and eventual improvement of clerical income, it should be noted that by 1800, the secular, or parish clergy, had won their struggle with their chief rivals, the regular clergy, or friars, for scarce resources by ironically taking a leaf out of friars' book in successfully substituting stations for the friars' traditional mode of questing among the

---

or 2,700,000. See David W. Miller, 'Irish Catholicism and the great famine', *Journal of Social History*, 9 (1975), 81–98. **17** For the figure of 500,000 Catholic tenant farmers holding more than three acres, see 'Returns of agricultural produce in Ireland, 1847,' *Parliamentary papers*, sessional papers, 1847–8, House of Commons, lvii, 112. The total number of farmers who held more than three acres was 660,489. If that figure is reduced by 20% for those farmers who were Protestant, and further reduced by 5% to distinguish the occupiers from the holders of land, the number of Catholic tenant farmers is 501,972, which if multiplied by 5.5 to determine family size comes to 2,858,471. If to that number is added their shopkeeper cousinhood in the towns of some 200,000, the total comes to 3,058,471. See Emmet Larkin, 'Church, state, and nation in modern Ireland', *American Historical Review*, 80:5 (1975), pp 1145–6, note 3. **18** Emmet Larkin, 'The rise and fall of stations in Ireland, 1750–1850', in Michel Lagrée, *Chocs et Ruptures en Histoire religieuse fin XVIII–XIX siécles* (Rennes: Presses Universitaires de Rennes, 1998), pp 19–32.

laity for their support. By 1800, in fact, the friars had been eclipsed by the seculars as a vital force in the Irish Church, having been reduced from 800 in 1750 to some 400, most of whom had been obliged to become parish clergy in order to survive.[19] Between 1800 and 1840, the secular clergy further consolidated their economic position by increasing more than three-fold their annual parish incomes. In 1800, for example, the average annual income of the 1,000 parish priests was £85, which included wide regional differences, from £63 in the far west, to £114 in the heart of the Catholic economic heartland in the southeast.[20] The more than a three-fold increase by 1840 was not only further complicated by regional differences, but also by population growth and price movements.

The role of stations, however, in furnishing the core of that income and in augmenting its improvement was crucial. The essential core consisted of fees and dues. The fees were the customary payments for the rights of passage, namely, baptisms, marriages, and funerals. The dues included the voluntary payments by the head of each household of a shilling at the Christmas and Easter stations. These dues were also, of course, greatly augmented by the some eighty days of hospitality provided by the laity at the stations for the parish priest, his curate, his clerk, and their animals. In 1800, the proportion of dues to fees was on the order of about one to one, or half, while by 1830, it was more than two to one, or two-thirds.[21] The variable that most impacted on this proportion over time, especially outside the Catholic heartland, was the number of paupers, or 'insolvents', among the heads of households, who were exempted from paying dues. The greater the number of paupers, therefore, the greater was the tendency to reduce the proportion of dues to fees. In spite of the large increase in the number of the poor, however, the dues increasingly made up a greater proportion than the fees, especially in the Catholic economic heartland, because the more substantial among the tenant-farming class significantly increased their contributions.

Indeed, in 1831 the bishops of the province of Dublin in order to redress this increasing imbalance between dues and fees legislated in synod a new tariff for fees.[22] The bishops defined four economic groups in the Catholic community – the wealthy, the well-off, the less well-off, and the paupers. The fees for the rites

19 Ibid., p. 24. 20 See, for average annual income in 1800 of parish priests, Vane, *Castlereagh memoirs*, iv, pp 102–73. The evidence for the more than three-fold increase is too complicated to be presented coherently here and one example will have to serve for all. The income of the parish priest of Kenmare, in the diocese of Kerry, averaged for the seven years (1839–1846) before the famine some £293. The return for the parish of Kenmare in 1800 was £65. For the averaged income of £293 see *O'Sullivan journal*, Kerry diocesan archives, p. 84. 21 For 1800 see Vane, *Castlereagh memoirs*, iv, p. 124 for report of the Archbishop of Cashel – 'The Easter and Christmas offerings constitute, on an average, one-half of all the emoluments of every parish in said Diocese', referring to Cashel and Emly. For 1830, see evidence of bishop of Kildare and Leighlin, 'State of Ireland, 1825', p. 185. For more than two-thirds see 'State of Ireland, 1825', p. 187. 22 *Statuta diocesana, per provinciam Dubliniensem, edita et promulgata, hebdomada quarta mensis Julii, A.D. 1831* (Dublin: Richard Coyne, 1831), pp 83–6, capitulum 24, de debitis colligendis.

of passage for the wealthy were confided, as was customary, to their traditionally generous and charitable disposition, while the well-off were now obliged to contribute twice what the previous tariff in force had enjoined, namely, 5s. for baptisms, £2 for marriages, and 10s. for funerals. The less well-off were left to enjoy their previous dispensation of half the newly imposed tariff, while the paupers continued to be exempted, unless they volunteered an offering. The dues collected at stations, however, continued to provide the stable core of clerical income into the 1840s, though the winds of change and reform were beginning to blow more strongly. Clerical incomes were, in fact, being further enhanced, independently of fees, and dues in cash and kind, by the increased earnings of the ubiquitous farmer priests, and the salaries afforded by the all the new chaplaincies to the poor houses, prisons, hospitals, and nunneries.[23] The very significant growth in clerical incomes between 1800 and the famine, and especially that of the parish priests, had certainly raised the clergy to an elite status in the Catholic community, and the system of stations had been the key element in the creation of that income and status. Perhaps it is best to leave the last word in this matter to the parish priest of Kenmare, John O'Sullivan, in 1843. 'We had,' O'Sullivan noted in his diary on 11 October, 'a station at Dirun this day, got 29 shillings there. How well the poor people pay in general.'[24] 'I certainly enjoy,' he then added most tellingly, 'more real independence than many estated gentlemen about me.'

In turning to the pastoral contribution of stations, to sustaining the Irish Church in pre-famine Ireland, it is once again necessary to emphasize how seriously religious practice continued to be impaired by the worsening of priests to people ratios between 1770 and 1840. That practice, therefore, especially in regard to the sacramental system, was not only severely limited for most of the Catholic community, but particularly for those who occupied the bottom half of the socio-economic pyramid. The sacraments of confession and communion were generally received only twice a year at the Christmas and Easter stations. The defining obligation for a practicing Catholic before the famine was not mass attendance, but the fulfilling of one's Easter duty, which entailed going to confession and receiving communion between Ash Wednesday and Ascension Thursday, the neglect of which was not just a mortal sin, but also involved the threat of excommunication and deprivation of a Christian burial. In the diocese of Kildare and Leighlin in 1829, for example, the bishop, James Doyle, made the distinction between Easter duty and regular communion clear when he reported that 74 per cent of his flock made their Easter duty while only some 10 per cent were monthly communicants during the year.[25]

---

23 The number of nunneries, for example, expanded from 6 in 1800 to 91 in 1846. For 1800, see Vane, *Castlereagh memoirs*, iv, p. 101, and for 1846 see *Irish Catholic Directory, 1846*, p. 332. All of these nunneries required a Catholic chaplain. The Irish Poor Law in 1839 authorized the building of 130 poor houses and in 1848 authorized the building of 33 more, many of which were provided with chaplains. **24** Kerry Diocesan Archives, O'Sullivan papers, *Diary*, 11 October 1843. **25** Thomas McGrath, *Religious renewal and reform in the pastoral ministry of*

Nearly twenty years later in May 1847, in the midst of the great famine, the archbishop of Dublin, Daniel Murray, in writing to the prefect of Propaganda in Rome, continued to emphasize the crucial role of stations in sustaining the fundamental obligation of going to confession and receiving communion at Easter. 'In order that all could comply with this precept,' Murray reminded the cardinal, referring to the requirement of Easter duty, 'it was conceded by the Holy See, because of the scarcity of priests, that the time within which it could be done would be extended from Ash Wednesday to the Feast of the Ascension of the Lord, and in certain dioceses to the Feast of SS. Peter and Paul.'[26] 'If an interruption of this kind should happen abruptly,' Murray then warned, alluding to the abolition of stations, 'it is feared the farmers, who are far away from the parish church [...] would neglect the Divine Altar longer than might be warranted, and gradually they would neglect the precept to attend to their Easter duty.'

Archbishop Murray's chief concern in 1847, it would appear, was for the neglect by the farming class of their religious duties if stations were suddenly abolished. What, however, was the pastoral situation with regard to sacramental practice of that class that made up the other half of the socio-economic pyramid, and especially the quarter that occupied the very bottom of that pyramid? Some insight into their condition was provided in a long affidavit in November 1843 submitted by Thomas Chisholme Anstey to the Propaganda authorities, complaining bitterly about the pastoral neglect by the Irish clergy of their people.[27] In the course of his 12,000-word indictment, Anstey told the story of having been invited by a local gentlemen in the diocese of Elphin to attend the first communion of the children who had been catechized by his daughter at the charity school he had founded in his parish. 'And this Affirmant accordingly,' Anstey reported, 'attended at the Function, and saw many old and young, having Tapers lighted in their hands':

> and these the said Lady informed him, were First Communicants, and she said that the Parents, and Grand parents and other adult and aged relatives of the Children had taken the opportunity of her coming to instruct the latter, to receive instructions themselves with a view to receiving their first Communion; and amongst others an old man then kneeling at the Rails, who only a fortnight before had been all his life ignorant of the real presence of Christ in the Eucharist, having never heard of the existence of such a Doctrine. Nevertheless he and all the rest were always Catholics, and so had their Ancestors been before them, and had received Baptism in the Church, and many had been married therein and all meant therein to live and die.

Bishop James Doyle of Kildare and Leighlin, 1786–1834 (Dublin: Four Courts, 1999), p. 231, 'Appendix 5: annual and monthly communicants, 1820–3, 1829'. **26** Archives of the Sacred Congregation for the Evangelization of Peoples, Rome, *Scritture referite nei congressi, Irlanda (S.R.C.)*, xxix , fols. 128–31. **27** Ibid., xxviii, fols. 121–45.

Anstey concluded with the following observation:

> [a]nd she said that there were many such cases as these, and it was a
> common thing for the people to pass from Birth to Burial without any
> other Sacraments than Baptism in Infancy, and the last Sacraments at the
> hour of death; with perhaps marriage in the interval; all which was
> owing to the neglect of the Priests, and never the less the Parish priest of
> that Parish derived for himself, without counting what his Curates
> received out of the parochial Revenues, an income of not less, as this
> Affirmant believes, something more than Four hundred pounds a year.'

Anstey's charge of willful neglect on the part of the Elphin clergy, as the
cause of the spiritual destitution of which he was an actual witness, however, is
certainly mitigated by the fact that the ratio of priests to people in that diocese
in 1840 (see table three), was among the worst in Ireland at one to 3,530. What
has not been generally appreciated, moreover, is that this appalling pastoral
workload in pre-famine Ireland was both increased and aggravated by a whole
series of additional activities and commitments on the part of the clergy, some
baneful and others salutary, that further impaired their pastoral effectiveness. The
more baneful of these activities was the result of an increased incidence in clerical misbehaviour, which included avarice, drunkeness, immorality, contumacy,
and faction.[28] The more salutary included the efforts of the clergy to provide
chapels, schools, and charity for the poor as ministers of God, as well as their
deep commitment to secular politics as tribunes of the people in the movements for Catholic emancipation and repeal of the union. The point to be
made, of course, is that all these extra-curricular activities, both baneful and
salutary, had the effect of further reducing the time and energy they could
devote to their more strictly pastoral and religious obligations.

In order to bring this discussion full circle, and also by way of concluding it,
I will now consider the constitutional implications of the emergence of a unique
Irish Church in pre-famine Ireland. Though a society and its institutions, as has
been premised in this essay, may be constrained by the blind economic and social
forces that shape it, those forces are in turn tempered by the political response of
that society and its institutions to those forces. So it was with the workings of the
legislative and executive dimensions of the constitution of the Irish Church that
emerged in pre-famine Ireland. In regard to legislative reform, for example, the
thrust of virtually all the legislation enacted by the Irish bishops in pre-famine
Ireland was the result of purely practical rather than Tridentine considerations.
The regulations and ordinances provided by the bishops, in fact, were pragmatic
and *ad hoc* measures designed to correct pressing abuses. The regulation of fees
and dues, and hospitality at stations, by the Cashel bishops in the 1780s in

---

28 Emmet Larkin, 'The devotional revolution in Ireland, 1850–1875', *American Historical Review*, 77:3 (1972), pp 627–31.

response to the protests and threats of the Whiteboys, for example, is an appropriate case in point.[29] When the bishops of the province of Tuam met formally in synod in May 1817, moreover, they proceeded to regulate the perceived abuses in the conduct and behaviour of their secular and regular clergy. On forwarding their decrees, as required, to Rome for approval, they found that the Propaganda authorities were very disturbed by their failure to observe the Tridentine norms in their legislation.[30] The decrees were returned for revision and were not finally approved until some eight years later in 1825, after they had been minutely corrected and revised to Rome's satisfaction.[31] When the four bishops of the province of Dublin, therefore, decided to take collective legislative action in synod in 1831, they took the unprecedented step of meeting collectively and privately to prepare their legislation and then simultaneously convening four diocesan synods, which were not formally required, as provincial synods were, to submit their legislation to Rome for approval, thus avoiding a Roman review of their decrees.[32] Three years later, in 1834, the nine bishops of the province of Armagh followed the precedent of their Dublin colleagues and assembled individually in nine diocesan synods to enact their also preconcerted provincial legislation.[33] This extraordinary behaviour on the part of the Dublin and Armagh prelates was apparently the result of not only their fixed determination to avoid the unfortunate consequences of Roman procrastination, but also an indication of their perception of the needs of a Church in a state of crisis.

In turning finally to the exercise of executive authority in the governing of the pre-famine Church, that constitutional development may be easily traced in the emergence of the Irish bishops as a self-conscious, corporate, and national body in the sixty years before the famine.[34] The birth of that body, in fact, may be dated from the first meeting of the four archbishops in November 1788, which was soon extended to meetings that included their representative suffragan bishops, and then eventually to meetings of the whole of the some twenty-six Irish bishops. By 1820, the bishops as a body had begun to meet annually for the next thirty years on a regular basis. These annual meetings were not taken to be synodical because the solemnities of that mode were not observed in either their form or procedure. As to their form, for example, there were no requirements in regard to either dress or attendance, and as to procedure, they were parliamentary, civil, and majoritorian in contradistinction to the synodical, hierarchical, and consensual mode. The

29 Larkin, 'Rise and fall', pp 25–6. **30** Archives of the Sacred Congregation for the Evangelization of the Peoples, Rome, *Acta*, clxxxii (1819), fols. 127–51, 'Esame dei decreti del sinodo provinciale Tuamense in Ibernia tenuto nei giorni 6, 7, e 8. di Maggio, 1817.' **31** *Acta*, clxxxviii (1825), fols. 259–274, 'Ristretto con summario sulla approvazione dei decreti del sinudo provinciali di Tuam tenuto nei Maggio, 1817.' **32** See note 22. For an account of the background to the meetings, see William Meagher, *Notices of the life and character of His Grace, Most Rev. Daniel Murray, late Archbishop of Dublin* (Dublin: Gerald Bellew, 1853), pp 128–31. **33** Ambrose Macaulay, *William Crolly, archbishop of Armagh, 1835–1849* (Dublin, Four Courts, 1994), pp 108–11. **34** Sean Cannon, *Irish episcopal meetings, 1788–1832* (Rome, Pontificia Studiorum Universitas a S. Thoma Aq. in Urbe, 1979), pp 44–124.

meetings, moreover, were presided over by one of the Irish archbishops, who was
not invested with any pontifical authority, while the agenda was prepared by the
body, and the resolutions arrived at were not referred to Rome, unless there was a
serious difference of opinion among the bishops, and the minority formally
decided to appeal to Rome. This gradual emergence of the body of the Irish bishops as a constitutional presence in the governing of the Irish Church, needless to
say, did not sit well with the Roman authorities, and throughout this whole
period, the Romans were very suspicious and wary about what they believed to
be the incipient Gallican and Febronian tendencies of the Irish Church, which
was yet another worriesome sign of the unique nature of the Church in pre-
famine Ireland.[35] The point, of course, is that the pre-famine Church was not an
Ultramontane Church, much less a Tridentine Church.

What is there to be said finally about pre-famine Ireland? In fine, that society and its Church were *sui generis* because what came both before and after
them were essentially different. The structure of Irish society was fundamentally
transformed by the demographic factor after 1750, and again more dramatically
in 1847. In the interim there emerged a singular world and a way of life that has
been best described in *The traits and stories of the Irish peasantry* by William
Carleton. That world was often very ugly and life was nasty, brutish, and short.
The poverty, the hunger, the ignorance, the violence, and the sectarianism, however, were all partially redeemed by an extraordinary zest for life, which became
the hallmark of that society and its Church. Indeed, the most remarkable characteristic of the Irish people and their clergy in this period was their enormous
vitality. From their monster meetings, temperance processions, house stations,
and chapel building to their secret societies, endemic drinking, faction fighting,
and clerical misbehaviour, they displayed a prodigious energy and determination.

The great famine dealt a mortal blow to this world and its way of life by
sweeping away the largest part of the bottom of the social pyramid. 'Every day,'
the *Limerick and Clare Examiner* explained sadly on 5 January 1850, more than
three years after that awful social catastrophe, 'brings a fresh bundle to the faggot
heap by which the funeral pyre of the old Celtic race is burned to cinders.
Landlords crippled – farmers crushed – shopkeepers ruined – and the poor rot-
ting in heaps – aye in heaps among the bogs and ditchpits of the country.'[36] Not
only does that remarkable world and way of life that was laid low by the famine
require a more dignified historical epitaph, but the Church that informed that
world and its way of life deserves a better historical fate than being reduced to
a mere Tridentine precursor or prolegomenon to the devotional revolution.

---

35 Roman-Irish relations became especially tense after 1815. The lowest point in that rela-
tionship perhaps was reached under Pius VIII (1829–31). See Dublin Diocesan Archives,
Murray Papers, 1830, 30/2, Patrick Curtis, Archbishop of Armagh, to Daniel Murray, 4
December 1830, for a good summary of the existing tensions in regard to the alleged Irish
Gallicanism by Rome.   **36** Quoted in Ignatius Murphy, *The diocese of Killaloe, 1850–1904*
(Dublin, Four Courts, 1995), p. 13.

APPENDIX: CATHOLIC POPULATION AND PRIESTS IN PRE-FAMINE IRELAND

Dioceses	Pop. 1834	Pop. 1800 est.	Priests 1800	Pop. 1840 est.	Priests 1840
ARMAGH	309,564	202,013	85	317,449	126
Ardagh	195,056	127,288	67	200,025	87
Clogher	260,241	169,826	53	266,870	86
Derry	196,614	128,305	52	201,622	73
Down and Connor	154,029	100,515	48	157,952	60
Dromore	76,275	49,775	22	78,218	35
Kilmore	240,593	157,005	53	246,721	82
Meath	377,562	246,387	114	387,179	134
Raphoe	145,385	94,874	35	149,088	44
TOTAL	1,955,319	1,275,988	529	2,005,124	727
CASHEL	296,667	193,597	85	304,224	115
Cloyne and Ross	436,627	284,931	85	447,749	131
Cork	303,984	198,372	70	311,727	89
Kerry	297,131	193,900	75	304,700	82
Killaloe	359,585	234,656	83	368,744	119
Limerick	246,302	160,730	68	252,576	108
Waterford and Lismore	253,091	165,160	77	259,538	114
TOTAL	2,193,387	1,431,346	543	2,249,258	758
DUBLIN	391,006	255,160	169	400,966	195
Ferns	172,789	112,758	76	177,190	105
Kildare and Leighlin	290,038	189,271	90	297,426	120
Ossory	209,848	136,941	72	215,193	88
TOTAL	1,063,681	694,130	406	1,090,775	508
TUAM	405,306	264,492	110	422,363	122
Achonry	108,835	71,023	38	111,607	40
Clonfert	119,082	77,710	46	122,115	48
Elphin	309,761	202,142	94	317,651	90
Galway	62,664	40,893	35	57,527	40
Killala	136,383	89,000	30	139,857	38
Kilmacduagh & Kilfenora	81,642	53,278	28	83,721	29
TOTAL	1,223,673	798,538	381	1,254,841	407
IRELAND	6,436,060	4,200,002	1,860	6,599,99	2,400

Sources: See for Catholic population in 1834, 'First report of the commissioners of public instruction, Ireland', *Parliamentary papers*, sessional papers 1835, xxxiii (45), appendix three, pp 68–74. The estimates of the Catholic population for 1800 and 1840 are derived from a proportion of the total population and Catholic population in 1834 and the total population in 1800 and 1840. The number of priests in 1800 is derived from Vane, *Castlereagh memoirs*, iv, pp 97–173, and those for 1840 from the *Irish Catholic Directory, 1840*.

Did Ulster Presbyterians
have a devotional revolution?

DAVID W. MILLER

The question which I posed for myself in the title of this essay may seem to have an obvious answer. In 1859, squarely within the quarter-century, 1850–75, which Emmet Larkin identified in his 1972 article as the period in which Irish Catholicism underwent a 'devotional revolution', Ulster Presbyterianism experienced a religious revival of cataclysmic proportions. At least in the short run the 1859 revival had an impact on religious behaviour comparable to, say, dozens of Marian apparitions, hundreds of parish missions, thousands of novenas. Whether all that short run change adds up to a 'revolution' in the long run is another matter.

Revivals are relatively brief, intense, episodes generally associated with a long-run change known as the rise of something called *evangelicalism*. To make sense of the 1859 revival we must consider how Ulster Presbyterianism fits within the rise of evangelicalism in the Atlantic world. In my view much of the substantial historical literature on evangelicalism written in the past three decades is flawed by its preoccupation with theology, the ideas of the religious professionals.[1] Certain sociologists of religion in this same period have come up with a model which at least marginally improves on this approach.[2] Religious systems are seen as operating in a marketplace: the high levels of religious practice in contemporary America, when compared to Europe, result from a 'free market' rather than a 'monopoly' in religious 'products'. I myself find this market *model* to be shallow and mechanical, but I think that a market *metaphor* can be quite useful. Yes, of course, religion is a commodity, but as a commodity it closely resembles whiskey:

---

1 See Mark A. Noll, David W. Bebbington and George A. Rawlyk (eds), *Evangelicalism: comparative studies of popular Protestantism in north America, the British Isles, and beyond, 1700–1900* (New York: Oxford UP, 1994); George Rawlyk and Mark A. Noll (eds), *Amazing grace: evangelicalism in Australia, Britain, Canada, and the United States* (Montreal & Kingston: McGill-Queen's UP, 1994); D.W. Bebbington, *Evangelicalism in modern Britain: a history from the 1730s to the 1980s* (London: Unwin Hyman, 1989); David Hempton and Myrtle Hill, *Evangelical Protestantism in Ulster society, 1740–1890* (London: Routledge, 1992); George M. Marsden, *Fundamentalism and American culture: the shaping of twentieth-century evangelicalism, 1870–1925* (Oxford UP, 1980); Michael J. Crawford, *Seasons of grace: colonial New England's revival tradition in its British context* (New York: Oxford UP, 1991).   2 Roger Finke and Rodney Stark, *The churching of America, 1776–1990: winners and losers in our religious economy* (New Brunswick, NJ: Rutgers UP, 1992).

it is a commodity which can readily be manufactured by the consumer. The professionals of different religious systems compete not only with each other's products but also with the home-brewed output of their own customers. A good example of such marketing initiatives is the Church of Ireland's movement in the two decades following the 1798 rebellion toward the vital religion promoted by Wesley and his followers. Before 1816 there was no Methodist denomination to compete with, but there were numerous Methodist lay fellowships among ordinary Anglicans. The 'evangelical' turn in the Church of Ireland was an adaptation of official religion to popular demand among its own devout. This marketing ploy, I might add, was accompanied by the development by elite laymen and some clergy of a new product line, the Orange Order, which provided rituals by which less devout Anglicans might act out their Protestantism without the inconvenience of regular church attendance.

So I see religious change primarily as an outcome of complex interactions between religious professionals and ordinary folk – between official religion and popular religion. In the Ulster Presbyterian case we have terms to describe the principal doctrinal products on offer by the clergy: they are called 'old light' and 'new light'. However, we lack a comparable set of terms for what was invented and/or demanded by lay folk. I propose two terms to fill that vacuum: 'old leaven' and 'new leaven'. By 'new leaven' I mean the conversionist enthusiasm associated with pietism in Germany and with Methodism in the English-speaking world in the eighteenth century. When most historians use the term 'evangelicalism' they have in mind the intellectual and organizational structures crafted by religious professionals since about 1740 as they came to terms with these powerful – sometimes frightening – popular movements. By 'old leaven' I mean the much more politicized sources of popular enthusiasm which Protestantism enjoyed *prior to* about 1740. In England the old leaven was most spectacularly on display in the 1640s and 1650s when a welter of movements – Diggers, Levellers, Baptists, Fifth Monarchy Men, Muggletonians, Quakers, etc. – threatened to overturn the social and political order. The erastian confessional state of the eighteenth century had considerable success in stamping out whatever remained of the old leaven of the 'rude mechanic preachers' and their enthusiastic audiences. Wesley himself had to contend with elite suspicions that since his preaching drew large and excited crowds it must be a reappearance of the old leaven.[3] However Methodism eventually convinced the authorities that it was a new leaven purged of the political agenda of the old and became a respectable, if not quite a fashionable, religion in nineteenth-century England.

Although the English old leaven was largely eliminated in the eighteenth century, the same was not true for Scotland where politico-religious enthusiasm had taken the name of Covenanting. The Williamite settlement incorporated most of the old leaven into the Church of Scotland; initially only a tiny

---

3 Bernard Semmel, *The Methodist revolution* (New York: Basic Books, 1973), pp 13–17.

minority of the Presbyterian enthusiasts – those revolutionaries who were unwilling to settle for 'Presbyterianism in one country' – remained outside the establishment. For the first two decades after the revolution the main components of the popular Presbyterian vision of an established church which was not a state church – a situation in which *the* Church was controlled by the godly, not by the wealthy and well-born – seemed to be secure. After the union of 1707 English politicians, with the collaboration of the Scottish ecclesiastical party known as the 'moderates', chipped away at the elements of the Scottish establishment central to the old leaven vision – most notably through the reintroduction of lay patronage, the right of the laird – or sometimes the crown – to appoint the minister without the approval of the congregation. As a result, at about the same time Wesley was beginning his career of preaching the new leaven, a number of clergy seceded from the Church of Scotland because of its deviations from the old leaven. Although the moderates continued to dominate the General Assembly until the 1830s, a strong minority sympathetic to the seceders' position remained. This 'popular party' – one is tempted to call them the 'immoderates' – came to be known as the 'evangelicals' even though, in the words of a recent student of their theology,

> their perceptions of the nature of saving faith and such central doctrines as the Atonement were orientated towards an intellectual rather than an experiential conception of conversion and faith, and their preaching was not directed to the emotions of their hearers in the way that later nineteenth-century evangelical preaching often was.[4]

Although the meanings of 'evangelical' in English and Scottish Christianity did eventually converge, we will misunderstand developments well into the mid-nineteenth century if we fail to distinguish between their origins in the peculiar enthusiasms of new and old leaven respectively.

The power of the new leaven to evoke religious commitment is relatively easy to understand. By appealing to the emotions and fostering an experience in which the individual might attain a sense of assurance of his or her own salvation, the new leaven might seem to enjoy a clear advantage over more intellectual preaching in reaching ordinary folk of limited education. However, to understand the appeal, and even the nature, of the old leaven we need consider some specifics of the history of Presbyterianism in Scotland and its diaspora, and the north of Ireland is actually quite a good place to start. It was in Ulster that the terms 'old light' and 'new light' were coined during a protracted crisis in the Synod of Ulster in the 1720s. The new lights were a Belfast-centred group of ministers who were seeking alternatives to rigid Calvinism. From what we can

---

4 John R. McIntosh, *Church and theology in Enlightenment Scotland: the popular party, 1740–1800* (East Linton: Tuckwell, 1998), p. 237.

tell the alternative which most attracted them was Arminianism – the century-old reformed heresy which allowed the individual more agency in bettering his moral status than Calvin would admit.[5] And indeed, when the old light/new light controversy replicated itself a few years later on the Pennsylvania frontier the term new light was applied to revivalists who, almost by definition, were subject to suspicion of Arminianism. Over the next century the Irish and American usages of 'new light' diverged as the Irish new lights drifted toward Unitarianism. The term 'old light', however, was virtually unchanging in its connotation: it signified insistence that every minister must subscribe to the Westminister Confession of Faith.

What is interesting for our purposes is that the pressure to require subscription, from at least the 1720s, came principally from laymen. Why should it be so important to country folk whether their ministers espoused such Calvinist abstractions as limited atonement and unconditional election? To answer this question we need to understand that Scottish Presbyterianism was, to use a term coined by Margo Todd, 'logocentric'. Between 1560 and 1640 a largely illiterate Scottish laity was systematically indoctrinated with Calvinist teachings, an effort which was supported by the power to withhold communion and the vigilance of a Taliban-like religious police.[6] One can scarcely wonder that simple folk still accustomed to view access to the host as necessary to avoid physical disease as well as eternal punishment might now come away with the notion that the way to salvation was primarily a matter of having the right answers. Although this wholesale catechizing certainly subordinated ordinary laity to the religious elite in the short run, the persecutions of the later seventeenth century meant that clergy found themselves no longer imposing their theological system upon the indifferent, but rather celebrating the faithfulness of the godly. We should not be surprised if godly lay folk took from the experience a heightened sense of their own agency in maintaining doctrinal purity. A conviction among laymen that their order bore special responsibility to protect the old light from clerical derogation became central to the old leaven.

When the American historian George Marsden describes the Scotch-Irish as 'notorious hagglers over doctrinal detail,'[7] he identifies, perhaps unintentionally, a ritual manifestation of the old leaven: contesting by various means the orthodoxy of the minister, or ministerial candidate. Since Presbyterianism was not the established church in Ireland, we do not find in Ulster the most dra-

5 I.R. McBride, *Scripture politics: Ulster Presbyterians and Irish radicalism in the late eighteenth century* (Oxford: Clarendon, 1998), p. 45; A.W. Godfrey Brown, 'A theological interpretation of the first subscription controversy (1719–1728)', in J.L.M. Haire et al., *Challenge and conflict: essays in Irish Presbyterian history and doctrine* (Antrim: W. & G. Baird, 1981), pp 28–45. **6** Margo Todd, *The culture of Protestantism in early modern Scotland* (New Haven: Yale UP, 2002), pp 1–126. **7** George M. Marsden, *The evangelical mind and the New School Presbyterian experience: a case study of thought and theology in nineteenth-century America* (New Haven: Yale UP, 1970), p. 39.

matic Scottish ritual of this sort: the riot to prevent the new minister and his military escort from entering the church – or to force him to enter through a window or some door other than the main entrance, which, in the popular mind invalidated his installation.[8] Nevertheless, Ulster does present various less drastic rituals of social inversion in which the literate but unreflective could challenge the well-read, perhaps even well-born, minister and thereby act out the role in the kingdom of God which the old leaven, as they understood it, conferred upon them. Such rituals might include grilling the ministerial candidate, registering complaints about a minister at periodic presbytery visitations of the congregation, attending the outdoor sermon of an itinerant Covenanting minister, or withdrawing altogether from the pastoral care of one's minister to join a nearby Seceding congregation. We should think of these challenges of the well-read leader of the community as a peculiarly Scottish ritual comparable to carnival in southern Europe; it was a means of sustaining the social order by turning the world upside down, if only for a day.[9] The satisfactions of haggling were as central to the appeal of the old leaven as were the ecstasies of palpable conversion experience to the new leaven.

Just as official Presbyterianism conceived its mission, in Calvin's terms, to be a ministry of sacrament as well as of the word,[10] so also popular Presbyterianism of the old leaven supplemented its logocentric haggling rituals with a sacramental ritual reminiscent of the days of persecution. This ritual was the festal communion or 'holy fair'. The outdoor clandestine communion services of covenanting days evolved into a post-1690 procedure by which in many parts of Scotland and the north of Ireland communion was typically observed once or twice a year at an outdoor location where members of two or more congregations gathered for several days of preaching and prayer, culminating in the actual partaking of bread and wine around rustic tables. Since the participants came from different parishes, the communion token – that peculiarly Presbyterian contribution to sacramental apparatus – was invented to insure that only those certified as worthy by lay elders of their kirk sessions were admitted to the sacrament at that dramatic moment known as the fencing of the tables. In Ulster we should see the festal communion as complementary to the haggling. Where the latter was a ritual of social inversion, the former was a ritual of social integration. The fencing of the tables did certainly draw a boundary around the godly, but a penumbra of the less devout who attended the event mainly in the interest of sociability, refreshment and dalliance ensured that, in Ulster at least, these occasions functioned

8 Kenneth J. Logue, *Popular disturbances in Scotland, 1780–1815* (Edinburgh: John Donald, 1979), pp 168–76.   9 Emmanuel Le Roy Ladurie, *The peasants of Languedoc* (Urbana: University of Illinois Press, 1976), pp 192–7; Peter Burke, *Popular culture in early modern Europe* (New York: New York UP, 1978), pp 185–91; see H.G. Graham, *The social life of Scotland in the eighteenth century* (London: A. & C. Black, 1937), pp 366–71.   10 John Calvin, *Institutes of the Christian religion* (Grand Rapids: Eerdmans, 1989), IV, i, 9.

to affirm an ethnoreligious community which transcended godliness. In that respect they resembled patron saints' days, known as 'patterns' among Catholics in rural Ireland.

Here I must pause to address an historiographical problem. It is a commonplace that the Scottish Presbyterian festal communion evolved into the revivalist camp meeting in America. In recent years this development has been explored by several scholars – most brilliantly by Leigh Eric Schmidt. It is important to understand, however, that this historical process involved discontinuities as well as continuities. In Scotland the old leaven and the new intermingled as early as the Cambuslang 'Wark', a 1742 festal communion which took on the appearance of what came to labelled after 1800 a 'revival',[11] and further examples occurred over the succeeding century. Schmidt points out that in such sacramental occasions in Scotland the ecstasy reported by communicants was understood not as a once-for-all conversion, but as a recurring annual experience. Its function was 'to rejuvenate those who were already God's people as much as to convert the unregenerate'.[12] In the terms which I am using, the old leaven was not completely driven out by the new until the early nineteenth century when the sacrament itself was dropped from such occasions in America. A shortcoming of Schmidt's work is that he pays practically no attention to Ulster which was so often a one- or two-generation staging area for a family's passage from Scotland to America. In the case of Ulster, no evidence of Presbyterian festal communions turning into revival-like occasions has come to light for the period from the crucial 1730s until 1859.[13] What did happen was the *invention* of a tradition of Ulster revivalism. A manuscript account of religious commotions in the 1620s which resembled a modern revival was discovered by James Seaton Reid and reported in 1834 in the first volume of his history of Irish Presbyterianism. Advocates of a revival seized upon this event as a living tradition in the spiritual repertoire of their community, but in fact whatever happened in the 1620s had been generally forgotten in the intervening two centuries.[14]

---

11 In all the *Oxford English dictionary*'s eighteenth-century quotations illustrating usage of 'revival' to mean a religious reawakening, the word is followed by a modifier such as 'of religion.' Only from 1818 does the *OED* document the elliptical usage which we now take for granted: 'The Methodists of Cincinnati are very zealous and have what they call "a revival" in the country.' However, a search of a large on-line database of published books (WorldCat) reveals a spate of titles containing this elliptical usage beginning in 1801. **12** Leigh Eric Schmidt, *Holy fairs: Scottish communions and American revivals in the early modern period* (Princeton: Princeton UP, 1989), pp 153–58. **13** Marilyn J. Westerkamp, *Triumph of the laity: Scots-Irish piety and the great awakening, 1625–1760* (New York: Oxford UP, 1988), p. 134. Westerkamp probably means that such Irish Presbyterian revivals did not happen in the 1740s, but no evidence of any such events between then and 1859 seems to have come to light. **14** James Seaton Reid, *History of the Presbyterian church in Ireland* (Belfast: William Mullan, 1867) [vol. i originally published 1834], i, 106–12. We know that these events had been forgotten because S.M. Stephenson in a carefully-written local history, *A historical essay on the parish and congregation of Templepatrick: compiled in the year 1824* (Belfast: Joseph Smyth,

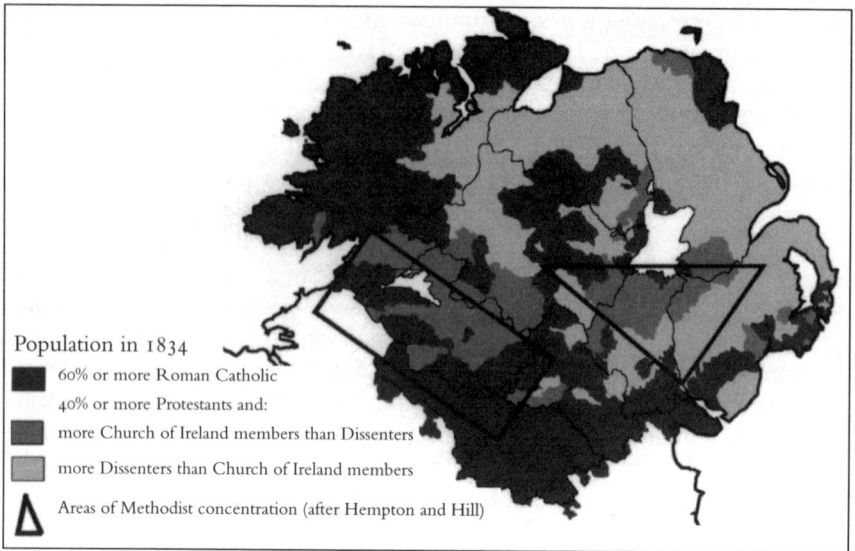

Figure 1 Sectarian zones in 1834

Festal communions did certainly continue to be celebrated in Ulster as late as the first decade of the nineteenth century, but it was the Seceders – the champions of the old leaven – who kept them alive. No doubt these sacramental occasions quietly nurtured the spiritual development of the godly, but without the outward manifestations of emotional convulsion in which the new leaven came to Scotland. The likeliest way for Ulster Presbyterians to come into contact with the new leaven was through John Wesley and other Methodist itinerants, but in fact Methodist impact in Ulster was largely confined to Church of Ireland folk, as can be seen in figure one. Indeed, why bother to listen to a Methodist preacher denounce your minister as unconverted when you and your peers enjoyed so much latitude, through the Presbyterian haggling rituals, to take such matters into your own hands? Between the late seventeenth and early nineteenth centuries, the old leaven actually worked better in the Scottish settlements of Ulster than in Scotland itself as the demotic component of a stable religious system. Because Ulster Presbyterianism was not an established church and because within the rural Presbyterian community there were only modest differences in wealth, as the landlords were nearly all Anglicans, the Presbyterian rituals of inversion and integration functioned well enough to sustain that system.

This happy consummation was not to last. By the early nineteenth century, Presbyterianism was increasingly defined by social and intellectual respectabil-

1825), pp 30–5, recounts Presbyterian origins in the valley in the 1620s without once mentioning the incidents which would be labelled a 'revival' by Reid nine years later.

ity and by a regimen of decorous weekly worship, better-suited to the sched-
ules, wardrobes and residential patterns of the middle class at the cost of active
participation by humbler members of their traditional ethnic community. The
festal communions failed the respectability test and, as in Scotland and
America,[15] Presbyterian eucharistic practice in Ulster moved decisively indoors.
There it would increasingly serve well-dressed, well-scrubbed communicants.
By around 1840 it appears that about three-quarters of the nominal
Presbyterians in Ulster were in some sense affiliated with a particular congregation, but that probably fewer than one-quarter attended worship services on
a typical Sunday.[16] While it is impossible to say whether these figures represent
a decline in Sunday churchgoing over the preceding century or so, by the 1830s
outdoor festal communions were largely extinct and the Sunday worship service was increasingly the central Presbyterian ritual. It took place in a meeting-
house which might be quite distant from the residences of the poorest (probably horseless) Presbyterians, and its regular participants dressed respectably, and
expected the same of their co-worshippers. In the absence of the festal communions, plain folk found it hard to act out their identification with the
Presbyterian community on a seasonal timetable which reflected the rhythms
of agrarian life. Perhaps more important, it came at a time when Ulster
Presbyterians were realizing that, like the churches in industrialized regions of
Britain, they had a serious problem of lapse from religious practice especially in
Belfast and among the deskilled domestic linen workers of its hinterland.

Meanwhile, in a number of the Presbyteries of the Synod of Ulster –
though not, of course, the Seceding Synods – the requirement that ministers
subscribe to the Westminster Confession had been quietly relaxed. Old light and
new light clergy co-existed amicably in the Synod, but among the less-educated
lay folk there continued to be deep suspicion of new light clergy which mani-
fested itself in the old leaven ritual of haggling. A crude measure of the presence
of the old leaven is the incidence of disputes within congregations depicted in
figure two.[17] Henry Cooke, a minister who, from about 1825 to 1843, was the
'acknowledged leader' of Ulster Presbyterianism, set out to rid the Synod of
Ulster of the new light. He attained this goal in 1829 when seventeen ministers

15 Schmidt, *Holy fairs*, pp 198–205.   **16** The data on which these calculations are based are
found in *First Report of the Commissioners of Public Instruction, Ireland*, H.C. 1835, xxxiii, and in
the National Archives of Ireland, Presbyterian Certificates, 1841, Room VI, 3/372; VIC/15/5.
17 The data in figure two were drawn from the congregational histories in *A history of the
congregations in the Presbyterian Church in Ireland, 1610–1982* (Belfast: Presbyterian Historical
Society of Ireland, 1982). Only disputes which seem to have involved popular participation
(as opposed, for example, to disputes solely between a minister and a higher judicatory) are
included. Disputes which involved two or more congregations (e.g. those which resulted in
formation of a second congregation) are counted only once. The analysis is limited to disputes originating in congregations in Ulster which, at the time of the dispute, were affiliated
with the General Synod, the Burgher Synod, the Antiburgher Synod, the Secession Synod
or the General Assembly.

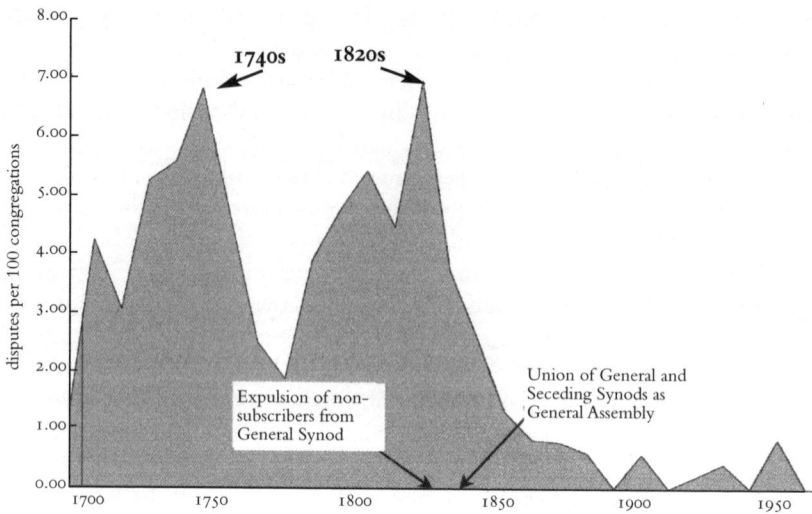

Figure 2   Dissension in Ulster Presbyterian congregations (within judicatories
which became the General Assembly in 1840), by decade.

withdrew from the Synod, with their congregations, rather than accept stricter
rules for enforcing subscription to the Westminster Confession by new ministerial candidates. After 1829 candidates for Ulster pulpits were clearly certified
as subscribers to the Westminster Confession – after 1836 subscribers who were
not even allowed to state and explain disagreements with particular phraseol-
ogy in the Confession. As is evident in figure two, congregational disputes
dropped sharply after the 1820s, for there was now little or no room for haggling; one might say that Cooke took all the fun out of being a Presbyterian.

The imposition of unqualified subscription in the General Synod paved the
way for its reunion with the Seceders as a General Assembly in 1840, and Ulster
Presbyterianism gave the appearance of a renewed institution able to address its
problems with unity and dispatch. However, having attained his objective of
expelling the new lights, Cooke had overreached by adopting a second major
goal which would ultimately cost him his domination of the Assembly and
leave it without united leadership. Starting in 1834 Cooke had sought to take
advantage of the crisis in church-state relations in the United Kingdom
reflected in Catholic emancipation in 1829 and the Irish Church Temporalities
Act of 1833 to forge an alliance between the Presbyterian Church and the
Church of Ireland in which the Presbyterians would be understood to be not
mere Dissenters but a branch of the established Church of Scotland.[18] There

18 Cooke himself rejected the term 'dissenter' to describe himself. J.L. Porter, *The life and
times of Henry Cooke* (London: John Murray, 1871), p. 267.

was a serious disconnect between Cooke's two goals. While unqualified sub-scription to the Westminster Confession owed its popularity among godly lay folk to its reaffirmation of Presbyterian distinctiveness and rightness, for Cooke it was a step toward reconciliation with Anglicanism. In his mind there was no essential doctrinal difference between The Confession and the Thirty-nine Articles; such differences as there were between the two communions related to mere 'outward forms'.[19] He had himself undergone an emotional conversion experience, and the 'Protestant peace' which he envisaged would rely on the new leaven for its popular base.

So Cooke's two major goals, taken together, amounted to a project for safe-guarding the old light while ditching the old leaven, for central to the old leaven was the sacred memory of persecution by 'prelacy' in the covenanting days. His failure to attain his second goal was no doubt overdetermined, but the occasion for his abandonment of it arose out of the Great Disruption in Scotland. Cooke tried doggedly in the early 1840s to use his Tory connections, especially his friendship with Sir Robert Peel, to broker a compromise over the Scottish evangelical party's demand for an end to lay patronage. When he failed and the evangelicals left the Church of Scotland, the logic of his proposed détente with Anglicanism fell apart, and the Irish General Assembly, in implicit repudiation of his policies, passed a resolution intended to promote the election of Presbyterians, rather than Cooke's Tory landlord friends, to parliament. Cooke announced his withdrawal from the General Assembly's jurisdiction until such time as the resolution was rescinded.[20] Although this condition was met four years later and Cooke resumed his seat in the Assembly, he played more the role of elder churchman than ecclesiastical politician for the remain-der of his career.

Cooke had succeeded in transforming his communion into a solidly old light body. His other project, however, was a shambles; the Assembly had no consistent strategy for how to recover its popular appeal in light of its increasingly obvious failure to maintain its full traditional constituency. Urbanization, industrialization, and the decline of the domestic linen industry were transforming Ulster Presbyterianism from a communal religious system serving an entire ethnic com-munity to a middle-class religion. One solution advocated by some of the younger ministers was the undiluted new leaven – in other words, promotion of revivals. Advocates of this solution were at pains to distance themselves from the excesses of revivalism in America. Moreover, the lines of communication with American Presbyterianism were tangled because after 1837 their potential theo-logical allies, the Old School, were suspicious of revivals, and were under suspi-cion themselves for harbouring most of the pro-slavery presbyteries.

Several strategies which owed more to the old leaven than to the new were also being floated. The most revolutionary of these was, in effect, to transform

---

19 Ibid., pp 274, 341. 20 Ibid., p. 442.

Presbyterianism from an ethnic religion to a multi-ethnic one by seeking to convert Catholics – a 'home mission' project strongly supported by John Edgar, the leading figure among the former Seceders. Although in Irish historiography this effort is usually treated as a mere offshoot of the Church of Ireland's 'second reformation', it actually emulated a more venerable and promising precedent: the conversion over the preceding century of many of the Scottish highlanders to Presbyterianism. The principal technique was not new leaven emotionalism but old leaven logocentrism: literacy in Irish would be taught to illiterate monoglot Irish speakers through the medium of the Irish-language bible. It was a classic logocentric project; it assumed that mere access to the very words of scripture could cause the scales to fall from Catholic eyes. Because virtually the only available teachers of literacy in Irish were Catholics, it was fraught with accountability problems in the early 1840s.[21] The famine, however, breathed new life into the project because it offered an answer to the troubling question: what did providence intend in visiting this calamity upon Ireland? Among Presbyterian clergy that answer – that God was opening a door for Presbyterians to convert the Catholics – gained broader support than any of the various other theories of divine intent in circulation. Lay liberality did not match clerical conviction on this point, however, and expectations of an abundant harvest of elect but benighted Catholics were disappointed.[22]

A second strategy was also occasioned by the famine, but it arose among clergy who more candidly recognized that not just Catholics, but poor Presbyterians also, were victims of the calamity. Ministers who pursued this policy associated themselves with the tenant right movement of the early 1850s. The most gifted member of this group was Alexander Goudy, minister of First Strabane congregation, grandson of the celebrated Revd James Porter who was hanged for complicity with the 1798 Rebellion. When reminded of his ancestry he would wryly remark, 'My grandfather was suspended.' Goudy articulated a rationale for his social vision in explicitly old leaven terms: Ulster was 'our own Zion' in which the Presbyterian Church had a mission to preach the Word which 'would forbid the rich to grind the faces of the poor'. In opposition to the ecumenical tendencies promoted by the new leaven, he argued that Presbyterian polity was the true teaching of the New Testament, 'diametrically opposed' to 'black Prelacy'. Presbyterians held the true principles of William of Orange: 'toleration – progress – reform – constitutional Government – civil and religious liberty,' and the very reverse of principles 'that have so long usurped,

---

21 In the early 1840s one of the teachers, the poet Aodh MacDomhnaill, admitted publicly that he had falsified reports of Irish language instruction in the Glens of Antrim. Breandán Ó Buachalla, *I mBéal Feirste Cois Cuain* (Baile Átha Cliath: An Clóchomhar, 1968), pp 103–15; Luke Walsh, *The home mission unmasked* (Belfast: James M'Convery, 1844).   **22** David W. Miller, 'Irish Presbyterians and the great famine', in Jacqueline Hill and Colm Lennon (eds), *Luxury and Austerity*, Historical Studies 21 (Dublin: University College Dublin Press, 1999), pp 165–81.

and caricatured, and prostituted' King Billy's name. Naturally, Goudy also conceived the realization of 'Zion's good' in terms of 'the overthrow of the Roman Antichrist' – especially in a sermon preached in that revolutionary year, 1848 – stressing that this was a task for Presbyterianism since the 'corrupt' established church had 'shewn herself to be utterly unfitted for it.' There is a relentless logic in Goudy's writings, and although he seems to have genuinely wished for social justice for Catholics as well as Presbyterians, that logic stood in the way of his offering effective leadership to the tenant right cause. He could not bring himself to share a platform with Catholic priests. Of course the failure of the so-called 'League of North and South' in the 1850s is more complicated than the mentality of this one minister, but his career illustrates the difficulty in basing a popular renewal of Presbyterianism at this moment upon the old leaven.[23]

A third approach to the problem was open-air preaching to reach the poor and 'careless' who did not 'come directly under the influence of the means of grace, even where they are most abundantly provided in the ordinary way'.[24] Such a proposal had been made at the 1845 General Assembly for an organized campaign of open-air preaching but had been dropped for fear that it would mobilize Catholic resistance to the home mission.[25] Once the famine had come and gone without producing any abundant providential harvest of Catholic converts, however, the way was clear in the early 1850s for such a campaign to be launched. Although open-air preaching was championed by proponents of the new leaven, it took advantage of old-leaven memories of outdoor spirituality, though without a sacramental component. In 1857 major sectarian riots were triggered in Belfast by open-air preaching,[26] but as Janice Holmes has recently argued, territorial aggrandizement *vis-à-vis* the Catholic community was not the primary cause for the preaching campaign. Figure three, which depicts the routes to be followed by the preachers in the summer of 1858, demonstrates that the system was clearly designed primarily to reach lapsed Presbyterians. The few incursions into Catholic territory were typically incidental to travel from one Protestant, usually Presbyterian, district to another. The object of the exercise was evident in the Revd William Patton's description of the audience to whom he preached in Glenarm: 'All were poor people – of that class for whom open-air preaching is designed.'[27] The Revd Richard Smyth of

---

23 Alexander P. Goudy, *Zion's good, or, The position and duty of the Irish Presbyterian Church at the present time* (Derry: 'Standard' office, 1848); and *'Buy the truth and sell it not': a sermon preached before the General Assembly of the Presbyterian Church in Ireland* (Belfast: C. Aitchison, 1858); Thomas Croskery and Thomas Witherow, *Life of the Rev. A.P. Goudy, D.D.* (Dublin: Humphrey and Armour, 1887. **24** *Irish Presbyterian*, 1:7 (1853), p. 196. **25** *Banner of Ulster* (Belfast), 4 July 1845, p. 4, cols. 3–6. **26** Janice Holmes, 'The role of open-air preaching in the Belfast riots of 1857', *Proceedings of the Royal Irish Academy* (2002) Section C, 102, pp 47–66; John M. Barkley, *St Enoch's Congregation, 1872–1972* (Belfast: St Enoch's Church, 1972), pp 45–9. **27** *Eighth annual report of open-air preaching by ministers of the General Assembly of the Presbyterian Church in Ireland. 1858* (Belfast: 'Banner of Ulster' office, 1859), observations of

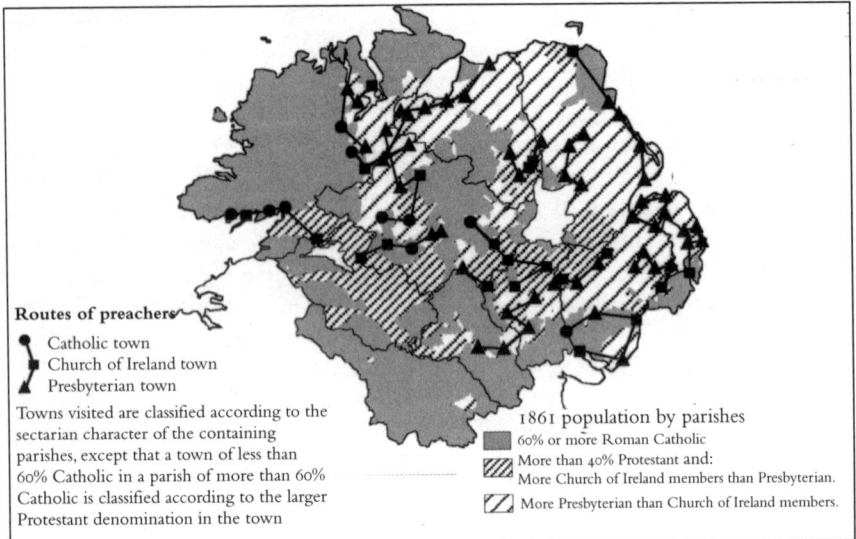

Routes of preachers

- Catholic town
- Church of Ireland town
- Presbyterian town

Towns visited are classified according to the sectarian character of the containing parishes, except that a town of less than 60% Catholic in a parish of more than 60% Catholic is classified according to the larger Protestant denomination in the town

1861 population by parishes
- 60% or more Roman Catholic
- More than 40% Protestant and: More Church of Ireland members than Presbyterian.
- More Presbyterian than Church of Ireland members.

Figure 3 Presbyterian open-air preaching, 1858, and sectarian geography

Derry bluntly captured the social reality when he wrote that at one of his sermons '[m]any of the non-church-going class were present.'[28]

Open-air preaching may well have helped to make the fourth solution, revival, more acceptable merely by not triggering the kind of excitements which so troubled many clergy. The lyrical tone of a lead article entitled 'Times of Refreshing' in the June 1853 number of a newly-established denominational magazine[29] contrasted sharply with the more defensive appeals for revival which had appeared prior to the famine. It conveyed the impression that 'glorious effusions of the Spirit' might be expected without any of the excesses associated with American revivals earlier in the nineteenth century. This impression seemed to be confirmed in 1858 when the news of a very extensive revival began to arrive from across the Atlantic. This event was indeed remarkably free of embarrassing popular commotions, no doubt partly because of its social origins. Triggered by a financial crisis, it came to be known as the 'businessmen's revival'.

Businessmen were especially thin on the ground, however, in the parishes of Ahoghill and Connor, Co. Antrim. In the latter the Revd J.H. Moore had for sev-

William Patton concerning preaching at Glenarm, 25 August 1858. **28** Ibid. Typically a minister would sign up for five sermons at five locations during a given week. Each preacher was asked to record his observations in a diary, and many of those observations focus on the social class division which increasingly marked the boundary between 'church-goers' or 'the respectable classes' on the one hand and the 'working classes' or 'poorer classes' on the other. The Revd Robert Rule was pleased that a sermon he preached at Ship Quay in Derry was heard by '[a] large number of people who are too poor to attend the public worship of God on the Sabbath.' **29** *Irish Presbyterian*, 1:6 (1853), pp 145–50.

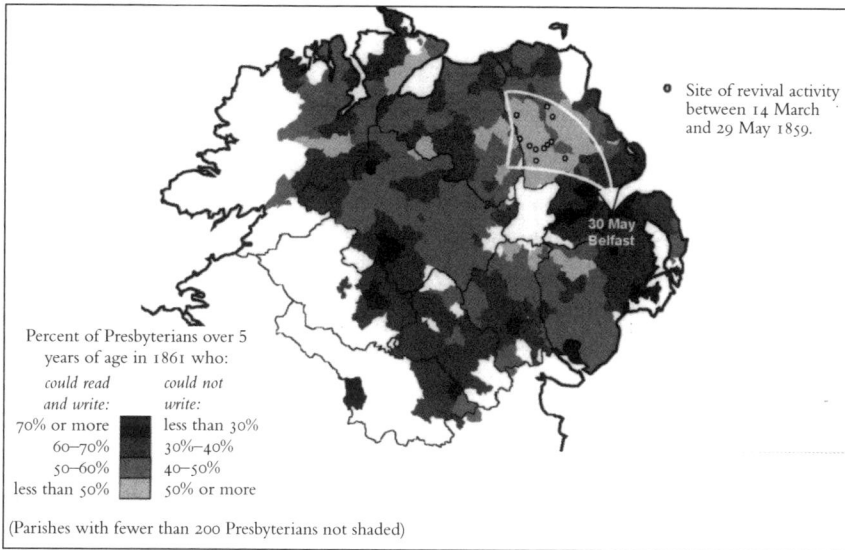

Figure 4 Literacy (as an indicator of social class) among Presbyterians in Ulster, and the early phase of the 1859 Revival

eral years been preaching up and praying down a revival in special services 'designed for the outlying population, who had no regular church connexion, and who could not find accommodation in the crowded pews in the previous part of the day'.[30] On 14 March 1859, in First Ahoghill Presbyterian Church, at the traditional Monday thanksgiving service to close a communion season was interrupted by an outburst which led to a scene outside the church marked by the prostration of 'scores' of people 'under intense conviction of sin'.[31] With the appearance of such 'bodily manifestations', religious enthusiasm spread quickly during the next two months to nearby localities in mid-Antrim, as shown in figure four.

As can be seen in figure four, which utilizes literacy as a proxy for social class, the mid-Antrim 'revival district' was distinguished by a substantial population of poor Presbyterians. At the end of May several revival converts were invited to speak to Belfast congregations. The fervour induced by these events soon spilled out of the churches into working-class streets and workplaces. Newspapers in the provincial capital were filled with revival intelligence; the revival became a media event and was quickly diffused to Protestant areas throughout the province.

30 William Gibson, *The year of grace: a history of the Ulster revival of 1859* (Edinburgh: Andrew Elliot, 1860), p. 19. 31 Eull Dunlop (ed.), *Alfred Russell Scott. The Ulster revival of 1859: enthusiasm emanating from mid-Antrim* (Ballymena: Mid-Antrim Historical Group, 1994), p. 61, quoting J.E. Orr, *The second evangelical awakening in Britain* (London: Marshall, Morgan & Scott, 1949) p. 40.

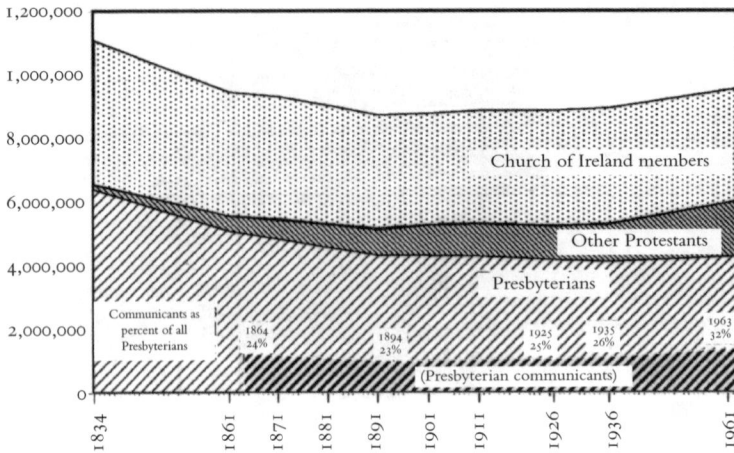

Figure 5 Protestants in Ulster by major denominational grouping, 1834–1961,
with number of Presbyterian communicants, 1864–1963

Once the revival reached Belfast the city's ministers assumed leadership in a
concerted effort to gain control of it, and they had ample reason for doing so.
As early as the Ahoghill incident, converts had declared that a farmer whom the
minister tried to restrain from excitedly praying aloud, 'spoke by the command
of a power superior to any ministerial authority'.[32] In the popular mind, public
testimonies by those who had experienced the prostrations, dreams, visions, and
yes, stigmata, became more central to the revival experience than clerical min-
istrations. Like Lawrence Taylor's 'drunken priest' whose lack of self-control has
alienated him from his bishop,[33] the converts were believed to enjoy access to
the supernatural which the clergy had forfeited in their pursuit of careers in the
institutional church. Most clergy genuinely hoped that the revival might
improve religious observance among the lower classes, but many were also
aware, especially in Belfast, of their increasing dependence on the middle-class
sector of their flocks. To meet the respectability test, the 'bodily manifestations'
and altered states of consciousness had to be relegated to an ancillary and dis-
pensable place in the salvation process, and the ministers undertook that task
both in their pastoral activity and their editorial role in the publication of
revival narratives.

To return the question posed in my title, '*did* Ulster Presbyterians have a
devotional revolution?' Both Ulster Presbyterianism and Irish Catholicism, like
nearly every other church in western Christianity, did experience significant

---

32 Scott, *Ulster revival*, pp 61–3, quoting *Ballymena Observer*, 26 March 1859. 33 Lawrence J.
Taylor, *Occasions of faith: an anthropology of Irish Catholics* (Philadelphia: University of
Pennsylvania Press, 1995), pp 145–66.

devotional change in the nineteenth century in a qualitative sense. What made the change in Irish Catholicism worthy of the label 'revolution' is the fact that it initiated a period of about a century during which canonical religious practice became virtually universal. Nothing like this seems to have occurred in Ulster Presbyterianism. Of the Ulster population returned as Presbyterians by the census, 24 per cent were reported by the denomination in 1864 to be 'communicants'. As figure five shows, there was no sustained rise in this figure until the mid-twentieth century.

To understand these strikingly different quantitative outcomes of devotional change we should think of Catholic seasonal practices such as the landscape-based devotions at holy wells and the neighbourhood-based station masses as roughly analogous to the Presbyterian old leaven, and the more universalistic Catholic devotions which appealed to the senses and the emotions and were introduced from the continent in the mid- and late-nineteenth century as analogous to the new leaven. In both communities the older popular practices fostered religious systems in which annual or semi-annual official observance might be more common among the poor than weekly attendance at chapel or meetinghouse. Patterns of religious practice in both denominations were crucially affected by the development in the nineteenth century of a strong middle class fixated on the respectability, which could most easily be demonstrated by attendance at weekly worship. The elimination during the famine and in the continuing emigration thereafter of so much of the agrarian underclass of cottiers and labourers probably facilitated the extension of the respectability culture to nearly all remaining Catholics.

The respectability culture affected Presbyterianism differently. Middle-class Presbyterians were offended by the excesses of the revival which, for mill girls and farm labourers were its very essence. The uncomfortable division along class lines was evident in a pseudonymous letter to a Presbyterian magazine in 1867. The writer complained of 'the absence of personal intercourse between our ministers and elders and their people on the subject of their individual religious experience', making plain that he (or she) had in mind especially those members lacking in 'refinement and education'. This 'remissness', the writer claimed, had already caused the Presbyterian church to lose 'some of her most sincere and pious members', to 'some denominations closely approaching to our own in doctrine and discipline, but far exceeding her in this – shall I call it fellowship or communion of saints?'[34]

Such defection to other denominations does seem to have occurred on a large scale. A generation after the revival, the Presbyterian historian W.T. Latimer wrote of the tendency of its converts to desert 'the faith of their forefathers' for 'various sects of religious enthusiasts'.[35] Indeed, the proportion of the Ulster

34 Letter from 'A Church Member', *Evangelical Witness and Presbyterian Review*, 5:10 (1867), p. 252. **35** William Thomas Latimer, *A history of the Irish Presbyterians* (Belfast: James Cleeland,

Protestant population who identified with Methodism and other smaller denominations doubled, from 5.5 per cent to 11 per cent between the 1861 and 1901
censuses,[36] and since non-churchgoing Protestants no doubt continued to report
their religion as Church of Ireland or Presbyterian, members of the smaller
groups would have bulked larger among the observant (see figure five). The
clergy having constructed and endorsed a 'proper' revival – that is one without
'excesses' – could hardly deliver on the implied promise of more emotion-
charged devotion in a denomination which continued for another four decades
after the revival to debate bitterly the admissibility of instrumental music in worship and of hymns to supplement the Scottish metrical Psalter.[37] Insistence on the
continued importance of these relics of the old Presbyterian leaven made little
sense in a clergy which had worked so furiously to associate themselves with a
new leaven which was inherently indifferent to differences within Protestantism.
They should not have been surprised at the defection of their most devout working-class adherents, leaving them with a working class whose Presbyterianism was
little more than a response to the census-taker once a decade. The Catholic
Church made no such foolish error – at least not until our own day.

1902), pp 492–7. **36** W.E. Vaughan and A.J. Fitzpatrick (eds), *Irish historical statistics: population,
1821–1971* (Dublin: Royal Irish Academy, 1978), pp 53, 65; Presbyterian Church in Ireland,
General Assembly, *Minutes*, 1864, 1894, 1925, 1935, 1963. **37** Latimer, *History*, pp 509–12, 522,
533.

Unremembering the devotional revolution

JAMES H. MURPHY

Over three decades have now passed since Emmet Larkin published his ground-breaking article 'The devotional revolution in Ireland, 1850–75'.[1] The article makes four principal claims: that the Irish people only became practicing Catholics in the latter half of the nineteenth century; that the nature of religious practice among Catholics changed dramatically and became much more Tridentine in character; that the institutional church, under Paul Cullen, underwent significant reform; and, finally, that Catholicism supplanted the Irish language as a badge of national identity. The last of these points has been the most contentious, inevitably so, because it is a matter of historical sociology which must always remain somewhat speculative as the tools of the behavioural sciences are not available to the historian.

As for the other elements of the Larkin thesis, there is now little disagreement among historians that very significant changes took place within Irish Catholicism in the middle of the nineteenth century, though the roots of those changes may go back somewhat further than the 1972 article allowed. Even a scholar such as the late Donal Kerr who was uncomfortable with the claim that prior to 1850 the mass of the Irish people outside the north-eastern counties were not practicing Catholics admitted that 'Easter communion, rather than regular Sunday mass attendance, with the difficulties that such attendance involved, was probably regarded as the criterion of a practicing Catholic.'[2] At the very least he is here conceding that the definition of what constituted a practicing Catholic changed dramatically after the famine. My own work on parish missions, on the fiction of Catholic Ireland and on Irish education is deeply indebted to the devotional revolution thesis.[3]

This essay asks two related questions. Firstly, what happened to the memory of the devotional revolution and of the religious practice which predated it, that is to the memory of the time when the religious practices of the people were

---

1 Emmet Larkin, 'The devotional revolution in Ireland, 1850–75', *American Historical Review*, 77:3 (1972), pp 625–52. 2 Donal Kerr *'A nation of beggars?' Priests, people and politics in famine Ireland, 1846–52* (Oxford: Clarendon, 1994), p. 319. 3 James H. Murphy, 'The role of Vincentian parish missions in the "Irish counter-reformation" of the mid-nineteenth century', *Irish Historical Studies* 24 (1984), pp 152–71; James H. Murphy, *Catholic fiction and social reality in Ireland* (Westport CT: Greenwood, 1997); James H. Murphy, 'A history of Castleknock College,' in James H. Murphy (ed.), *Nos Autem: Castleknock College and its contribution* (Dublin: Gill and Macmillan, 1996), pp 1–154.

different from what they subsequently became in the latter part of the nine-teenth century? Secondly, why was it, to quote Sean Connolly, that 'the real his-tory of Irish Catholicism, with its complex interaction of popular and official traditions, was obscured beneath a legend of long suffering but unwavering piety which it is only now becoming possible to dismantle.'[4]

In answer to the first question what I want to suggest is that the older pat-tern of religious practice may not simply have been forgotten, it may have been deliberately unremembered. Within the limits of this essay, I would like to adduce one piece of evidence to support this tentative assertion, albeit a signif-icant piece of evidence. In 1894 the *New Ireland Review* published an article entitled, 'What Our Country Folk Read'. Referring to the parish libraries which were the main source of reading material for country people, it con-cludes, 'Time after time *Knocknagow* [by Charles J. Kickham] is recommended by one reader to another as the very best novel in the collection.'[5] Kickham's biographer has noted that '[i]n the decades when the great figures of the Irish renaissance were attaining their finest achievements, the most consistently pop-ular book in Ireland was *Knocknagow.*' It embodied 'the virtues that . [...] soci-ety prized, the emotions that if felt, and the values that it exalted.'[6]

The people depicted in Kickham's novel, which was published in 1873, are all more or less practicing Tridentine Catholics. Perhaps more importantly the community itself is a practicing Catholic community. Thus the chief commu-nal events in the opening chapters of the book are Christmas morning mass in Kilthubber chapel and a station mass held in the home of the principal family in the novel, the middle-class Kearneys. Mary Kearney's explanation of the pur-pose of the station mass to a visitor from England reflects its origins in the pre-devotional revolution practice of religious life, 'Catholics go to Confession and Communion at Christmas and Easter. And, in country districts, instead of requiring the people to go to the chapel, the priests come to certain houses in each locality to hear confessions and say Mass.'[7]

Kickham, however, is keen to present the station mass as being a custom which is in harmony with a supposedly immemorial Tridentine practice, rather than in competition with it. For example, when Fr Hannigan addresses the people after the station mass he tells them that it is acceptable to go beagling on Sundays, 'As long as ye are sure not to lose Mass, I won't say anything against the beagles [...] And if ye meet after Mass – mind I say, *after* divine service – I don't see much harm in it.'[8] This statement assumes that everyone attends Sunday mass. In *Knocknagow* attendance at the station mass is not a substitute for weekly mass

4 Sean Connolly, *Religion and society in nineteenth century Ireland*, Studies in Irish Economic and Social History 3 (Dundalk: Dun Dealgan, 1985), p. 60.   **5** *New Ireland Review* 1 (1894), p. 67.   **6** R.V. Comerford, *Charles J. Kickham: a biography* (Dublin: Wolfhound, 1979), pp 209–10. **7** Charles J. Kickham, *Knocknagow, or, The homes of Tipperary* (1873; Dublin: Anna Livia, 1988), p. 26.   **8** Kickham, *Knocknagow*, p. 68.

attendance in the local 'chapel'. It is not an indicator of the existence of an alternative mode of Catholic religious practice to Tridentine orthodoxy.

In fact, the station mass was seen as one of the principal 'abuses' which the Tridentine reformers, only a decade or two before the writing of *Knocknagow*, had sought to correct.[9] In his original devotional revolution article Emmet Larkin draws attention to two accounts from the 1840s which are critical of station masses.[10] The criticisms can be divided under a number of headings: that mass is celebrated in unworthy, squalid settings; that the greedy clergy use station masses and the celebration of the sacraments to charge exorbitant fees; that the host family for the occasion is obliged to offer lavish hospitality to the clergy; and that confessions are heard in cramped and confused circumstances in which the penitent can be overheard by others and in which the priest is constrained from offering proper counsel. Larkin summarizes the situation thus, 'The complaints of the reformers, who were concerned about the abuses attendant on the system, had mainly to do with the exorbitant "offerings" extracted by the clergy for the administration of the sacraments and the undignified if not unholy celebration of sacred rites in profane places.'

None of these abuses is present in Kickham's description of the station mass in *Knocknagow*. However, the thorough Tridentinism of religion in *Knocknagow* and the impression that the novel gives that things were ever thus is I believe not simply because Kickham knew no different or because he had forgotten that things had changed but because he was actively seeking to unremember that the past had been different. His unremembering though bears the imprint of the very past he is seeking to forget. The station mass in *Knocknagow* is thus attended by concomitant virtues to the vices with which station masses were once historically associated.

What I want to suggest is that the unreformed practices of the station mass are not simply absent, they are demonstratively absent in Kickham's account. In other words, Kickham's description, in its keenness to forget the past, draws attention to it by highlighting the absence of abuses, especially those which Larkin's analysis showed to be of central concern to reformers: clerical avarice and the undignified celebration of the sacraments. The memory of the older pattern of religious practice is thus paradoxically present through its pronounced absence.

In *Knocknagow* the station masses is conducted with decorum and piety. There is a detailed description of the hearing of confessions.[11] Far from being

---

9 In the 1840s, according to Donal Kerr, Easter communion was accepted by the clergy in the diocese of Cashel in Co. Tipperary as the criterion of Catholic practice. See *'A nation of beggars?'*, p. 319. Though it was one of the targets of the reformers, the station mass was to survive into the twentieth century in parts of the south and west of Ireland, albeit in a more Tridentine form as in *Knocknagow*. **10** Larkin, 'Devotional revolution,' pp 635–6. **11** Before the station mass at the Kearneys house confessions are heard with propriety. Three priests hear confessions, two in rooms in which the priest is alone with the penitent. The third hears

avaricious, the parish priest Fr McMahon is someone who when he dies 'will not have as much money as will bury him'.[12] Station masses are part of the great 'amount of labour an Irish priest has to go through.'[13] And when the conversation turns briefly to an isolated and regretted case of clerical avarice in another parish it only serves to emphasize the piety and lack of avarice which have characterized the station mass at the Kearneys' home. In sum Kickham's detailed account of the conduct of confessions and repeated return to the topic of clerical avarice in his description of a station mass within a Tridentine religious system indicate, in my view, the influence of the memory of the vices that had once been associated with station masses and which his description is seeking to unremember.

It is now time to return to the second question posed in this essay and to attempt to answer it at least in terms of *Knocknagow*. Why was this happening? Why does Kickham actively wish to bury the memory of the past? The novel, indeed, provides an answer to this question though it is an unsurprising answer. Inappropriate behaviour is unrespectable and respectability in the eyes of others is of prime concern. During the confessions at the station mass at the Kearneys' a humorous minor fracas develops as one woman tries to overtake others at the head of the queue for confession. Henry Lowe, the Kearneys' English visitor, witnesses the incident. Mildly rebuking the woman concerned, the confessor Fr Hannigan says, 'There's a strange gentleman from England looking at ye; and what will he say of the Island of Saints when he goes back, if this is the way ye behave yourselves.'[14]

Henry Lowe, however, is 'struck by the fervour of the people' at the station mass.[15] In fact the station mass marks the conclusion the novel's early concern to establish the general respectability of Irish Catholicism through Henry Lowe's experience of it. He is presented as being a fair-minded Englishman and is an example of a literary type which is found throughout nineteenth-century Irish fiction and whose function is to vindicate Irish respectability in the face of the unfavourable stereotypes of the Irish which were prevalent in Britain.

Chapter one of the novel focuses on the Christmas morning mass at the local chapel but does so from the perspective of Lowe who attends with his

confessions in the kitchen and has to erect a barrier of chairs to keep the line of penitents at a sufficient distance for confidentiality. This is said to be 'by his own choice (Kickham, *Knocknagow*, p. 40), meaning presumably that the Kearneys had planned to furnish him with a more suitable room. One minor, humorous incident of rowdiness occurs. The offering of the mass itself is not described, perhaps because there has been a description of mass in chapter one. **12** Kickham, *Knocknagow*, p. 26. **13** Ibid., p. 27. **14** Ibid., p. 41. Kickham has Hannigan go on hold up the behaviour of the local men as an example to the women, 'Look at the men, how quiet and dacent they are.' Later he criticises the men for being drunk at a funeral. However, this is after they had carried the remains of the deceased for thirteen miles through teeming rain to fulfil his dying wish to be buried with his wife and children, p. 69. **15** Ibid., p. 66.

hosts, the Kearneys. He and they take their seats in pews in the gallery where middle-class proprieties obtain, as Lowe feels awkward at sitting beside some-one to whom he has not been formally introduced. By contrast the ordinary people, down in the main body of the church where there are no pews, become almost a collective entity. Thus they stand and press forward together towards the altar to hear the sermon.

The sermon by Fr McMahon seemed to Lowe to be 'a torrent of barbaric eloquence, which rose into a kind of gorgeous sublimity, or melted into pathos, sometimes homely, sometimes fancifully poetical.'[16] During the more lyrical pas-sages in the sermon describing the plight of the Virgin Mary in search of accom-modation in Bethlehem 'a cry burst from the congregation, and the sobs were so loud and frequent that the preacher was obliged to pause till the emotion he had called forth had subsided.'[17] The conclusions which can be drawn from this description are that Irish Catholicism maintains a proper sense of social hierarchy and that it encourages docile child-like qualities of wonder and awe of among its adherents in the lower classes of society. Kickham is presenting Irish Catholicism as a force which tends to reinforce a Victorian respectability.

This impression is confirmed later in the novel when people are under severe pressure from the evils of the land system. During mass Fr McMahon denounces the 'damnable government' and a woman from the workhouse becomes agitated when she learns of her husband's death. Describing the latter event to a friend in a letter Mary Keaney writes that it was 'a very affecting incident' which turned the people's 'anger into pity, though one would think it ought only to incense them all the more against their rulers.'[18] Here indeed is a religion of exemplary respectability. At a time when priests and the middle classes are roused to anger, it continues, in the world of *Knocknagow* at least, to foster docility and compliance among those of its members who could be con-sidered most prone to social discontent.

Early on in the novel, Catholicism's respectability at both social and personal levels receives Henry Lowe's stamp of approval: 'in spite of his prejudices the evidently earnest devotion of the worshippers impressed Mr Lowe with a respect for their form of religion which he never had felt before.'[19] Devotion thus earns respect for Irish Catholics. That which prevailed before the age of Tridentine devotion is unremembered.

There are of course well-known perils in dealing with fiction as a source for social history. What applies within the pages of Kickham's novel may not apply beyond them. At the very least though *Knocknagow* is suggestive about the rea-sons why the religious changes of mid-nineteenth-century Ireland were lost to the popular memory.

This essay has been about historiography. Emmet Larkin's devotional revo-lution thesis was and is a shaping factor in the twentieth-century historiogra-

---

16 Ibid., p. 6.   **17** Ibid., p. 7.   **18** Ibid., pp 540–1.   **19** Ibid., p. 6.

phy of nineteenth-century Ireland. The historiography, especially the popular historiography, of the nineteenth century itself is a subject which would repay greater investigation.[20] This essay has attempted to read *Knocknagow* as one piece of evidence in the popular historiography of what Emmet Larkin has called the devotional revolution. That it is an historiography of apparent absence does not diminish its significance, for historiography is surely just as concerned with what is forgotten, and how and why it is forgotten, as it is with what is remembered, and how and why it is remembered.

---

20 Of particular note are the tropes of nineteenth-century popular history such as the wild geese and the penal laws. See James H. Murphy, 'The Wild Geese', *Irish Review* 16 (1994), pp 23–8 and Murphy, *Catholic fiction*, pp 137–42.

'Perge, signifer' –
or, where did William Maginn stand?

DAVID E. LATANÉ, JR

After one meeting with William Maginn, Thomas Carlyle had a conviction: the 'rattling Irishman' was 'without ill-nature, without earnestness, certainty of conviction or purpose in regard to *any* subject, except this one: *Punch* is *Punch*.' Carlyle wasn't talking, either, about the magazine, which made Maginn the subject of its first obituary after his death in 1842, but strong drink. Maginn, he wrote his brother John, 'talks horribly of *drink*.'[1] Carlyle weighed in on Maginn because his need for a publisher had brought him within the orbit of *Fraser's Magazine*, launched by Maginn in 1830. And *Fraser's* is Maginn's claim to fame. As Patrick Leary describes it, 'Ultra-Tory in politics and antisentimental in literary taste, its slashing commentary on eminent political and literary figures quickly made it the most talked-about magazine in London.'[2] In addition to *Fraser's* Maginn helped found the *Standard* newspaper, was one of the writers who brought *Blackwood's* its early success, and wrote innumerable political leaders for several different papers that helped shape the course of the Tory party in the era of reform.

But Maginn, who not only talked but wrote profusely about the joys of intoxicating beverages, is generally remembered not for his writing or editing but for his bohemianism. As a writer, nothing so unbecame his reputation as the manner of his leaving life, destitute and drunk.[3] Maginn's raffishness and propensity to satirize friend and foe alike, combined with the sprezzatura public persona remarked by Carlyle, also led to the libel against Maginn that he was a 'literary Swiss', willing to hire his pen to whomever would pay – a grave charge that puts journalists on a par with lawyers.[4] Champions of Maginn have laboured long against unheavenly twin accusations: alcoholism and insincerity.

---

1 Charles Sanders, Kenneth Fielding, et al. (eds), *The collected letters of Thomas and Jane Welsh Carlyle*, 30 vols. to date (Durham, NC: Duke UP, 1970–), v, p. 217. Research for this essay was made possible by an NEH College Fellowship, 2000–01. 2 Patrick Leary, '*Fraser's Magazine* and the literary life, 1830–1847', *Victorian Periodicals Review*, 27:2 (1994), p. 106. 3 His death was caused by tuberculosis contracted in the Fleet debtors' prison, and he continued producing high quality work in abundance until the last few weeks of his life. Most posthumous accounts, however, simply assert that he drank himself to death. 4 The source for this charge is most often the writings of Samuel Carter Hall, the teetotalling Cork contemporary of Maginn, who published as an old man several volumes of memories of the great men of his youth for a later Victorian readership. Miriam Thrall vigorously, though not completely con-

What did Maginn believe in other than punch? Where did he stand? My title comes from a remark in *Blackwood's* 'Noctes Ambrosianæ' – 'North' remarks to 'Odoherty,' '*Perge, Signifer*', which in turn alludes to a passage in Livy: *Signifer statue Signum: Hic optime manebimus*[5] – 'Plant here the Standard. Here we shall best remain.' The 'Signifier' or 'Standard-bearer' in *Blackwood's* slang was the 'Ensign', Sir Morgan Odoherty. This signature was taken by a number of writers, but gradually became a persona for William Maginn. Just as Odoherty was staunch but many-personed, Maginn has a surfeit of stands, and because the two nineteenth-century collections that are all the Maginn we have in book form are full of writings that he did not write, Maginn sometimes appears more inconsistent than he really was. Maginn doesn't so much flip-flop as constantly present a manifold or constellation of sometimes paradoxical viewpoints, ranging the gamut from the seemingly reactionary to the radical, sometimes aphoristic in style, often Rabelaisian, occasionally in the manner of Swift or Sterne. There are, however, constant stars in his constellations and most of them can be traced back to Ireland and Cork. While little is known about his family or childhood, clues exist in that record to his core beliefs.

His father, John Maginn, who was from an Ulster family that included both Catholics and Protestants, was appointed a schoolmaster at the Protestant Cathedral of St Fin Barre by Bishop Mann on 29 March 1777.[6] He was for decades an assistant to the Revd Giles Lee in the Diocesan School. His wife was Anne Eccles, daughter of William Eccles, Esq. of the Scotch-Irish family of Ecclesville, Co. Tyrone. She was remembered in the family as 'a woman of humor as well as of judgment.'[7] John Maginn, according to a newspaper obituary, was 'a tender and affectionate husband' and a 'fond an indulgent father' who 'with unremitting attention bestowed' on his children 'a finished education rarely to be found in any rank of society.'[8] Their eldest child William was born 10 July 1794, and he became a locally celebrated educational advertisement for Giles Lee, John Maginn and the Diocesan School. Most of the surviving anecdotes about his childhood relate to his precocious ability with languages. Not emphasized in the biographies is that he formed a strong bond with his 'little platoon' – specifically Southern Irish protestants with a strong stake in the established Church of Ireland. William was originally intended for this Church, and both his brothers became its ministers. Maginn's platoon was under great stress during his years in Cork. As he pleaded in a private note to William Blackwood about 1821, 'do not admit any severe things on the Church of Ireland; for you really have no notion of how sore we are.'[9] His childhood

vincingly, refutes it in her 'Enemies' chapter in *Rebellious Fraser's* (New York: Columbia UP, 1934), pp 208–28.   **5** R. Shelkton Mackenzie (ed.), *Noctes Ambrosianæ*, 5 vols (New York: Redfield, 1855), i, p. 323. Livy, *Ammiani Marcellini historiae*, bk 16, par. 18.   **6** William Maziere Brady, *Clerical and parochial records of Cork, Cloyne, and Ross*, 3 vols (Dublin: 1863–4), i, p. 271. **7** Thrall, *Rebellious Fraser's*, p. 165. Her source was Miss Elizabeth Maginn, William's great-niece.   **8** *Southern Reporter* (Cork), 24 January 1819, p. 3.   **9** Ann Kersey Cooke, 'Maginn-

would have been shaped in part by a prevailing siege mentality. He was born in
the month of Thermidor of the terror in France, and between ages four and
seven he lived through the 1798 rebellion and the uproars surrounding the
union – both of which must have heightened his infant political consciousness
– or at least his anxieties. In politics and religion, Giles Lee and his father combined Swift and Burke with broad Church doctrine. Lee preached a sermon in
1797 that argued '[m]an, in his present corrupted state, is incapable of perfect
freedom: to be susceptible of such high perfection, the empire of reason must
be invariably established – the dominion of passion be totally extinct.' For Lee,
reformers and French revolutionaries were 'all those iniquitous projectors
against the happiness and virtue of the human race.'[10] Maginn's childhood was
also shaped by his college tutors, for he matriculated at Trinity College in 1806
at age eleven. After placing first on the Hebrew examination given by the
famously eccentric 'Jacky' Barrett, he was assigned to the tutelage of Dr Samuel
Kyle, a Londonderry man. Kyle was a nurturing figure. Looking back on the
Trinity of his youth, Kyle criticized 'little if any special attention [was] paid to
individual Pupils – *nothing paternal – nothing kindly* – .'[11] In Maginn's case, as one
friend recorded, Kyle 'suffered the affections of the man to supersede the rigour
of the tutor, and he may be said to have stood to him "*in loco parentis*".'[12] As
such, Kyle – along with Giles Lee – inevitably shaped Maginn's Protestant and
Unionist positions in politics. In the rebellion of 1798, which split the college
and resulted in a number of expulsions and prosecutions of students, Kyle had
gone out with a loyal troop from the college to guard the bridges over the
Liffey, and he would later in the House of Lords vote against the Reform Bill
of 1832 because of the threat of the admission of more Catholics to Parliament.
Kyle and Lee saw in the young William a brilliant scholar and a potential
defender of the faith. In this they would be more disappointed than not –
though Kyle remained close to Maginn and was one of the sponsors of the fund
collected for his family after his death.

   Maginn's father I believe influenced Maginn in a different direction. He was
a naturally tolerant man, well known in Cork society for his warm friendships
and rich 'vein of wit and humour'[13] and the Maginns, who were acquainted
with many in Cork City's growing Catholic middle classes, were in the thick of
the astonishing flurry of Cork culture documented recently by Terry Eagleton
in his essay 'Cork and the carnivalesque'.[14] Though prepared for a fellowship by

Blackwood Correspondence' (MA, Texas Technological College, 1955), p. 111. Quotations
from the Blackwood correspondence in the National Library of Scotland are, unless otherwise noted, taken from her 714 pages of transcriptions. I have checked the accuracy of many
of these transcriptions against the manuscripts.   10 Giles Lee, *A sermon preached at Inniscarra,
on the sixteenth of February, 1797, being the day appointed for a general thanksgiving; before the barony
of Barrett's Cavalry* (Cork: A. Edwards, 1797), pp 6, 18.   11 'Memoir' (TCD MS 10978).
Quoted with permission of Trinity College Library.   12 'The Late Dr Maginn, LLD,' *The Age*
(London), 28 August, 1842, p. 5.   13 *Freeholder* (Cork), 26 January 1819, p. 3.   14 Terry

Kyle, Maginn was repelled by the 'cold morality and uncompromising theology' of the examiners, who failed to perceive the merit – or humour – of his Latin poem in which Æneas is made out to be a eunuch.[15] He returned to his family in Cork, where his father had decided to make an amicable break with the Diocesan School and start, with his son's aid, his own school. Between 1811 and 1819 he assisted his father in this new classical academy (located in the family home), deepened his philological knowledge, wrote anonymously for the newspapers, and raked around town.[16] Eagleton's description of him as a 'lusty orange apologist' with 'virulently anti-Catholic sentiments' is I think excessive.[17] For one thing, the record we have of his writings prior to 1819, when he began his remarkable (and well documented) career with *Blackwood's*, is one in which variety of fun rather than virulence of politics predominates. For another, Maginn's friendships extended across all Corkonian classes, and he made few distinctions in his private life between Protestant and Catholic. In a small city a polylingual and fun-loving teenage schoolmaster stood out. As he wrote to Blackwood, '[a]s for me, you may tell any Cork man, any thing you like, true or untrue about me; for I am known by every body gentle and simple in this city.'[18] In the 1820s, his catholicity of connection may be instanced by his ability to recruit for the ultra-Tory *Blackwood's* the young J.D. Murphy, from a wealthy Catholic family, a middle-class Catholic Whig lawyer, and the impoverished Catholic poet J.J. Callanan (hired later to teach in his school), as well as the expected Protestant apologists such as the Revd Horatio Townsend. Some have found it an 'enigma of his career'[19] that Maginn could have so many Catholic friends and still hold his anti-Catholic political views. Getting along, however, was a habit inherited from his father, as well as a prudent business practice.

One other Cork influence should be mentioned. A very short distance from the Maginn family home was the printing shop of John ('Jack') Boyle, who published the liberal (and generally pro-Catholic) *Freeholder*. The paper, termed by B.G. MacCarthy a 'journalistic excrescence' did not campaign for causes so much as provide a venue for freewheeling and eclectic waggery.[20] As a writer, it was Maginn's grammar school, with a 'quiz' every day. He learned in the *Freeholder* the inveterate habit of satirizing both sides, and especially at the time of his wedding found himself the target of much good-natured fun in return. In an autobiographical story in *Blackwood's* just before he left Ireland, he has his narrator confess,

> I have dirtied my fingers with ink, you say, and daubed other people's faces with them. I admit it. My pen has been guilty of various jeux d'e-

Eagleton, 'Cork and the carnivalesque', in *Crazy John and the bishop* (Cork: Cork UP, 1998), pp 158–211.   **15** 'Late Dr Maginn', p. 5.   **16** John Maginn died on 22 January, 1819, when Maginn was twenty-four.   **17** Eagleton, 'Cork and the carnivalesque', p. 167.   **18** 25 Feb. 1822, Cooke, 'Maginn–Blackwood', p. 255.   **19** Davis and Mary Coakley, *Wit and wine: literary and artistic Cork in the early nineteenth century* (Dublin: Glendale, 1985), p. 26.   **20** B.G. MacCarthy, 'Centenary of William Maginn, 1794–1842', *Studies*, 32 (1943), p. 348.

sprit, but let me whisper it, Jemmy, on *both* sides. […] I write with no ill feeling; public men or people who thrust themselves before the public in any way, I just look upon as phantoms of the imagination, as things to throw off common-places about.[21]

Maginn regarded publishing 'quizzes' on both Whig and Tory as, in some way, an act that transcended politics, and in this regard it shows that his politics, while sincere, were subservient to this impulse. These 'quizzes', however, require someone else to take an action, to thrust themselves before public attention so that the quizzer may react. Maginn's positions may best be understood as reactionary, or to give it a more palatable spin, instinctively oppositional. I believe Maginn's 'Standard' was a fourfold one, and will examine his core beliefs of anti-whiggism, anti-papism, anti-humbug, and anti-political economy.

Maginn's anti-Whiggism was constant. Maginn was raised to believe that the Whigs were wrong on the French Revolution, wrong on Napoleon, and wrong on Ireland. He found irksome the insincere or tactical use of the Irish issue by English Whigs, without any concern for the effect of their policies on people like him. *Edinburgh Review* writers such as Henry Brougham and Sydney Smith hammered in their journal about Ireland: 'the great mass of the population is completely subjugated and overawed by a handful of comparatively recent settlers,' Smith wrote in 1820, 'who have been reluctantly compelled to desist from still greater abuses of authority, – and who look with trembling apprehension to the increasing liberality of the Parliament and the country towards those unfortunate persons whom they have always looked upon as their property and their prey.'[22] For people like Maginn who were Protestant but saw themselves as Irish through and through, and who lacked the options and protections of the rich, this 'trembling apprehension' was all too real. In the 1820s Munster was riven by agrarian violence, which Maginn documents in essays and in private letters, generally laced with his ironic humour. Comparing Irish radicals to London ones, he writes that '*our* Whigs display their spleen in burning houses & cutting up his Majesty's subjects – while *their* Whigs vent their ire in talk, and murder nothing but the King's English.'[23]

Once in London, his antipathy to the Whigs as a jobbing club dedicated to getting place at any cost deepened – but his connections to the Tories were shaken as well, and not only by the defection of Peel and Wellington to the other side of the Catholic question in 1829. R.P. Gillies had met Maginn when he visited Scotland in 1823; later in London in 1827 he found a man more inclined to make sarcastic comments about both Whig and Tory.[24] His opposition to Whiggery shifted in England towards disgust with what he thought of

21 'Pococurante', *Blackwood's*, 14 (1823), p. 134. **22** *The works of the Rev. Sydney Smith* (London: Longmans, 1869), p. 346. **23** 24 Jan 1822, Cooke, 'Maginn-Blackwood,' p. 243. **24** R.P. Gillies, *Memoirs of a literary veteran*, 3 vols (London: 1851), iii, p. 169.

as their pandering, snobbery, and hypocritical advocacy of pseudo-radical views. Maginn gave carte blanche to William Blackwood to manipulate and revise his contributions; in 1825, however, he wrote in a letter 'Whigs, be they Lords, or be they plebeians, I shall not praise directly or indirectly — and I only request that no panegyric on one of such persons be ever inserted in any article of mine on any account whatsoever —That is the only stipulation I make.'[25] By the 1830s Maginn's vitriolic anti-Whiggism encompassed views that seem, at first glance, to be quite radical. He argued, for instance, that the best way to dish the Whigs would be for the Tories to push for universal male suffrage and he became more hostile to the aristocracy *per se*.[26]

Punch, as Carlyle said, is Punch — that is, when it's not Ireland, and the nature of Maginn's Irishness has always been contested; some have never forgiven him the 'Lady of Leith' song that seems the archetype of the stage Irishman, or his role in transforming 'blarney' from a place name to an Irish characteristic.[27] Maginn thought that a 'jug of punch' was an 'accurate and truly philosophical emblem' for Ireland:

> There's the Protestant part of the population inferior in quantity, superior in strength, apt to get at the head, evidently the whiskey of the compound. The Roman Catholics, greater in physical proportions, but infinitely weaker, and usually very hot, are shadowed forth by the water. The Orangemen, as their name implies, are the fruit, which some palates think too sour, and therefore reject, while others think that it alone gives grateful flavor to the whole.

Asked 'what's the sugar?' he replied, 'Why, the conciliators dropped in among us to sweeten our acidity [...] very much at the risk of turning the stomachs of the company.'[28] Odoherty's Ireland and punch analogy appeared in 1823, just as Maginn was making plans to go to the land of the sugar, England. He was only waiting for his brother John to finish at Trinity so he could take over the family business. Maginn had abandoned a career in the Church of Ireland, and his emigration is tinged by an awareness of the untenable nature of the Protestant Ascendancy. Terry Eagleton notes that a 'governing bloc with its political back to the wall is likely to react rather more hysterically than those accustomed enough to being victimized, given the contrast with their previous condition.'[29] Maginn does show symptoms of this hysteria during the Rockite and Whiteboy

---

25 Cooke, 'Maginn-Blackwood,' p. 574. **26** James Sack notes that Maginn was by August 1831 suggesting the Tories add both 'male *and* female suffrage to the £10 franchise component of the Whig bill'; see *From Jacobite to Conservative: reaction and orthodoxy in Britain, c.1760–1832* (Cambridge: Cambridge UP, 1993), p. 154. **27** Maureen Waters, *The Comic Irishman* (Albany: State University of New York Press, 1984), p. 184. **28** *Noctes*, i, p. 189. **29** Terry Eagleton, *Scholars and rebels in nineteenth-century Ireland* (Malden, MA: Blackwell, 1999), p. 54.

'outrages' that attended the economic distresses of 1821–3, but as he also somewhat sardonically commented to William Blackwood, the outrages *are a matter of no moment in the end*, but during their operation they are terrifying, & afford fine commonplaces for antiliberal speakers & writers.'[30] He was himself an antiliberal manipulator – he apparently worked in 1821 to encourage Catholic priests to oppose emancipation. His jaundiced remark, I believe, shows another problem with Cork for Maginn: the same debate and the same conflicts had been played over his entire life, and there was no end in sight. He was bored with it all. In a slashing review of collections of Irish songs published in England, Maginn remarks '[i]t would, perhaps, be a good thing to go over some of the political speculations on Ireland in the same manner, but I never liked Irish politics, and now I particularly detest them.'[31]

He also I believe detested Irish politics because he recognized the bleakness of his cause, and that's one reason why he rejected Blackwood's repeated requests to take charge of the 'Irish' material for the magazine. 'As for Catholic Emancipation,' he replied, 'ask any body but an Irish Protestant for an article about that.'[32] Numerous factors account for his emigration to London, but the unrest in Munster was top of the list, especially once his marriage was planned to the daughter of a Church of Ireland clergyman, Ellen Bullen. They were wed in January of 1824 and the couple left Cork almost at once for the metropolis.

They found however that Cork went with them. Ellen socialized almost entirely with Irish friends, and Maginn's sister Margaret lived with the family for several years. Thackeray remembered how 'Maginn used always to have a half dozen tipsy fellows in his train, to whom he gave money and clothes.'[33] The Maginns welcome mat was out for almost anyone from Cork, regardless of religion or politics. He also moved easily among the Irish poor in London, partly to hide from creditors and their bailiffs, but also by choice. Maginn was fluent in Irish, and he was also able to 'talk St Giles's' slang.[34] He reiterates his preference for drinking with coal-heavers over club-men so frequently that one concludes he was sincere.

Despite these tolerant ways, Maginn's most sustained newspaper work began in an explicitly anti-Papist way, when he joined another Trinity College LLD, Stanley Lees Giffard, in editing the new Tory daily, the *Standard*. Giffard took his MA from Trinity in the same year that Maginn completed his BA, but it is unlikely, given the differences in age, that they were intimate at that time. Giffard's father was a Castle secret agent and 'vitriolic' enemy of Catholic emancipation.[35] According to one historian of the press, Maginn chose the title, the

30 26 Nov. 1821; Cooke, 'Maginn-Blackwood', p. 199.   31 'Odoherty on Irish songs', *Blackwood's*, 17 (March 1823), p. 321.   32 1821?, Cooke, 'Maginn-Blackwood', p. 111.   33 William Makepeace Thackeray, *Selected letters*, ed. Edgar F. Harden (New York: New York UP, 1996), p. 147.   34 'The election of editor for *Fraser's Magazine*', *Fraser's Magazine*, 1 (1830), p. 507.   35 Hereward Senior, *Orangeism in Ireland and Britain, 1795–1836* (London: Routledge & Kegan Paul, 1966), p. 72.

motto from Livy, and wrote the prospectus for the new venture.[36] The motto was dropped after the first issue, because the association of 'Signifer' with Maginn misleadingly pointed to 'The Doctor' as the prime mover and editor-in-chief. The goal of Giffard and the wealthy Tories behind the venture was always clear: to plant the *Standard* on the shaky ground of opposition to Catholic emancipation, and the tenor of their position is enunciated in all capital letters in a leader of 17 September 1827. Arguing against the proposition that emancipation would tranquilize Ireland, the paper booms: 'THE PAPISTS OF IRELAND HAVE NEVER BEEN TRANQUIL BUT WHEN KEPT DOWN BY SUPERIOR POWER' (p. 3).

It is not possible to separate Maginn's leaders from Giffard's on the *Standard*. Maginn recalled that 'Giffard was supposed to write from a real fanatical feeling against the Papists; – I was charged with satirizing them and Peel for fun and the love of mischief. Besides I was accused of writing much that I did not write. In fact I was accused of having made the libels that Giffard really wrote'.[37] *Fraser's* commentary on Ireland shows Maginn's mature thinking much more clearly. There he accepts the new reality: the constitution has been changed, the Catholics have been enfranchised, and no return to the *status quo ante* is possible; Maginn's introduction to the first issue simply states 'we shall not moot a question which […] is as useless in practice as the famous schoolboy controversy of ancient times, whether Hannibal ought to have marched upon Rome after the battle of Cannæ.'[38] In his own writings for *Fraser's* and in the political writings of David Robinson, the London essayist he imported from *Blackwood's*, anti-papism is mixed with an insistence on the historical context: 'England is chargeable,' Robinson writes in *Fraser's*, 'with a course of either vicious or guilty policy towards [Ireland] from the first year of her subjugation.'[39] Maginn's own forceful plea for humane Poor Laws for Ireland in 1833 shows his sympathy for the 'little cotters, who have been induced to take cabins and potato-gardens,' many of whom later swarmed to London to avoid starvation.[40]

Maginn returned to Ireland for the last time in the Summer of 1839, where he visited his brothers John, rector at Castletown Roche, and Charles, just ordained. Commenting on Maginn's Protestant family background, MacCarthy notes that '[h]e did not need to leave Ireland to become an expatriate Irishman'; his political opinions on Ireland remained rooted in the Church of Ireland, and in Munster Protestantism, but he took a perverse pride that Daniel O'Connell had once referred to him in a speech as 'that hoary-headed libeller, Dr. Maginn.'[41]

36 Frederick Knight Hunt, *The fourth estate: contributions towards a history of newspapers, and the liberty of the press*, 2 vols (London: D. Bogue, 1850), ii, p. 240.   **37** Edward Kenealy papers, Huntington Library, HM 38640. This item is reproduced by permission of The Huntington Library, San Marino, California.   **38** 'Our "Confession of Faith"', *Fraser's Magazine*, 1 (1830), p. 4.   **39** 'Ireland and the Progress of the "Repeal Question"', *Fraser's Magazine*, 9 (1834), p. 253.   **40** 'Poor-laws for Ireland', *Fraser's Magazine*, 7 (1833), p. 285.   **41** MacCarthy, 'Maginn-Blackwood', p. 349; Kenealy, p. 93.

Maginn might be considered an antitype of Scrooge. Both Ebenezer and Maginn come to the conclusion that society is comprised chiefly of 'humbug'. But where Scrooge hordes in response, is mean with others, and is personally surly, Maginn spends, freely loans money, and engages in ubiquitous cheerfulness. In Cork he gave deadpan presentations to various improving societies, while sending them up in the pages of the *Freeholder* and *Blackwood's*. While Cork's secular improving societies provided prime specimens of humbug, he ridiculed the humbuggery of both Catholic and Orangeman in his correspondence and in the pages of *Maga*.[42] Maginn's reaction to his perception that the world's all humbug is often through the hoax; the hoaxer, after all, has greatest fun when humbugs are caught taking themselves for real. Once in London, Maginn earned his living at first via Theodore Hook's *John Bull* Sunday newspaper. In Cork he had lampooned the pretensions of the provinces; in London he saw them magnified.

In July of 1824 he launched the *John Bull Magazine*, advertized as 'edited by a Committee of plain People, who dip into all sorts of books, frequent all sorts of company, drink ale with their cheese, and ask twice for their soup if they want it. Prospectuses being decidedly Humbugs, none will be given.'[43] His abettors were probably Theodore Hook and William 'Tiger' Dunlop, a scalawag Scottish half-pay Army doctor and future Canadian founding father. The sensational first issue featured a forged bit of the Byron *Memoirs* titled 'My Wedding Night', which immediately placed the magazine outside society's pale; friends such as John Gibson Lockhart were appalled. In the same issue a series titled 'The Humbugs of the Age' began with an extraordinary attack on Thomas de Quincey. Maginn defines lawful and unlawful humbug in his opening:

> There are some humbugs with which we have no patience. If we see a quack-doctor vending gin and rosemary-oil, under the name of the balsam of Rakasiri – or a mock-patriot bellowing loudly in a cause for which he does not care a pinch of snuff – or a pseudo-saint turning up the whites of his eyes, and rolling them about in all the ecstasies of hypocrisy, at a conventicle – or a poor anxious author sitting down to puff himself up in a review, got up for the occasion – or twenty thousand more things of the kind, we can appreciate and pardon them all. The quack mixes – the orator roars – the saint prays – the author puffs – for a tangible and intelligible reason, money. This is the lawful object of humbug. Even with those who go through similar operations for fame, which is a secondary scope of the humbuggers, we are not very angry if that fame be for anything worth looking after. But the sort and description of humbugs which we cannot tolerate, even in thought, are

---

42 See for instance the postscript to 'Letters of Timothy Tickler, Esq. No. IX' in *Blackwood's*, 14 (1823), p. 312.   **43** Advertisement in the *Examiner*, 27 June 1824, p. 414.

the fellows who, on the strength of some wretched infirmity, endeavor
to puff themselves into notice, and not satisfied with being thought
worthy of being objects of charity and compassion, look about the company, into which they introduce themselves, for wonder or applause.[44]

Even after he had been convinced to pardon De Quincey, Maginn continued
to humour professional humbug but react viscerally to what we might call psy-
chologically needy humbuggery. He warns the new readers of *Fraser's* in 1830,
'I have written for all sorts, kinds, manners, and persuasions of periodicals, and
I find them all pretty much the same – very considerable damned deal of
humbug in the internal regulation of their affairs.'[45] The targets of *Fraser's* sustained literary attacks – Edward Bulwer, Alaric 'Attila' Watts, Robert 'Satan'
Montgomery – could all be said to fall into the second category of humbugs
who lusted after 'wonder or applause'. In the war on publisher 'puffing' that
Maginn and *Fraser's* famously waged, the professionals at Colburn and Bentley
never received the harshest treatment.

Maginn's most personal writings for *Fraser's* were undoubtedly filler he supplied at the back, written over the bottle in the publisher's back parlour with
the printer's devil at his elbow. In one such production, 'Rumbling Murmurs of
an Old Tory over the Fate of his Quondam Friends' he returns to the voice of
the plain man who drinks ale with his cheese:

> And having all my life a particular hatred of humbug, quackery, lying,
> and deceit, it is quite needless to say that I hate, in politics, Whigs, *i.e.*
> Jacobins in a cloak – in religion, Socinians, *i.e.* Deists in a cloak – in phi-
> losophy, useful knowledgers, that is, blockheads in a cloak – and in all
> branches of human concernment rats, that is to say, rascals, who, to do
> them justice, seldom wear any cloak, but walk forth stark naked in all the
> majesty of scoundrilism.[46]

Maginn's particular hatred is of course partial; his chief weapon against the
humbugs was, after all, the outrageous spoof.

One of the most dependable and consistent beliefs – if that's the right word
for it – of the adult Maginn derives from the 1790s – that one should be skep-
tical of all 'projectors'. It is this antipathy that partially accounts for Maginn's
shameful support for the West Indian planters, since the leading abolitionists
were so closely associated with Bentham's projectors on the one hand, and
evangelical killjoys on the other. In both cases Maginn found the enthusiasm for
abolition abroad combined with a seeming indifference either to the suffering

---

44 'Humbugs of the Age. No. I. – The Opium Eater', *John Bull Magazine* 1 (1824), p. 21.   **45**
'Election', *Fraser's*, 1 (1830), p. 507.   **46** 'Rumbling murmurs of an Old Tory over the fate of
his quindam friends', *Fraser's*, 3 (1831), p. 649.

or the pleasures of the lower classes at home, and faulted the latter. David Levy has recently shown how *Fraser's* was thus able to obtain a 'progressive' reputation among scholars more concerned with the abuses of the factory system and the poor law despite its reactionary stance on slavery.

Miriam Thrall, in *Rebellious Fraser's*, her 1934 book that is still the sole monograph to treat Maginn in depth, notes that prior to the 'mighty remonstrances of Carlyle, Maginn's articles against utilitarian policies were unparalleled in audacity.'[47] In 1832, the magazine was rededicated and its politics redirected towards the reformers: 'we despise those political economists who swallow the jargon of Malthus or Macculloch with good faith, and pure ignorance of the consequences of the doctrines they preach.'[48] The *Fraser's* attacks on political economy, the New Poor Law, Malthus, etc. were, however, not really proto-serious Victorian; they were more frequently written in high glee. For Maginn – in contradistinction to Carlyle and those in his wake – the gravest sin of the economists was their ridiculous earnestness. Bentham's follower John Bowring, for example, was the target of a barrage of bizarre quizzes. Like Maginn, Bowring was polylingual, and an LLD, but unlike Maginn he put his signature constantly before the public. His translations from unfamiliar languages quickly became the fodder for Fraserian hoaxes. In 'Poetry of the Magyars' of 1830, a manuscript slips out of the review copy that shows Bowring describing a meeting of 'they who sit at Jerry's table' as if it were a 'Noctes Ambrosianæ':

> Then Jerry grows enamoured of his pot
> Of Barclay's best, and opening wide his gullet,
> Like Chops of Channel or Tom Thumb's big giant,
> He gulps down what would full swill Glumdalglitch;
> And when his face glows like the setting sun
> […]
> He cries aloud, being quite inebriate: –
> […]
> Say, am I not a cleverish fellow?[49]

A Rabelaisian Jeremy Bentham provokes mirth, presumably, on the face of it. Bowring was enrolled in the company of constant target of jokes as 'Our Man of Genius, Tydus Pooh-Pooh' – a late example, almost certainly Maginn's, may be found in some verses ascribed to Bowring in *The Age* in 1836: 'Sir, I say 'tis not right in "ridiculous" light / Should be render'd my genius so tow'ring; / If the Commons' bad taste made their fun so ill-placed, / It must not be said *I'm*

---

47 Thrall, *Rebellious Fraser's*, p. 122. 48 'Our first double number, and the reason why', *Fraser's Magazine*, 6 (1832), p. 626. 49 'Poetry of the Magyars', *Fraser's Magazine*, 1 (1830), p. 169. John Heraud also wrote part of this article.

"Butt Bowring".[50] In Bowring's case all Maginn's 'anti's' converge, but it is with delight rather than rage that he picks up his pen. To the smugness of the Whigs, projectors such as Bentham and Bowring add the grave sin of sobriety.

Which is not to say that Maginn was not genuinely moved by the plight of the poor in the industrial age, or outraged by the theorists who seemed to countenance such conditions. When Maginn moved to London he did not leave the Irish poor behind, and in his debt-ridden last decade he often hid from bailiffs in the slums of St Giles. He felt the political economists, removing religion from their calculus, could never come to grips with the nature of Ireland. At the end of his life Maginn found himself within the bounds of the Fleet Prison and in close company with its most celebrated denizen, Richard Oastler, the so-called 'Tory Radical' and leader of the anti-Poor Law movement whose imprisonment for debt was part of a campaign to silence him. The two men sat together in the evenings and wrote, the more earnest Oastler penning his *Fleet Papers*, and Maginn turning out leaders for the *Argus* newspaper, sometimes taking Oastler's advice on factory questions. (He also probably wrote the articles advocating Oastler's release in both the *Standard* and *The Age*.) Maginn predictably astonished Oastler with the depth of his learning, as well as his witty facetiousness. In his fond obituary notice of Maginn Oastler proclaimed that 'Dr. Maginn's politics were in unison with my own – they were all of the Saxon school.'[51] The Saxon school: that would have amused Maginn immensely; Saxon was one of the few languages he did not speak.

Maginn's twenty-five year career is extraordinarily rich and difficult to categorize. Given a target to lampoon, he almost always lampooned, though he was famous for his lack of personal malice. Maginn's reaction to his times represents one strategy among the supporters of the Established Church in Ireland – to confront change with rhetorical fireworks, mixed with an ironic appraisal of the chances of success at turning back Whig and Radical reform and rising Catholic nationalism. With the more proactive (and ultimately influential) strategy of the evangelical movement, which gained ground among members of the Church of Ireland, he had little sympathy. Throughout his life there are glimpses of an extraordinarily intelligent mind that has a hard time escaping from his sense of the absurd. I believe he regularly glimpsed Hardy's 'purblind doomsters' from 'Hap' dicing with fate, but instead of writing grim poems he sauntered up to ask if they'd like a drink and a drisheen. But first, I would argue, he would have ascertained that they were not Whigs, or Irish political bores, or Benthamites, or the second sort of humbugs.

---

50 'The Lament of Tydus Pooh-Pooh', *The Age*, 21 February 1836, p. 61.   **51** Richard Oastler, untitled obituary for Dr Maginn, *The Fleet Papers*, 2 (1842), p. 295.

The siege of O'Connell:
Charlotte Elizabeth Tonna's historical
novels of Ireland

KARA M. RYAN

In her autobiographical work, *Personal reflections*, British author and activist Charlotte Elizabeth Tonna recalls how, as a young child, she was greatly affected by the French revolution and its reverberations:

> Connected with [...] my early life are recollections that I would not lose. They are vivid, because, as I have said, I was a thinking child, and having been accustomed to listen with eagerness to the conversation of my seniors, I had insensibly imbibed their feelings. The recent horrors of the French Revolution, and the kindred spirit that had burst out with sanguinary violence in Ireland, while the social flame of England herself was deeply shaken by the roll of those waves that were not permitted to burst over her favored soil, of course formed a very permanent topic of conversation.[1]

Tonna's remarks are interesting and illuminating, particularly if one is familiar with her historical novels of Ireland, *The Rockite* (1823) and *Derry, a tale of revolution* (1833). The above passage reveals how the adult Tonna retrospectively accorded her epistemological and intellectual precociousness to particular historical events.[2] Like her better-known works, *Helen Fleetwood* (1839) and *The wrongs of women* (1844), Tonna's historical novels of Ireland act as interventions in the public arenas of history and political policy while they are also assertions of authorial and feminine subjectivity. As such, *The Rockite* and *Derry* warrant analysis from the perspectives of both Irish historiography and feminist literary criticism.

That Tonna's social protest fictions have been critically heralded for incepting legislative reform make her reactionary writings on Ireland all the more fascinating. Put plainly, Tonna is a paradox: her literary agitation against the anti-

---

1 Charlotte Elizabeth Tonna, 'Personal reflections', *The works of Charlotte Elizabeth, with an introduction by Mrs H.B. Stowe*, 2 vols (New York: M.W. Dodd, 1852), i, p. 14.   2 That she engages in such logic introduces a materialist, specifically Lukácian, insight to her self-analysis. See Georg Lukács, *History and class consciousness: studies in Marxist dialectics* (Cambridge, MA: Massachusetts Institute of Technology, 1968); Georg Lukács, *The historical novel* (Lincoln: University of Nebraska Press, 1968); and the debate that Lukács engages in with Theodor Adorno, Ernst Bloch, and Bertolt Brecht in Ernst Bloch (ed.), *Aesthetics and politics* (London: Verso, 1977).

domestic (and thus, in her eyes, immoral) tendencies of industrialism came to be expressed in a public forum resulting in some very definitive political reforms.[3] Unlike George Eliot who transferred her anxieties over the irreconcilability of women and history into her novels and characters – think of the prelude to *Middlemarch* and the crisis of Dorothea Brooke – Tonna does not seem to recognize the inherent subjectivity of historical representation, much less does she concern herself with displacement of women from that larger historical narrative. In her historical novels of Ireland, Tonna confronts the messiness of the Irish context with a temerity that leads to a misreading of Ireland's historical woes. She overlooks foundational material inequity in order to read historical tumult as synonymous with Catholicism and, while this results in formulaic, tract-like narratives, nonetheless, her characterizations of the various types on either side of the Irish question are revealing. Tonna's remedy for the Irish question is that disaffected Irish Catholics must be converted by a revitalized evangelical Protestantism. More specifically, in *The Rockite* the crisis of Ireland is presented as one of agency: once Catholics have exchanged their desire for historical agency with a properly situated spiritual agency – having, as it were, a direct line to Christ – the woes of Irish history will cease. *Derry*, on the other hand, emanates from the perspective of an evangelical Protestant affected by O'Connell's popular movement for Catholic emancipation. The spectacle of O'Connell's mass meetings arguably widened Tonna's hostility beyond Catholics to include those liberal Protestants whom she perceived as abetting Catholic emancipation. Her second historical novel of Ireland resurrects the events of 1688–9 to invigorate and unify the Protestants of Ireland.

In *The Rockite,* the seemingly ubiquitous turmoil of Irish history is attributed to Catholicism, a religion to be disdained for its inherent and contagious effeminacy. And while this work does indeed narrativize contesting interpretations of Ireland's crises – that is, we hear the Rockite version of history – Tonna's text ultimately promulgates a colonialist, Protestant historiography. Because Catholicism is a force that has bewitched its adherents, Tonna regards peasant rebellions as both produced from, and endemic in, a religion denying individual subjectivity. Herein lurks the irony of Tonna's historiography: rather than seeing peasant unrest as born out of colonial oppression and, as such, expressive of a genuine desire for political subjectivity, Tonna reduces the

---

3 Joseph Kestner, *Protest and reform: the British social narrative by women, 1827–1867* (Madison: University of Wisconsin Press, 1985), pp 91–102; Zipporah Batshaw, *Representing women: law, literature, and feminism* (Durham: Duke UP, 1994); Mary Jean Corbett, 'Feminine authorship and spiritual authority in Victorian women writers' autobiographies', *Women's studies: an interdisciplinary journal,* 18:1 (1990), pp 13–29; Deborah Kaplan, 'The woman worker in Charlotte Elizabeth Tonna's fiction', *Mosaic: a journal for the interdisciplinary study of literature,* 18:2 (1985), pp 51–63; and Elizabeth Ann Kowaleski, 'The dark night of her soul: the effects of Anglican evangelicalism on the careers of Charlotte Elizabeth Tonna and George Eliot' (PhD, Columbia University, 1981).

Rockite movement as merely emblematic of spiritual miscarriage. In her recon-figuration of history, Tonna supplants material poverty with spiritual emptiness, thereby decolonizing and neutralizing oppression. Hence, her solution to the woes of Ireland remains as contained as her perception.

The discursive excesses of Tonna's story correlate to the spiritual excesses of the Rockite movement itself: atop the litany of political grievances concerning mandatory tithes, land tenure insecurity, and climbing rents, the Rockites believed in a messianic second coming once the Protestant Irish and their polit-ical infrastructure had been destroyed. Although the Rockite movement was indeed unique for its millennial component, systematic peasant disturbances in the nineteenth century were anything but rare: historians James S. Donnelly, Jr, and Samuel Clark note at least one major outbreak every decade throughout the first half of the century.[4] Moreover, in spite of Tonna's presentation of the Rockite movement as primarily motivated by anti-Protestant sentiment, it is important to understand how the veritably unjust system of Irish land propri-etorship was foundational to Catholic disaffection and desperation. By 1804, out of Ireland's total population of 5.4 million, there were approximately 9,000 landed proprietors, and within that figure, 95 per cent were identified as Protestant.[5] Although Catholics were legally permitted to own land, the resid-ual effects of the penal laws had resulted in a class structure drawn upon sectar-ian lines, thus, most Catholics simply could not afford landownership. The land-less Catholic laborers, the poorest of the poor, made up the majority of the Rockites, although there were some middle-class Catholics drawn to the move-ment as an expression of religious solidarity.[6]

A Rockite handbill is illustrative of how concrete grievances intertwined with subtler anxieties exacerbated by years of subjugation:

> Hearken unto me, ye men of Ireland, and hear my voice? Arise, O! [*sic*] Milesians the day of our deliverance is coming, when the trumpet beat to

4 Samuel Clark and James S. Donnelly, Jr (eds), *Irish peasants: violence and political unrest, 1780–1914* (Madison: University of Wisconsin Press, 1983), p. 25.   **5** James S. Donnelly, Jr, *Landlord and tenant in nineteenth-century Ireland* (Dublin: Gill and Macmillan, 1973), p. 5.   **6** Bishop Charles Walmesley's *General history of the Christian church* provided the source of the mil-lennial rumor. Written in the 1790s under the pen name Signor Pastorini, 'Pastorini's prophe-cies' (as it became known) was ostensibly a commentary on the Book of Revelation, although its popularity among the peasantry can be traced to one textual line prophesying that Protestants would undergo punishment fifty years after 1771. Indicative of the Rockites' sweep-ing appeal is that notwithstanding denunciations by both the bishop of Limerick and the Great Liberator himself, Daniel O'Connell (the latter claimed the phenomenon was part of a Protestant conspiracy), by 1820, 'Pastorini's prophecies' had gone through at least six printings, while excerpts of it circulated widely throughout the countryside, particularly in the south. See James S. Donnelly, Jr, 'Pastorini and Captain Rock: millenarianism and sectarianism in the Rockite movement', in Samuel Clark and James S. Donnelly, Jr (eds), *Irish peasants: violence and political unrest, 1780–1914* (Madison: University of Wisconsin Press, 1983), pp 106–22.

arms [...] your eyes shall have no pity on the breed of Luther, for he had
no pity on us. Behold, the day of the Lord cometh, cruel both with wrath
and fierce anger, to lay the land desolate [...] Their children shall ye dash
to pieces. Before their eyes their houses shall be spoiled, and their wives
ravished [...] You see misery upon misery is come upon us. Seldom a day
passes that our cattle is [*sic*] not canted by the roguery and oppression of
our landlords. We have nothing left but to die valiantly or starve. We are the
most miserable people on the face of the earth, while our sons of perdition
are satisfying their appetite, luxury, and gluttony abroad [...] Oh when their
belly is full and warm, what a feeling they have for the poor [...] Lament
and mourn; ye hereticks, for the day of your destruction is come.[7]

Nancy Curtin's work on nationalism's usage of gender ideologies helps us
perceive how, within Rockite ideology, the reclamation of masculinity through
violent retribution became interchangeable with assertions of subjectivity, while
colonial oppression and civic powerlessness was seen as analogous to castration.[8]
For the many peasants who made up the Rockite movement, the ultimate act
of rebellion was the valiant death for the cause or, to use Curtin's phrase, 'patriotic self-immolation' – an exaggerated gesture emanating from a populace rec-
ognizing its utter disempowerment and historical absence.[9] Self-sacrifice in the
name of Ireland, although central to the United Irishmen, also became a recurring motif within various pro-union factions. Tonna's text is exemplary of the
pro-union attempt to reclaim certain motifs and stereotypes from the nationalist cause.

In *The Rockite,* Tonna utilizes the trope of literacy to draw an association
between Protestantism and historical agency as opposed to Catholicism and historical objectification. Her evangelical Protestantism posits her on the side of
viewing events as divinely determined and this is the prism through which she
reads Irish history. From the preface to *The Rockite,*

Among civilized nations, Ireland may be said to stand alone in the peculiar hardship of a destiny from the inflictions of which other countries are
generally exempt. The singularity of her misfortune consists in this: –
Nations may in their turn have been assailed by the hostile arm of foreign
invasion, but the inhabitants have bravely united in defence of their

7 Ibid., p. 123. **8** See Nancy J. Curtin, '"A nation of abortive men:" gendered citizenship and
early republicanism', in Marilyn Cohen and Nancy J Curtin (eds), *Reclaiming gender: transgressive identities in modern Ireland* (New York: St Martin's Press, 1999), pp 33–52. For a broader
discussion of nationalism, colonialism, and gender, see Anne McClintock, *Imperial leather: race,
gender, and sexuality in the colonial contest* (New York: Routledge, 1995). Although McClintock
discusses Ireland only briefly, nonetheless, her book is a seminal examination of gender ideologies, imperialism, and nationalism.   **9** Nancy J. Curtin, '"A nation of abortive men"', in
Cohen and Curtin, p. 34.

hearths, or sunk down together, powerless, beneath the overwhelming stroke. Ireland alone has been fated, from age to age, to furnish, from among the children of her soil, those enemies who should drench it in kindred blood; and devastate their mother land more effectually, more hopelessly, than a host of stranger foes would have aimed to accomplish.[10]

The evocation of a third-person narrator employing overwrought language works to create an initial tone of sympathy for Ireland that becomes swiftly undercut when one attempts to untangle meaning from the multiple instances of passive-voice construction and to discern the definitive nouns lurking under such ambiguities as 'peculiar hardship', 'inflictions', and 'singularity of […] misfortune'. Who are those who are assailing and devastating Ireland by drenching it 'in kindred blood'? Any assumption that the narrator wants us to consider British subjugation as the implied offense is dispelled by the final sentence denying the presence within Ireland of any 'stranger foes'.

These opening remarks reveal a historiography that is conveniently devoid of human agency. Imperial acts of conquest are robbed of their initial violent oppression; instead, colonialism is presented as an historical *fait accompli* – one of Homi Bhabha's 'fixities' of colonial discourse – while rebellion occurs without any sort of predicating oppression or cause.[11] Tonna's assertion that 'nations may in their turn have been assailed by the hostile arm of foreign invasion' never turns back upon itself to question the ethics of that initial act of aggression; rather, she locates historical criminality within the ranks of the Irish peasantry and implies that their incessant unwillingness to acquiesce in defeat is the reason for the continued bloodshed. 'If only Ireland would make it easy for the British' is Tonna's underlying sentiment. By constructing the continuous turmoil of Irish history in this way, Tonna engages in a rhetorical sleight of hand: if the Irish are victimizing the Irish, with the British nowhere to be seen, she can create from among the Irish both victims and perpetrators, playing upon her reader's emotions while simultaneously obscuring any foundational material transgressions.

In Tonna's reading of Irish history, rebels become rebels because they have no satisfactory outlet for their ambitions. At the onset of the narrative, the protagonist and future Rockite rebel Maurice Delany is shown to be in the throes of a crisis of agency rooted in Catholic ignorance and post-war uselessness:

In the Autumn of 1821, several regiments of cavalry were disbanded, both in Dublin and the provincial towns of Ireland. This step was inevitable; reduction to a moderate peace establishment having been for some years in progress; but those who best knew the actual state of public feeling among the lower classes, beheld with dismay a body of

---

10 Charlotte Elizabeth Tonna, 'The Rockite', in *Works of Charlotte Elizabeth*, i, pp 159–240.
11 Homi Bhabha, *The location of culture* (London: Routledge, 1994), p. 67.

fine enterprising young fellows, long unaccustomed to manual labour, and burning distinction, thus turned loose into the mass already fermenting in an alarming degree.[12]

Tonna's narrative seeks to counter associations between hypermasculinity and nationalism through the depiction of the nationalist rebel as effeminate and intellectually degenerate. While Maurice Delany's crisis of masculinity – his idleness – is shown to have pushed him toward nationalism, Tonna dismantles the nationalism-equals-manliness equation by depicting Maurice's devolving physiognomy. After joining the Rockites, his once 'manly stature' degenerates, the 'beauty of [his] manly countenance' is 'marred', his 'martial gait' and 'exact personal neatness' devolve to resemble the insolent, slovenly clownishness of his comrades.[13] Maurice's fate, least he denounce the agrarian cause, is epitomized by the Rockite superior: '[i]n his dress he was slovenly, and in person most uncleanly; his manners were savagely repulsive, and the notices penned by him were couched in a language more dreadful than those of any other person.'[14] Not only is this person a boor, but he is illiterate to boot.

Ignorance and arbitrariness govern the Rockites: Maurice joins the rebels out of naïveté about their political aspirations, which the narrative discloses to be mere sexual opportunism. Rockite rhetoric is presented as empty of substance and immaterial. When Maurice is on the run from his Rockite comrades after having refused to abduct a wealthy Protestant landholder's daughter, the rebels post a warning to those housing him: 'It wont do – we will have your blood, if you dont turn out the solger. It isn't the Peeler rascals, nor any Orange villains that shall protect you from me, John Rock.'[15] The gross grammatical errors are intentional on Tonna's part and they underscore a central tenet of her own perspective on the Irish question: that is, the circular reasoning that Catholicism breeds ignorance which, in turn, engenders greater allegiance to Catholicism. Rockite language becomes the mere recitation of political platitudes and Catholic ritual prayers. In their alliance with Satan, the Rockites use their historical agency for sadistically violent and grammatically incorrect purposes. Ultimately, illiteracy and ignorance become indistinguishable from Rockite allegiance and its correlative, degenerate masculinity.

This becomes further apparent in that countering the savage buffoonery of the Rockite rebel is the 'tall, sturdy, resolute-looking' Michael Donovan, the Catholic-turned-Protestant farmer whose narrated trials and political observations Maurice comes to equate with truth. Michael's first exposure to Protestantism is said to have come about by chance: he heard singing and followed the sound to a Methodist Church. After guiltily listening but not comprehending the sermon, Michael's infant spirit sought to overcome his Catholicism-induced ignorance:

12 Tonna, 'Rockite', p. 162.   13 Ibid., pp 168–9.   14 Ibid., p. 169.   15 Ibid., p. 227.

a congregation of Methodists had assembled for evening service. Not knowing what to make of the party, Mike lingered and listened, and heard from a blunt-looking man, slightly elevated above the rest, an address that filled him with astonishment and curiosity: but recollecting the guilt that he would incur attending to heretical teachers, he tore himself from the spot. One thought alone took full possession of his mind – a vehement desire of learning to read.[16]

Michael's spiritual awakening thus goes hand in hand with his intellectual birth: he teaches himself to read and shares his talent by becoming a proselytizer himself. After being driven out by the local priest, Michael settles in the west where 'it was his highest joy to assemble around him a party of his western countrymen, among whom the original language still retained its powerful *ascendancy*, and in that tongue read the Scripture, to explain, admonish, and pour forth his supplications.'[17] The now literate, now Protestant Michael Donovan ascends to the ideal Irishman as signified by his residency in the west of Ireland and fluency in Irish.

The climax of *The Rockite* incorporates a mélange of cultural stereotypes and religious iconography: as the Michael Donovan family is gathered around listening to the father read from the bible, a Rockite bullet, meant for Maurice, instead kills Michael's young son Paddy, who lies prostrate and bleeding in his mother's arms (an Irish pieta), while his forlorn twin-brother, appropriately named Johnny, wonders what made him so 'dirty'. The distraught father Michael comforts the even more guilt-ridden and distraught Maurice and reassures him that he is not to blame; rather, the death of innocents is a 'blood bought blessing' meant to teach a larger lesson.[18]

Of course, Maurice does learn his lesson; a few days later, he is captured by the Rockites who issue a death sentence. Anti-climatic when read from a nationalist position, when read from a pro-union position, the tranquility with which Maurice goes to his death completes the construction of an ideal Protestant, authentically Irish, Christ-like manhood. In this final scene, Maurice stands bravely before his bloodthirsty accusers and, in a gesture reminiscent of St Stephen's heavenward glance, looks to the sky for divine wisdom:[19]

> [After] looking earnestly at the blue vault of heaven for a few moments, during which his features even glowed with animated hope, he spoke in a firm tone, 'Comrades, take my forgiveness, and may God pardon you.'
> Driscoll [the Rockite leader] stepped back some paces; he summoned all his strength, mental and bodily, for the last anathema.

---

16 Ibid., p. 223. **17** Ibid., p. 224 (my italics). **18** Ibid., p. 229. **19** See Acts of the Apostles 7:51–8; I am grateful to James H. Murphy for pointing out this allusion to St Stephen, a figure mythologized as the first martyr.

'Traitor, and heretic! the soil of your poor country, with whose enemies and destroyers you have leagued, opens to shroud you in a name-
less, a dishonoured grave. So perish all Ireland's foes! The Holy Catholic
church, whose pure faith you have abandoned, whose altars you have
profaned, and whose salvation you despise, levels her thunders at your
accursed head – Where they point they smite. – Fire!'[20]

Maurice's noble bearing returns: he is accorded 'manly fortitude' and restored
with the 'bloom of his handsome countenance'. Moments before he is shot,
Maurice completes his conversion by directly appealing to Christ with words
that echo Christ's own plea for final forgiveness. In her revisionist gospel, Tonna
accords the Rockites the spiteful last word thereby underscoring the martyr-
dom of the newly converted Maurice.

But Tonna does not end it here. As a parallel to her prefatory remarks, she
concludes *The Rockite* with an epilogue affirming the vision of a Protestant-
governed Ireland as divinely ordained.

Unhappy Ireland! Long and deeply has her soil been saturated with the
blood of her children. Many a youth, like Maurice Delany, has been
lured from the paths of integrity, to pursue the down-hill road of guilt,
with more hardened offenders; destroying, until himself destroyed. Many
a gentle spirit […] is goaded into fiendish deeds by the false fervour of a
zeal that believes it is doing God service in murdering his people. Aye,
and there are Doyles and Donovans [Protestant proselytizers] too, pursuing at this day the unobtrusive work of peace and mercy. Themselves
enlightened, they are diffusing, each within his own little sphere, that
beam, beneath whose lustre the deluded soul strikes off its chain, and
rising into life and liberty, becomes the centre of another circle, widen-
ing until the kingdom of darkness already begins to totter at its base.[21]

Within Tonna's paradigm of history, colonialism is removed from material
reality and repositioned in a spiritual realm, while oppression is recast as voluntary religious servitude. Implicit in Tonna's colonial discourse is the notion
that the Catholic Irish will attain freedom and full subjectivity only once they
have liberated themselves from the 'darkness' and 'false fervour' of their blind
faith. In contrast, Tonna presents Protestant proselytizers enjoying complete
autonomy in their mission to save the Irish and Ireland from the dark abyss of
Catholicism.

The historian, Ian McBride, notes how the act of historical reconstruction
involves a intermingling of fact with myth, memory, and imagination, the order
and proportion of each determined by the particular subjectivity of the person

20 Ibid., p. 239.   21 Ibid.

constructing the narrative.[22] McBride has applied his insights onto the changing historical meaning of the siege. The siege, McBride remarks,

> represents in dramatic form a series of lessons regarding the relationship between Ulster Protestants and their traditional enemies. Like other political myths, the story of the siege is invoked to legitimate present actions and attitudes, and while the narrative has retained its basic structure, each generation has found fresh meanings, emphasizing or suppressing different components according to its own ideological needs.[23]

Written contemporaneously to O'Connell's movement for Catholic emancipation, *Derry, a tale of revolution* has two central and interrelated concerns: the first is to sermonize over what it means to be a Protestant in the age of secular liberalism and the second is to resurrect and reinterpret the events of 1688–9 in order to forge a spiritually-renewed, united Ascendancy. In her novel, Tonna challenges earlier histories of the siege that had depicted the Protestants as a vengeful and disunified mob; rather, in *Derry*, the Catholics assail the fortified city as a mob (made up of women and children no less), as the majority of the Protestants are depicted as sanctified martyrs. Tonna's history furthermore re-envisions the role of class as it was involved in the siege: through the depiction of the aristocratic McAlister family as the literal and spiritual heroes of Derry, Tonna elides earlier siege histories that presented lower-class Protestants as central and heroic agents in the city's defense.[24]

Tonna recounts her history seemingly conscious of her task and of her craft. From the very onset, she asserts her text's realism. In the preface to her novel, Tonna declares that she wrote *Derry* in order to counter 'that false and mischievous liberalism which is eating out the very heart of Protestant principle'.[25] She delineates between genres – there are 'wild romances' but then there are the 'simple [facts] of history' – this latter category is clearly the one in which she posits her tale; she asserts that 'she strongly protests against having her book classed with works of fiction, or considered amusement for an idle hour.'[26] And, in a further effort to establish historical validity, Tonna's narrative contains footnote references to various histories of the siege, including Graham's *Derianna*, published just a few years before her own work.[27]

However, running counter to Tonna's insistence on the verisimilitude of her text are frequent (and I would argue, disingenuous) admissions of aesthetic humility in the face of what she sees as such raw, violent history. The very beginning of her tale contains this remark:

22 Ian McBride, 'Memory and national identity in modern Ireland', in Ian McBride (ed.), *History and memory in modern Ireland* (Cambridge: Cambridge UP, 2001), pp 1–42. **23** Ian McBride, *The siege of Derry in Ulster Protestant mythology* (Dublin: Four Courts Press, 1997), p. 11. **24** Ibid., p. 16. **25** Charlotte Elizabeth Tonna, 'Derry', in *Works of Charlotte Elizabeth*, i, p. 246. **26** Ibid., pp 250, 245. **27** Ibid., p. 250.

Surely there is little danger of exaggeration of treating such a subject as this. Language cannot convey an adequate idea of what must have been endured by these martyrs to Protestantism, nor can the mind grasp a scene of such accumulated horrors as must have glared out on every side to sicken the hearts of the fainting multitude for many weeks prior to their deliverance.[28]

Tonna's statement that there is 'little danger of exaggeration' can be read straight on – that is, we might consider it yet another authorial declaration meant to justify and to emphasize a hard-line Protestant reading of the siege – or, we can read into her words a subtle and ironic threat. If we omit the prepositional phrase 'of exaggeration', we are left with 'surely there is little danger [...] of treating a subject such as this.' But we know that Tonna is aware of the danger that goes in recounting an event that draws from myth, memory, history, and religion. Not only does Tonna state in the preface to *Derry* her awareness of literature's intersection with history but her *Letters from Ireland* illustrate an astute ability at ethnographic analysis; in short, Tonna knows precisely the danger that may result from exaggeration.

Language is Tonna's weapon and she wields it deftly. Her contrasting images of the assailed Protestants and the ravaging Catholics further disclose her narrative calculation. Here is the passage describing Lady McAlister, matriarch of the heroic Protestant family:

Amid the interesting group now assembled, a stranger's eye would have involuntarily rested on the form and features of the venerable parent. Both were strikingly noble, nor had the pressure of near threescore years and tend diminished the sparking intelligence of the face, or bowed perceptibly the stately figure of the old lady. Highly intellectual and marked with decision of character, her countenance yet bespoke a meek benevolence which endeared what had otherwise been too commanding to inspire affection; and there were traits of long and patient endurance, sufficient to show that a cross had indeed been bourne by her, whose whole deportment told a tale of pious resignation.[29]

The physiognomy of the matriarch testifies to the supremacy that Tonna's narrative sketches out. She is stalwart, reserved, and graceful, both saintly and strong; she evokes a sort of muscular Madonna. Moreover, we discover that her she is a convert to Protestantism and having been born an O'Neill, her claim on Ireland is without question.

In contrast to the rhetorical fluidity with which she describes the heroic Protestants, Tonna prefaces the passages devoted to describing Catholics with

28 Ibid., p. 246.   **29** Ibid., pp 247–8.

more qualifiers such as 'to describe the state of the mob is utterly impossible' and a paragraph later, 'a more formidable body of assailants the imagination cannot picture'.[30] This is not to say, however, that Tonna does not encourage our imaginations: we are told that the mob consisted of mostly 'women and young boys' and we find out by way of Ross, one of the apprentice boys that 'two companies of infernals arrived at the Water-side, attended by a host of furies, actually drunk with rage, and yelling for blood; while the little butchering ruffians boys from eight or ten years old, are brandishing their knives, and prepared to take their initiatory lesson in the art of torturing from their more practiced companion.'[31] The sheer physicality of these enraged women and young boys underscores the reserve and immateriality of the Protestant Madonna, Lady McAlister.

Tonna accomplishes several feats in these contrasting passages: by emphasizing the humanity and suffering of the Protestants, the savagery of the Catholics is highlighted while she also isolates historical events within the realm of innate behavior. Material grievances do not motivate rebellion; rather, the mob converges upon Derry merely because such brutal behavior comes naturally to a race that adheres to such an ungodly belief system. However, Tonna's simplistic rendering of history ultimately undermines her call for a compassionate Protestantism. In a passage obviously meant to counter the scene of the Catholic mob, we read of a crowd of captive Protestants:

> A crowd appeared, comprising several thousands of Protestants – not captives taken in battle, but victims dragged by force from their peaceful habitations, of whom the great majority were females of every age, from extreme decrepitude of years to the infant newly born; the rest were old men and young boys, or invalids brought from their sick-rooms, with some more vigorous in appearance, seized in the moment of unarmed security, overpowered, and compelled to mingle in the wretched throng. Half naked, with bleeding feet and tottering knees, they staggered on, raising their supplicating voices to the besieged to spare their helpless friends; while the latter, in the very attitude of reloading their pieces, stood petrified with horror, staring as on some hideous vision which they wished to dispel. *It was, however, no vision*; still the crowd advanced; and they might see the ruffian soldiery behind, violently pushing and goading with their swords, the fainting forms that lingered last from inability to proceed; or dragging them along the ground, to which some had fallen.[32]

Despite the nearly buried disclaimer – 'It was, however, no vision' – we realize that it is but a vision and that the entirety of *Derry* – that is, the very nature of fiction – renders it all a vision. This short phrase, coupled with the narrative's repeated emphases on its truth both call attention to *Derry*'s very textuality.

30 Ibid., p. 254. **31** Ibid. **32** Ibid., p. 322 (my italics).

Moreover, Tonna's overuse of melodrama, drawn as it is upon sectarian lines, belies the meek and merciful form of Protestantism espoused by her heroes. Ultimately, Lady McAlister may preach a compassionate brand of Christianity, but vengeance and retribution lurk within the very rhetoric of this character's creator.

The Marxist literary critic, Georg Lukács, saw the potential of the historical novel to be the inception of a collective historical consciousness. Lukács celebrated the early nineteenth-century realist novels of Sir Walter Scott, specifically, because the hero of these stories was a normal citizen, rather than a person of extraordinary means or abilities.[33] It was Lukács's belief that historical novels written in the style of Scott would ultimately facilitate the emergence of proletarian class consciousness and then, eventually, revolution. Clearly, Lukács's theories have been both right and wrong. Despite the fact that many of his assertions read today as too dogmatic, the rigorous Lukácian methodology has proven valuable and influential beyond the confines of literary criticism. More specifically, a hermeneutics that incorporates what we have learned from the theories of historical materialism and feminism allows us to see how *The Rockite* and *Derry, a tale of rebellion* further afford insights into the complex machinations of nineteenth-century Irish history. And, finally, we observe that any discussion of a so-called nineteenth-century Irish historical consciousness must take place concurrently with an analysis of religious identity.

33 Lukács, *Historical novel*, p. 38.

'Second spring' and 'precious prejudices': Catholicism and anti-Catholicism in Hampshire in the era of emancipation

SHIRLEY MATTHEWS

Hampshire provides a good example of the southern English counties in the first half of the nineteenth century. Close enough to the centre of power to be aware of national politics (the duke of Wellington's country house, Stratfield Saye, was in the north of the county and Viscount Palmerston's at Broadlands near Romsey in the south), but sufficiently distant to retain an identity distinct from the urban culture of the metropolis. An essentially rural county, Hampshire nevertheless had two large maritime centres, Portsmouth and Southampton, which opened the south of the county to cosmopolitan influences, but which had not, before the 1830s, the necessary attributes to foster the technological innovations which attracted large-scale immigration, as did the mill towns of the north and the midlands. There was also Winchester, the ancient capital of England, an important ecclesiastical centre and a garrison town. Hampshire provides a suitable case for the study of the issues surrounding religious toleration, liberty and national identity, given its rural and urban constituencies, and its apparent quintessential Englishness.

After 1791 Catholics in England were able to profess and practise their faith publicly without fear of prosecution. Despite the restrictions placed on Catholics by the 1791 Act, it gave Catholicism in England the opportunity to expand. Bernard Ward argued that the Act added impetus to an expansion which had already begun in the mid-eighteenth century.[1] The registers of the Hampshire Catholic chapels suggest that before 1829 there was little in the way of expansion in the county and that rural communities remained stagnant or even declined.[2] What growth there was appears to have occurred mainly in the urban areas of Gosport and Portsea Island (which includes Portsmouth), which bears out Michael Mullet's argument that Catholicism was increasingly an urban

---

[1] Bernard Ward, *The dawn of the Catholic revival in England 1781–1803*, 2 vols (London: Longmans, Green, 1909), i, p. 298. In his discussion of the effects of the 1791 Act, Ward asserts that church-building and other activities were already in place, and that the act was rather the consequence than the cause of this. [2] Robert E. Scantlebury, *Hampshire registers*, 4 vols (London: Catholic Record Society, 1948–1955). Registers cover Winchester (i), Sopley, Canford, Stapehill, Tichborne and Hants Clergy Fund (ii), Brockhampton (iii) and Gosport and Portsea (iv).

religion and that rural Catholicism declined in the early nineteenth century.[3] Only two new missions were created in Hampshire after the 1791 relief act, in the urban areas of Portsea Island and Southampton. Problems of personnel and funding meant that the Catholic revival feared by those who opposed any measure of relief did not occur to any great extent in Hampshire prior to 1828. Nevertheless, there remained an innate distrust of Roman Catholics, and of Irish Catholics in particular.

Are the arguments of Edward Norman and John Bossy[4] about Catholic expansion and urbanization after 1829 borne out by the evidence from Hampshire, or do they apply only to the traditional areas of the study of Catholicism in England? Did the Catholic community in the county grow in relation to the population as a whole or remain proportionately relatively stable? The returns of the 1851 census and the religious census of the same year suggest that the Hampshire Catholic community was in a reasonable state of health in 1851 and that numbers had increased significantly, even if not in proportion to the growth in population. In all there were 2,729 attendances at the Roman Catholic chapels in Hampshire on 30 March 1851, a relatively high figure for the southern English counties, and while the religious census returns may have a range of shortcomings in assessing the size of the Catholic community, they do give an indication of the extent to which it had expanded during the first half of the nineteenth century.[5]

Accepting that Catholic numbers increased in Hampshire between 1829 and 1851, to what extent was this due to Irish immigration? This has been regarded as a major factor in the growth of the Catholic Church in England, and in the transformation of English Catholicism, although Bossy argues that this would have occurred without Irish influence.[6] While not one of the traditional areas of Irish immigration, Hampshire nevertheless attracted the Irish to the docks of Portsmouth, the railway and road building in the county[7], and the transfer of the Ordnance Survey office to Southampton in 1843 which brought an influx of young Irishmen.[8] The number of Irishmen serving in both the army and the navy ensured that Winchester and Portsmouth kept an appreciable level of Irish-

3 M.A. Mullett, *Catholics in Britain and Ireland, 1558–1829.*(Basingstoke: Macmillan, 1998), p. 140.   **4** E.R. Norman, *The English Catholic Church in the nineteenth century* (Oxford: Clarendon, 1984); John Bossy, *The English Catholic community, 1570–1850* (London: Dartman, Longman & Todd, 1975). **5** The 1851 census returns show an average population growth for Hampshire as 78% between 1831 and 1851. See W. Page (ed.), *Victoria county history of Hampshire*, 5 vols (London: Constable, 1911), v, pp 436–50. For the figures for Catholic chapel attendance see J.A.Vickers (ed.), *The religious census of Hampshire 1851* (Winchester: Hampshire Record Series xii, 1993), pp 13, 37, 77, 245, 273, 371, 476, 477, 503, 574.Vickers claims that Hampshire had a high proportion of Catholics for the south of England but communities were 'isolated and localized', p. xix.   **6** Bossy, *English Catholic community*, pp 298–316. **7** Frank Neal, *Black '47: Britain and the famine Irish* (Basingstoke: Macmillan, 1998), pp 52–3. **8** M. Skrimshire, *St Joseph's, Bugle Street, 1830–1980* (Southampton: Paul Cave, 1981), p. 23.

born residents (although this fluctuated with the varying nature of the deployment of regiments). In the 1841 census, Southampton had 420 Irish-born residents; this increased to 688 by 1851, while Portsmouth's Irish-born population more than doubled in the same period to 2,156.[9] Given the preponderance of Catholics in the Irish population, it is probable that the majority of these immigrants were Roman Catholics.

The incidence of Irish names in the *Hampshire Registers* demonstrates the impact of Irish immigration on local congregations. The Irish may have been reluctant churchgoers but they married and had their children baptized in the Catholic chapels. The 1803 list of Winchester Catholics shows only one name which could possibly be Irish, Callagan,[10] and up to 1840 there are relatively few entries which indicate an Irish connection. The list of confirmations in 1851, however, shows an increase in Irish surnames, nine out of thirty-four,[11] and throughout the 1840s, more Irish names appear in the registers. The presence of Irishmen at the garrison contributed to this, many of the marriage entries showing the groom as a member of a foot regiment.[12] The Gosport registers show a substantial number of Irish surnames in the late eighteenth century, probably due to the presence of Irish soldiers during the revolutionary and Napoleonic wars. In the Portsea and Gosport registers in the 1840s, Irish names predominate. The presence of the Irish undoubtedly increased the size of the Catholic population of Hampshire, but whether they contributed significantly to the vitality of the church is open to question.[13] The Irish among the Catholic community were not particularly well-served in terms of Irish priests; James Delaney, a Douai-trained Irishman served Winchester from 1825–45, but it was 1848 before a Maynooth-trained Irish priest, William Kelly, arrived at Portsea where he oversaw the enlargement of the chapel and the building of a school.[14] This deficit is hardly surprising given the difficulties faced by the Irish Catholic Church in providing sufficient clergy for Ireland as Emmet Larkin has demonstrated.[15]

Edward Norman asserts that by 1840 'the physical signs of Catholic advance were becoming very clear.' Across England, the architect Augustus Welby Pugin was building seventeen churches. St Chad's in Birmingham was the first Catholic cathedral consecrated in England since the reformation and opened in 1841.[16] The 'second spring' theory, however, was over-hopeful. In London, indeed, new missions and religious communities were formed, but this was not

9 *Hampshire Census Reports, 1801–1891* (Great Britain Office of Population Censuses and Surveys, n.d).   **10** Scantlebury, *Registers*, i, *p.* 121.   **11** Ibid., p. 83.   **12** Ibid., i, pp 51, 53.   **13** For a discussion of the churchgoing habits of Irish Catholics in Britain see G.P. Connolly, 'Irish and Catholic: myth or reality? Another sort of Irish and the renewal of the clerical profession among Catholics in England 1791–1918', in R. Swift and S. Gilley (eds), *The Irish in the Victorian city* (London: Croom Helm, 1985), pp 225–54.   **14** Scantlebury, *Registers*, i, pp 15–16; V.J.L. Fontana, *Rebirth of Catholicism in Portsmouth* (Portsmouth: Portsmouth City Council, 1989), pp 21–2.   **15** E. Larkin, 'The devotional revolution in Ireland, 1850–75', *American Historical Review,* 77:3 (1972), 625–52.   **16** Norman, *English Catholic Church*, p. 201.

necessarily the case outside the established areas of Catholicism. Hampshire itself had no new religious houses; although land had been purchased in Southampton in 1850 for a convent, the sisters did not in fact arrive until the 1880s.[17] The hopes of the Catholic Church, and the fears of Protestants, that Catholicism would advance to the extent of bringing down the established church and converting all England back to Catholicism were never realistic, despite the seeming promise of the Oxford converts. However, the perceptions of Catholic progress elicited an anti-Catholic response among Protestants of all hues who feared for their personal and religious liberties.

If Newman's 'second spring' did arrive, it was in the areas where Catholicism before 1829 had a firm hold, and where the influx of Irish immigrants made a significant contribution to Catholic life and worship. It appears that the Catholic numbers in Hampshire remained a stable proportion of the total population, and that Irish immigrants were not of sufficient numbers to change the face of the towns or to create the 'little Irelands' which existed in Manchester and other northern cities. There may have been no new convents or monasteries, and only a minimal amount of church building in the county, but the increased confidence among the Catholic community, more Catholic periodicals, open debates on doctrine and practice, and the questioning of Protestant beliefs offended Protestant sensibilities and created tensions which erupted in times of political crisis.

Was there a correlation between the level of anti-Catholicism and a Catholic or Irish presence? Despite the limited numbers of Catholics in Hampshire, the debate about Catholic relief in 1828–9 was vigorous. The newspapers reported public meetings throughout the county for the purpose of raising anti-emancipation petitions to parliament, although none matched the scale of the Penenden Heath meeting in Kent. A Brunswick Club, founded on Orange principles, was formed in Portsmouth and the Tory *Hampshire Advertiser* called upon the 'populous town' of Southampton similarly 'to evince the attachment to the Protestant cause.'[18] The arguments presented against emancipation reflected those in the parliamentary debates and in the nationwide pamphlet campaign. Catholic loyalty was suspect, Catholics were intolerant, bigoted, idolatrous and superstitious. The *Hampshire Advertiser* printed the letter of the anti-Catholic duke of Newcastle, as well as advertisements for anti-emancipist pamphlets and tracts, and supported the repeal of the Test and Corporation Acts because that would ensure Protestant unity against 'the tyranny of Papal usurpation [...] and its despotism.'[19] The petition against relief was held at the paper's office in Southampton for signature. The anti-Catholic rhetoric of the *Advertiser*

---

17 Skrimshire, *St Joseph's*, p. 44.   18 Brunswick Clubs were founded in 1828 in order to defend the Protestant constitution, adopting the role of the Orange Order which had been suppressed in 1825; see G.I.T. Machin, 'The no-popery movement in Britain in 1828–9', *Historical Journal*, 6:2 (1963), pp 193–211, for an account of the English Brunswick clubs; *Hampshire Advertiser*, 18 Oct. 1828.   19 *Hampshire Advertiser*, 18 Oct. 1828

reflected the Tory Anglican views of its proprietor, John Coupland, who also published anti-Catholic pamphlets. In Portsmouth, the language of the local paper the *Hampshire Telegraph* was less hysterical, perhaps reflecting the strong liberal Dissenting tradition among the ruling oligarchy of the town led by the Unitarian John Carter. The Portsmouth corporation called a meeting to raise a petition in favour of emancipation, in contrast to that of Southampton which refused to sanction a public meeting on the issue. Of the seven Hampshire pro-petitions listed in the Commons journals, four came from Portsmouth, while three of the twelve antis from the county emanated from that area. Other peti-tions against emancipation came from parishes where there was no significant Catholic or Irish presence, suggesting that it was among the Anglican clergy, who were often in the forefront of petition-raising, that anti-Catholicism was most prevalent.

As was suggested earlier, the passing of the Catholic relief act of 1829 did not bring about a 'second spring' in Hampshire; nevertheless the county was not immune to the 'precious prejudices' which the work of John Wolffe, Denis Paz and Walter Arnstein has shown persisted throughout the country.[20] The Protestant Association, founded to work for the protection of Protestantism in Great Britain and Ireland, had branches in Gosport and Portsmouth, and the Reformation Society in Southampton and Portsea, all areas where there was a sizeable Catholic (and in Portsmouth's case Irish) presence.

The anti-Catholic rhetoric of the post-emancipation decades in Hampshire shows some evidence that anti-Catholicism was linked with anti-Irish feeling. However, the type of anti-Irishness which Mark Harrison and Frank Neal have discovered in Bristol and Liverpool respectively is largely absent.[21] The Catholic clergy in Ireland were occasionally criticized, and in 1850 the *Advertiser* pub-lished an editorial explicitly linking the Irish with Wiseman and popery.[22] Most references to the Irish in the county's papers were, however, taken from the national press, and reflected the national concerns about the state of Ireland in the 1830s and 1840s, the repeal movement, the poverty and backwardness of the country, the influence of Catholic priests, and from 1846 on the famine. The furore over the Maynooth grant gives some indication of the perceived rela-tionship between Catholicism and Irishness. Hampshire residents were not remiss in petitioning against support for the Catholic college. The annual grant to Maynooth was objected to in 1837–8 by Gosport and Alverstoke, in 1839 by Hartley Wintney, Hook and Verwood, in 1840 by Blendworth, and in 1841 by

---

20 John Wolffe, *The Protestant crusade in Great Britain, 1829–1860* (Oxford: Clarendon, 1991); D.G. Paz, *Popular anti-Catholicism in mid-Victorian England* (Stanford: Stanford UP, 1992); W.L. Arnstein, *Protestant versus Catholic in mid-Victorian England: Mr Newdegate and the nuns* (Columbia, Missouri: University of Missouri Press, 1982). **21** Mark Harrison, *Crowds and history: mass phenomena in English towns, 1790–1835* (Cambridge: Cambridge UP, 1988), pp 113–15, 153–9, 187–9; Frank Neal, *Sectarian violence: the Liverpool experience, 1819–1914* (Manchester: Manchester UP, 1988), passim. **22** *Hampshire Advertiser*, 30 Nov. 1850.

Portsmouth. Petitions were sent from the Wesleyan Methodists of Andover and Portsmouth in 1842, and in 1845 Peel's bill to make the grant permanent and to increase it from £8,928 to £26,360, drew no fewer than sixty anti petitions from the county and none in favour. Portsmouth, Portsea and Southampton sent twenty-two petitions between them, Romsey and Winchester sent three each.[23] The *Hampshire Chronicle* reported that the petition from Winchester had been 'numerously and respectably signed by the clergy and laity' of the city, and that 'similar petitions ha(d) been forwarded by the bodies of Wesleyan and Independent dissenters' of the city. In Portsmouth, Portsea and Gosport 'considerable excitement' had prevailed on the subject, the matter had been alluded to in several chapels and 'strongly worded bills ha(d) been issued, calling upon all interested in the safety of the Protestant Church to come forward and sign the petitions against the grant.'[24]

The anti-Maynooth petitions of 1845 were an outpouring of public opposition to a government measure which proved even more unpopular than Wellington's emancipation bill. Despite public opinion, however, the bill became law. Public resentment of the measure remained active and surfaced on numerous occasions, most notably in the general election of 1847. The two candidates for the southern division of Hampshire, Henry Compton and Charles Wellesley, wrote to the electors about their devotion to the Protestant establishment and the constitution. Wellesley specifically declared his opposition to any proposal for endowing the Roman Catholic clergy.[25] Sir William Heathcote, the MP for north Hampshire, also assured electors of his 'unshaken attachment' to the institutions in church and state, and he admitted that the Maynooth issue had broken up party connections in parliament, because of Conservative opposition to Peel's bill.[26] The level of anti-Catholic sentiment among Conservatives was demonstrated by the case of the two Conservative members for Southampton, Humphrey St John Mildmay and George Hope. They wrote to Peel on 31 July 1847 complaining that the support of Conservatives in Southampton could only be obtained if they declared 'an intention of opposing, during this Parliament, at least, every grant of public money for the benefit of Roman Catholics, even though limited to the promotion of education among their children.' They believed that tensions and jealousies between Anglicans and dissenters in the town lay behind the demand, but nevertheless, announced the withdrawal of their candidacy.[27]

Wolffe argues that the rhetoric of the 1847 general election, while not resulting in the election of a large number of anti-Catholic members of parliament, nevertheless succeeded in airing Protestant views 'in such a way as to ensure that the new Parliament would be more responsive to their wishes than

23 *General index to the reports on public petitions 1833–1852* (House of Lords Record Office, 14 Aug. 1855), pp 598–634. 24 *Hampshire Chronicle*, 12 Apr. 1845. 25 *Hampshire Chronicle*, 31 July 1847. 26 *Hampshire Chronicle*, 24 July 1847. 27 Papers of the prime ministers of Great Britain, series two: the papers of Robert Peel, British Library Add. MSS 40599, fols. 127–9.

the old one in 1845 had been,' and thus prevent further grants and concessions to Roman Catholics.[28] Objections to the grant continued with petitions calling for repeal of the endowment being sent from Holy Rood parish in Southampton in 1851, and from Soberton, Gosport, Southampton and Winchester in 1852.[29]

For many Protestants, the Maynooth grant was an affront to divine providence, which Denis Paz has argued was one of the fundamentals of anti-Catholicism.[30] God had decreed that England should be Protestant and had given her the wherewithal to spread Protestant Christianity through her empire and colonies. Support for a Catholic college in Ireland was seen as a dereliction of duty on the part of the government. On 27 December 1845, an announcement appeared in the *Hampshire Chronicle* concerning a new paper to be published the following month, the *Hampshire Guardian*. The prospectus for the paper asserted that 'the Protestant feeling of this country ha(d) long been most inadequately represented, both in the Legislature, and by the public press.' The proprietors of the paper meant to raise the 'low tone' of public morals, to maintain the Protestant constitution and to elevate the 'national religious character'.[31] The correlation of Protestantism with national character is interesting in the light of events in Ireland, where Daniel O'Connell's Repeal Association was pressing for an end to the union of Ireland and Britain.[32] If the national religious character was Protestant, then Catholics, especially Irish ones, were outside that definition. If national identity rested on religion, then Catholics were outside that identity.

In 1845, too, Bishop Charles Sumner of Winchester repented of his decision to support emancipation in 1829, when the evangelical bishop had seen the measure as the means by which Ireland would be pacified, and prospects for the conversion of Irish Catholics increased.[33] But in his 1845 visitation charge, Sumner expressed his disillusion at the failure of the Act to achieve those aims.[34] Moreover emancipation had given rise to greater arrogance among Catholics; tolerance had given way to insolence, 'the humble supplicant of 1829 is now the rebel with the strong hand and the sharp knife at our throats' declared the *Hampshire Advertiser,* in 1850, during the papal aggression 'crisis'.[35]

The anti-Catholic rhetoric over the restoration of the Catholic hierarchy echoed that of earlier times insofar as it concentrated on the evils of 'popery' rather than on Catholics themselves. It focused on the claims of the pope to jurisdiction over all Englishmen except Quakers, Jews and unbaptized

---

28 Wolffe, *Protestant crusade, p.* 223.   **29** *Public petitions*, p. 632.   **30** Paz, *Popular anti-Catholicism,* pp 2–3.   **31** *Hampshire Chronicle,* 27 Dec. 1845.   **32** For a full account of the Repeal Association see Oliver MacDonagh, *The emancipist: Daniel O'Connell, 1830–47* (London: Weidenfeld and Nicholson, 1989).   **33** A. Aspinall (ed.), *The letters of King George IV, 1812–1830,* 3 vols (Cambridge: Cambridge UP, 1938), iii, no. 1558, pp 455–6.   **34** G.H. Sumner, *Life of Charles Richard Sumner DD, bishop of Winchester* (London: Murray, 1876), p. 163.   **35** *Hampshire Advertiser,* 2 Nov. 1850.

Protestants. A letter printed in the *Advertiser* called on Protestants to 'rise and in the might of God, shake off the vampire from (their) veins, purge the land from the mark of the beast' and drive 'every monk and priest and emissary of Rome' back across the Channel.[36] It is significant, however, that the purple prose of this letter does not apply to lay Catholics, only to those clergy who supported the pope's actions.

Anti-popery was demonstrated at Ringwood in the form of a mock procession, with effigies of the pope and Cardinal Wiseman 'exposed to the jeers of the populace,' and subsequently hanged from 'a lofty gallows, where they were committed to the flames.' This was anti-Catholicism as entertainment for the masses but was not a spontaneous outburst. Handbills had been posted and announcements made by the town-crier, a fireworks display by a 'London pyrotechnist' was arranged and the shops were closed. Clearly this was an orchestrated display of anti-Catholicism, and given its entertainment value, may not necessarily reflect a conscious anti-Catholicism among the lower orders.[37] Nevertheless it does demonstrate the relative ease with which such sentiments could be brought to the surface.

The reports of meetings at Winchester, Gosport, Petersfield, Romsey, Farlington, Portsmouth and Bitterne filled the papers and all carried the same message, indignation at papal audacity and undying loyalty to Queen Victoria, whose very authority was being questioned.[38] The addresses to the queen adopted at these meetings invariably stressed loyalty to the monarch and to the Protestant constitution, as well as an abhorrence of the perceived aggressive policies of Rome.

There appears, in the Hampshire papers at least, to be fewer references than in 1829 to the loyalty of Catholics, although one letter-writer did attempt to prove that Catholic canon law, which Wiseman intended to introduce into England, was seditious, intolerant and persecutory.[39] The *Advertiser's* editorial of 23 November 1850 concerned an address which the Roman Catholics of England proposed to present to the queen and which breathed 'a spirit of loyalty' for which the paper was 'willing to give them the fullest credit'. Individual Catholic loyalty to the crown was not in doubt and 'they need not be under the apprehension' that they would be called traitors. This acceptance of the loyalty of England's Catholics, however, was tempered by criticism of the political steps which had been taken to admit them into the political nation and thereby open the door to Roman incursion.[40] This was evident in the controversy over a sermon given by the Revd Ignatius Collingridge, the priest at Winchester, to the Catholic troops in the town. Objections were raised that the sermon was seditious and the troops were subsequently barred by the commanding officer

36 *Hampshire Advertiser*, 30 Nov. 1850.   **37** *Hampshire Advertiser*, 30 Nov. 1850.   **38** *Hampshire Advertiser*, 9, 23, and 30 Nov. 1850; *Hampshire Chronicle*, 7 Dec. 1850 and *Hampshire Telegraph*, 16 Nov. 1850.   **39** *Hampshire Chronicle*, 7 Dec. 1850.   **40** *Hampshire Advertiser*, 23 Nov. 1850.

from attending St Peter's Chapel.[41] Given that many of the Catholic soldiers would have been Irish, this may indicate the level of distrust felt for Irish Catholics. After all, the abortive Young Ireland rising had taken place only two years before and, despite the movement's most prominent leaders, William Smith O'Brien and John Mitchel, being Protestant, the perception of the inseparability of Irishness and Catholicism gave rise to fears that seditious tendencies could spread among the Irish element in the British army through the medium of Catholic priests, the issue of Irish 'priestcraft' being never far from the anti-Catholic mind. The Hampshire evidence points to differing perceptions of English and Irish Catholics, as one speaker put it in 1829, 'Ireland is but the puppet of a power which wishes to drink the blood of the whole earth.'[42] Concern for the conversion of Ireland was demonstrated in the existence of a Winchester branch of the Irish Society of London for Promoting the Education and Religious Instruction of the Native Irish through the Medium of their own Language; the religious education being of course that of the reformed church.[43]

In his work A. Temple Patterson asserted that anti-Catholicism in Southampton was weak because the Catholic community in the town was relatively small, and there were few Wesleyans, whose antipathy to the church of Rome was strong.[44] However, the activities of T.H. Croft Moody, a local solicitor, indicate that anti-Catholicism was not always a reaction to a perceived threat from a large Catholic presence. Croft Moody became secretary of the Southampton branch of the Reformation Society in 1833,[45] and was instrumental in organizing the 1851 petitions against papal aggression, collecting donations towards the cost of the organization.[46] Some of those who contributed were present at a meeting of the town council which discussed a motion to petition the queen on the issue, including the newspaper proprietor, John Coupland. The motion for the petition was carried. That the town council should discuss the issue at all (in spite of some reservations about the inappropriateness of the council chamber for such discussions) and subsequently vote to petition the queen, was a departure from the position in 1829 when the town corporation had been criticized for a lack of action.

There was also a branch of the Reformation Society in Portsmouth, but its activities are less well documented than those of the Southampton branch. Nevertheless, the commitment of the members can be measured in terms of its being one of the leading subscribers to Society funds. Contributing over £500 between 1827 and 1860, it ranked alongside Southampton, Preston, Liverpool, Sheffield, Leicester and Bristol.[47]

---

41 *Hampshire Chronicle*, 23 Nov. 1850.   **42** *Hampshire Telegraph*, 23 Feb. 1829.   **43** Page and Moody Papers, Southampton Record Office, D/PM/10/10. Collections for the society were made in Southampton by a Mrs Jeffreys.   **44** A. Temple Patterson, *A history of Southampton, 1700–1914*, 2 vols (Southampton: University of Southampton Press, 1971), ii, p. 72.   **45** Ibid., p. 70.   **46** Page and Moody papers, D/PM/10/1/7.   **47** Wolffe, *Protestant crusade*, p. 153.

In contrast to 1829, when many liberals and 'old' dissenters favoured emancipation, response to the restoration of the hierarchy among these groups was as antagonistic as that of the more conservative Anglicans. The *Hampshire Independent*, a new radical newspaper formed in Southampton in March 1835 with 'capital provided by some liberal gentlemen of the county,'[48] at first averred that it had no quarrel with the papal bull on religious grounds but objected to the 'political intrigues of the Court of Rome.' More problematic was the flirtation which leading Anglicans were conducting with Romanism. The paper's editor appeared content initially to treat the matter lightly, maintaining that 'apart from its impertinence [...] the establishment of the new hierarchy [would] be about as innocuous as would the creation of a new Dukedom of Wormwood Scrubs.'[49] By the next month, however, the *Hampshire Independent* found itself in agreement with 'the old and rancorous foes of civil and religious liberty' (that is, conservative Anglicans against whom they had previously fought) in deploring papal aggression.[50]

The response of Hampshire Protestants to Catholic emancipation, the Maynooth grant and to papal aggression indicates a significant level of anti-Catholic and anti-Irish sentiment in the county. They may have coated the pill by claiming opposition only to the endowment of education or payment of the Catholic clergy, or to the impudence of a foreign prince in arrogating power, but it is likely that the underlying motive for all this activity was a deep distrust of Catholicism and of Catholics, and often by definition, the Irish. Efforts to separate the people from the religion, at a time when religion was a dominant feature of many people's lives, especially among the middle classes, were fruitless. Men like Croft Moody were well aware of the situation in parts of England where Catholic numbers appeared frighteningly large, and Catholicism was enjoying greater success among the working classes than was the Church of England. Fear of Catholic expansion perhaps drove such men and women to issue warnings of its consequences and to struggle against further encroachment.

John Wolffe suggests that anti-Catholicism increased in response to the growth of Catholicism after emancipation and there is some evidence of this in Hampshire, with the formation of Protestant associations in the county. The Catholic Church no longer shunned the light of day by 1850. Its missions and its schools underwent rebuilding and expansion, and in Southampton, a newly-appointed Cardinal was invited to open the refurbished St Joseph's in 1851.[51] Such confidence and presence may have exacerbated anti-Catholic feelings.

---

48 Temple Patterson, *Southampton,* i, p. 175.   **49** *Hampshire Independent*, 26 Oct. 1850. This is a reference to Wormwood Scrubs as a small area of London, and not the prison of the same name which was not built until 1875.   **50** *Hampshire Independent*, 16 Nov. 1850.   **51** Page and Moody Papers, D/PM/10/10.

Wolffe also argues that anti-Catholicism was a nuanced and complex phenomenon, often an expression of anti-Irish sentiments;[52] so although strident anti-Irishness was lacking in the Hampshire press (no-one displayed the antagonism of the country curate writing to the bishop of Chester in 1829, who called immigrants 'the spawn of its [the Irish population's] lowest dregs,' a drain on the poor rates, diseased, ignorant, and depriving honest Englishmen of jobs)[53] the residents were not immune to such feelings. It is interesting that there were Orange Lodges in both Southampton and Portsmouth perhaps indicative of an Irish Protestant presence in the town, as this was the group whose members were most drawn to Orangeism, and who were often the most anti-Catholic.[54]

The complexities of anti-Catholicism are demonstrated in the Hampshire evidence, but there remains one underlying theme, that of loyalty and with it, national identity. Both Catholics and Protestants of all hues constantly stressed their loyalty to the crown, but that Catholic loyalty remained questioned. The quiet English Catholics of the late eighteenth century had become a vociferous minority, confident enough to declare in favour of English bishoprics. If such confidence grew, what was to stop them eventually re-introducing Catholicism as the religion of England? Ireland was already predominantly Catholic, and Scotland and Wales might well follow suit. What future then for the Protestant constitution in church and state? What hope then for religious and personal liberty? If such apparent horrors were not to be realized, then Catholicism must be contested at every level, religiously, politically and socially. The threat to Protestant national identity must be contained. How all this was to be managed in terms of Ireland and Catholicism was the problem. That sense of British identity based on Protestantism, which remained a very significant factor until the middle of the nineteenth century, could not embrace the Irish or English Catholics, but constitutionally they were part of the United Kingdom and so must be accommodated. Given the increasing identification of Irishness with Catholicism in the mid-nineteenth century, and the growing ultramontanism of the Irish Catholic church, it seems likely Wolffe's assertion that anti-Catholicism reflected a deep-seated anti-Irishness was correct. The failure of the Irish to adopt the reformed religion made acceptance of Irish Catholics into an overarching Britishness almost impossible and they were destined to remain the 'internal other'. Peel's efforts in the 1840s to conciliate Irish Catholics only served to arouse anti-Catholic feeling and to highlight the

---

52 Wolffe *Protestant crusade*, p. 7.   53 *A letter to the Right Rev. John Bird Sumner, D.D., Lord Bishop of Chester, occasioned by the letter of His Lordship to the clergy of his diocese, on the Act of the Legislature granting relief to His Majesty's Roman Catholic subjects. By a Country Curate* (Kendal: 1829), p. 10.   54 Neal, *Sectarian violence,* pp 259–60. The rules and constitution of the Southampton Lodge for 1851 can be found in the Page and Moody Papers D/PM/10/10.

problem of integrating Ireland into a United Kingdom based on a Protestant constitution in church and state.

The Hampshire evidence demonstrates that anti-Catholicism was not necessarily a reaction to a large Catholic or Irish presence, but was often a fear of the unknown, and as Charlotte Yonge wrote, 'prejudices are very precious things [...] but [... the] history of England takes care of them because the R.Cs are always the enemy, and the burnings and Gunpowder Plot will keep an English mind well prejudiced.'[55]

---

55 Letter from Hampshire author Charlotte Mary Yonge 1850 cited in Christabel Coleridge, *Charlotte Mary Yonge: her life and letters* (London: Macmillan, 1903), p. 161.

Religious affinity and class difference in two famine poems from Young Ireland

KATHERINE PARR

Representations of the famine frequently applied religious imagery in arguments that ascribed guilt and levelled blame for the disastrous circumstances which precipitated starvation and disease in nineteenth-century Ireland. Some arguments called for reprisal against social malfeasance, and poets of the day joined the debate. For those loyal to British interests in Ireland, famine poetry served as a means to blame the Irish for Ireland's troubles and to ascribe to the famine divine a purpose in reprisal for Ireland's recalcitrance under colonial rule. For those who advocated repeal of the union with Britain, and especially the radical wing of Daniel O'Connell's Repeal Association, Young Ireland, famine poetry called attention to the abuses of imperialism and laid the blame for the famine squarely at the feet of the colonizers. Blame for the famine tended to align along religious lines, the Protestants tending to believe it retribution against the predominantly Catholic peasantry while Catholics blamed English economic practices.

However, laying blame on the helpless peasantry was not restricted to the Protestant community. Daniel Murray, Catholic archbishop of Dublin, in an uncharacteristic moment, attributed to the famine divine retribution for the casual practice of Catholicism among the Irish.[1] Thus even among those allied against the union with Britain, differences arose as to the blame for the devastating famine that gripped the island and the action that would forestall open rebellion. Seated in ideological differences, the debate penetrated the national poetry wherein poets utilized religious imagery to represent differing interpretations of the events, some blaming Britain for famine and others blaming Ireland. These differences are especially evident in the poetry of two popular Young Ireland poets: Jane Francesca Elgee (1826–96), a member of the Anglo-Irish establishment who embraced Young Ireland's romantic cause, and Richard D'Alton Williams (1822–62), a Catholic poet and a member of Young Ireland's inner circle. Both wrote for the *Nation* and both were well recognized as national poets. As was the fashion, Elgee wrote under the pseudonym Speranza while Williams signed as 'Shamrock', one of several aliases.[2] Two of their famine

1 Sean Connolly, *Religion and society in nineteenth-century Ireland* (Dundalk: Dundalgan Press, 1985), pp 50–2. 2 T.F. O'Sullivan, *The Young Irelanders*. (Tralee: Kerryman, 1944), pp 657–8. Elgee used 'Speranza' when writing poetry, but also signed her letters to the editor as 'John Fenshaw Ellis' and 'A'. Williams used various pseudonyms aside from 'Shamrock': 'Milton

poems are inspired by religious practice in the country and reflect similar frameworks. The structure of each poem reflects a liturgical element shared by both the Anglican and Roman churches – the Kyrie eleison. Each Young Ireland poet uses the litany form to lament the devastation of the famine, listing in highly emotive language the sights that had become all too familiar.

Translating as 'Lord have mercy!' the Kyrie has its origins in Greek liturgy that dominated Christian practice in the Middle Ages. Initially, the prayer was associated with processional litanies that opened the mass. By the sixth century, Roman practice added the Christe eleison (Christ have mercy!) and the long procession opening the mass was dropped so that, according to Pope Gregory I, more time could be given to other parts of the mass; eventually, only 'Kyrie eleison' and 'Christe eleison' were sung.[3] This practice remained in the Anglican liturgy after the break with Rome, albeit in English translation.

The structure of both poems, Elgee's and Williams's, reflects this ancient prayer form in the use of three-line stanzas followed by the response, which invokes God's mercy. Just as a litany lists supplications to God on behalf of a congregation, each stanza of each poem recalls the sufferings of the Irish people caused by the famine. Reflecting the original form of the Kyrie that accompanied the liturgical processional, these poems suggest a funerary quality – the procession in the mass for the dead. Thus, the two poems appear quite similar, despite their differing titles. Elgee entitled her poem 'A Supplication'; whereas, Williams used the Latin 'Kyrie Eleison' for his. Yet the poems also differ in several important aspects: firstly, in tone, secondly, in theme, and thirdly, in diction, denoting an intended audience that supports theme. These qualities align Jane Elgee with the Anglican or Anglo-Irish community while the tone, intent, and diction evident in Williams's poem denote solidarity with the Catholic peasantry. Both poets embraced images of guilt, blame, and reprisal, but the agents of these sensibilities differ considerably, and the conclusions drawn by each poet reflect subtle but deep-seated class ideological differences.

Jane Francesca Elgee was the granddaughter of Archdeacon Elgee, the rector of Wexford.[4] She was born into the Protestant Ascendancy, and both her social and intellectual tastes aligned with the upper class. Despite her fiery poems against British rule of Ireland, she was known to attend social functions sponsored by the British government at Dublin Castle.[5] In 1851, she married the Irish surgeon Sir William Wilde. As Speranza she wrote a seditious article 'Jacta alea est' (The die is cast) which became the focal point in the prosecution of her friend and editor, Charles Gavan Duffy. Called upon to admit authorship of the infamous tract, Speranza – always outspoken and the centre of attention – had an attack of modesty; she refused to defend her friend and mentor. Although she is

Bryon Scragge', 'The Haunted Man', 'The Jealous Stoneybatter Man'. **3** Francis Proctor, *A history of the* Book of Common Prayer *with a rationale of its offices* (New York: Macmillan, 1881), p. 251. **4** O'Sullivan, *Young Irelanders*, p. 107. **5** Joy Mellville, *Mother of Oscar: the life of Jane Francesca Wilde* (London: Allison and Busby 1999), p. 40.

reputed to have stood at Duffy's trial and claimed her authorship in his defence, it was Duffy's sister-in-law, Margaret Callan, who stood in the crowded court-room and declared that she had authored the text.[6] Jane Elgee, the socialite, main-tained her distance from the actions of Speranza; her family disapproved of her association with Young Irelanders.[7] She, however, did allow the myth that brought her fame as a patriot to survive, never having denied her cowardice. This is to say that Jane Elgee was something of a hypocrite; she wrote volatile verse and prose that indicted England for abuses against the Irish populace, yet when her identity was compromised, and she was asked to stand in public to defend Young Ireland, she chose other loyalties – to the aristocracy and to Dublin society.

As Speranza, Elgee aligned herself with the rebellious Young Irelanders, becoming attracted to the romance and drama surrounding the early death of its inspiration Thomas Davis. Yet her poetry set her apart from other Young Ireland poets in terms of poetic diction prescribed by Davis. He insisted that Ireland adopt a characteristically Irish literature drawn from traditional history, myth, and folklore. Poetic language was meant to be democratic and phrases were often taken from Irish Gaelic, albeit spellings were often phonetic and only approximated the language. Davis and his followers found their poetic lan-guage in Ireland's rural population. Hence, they subscribed to Wordsworth's tenet that poetic language should reflect the 'essential passions' or natural feel-ing present in 'rustic life.'[8] Most important to the vision of Young Ireland were democratic values, especially the erasure of class lines that had divided the Irish people under colonialism. Thus, the anticipated audience for Young Ireland poetry included the illiterate – the rustic who in the romanticism of Young Ireland embodied the natural, indigenous race.

On the contrary, Elgee's verses are marked by tropes from classical or high poetry. Her verse invokes the ancient cultures of the western world – Greek, Roman, and Hebrew – and her imagery is often obscured by references to antiquity. An elitist, Speranza wrote diatribes that bespoke a contempt for the illiterate Irish peasant. Her biographer reports that Elgee wrote in a letter to a friend, 'Why should a rude, uncultured mob dare to utter its voice? Let the best reign, Intellect and Ability.'[9] Such sentiment will become evident in the lines of her Kyrie where she attributed the cause of the potato failure and the ensuing pandemic to the Irish themselves.

First, we might examine the surface features of the poem that make it appear democratic and empathetic. The title of her poem 'A Supplication' is taken from a litany in the Anglican tradition still used in 'times of war, or of national anxiety, or of disaster.'[10] The poem also bears a subtitle in Latin, 'De profundis clamavi ad te

6 Eva O'Doherty, notebook. OM 71–6, envelope 5, John Oxley Library, South Brisbane, Australia. 7 Mellville, *Mother of Oscar*, p. 28. 8 William Wordsworth, 'Preface to the second edition of the *Lyrical ballads* (1800)', in Jack Stillinger (ed.), *Selected poems and prefaces by William Wordsworth* (Boston: Houghton Mifflin, 1965), p. 447. 9 Mellville, *Mother of Oscar*, p. 34. 10 *Book of common prayer and administration of the sacraments and other rites and ceremonies of the*

Domine', which alludes to Psalm 129 said in both the Anglican and the Roman office for the dead. The phrase translates, 'Out of the depths we call to thee, Oh God'; thus, the title and the subtitle establish the formality of the litany and align it with the office shared by both the Anglican and in Roman Catholic rites.

Elgee's litany is spoken in the first person-plural, suggesting the speaker's alliance with starving peasantry. It begins,

> By our looks of mute despair,
> By the sights that rend this air,
> From lips too faint to utter prayer,
> Kyrie eleison.

A dozen stanzas outline the scourges of the famine years and follow the formula of the Christian litany, yet the diction chosen by the poet betrays false sympathy. She depicts those most affected by the famine as

> Miserable outcasts we
> Pariahs of humanity
> Shunn'd by all where'er we flee.

These were frequent tropes used by Young Ireland to depict the Irish as a slave class, deemed an inferior race by some in Britain. In Speranza's poem, however, these outcasts of society have been cast out as well by heaven. They have sinned and in sinning have brought God's wrath:

> We have sinned – in vain each warning –
> Brother lived his brother scorning
> Now in ashes see us mourning.

This is the sin of Cain; the peasantry turning against the Anglo-Irish landlords meant brother against brother: they 'strove in senseless hate.' Here, the poet alludes to the violence that marked Ireland's history under colonization, from early resistance to the more recent raids by Whiteboys and Ribbonmen.[11] The speaker prays for unity among warring factions,

> Kneel beside me, oh, my brother,
> Let us pray each with the other,
> For Ireland, our mourning mother,
> Kyrie eleison.

Thus, the poet places the blame for the famine on class wars, not on economic policy. The Irish are portrayed stereotypically as a belligerent, slothful, warring

---

church (New York: Church Hymnal Corporation and Seabury Press, 1977), p. 154. **11** James H. Murphy, *Ireland: a social, cultural and literary history, 1791–1891* (Dublin: Four Courts, 2003), pp 33–5.

race that brought on the famine. According to the poet's reasoning, the peasants are punished because of their indigence and recalcitrance, a prevalent opinion in England.[12] The portrayal of the starving peasants refutes Young Ireland's position and betrays the Elgee's insensitivity, aligning her sensibility with the status quo.

On the other hand, the other poem demonstrates a much different stance toward the famine and the Irish. The poet Richard D'Alton Williams was Roman Catholic, schooled by the Jesuits, whom T.F. O'Sullivan, the Young Ireland biographer, called 'perhaps, the most versatile and popular of all the *Nation* poets'.[13] Williams was indeed a versatile poet; his verses addressed numerous subjects and ranged in tone from the highly serious to the ridiculous, in his parodies.[14] Using the pseudonym 'Shamrock', he contributed a series of comic poems to the *Nation* that he entitled 'Misadventures of a medical student'; he was in fact studying medicine at St Vincent's Hospital in Dublin. Williams also wrote verse in the Young Ireland tradition romanticizing Ireland and its rural populace. One such poem was his 'Dying girl', a romantic ballad about a rural beauty.[15] He wrote religious verses, as well, that found their way into books, such as *The manual of the Sisters of Charity*.[16]

Williams's work as a physician most certainly brought him into close contact with suffering famine victims and fuelled his resentment of British rule. In 1848, with another young physician Kevin Izod O'Doherty, Williams established his own radical newspaper the *Irish Tribune,* the *Nation* having been suppressed and its editor placed on trial. The paper ran only one month when Williams and O'Doherty were arrested and charged for treason. Although O'Doherty was convicted and sentenced to Van Dieman Island, the penal colony, Williams's attorney brought important character witnesses, including Dr. O'Brien Bellingham, William's mentor at St Vincent's Hospital, who were able to convince the jury of the young medical student's innocence. He continued to write patriotic poems for Ireland until he emigrated to the America in 1851.

In his poem, Williams applied the Latin title 'Kyrie eleison'.[17] Like Elgee's poem, Williams's incorporates the litany formula, three-line stanzas followed by the invocations, yet his stanzas open with doubled lines, ending first in the English translation 'Lord, have mercy!' and second in 'Christ, have mercy!' These operate rhetorically as epidictic recitations of facts that serve in evidence for the poet's theme and ultimate argument. These evidentiary statements are addressed to the primary audience in the poem, the Almighty as ultimate judge. Thus Williams's poem becomes an indictment of England and its representatives in Ireland, these evidentiary lines underscoring the poet's theme that the famine was a sin not just against humanity, but against heaven. The double lines that

12 James S. Donnelly, Jr, *The great Irish potato famine* (Gloucestershire: Sutton, 2001), pp 118–31. **13** O'Sullivan, *Young Irelanders*, p. 243. **14** William's parodied Davis' 'Oh! For a Steed' and Mangan's 'Time of the Barmecides', O'Sullivan, *Young Irelanders*, p. 244. **15** Ibid., p. 527. **16** Ibid., p. 243. **17** Richard D'Alton Williams, 'Kyrie eleison', in Chris Morash (ed.), *The hungry voice: the poetry of the Irish famine* (Dublin: Irish Academic Press, 1989), pp 236–38.

precede the tercets are followed in turn by the Latin phrase 'Parce nobis, Domine!' – 'Spare us, Oh Lord!' – a phrase used in the Roman rite with the Agnus Dei and at the end of litanies.[18] Thus, Williams's poem begins,

> Life and death are in thy hand,
> Lord, have mercy!
> The blight came down at Thy command,
> Christ, have mercy!
> The famine pang and fever pain
> Tear the nation's heart in twain –
> Human aid is sought in vain –
> Parce nobis, Domine!

As a devout Catholic, Williams would have believed in an all powerful God from whom all issues, yet the famine and its accompanying death causing disease were incomprehensible. According to Young Ireland ideology, the Irish had suffered because of colonial rule over centuries, and Williams's poem lays out those sufferings. Initially, the poet seems to subscribe to the prevalent notion that because the famine must have been divinely ordained, its outcome was punishment for unatoned sins:

> Outcast of the nations, long,
> Lord have mercy!
> We bear a foreign tyrant's wrong,
> Christ, have mercy!
> Black our fearful crime must be,
> With triple scourges lashed by Thee –
> Famine, Plague, and Slavery –
> Parce nobis, Domine!

Here, the poem seems to confirm the sentiment expressed by Elgee. However, in this poem, the imagined sin for which the Irish were punished, according to the speaker, is that they do not resist the alien foe:

> Oh! Had we fallen on the plain
> In rapid battle swiftly slain,
> We had not perished thus in vain.

Hence, it is the alien force that keeps Ireland in slavery and taunts those adhering to its religion, the Roman Catholicism: 'Their God is wroth, our foemen say.' Thus, the litany of suffering is punctuated with the cry for divine retribution, 'Avenger! When thine arm is bare, Parce nobis, Domine!'

18 H.T. Henry, 'Agnus Dei (in Liturgy)', *Catholic encyclopedia* (1907), i, http://www.newadvent.org/ cathen/01221a.htm, 2003.

The tone in this poem ebbs and flows between anger and resignation. The angry cry for vengeance turns to remorse and resignation in the next stanza. The petitioner expresses incomprehension that his God would withhold his intervention, but ultimately concludes that the almighty's will must be accepted:

> Before the isle is all a grave,
> Lord, have mercy!
> Arise! Mysterious God, and save;
> Christ, have mercy!
> But if the pestilential sun
> Must see us wither, one by one,
> Thy hand had made – Thy will be done –
> Parce nobis, Domine!

Even though the blame for the famine lies with the alien foe, the faithful speaker, witnessing for his nation, shows his resignation to Ireland's fate if it be God's will.

The uneasy conclusion of Williams's Kyrie, however, fails to offer a satisfactory closure. Its tension lingers, the speaker torn between the promise of faith and horrific reality. Thus, the poet demonstrates the peasant's struggle between maintaining faith and facing absolute and desolation. The unimaginable refusal of the divine to intervene indicates abandonment, ultimate damnation for the race, damnation that could not be averted despite penitential suffering. Although the speaker has pleaded the case for his people and appealed for justice, he resigns himself to the desperate reality that human history repeats. Never have the conquered successfully overthrown their conqueror:

> Six hundred years we toil in chains;
> We sow, but aliens reap our plains;
> The life is frozen in our veins –
> [...]
> Oh! Bitter is our Helot doom—
> In life no joy, in death no tomb –
> Despair and vengeance rule the gloom [...]

Here, the allusion associates the helpless and exploited image of the Irish race with the Helots who remained bound to the land, serving the Spartans. Only a higher power could reverse the repetition of history, so that power must be petitioned, through the litany, and implored through ritual prayer to avenge the faithful and release them from their foe. In this aspect, Williams's poem differs substantially from Elgee's. The Roman Catholic poet's presentation of the complexity of faith explores its contradictions and its mysteries; whereas, the Anglican sought a simplistic and superficial solution to the famine.

Elgee's performance reflects an intellectualism remote from the subjects of her poem, and prejudice seeps through her lines, blaming the peasants for their hapless condition. Thus, Jane Elgee echoes some British judgments that the famine was divinely ordained as punishment for an Irish refusal to accept the established social order. As a simply patterned tercet, her poem uses a simple and masculine rhyme scheme, with the stress falling on the last syllable in each line. The imagery of starvation pervades stanzas one through three while stanzas four through seven, however, connote the inferiority of Irish society: 'Miserable outcasts', 'pariahs of humanity', a 'death-devoted' race. The concluding stanzas place blame for the epidemic not on negligent landlords, not on the insufficient aid provided by Britain, not on the government's hands-off administration of economic policy, but on the exploited tenant-farmers and cottiers bound to an archaic, feudal system of agriculture. Using the first-person plural in sympathetic identification with peasants, the poet declares, 'We have sinn'd.' The poem's simplistic solution to the suffering depends on repentance, rejection of religious and social rivalries, and a show of solidarity as in a romantically inspired vision of a homogeneous nation. Speranza does not consider possible British blame for the famine.

Furthermore, 'A Supplication' originally spanned twelve stanzas when it appeared in the *Nation* in 1847.[19] Yet in a later revision, Elgee added a thirteenth:

> Golden harvests we are reaping,
> With golden grain our barns heaping,
> But for us our bread is weeping,
> Kyrie eleison.[20]

These lines indicate the poet's dismissal of the facts of the famine. Harvests were exported to support the empire, and it was not bread that was spoiled but the potato, the crop on which the Irish depended for sustenance. Elgee's awkward, metonymic use of bread in the place of food begs the question: why did the Irish starve if fields were golden with wheat harvests?

On the contrary, Williams's poem addresses the question directly, blaming Britain for the export of food during the famine: 'We sow, but the aliens reap our plains.' Despite his opening statement of faith that the blight came at God's 'command,' to this poet the ultimate sin causing famine was a 'foreign tyrant's wrong'.

Williams also applies a structure more complex than Elgee's. He uses five line stanzas with opening doublets punctuated by the English translated lines of the Kyrie to counter the simple, masculine rhyme of the litany. As we have seen, the tercet ends with another liturgical prayer taken from the Agnus Dei and written in the Latin: 'Parce nobis, Domine!' While the speaker implores in English, 'Lord have mercy' and 'Christ have mercy,' he chooses the Latin to reinforce the injustice of foreign occupation, 'Spare us, Lord.' The effect is a two-tiered poem: one that recounts Ireland's plight and rhetorically establishes evidence of oppression, and the other, a prayer for divine intervention that will punish the foe.

19 Jane Elgee, 'A supplication,' *Nation*, 18 Dec. 1847, p. 1003.   **20** Lady Wilde, *Poems by Speranza* (Dublin: M.H. Gill, n.d.), pp 15–16.

Furthermore, the inclusion of the Agnus Dei in refrain denotes a sacrificial quality to Ireland's suffering. Williams's choice of the Latin phrase coincides with its
use at the end of Roman Catholic litanies of the saints and of Loreto:

> Agnus Dei qui tollis peccata mundi,
> Parce nobis, Domine.
> Agnus Dei qui tollis peccata mundi,
> Exaudi nos, Domine.
> Agnus Dei qui tollis peccata mundi,
> meserere nobis.[21]

Translated, the lines read, 'Lamb of God who takes away the sins of the world,
spare us, O Lord; Lamb of God who takes away the sins of the world, Graciously
hear us, O Lord: Lamb of God who takes away the sins of the world, Have mercy
on us.' Because the supplication in Williams's poem first implores God in English,
one might mistakenly surmise that the poet assigned the Anglo-Irish reasoning
to the cause of famine, that it is God's will to punish the Irish, yet the interjec-
tion of the Latin phrase signifies the poet's intent. It aligns the Irish with the
Christ who asked that his sacrificial death be undone, 'Father, if thou art willing,
remove this cup from me; yet not my will but thine be done.'[22] Here is the key
to understanding William's poem: the speaker prays to be delivered from the
famine's effects that occurred through no real fault or sin of its victims. Faith
abides in the midst of the suffering and such a declaration brings the hope for
eternal salvation, despite the earthly sacrifice. With this passionate declaration of
faith, the poet empathizes with his people; he becomes their spokesperson: speaks
for his people – Williams's is the voice of the persecuted faithful.

The tension that hovers between bitterness and resignation makes the
ending ambiguous and unsatisfactory, but it also reflects complexity seldom recognized in Young Ireland poetry. Williams's poem replicates on one level the
helplessness of the famine victims who suffered inexplicably at the hands of
their enemy. On the other, it offers a reasoned explanation for the bitter cup
that has been served to the Irish. According to Christian faith, release comes
after death and another world awaits; the sacrifice made by starving men,
women, and children would ensure their entry into the heavenly hereafter.

On the surface, the Kyrie poems of Elgee and Williams appear to be quite
similar. Both take a solemn tone; both adopt liturgical litanies used by their separate but similar religions; both portray the famine as ravishing the indigenous
population of Ireland; both depict the helplessness of the Irish peasantry; both
apply religious themes of sin and repentance. Yet Elgee's verse reveals a distanced, aloof poet removed from the reality of famine. Her sympathy is a performance, a 'defect that is more dishonourable to the Writer's own character',

---

21 Henry, 'Agnus Dei'. **22** Luke 22:42. *New Catholic edition of the Holy Bible* (New York:
Catholic Book Publishing, 1960).

as Wordsworth had called this failing.[23] In contrast, Williams's verse reflects a sympathetic poet whose experience arose from his identification with the Irish farmers and his experience as a physician treating the suffering populace. His is a genuine expression, a romantically natural response that results in a more skilful rendering of Ireland's catastrophic history.

Although much of Young Ireland poetry has been maligned as 'occasional' and unworthy of serious study,[24] this comparison of two poets, important in their day, suggests subtle differences within Irish literature and culture of the nineteenth century. Further investigation of Young Ireland poets should provide further insights into Ireland's early cultural literacy, especially in terms of social ramifications. Ironically, of all the Young Ireland poets, Jane Elgee (Speranza) has received the most attention, this despite her questionable authority as a poet. 'A Supplication' was chosen by the composer Patrick Cassidy as lyrics for his 1998 famine memorial concert at St Patrick's Cathedral in New York.[25] Irish scholars have also made Speranza their subject for studies of famine poetry. Marjorie Howes offers a detailed explication of several poems in her essay 'Tears and blood: Lady Wilde and the emergence of Irish cultural nationalism'.[26] Sean Ryder has examined Elgee-Wilde's 'The stricken land' and points to 'the power of the political rhetoric which suffuses the poem'.[27] Yet famine poems by Williams and others have been neglected. More work should be done in reviving the famine poetry of poets Ellen 'Mary' Downing and Mary 'Eva' Kelly, who have received some attention for their nationalist poems.[28] Another prolific poet John Frazier has gone unnoticed even though the *Nation* published a significant tribute to him in 1851. The pages of the Young Ireland newspaper, now on microfilm, hold a treasure trove of poems that reflect a continuing commentary and debate during the four years of Ireland's historical famine period. Those pages hold various responses to the national catastrophe as well as valuable information about the revival of Irish culture and an emerging national conscience.

---

23 Wordsworth, 'Preface,' p. 447.   **24** Seamus Deane, 'Poetry and song, 1800–1890' in Seamus Deane (ed.), *Field Day anthology of Irish writing*, 3 vols (Derry: Field Day, 1991), ii, pp 1–6.   **25** Famine remembrance, Windham Hill, New York. 1997 (audio recording).   **26** Marjorie Howes, 'Tears and blood: Lady Wilde and the emergence of Irish cultural nationalism', in Tadhg Foley and Sean Ryder (eds), *Ideology and Ireland in the nineteenth century* (Dublin: Four Courts, 1998), pp 151–72.   **27** Sean Ryder, 'Reading lessons: famine and the *Nation*, 1845–1849', in Chris Morash and Richard Hayes (eds), *Fearful realities: new perspectives on the famine* (Dublin: Irish Academic, 1996), pp 151–63.   **28** Jan Cannavan, 'Romantic revolutionary Irish women: women, Young Ireland and 1848', in Margaret Kelleher and James H. Murphy (eds), *Gender and perspectives in nineteenth-century Ireland: public and private spheres* (Dublin: Irish Academic, 1997), pp 212–20; Melissa Fegan, *Literature and the Irish famine, 1845–1919* (Oxford: Oxford UP, 2002), pp 179–80; Maria Luddy, *Women in Ireland: a documentary history, 1800–1918* (Cork: Cork UP, 1995), pp 252–4; Spurgeon Thompson, 'Feminist recovery work and women's poetry in Ireland', *Irish Journal of Feminist Studies*, 2:2 (1997), pp 94–105.

William Carleton's literary religion

MARJORIE HOWES

This essay will examine Carleton's representations of religion in *Traits and stories of the Irish peasantry*, situating them in relation to conceptions of Irish culture on the one hand and literary tropes and forms on the other. Carleton is a fascinating figure through which to examine these relationships for several reasons. He is widely acknowledged as one of the founders of modern Irish literature. Yet we have relatively few sustained scholarly examinations of Carleton's work. In addition, scholars tend to locate Carleton's importance to the subsequent development of a national imagination and a national literature in Ireland in his ethnographic approach to the Irish peasantry. And critical debates about the meaning, value or validity of Carleton's representations of folk life and folk culture often hinge upon religion, in particular, upon Carleton's complex, and often confusing, relation to Catholicism. Finally, *Traits and stories* raises a series of difficult questions for scholars that have to do with literary form: the volumes are characterized by wild inconsistencies of tone, a mix of sympathy and condescension towards the peasantry and Catholicism, an extremely varied set of narrative voices and styles, and a combination of competing literary genres and vocabularies. I will argue that Carleton's representations of religion can best be understood, not in terms of his ideological or emotional relation to Catholicism, but through their relation to these formal and literary questions, and I will sketch some features of what I call his religio–literary imagination.

Scholars repeatedly cast Carleton as a central figure in the development of Irish literature. Terry Eagleton, for example, calls him 'the finest nineteenth-century novelist of all' and says that *Traits and stories* 'can surely lay claim to the status of premier work of the century's literature.'[1] Carleton is often cast as an important precursor of Joyce,[2] and Roy Foster has recently written an essay arguing his importance for the early Yeats.[3] His centrality for later writers and the problems his work raises are most often formulated through references to ethnogra-

1 Terry Eagleton, *Heathcliff and the great hunger* (London: Verso, 1995), p. 207.   2 Seamus Deane comments that 'the beginnings of the Joycean complex are discernable' in Carleton's representations of the Irish peasantry (*A short history of Irish literature* [London: Hutchinson, 1986], p. 112), and Paul Muldoon asserts that 'Carleton contains a powerful combination of intimacy with, and enmity towards, his subject matter that would not be seen again until Joyce' (*To Ireland, I* [Oxford: Oxford UP, 2000], p. 25).   3 Roy Foster, 'Square-built power and fiery shorthand: Yeats, Carleton and the Irish nineteenth century,' *The Irish story: telling tales and making it up in Ireland* (Oxford: Oxford UP, 2002), pp 113–26.

phy, religion, and literary form. Most critics agree that the importance of *Traits and stories* is primarily ethnographic, and that the two major problems that hindered Carleton's project, and the capacity of later readers to appreciate it, are his vexed relation to Catholicism and his formal unevenness. Seamus Deane claims that the tales in *Traits and stories* were 'truly memorable for the power with which they evoked the life of the Irish peasantry' but that 'most of Carleton's writings are miscellanies of prose styles, with stylistic breaks even in the midst of a single sentence'.[4] Declan Kiberd remarks that 'part of Carleton's achievement as a writer would be his rendition of a social panorama, a cross-section of peasant types', but also comments: 'it is sometimes said that a single Carleton sentence seems to have been written in two very different styles by two very different men.'[5] And Barbara Hayley characterizes the tales as 'a mixture of folklore and melodrama'.[6] Scholars may be fairly united on the subject of Carleton's formal fragmentation, but they are more divided on the subject of his religion and its impact on his role in the creation of an Irish national literature. I now turn to that subject more specifically, beginning with Carleton himself.

Traits and stories first appeared as an anonymous collection of eight stories in 1830. The critical reception was overwhelmingly favorable,[7] and the book was admired by many readers, from Karl Marx to Crofton Croker. It proved very popular, going through a number of editions, often expanded, re-arranged, and/or revised, over the next years.[8] By the time he wrote the preface to the 1842 edition, Carleton was explicitly casting his work as part of a burgeoning effort to create a truly national literature for Ireland. He lamented in particular the 'political' effects of the stage Irishman found in English letters, which, he said, 'passed from the stage into the recesses of private life, wrought itself into the feelings until it became a prejudice.'[9] He connected the literary situation with much-discussed political problems, claiming that previously Ireland had been laboring 'under all the dark privations of a literary famine'[10] and that Ireland's literary men had, by writing for the English market, become literary and intellectual 'absentees'.[11] He claimed that greater mutual knowledge between Irish and English was already leading to mutual respect, and praised the *Dublin University Magazine* as a 'neutral spot in a country where party feeling runs so high, on which the Roman Catholic Priest and the Protestant parson, the Whig, the Tory, and the Radical, divested of their respective prejudices, can meet in an amicable spirit'.[12] He predicted that 'Ireland in a few years will be able to sustain a native literature as lofty and generous, and beneficial to herself, as any other country in the world can boast of.'[13]

4 Deane, *History*, pp 108–9. **5** Declan Kiberd, *Irish classics* (Cambridge, MA: Harvard UP, 2000), pp 266, 274. **6** Barbara Hayley, *Carleton's* Traits and stories *and the 19th century Anglo-Irish tradition* (Gerrards Cross: Colin Smythe, 1983), p. 1. **7** Eileen A. Sullivan, *William Carleton* (Boston: Twayne, 1983), p. 59. **8** Barbara Hayley's book offers a definitive account of this process. **9** William Carleton, *Traits and stories of the Irish peasantry*, 2 vols (1842; Gerrards Cross: Colin Smythe, 1990), i, p. iii. **10** Ibid., p. v. **11** Ibid. **12** Ibid., p. vii. **13** Ibid.

Several features of Carleton's argument in the preface – his integrationist bent, his project to rescue the Irish from detractors and misunderstandings and to exhibit their positive characteristics, his belief that literature could heal the rifts of the political world, his determination to help establish a national literature, and the fact that he addressed himself, at least partly, to a non-Irish audience – mean that his work has something in common with the national tales written by authors such as Sydney Owenson or Maria Edgeworth. But if, as Ina Ferris and Joep Leerssen suggest, such tales in the early nineteenth century treated Ireland as an exotic, unknown place, in which the protagonist is nearly always an outsider who learns to put aside previous prejudices and forges a sympathetic connection to Ireland,[14] Carleton's work oscillates between the perspectives of insider and outsider. The preface to *Traits and stories* goes to some lengths to establish Carleton's status as an insider or native informant, claiming, as many later commentators would, that Carleton can accurately describe the Irish peasantry because he knows them and is one of them.

Carleton bolsters this claim to authenticity by recounting his biography and using his parents as exemplary figures for the peasantry as a whole. The parents embody different conceptions of the peasantry and Irish folk culture, however. In a famous passage, which Carleton reproduced in his autobiography, his father represents Irish country people as an inexhaustible mine of cultural vitality, perpetually available, co-existing comfortably with English language and culture. He knows the Old and New Testaments by heart, and

> his memory was a perfect storehouse, and a rich one, of all that the social antiquary, the man of letters, the poet, or the musician would consider valuable. As a teller of old tales, legends, and historical anecdotes he was unrivalled, and his stock of them was inexhaustible. He spoke the Irish and English languages with nearly equal fluency. With all kinds of charms, old ranns, or poems, old prophecies, religious superstitions, tales of pilgrims, miracles, and pilgrimages, anecdotes of blessed priests and friars, revelations from ghosts and fairies, was he thoroughly acquainted.[15]

As a result, Carleton says, he never came across a bit of Irish popular culture that was completely new to him. Carleton's mother, on the other hand, represents a conception of Irish peasant culture as fading, inaccessible, and incompatible with English. She was especially good at keening, 'had a prejudice against singing the Irish airs to English words' and some of her untranslated songs 'have perished with her'.[16] Those that were not lost with her are only partly known

14 See Ina Ferris, *The Romantic national tale and the question of Ireland* (Cambridge: Cambridge UP, 2002) and Joep Leerssen, *Remembrance and imagination: patterns in the historical and literary representations of Ireland in the nineteenth century* (Cork: Cork UP, 1996). **15** Carleton, *Traits*, i, pp vii–ix. **16** Ibid., p. x.

and interpretable: 'At this day I am in possession of Irish airs which none of our best antiquaries in Irish music have heard, except through me, and of which neither they nor I myself know the names.'[17]

Carleton's father represents retention and accessibility; through him, Carleton possesses the secrets of Irish culture before he goes looking for them. On the other hand, his mother is organized around loss and obscurity; even the cultural artifacts – the songs – he possesses directly through her cannot be fully known or accessed. Both conditions are the condition of an insider, but the latter is that of an insider who has been dispossessed of something that properly belongs to him. In one the insider's culture is vigorous and living, in the other, it is fractured and dying. This division bears a family resemblance to a dilemma that Joep Leerssen has argued was central to the language revival later in the century: 'the choice between the return to the pristine example of antiquity, or the vigour of the living demotic tradition'.[18] When Leerssen, in his extremely accomplished and wide-ranging account of how various thinkers represented Ireland in the nineteenth century, mentions Carleton, which is not very often, he sees him as part of the Romantic tendency to take the peasantry out of the present and the political realm and to locate them in various timeless realms, such as the past or folklore.[19] I would add that Carleton carefully constructed his own claims to authenticity and attached those claims to two competing (and equally Romantic) conceptions of the national, folkloric past: one that saw it as continually available for salvage and another that saw it as constantly slipping away.

Debates over the extent to which the authenticity Carleton claimed was genuine have often centered around his relation to religion. Born Catholic, Carleton converted to Protestantism, married a Protestant, produced some extremely anti-Catholic works early in his career, and moderated his views later, adopting a more liberal Protestantism and expressing considerable sympathy and admiration for Catholics. In 1826, before he began publishing his short stories, he wrote a letter to his friend William Sisson, deputy librarian of Marsh's Library in Dublin, and included a memorandum to be forwarded to Robert Peel, who was then home secretary. The memorandum is an argument against Catholic emancipation, which was of course then being hotly debated. Carleton draws connections between terrorist violence and the movement for Catholic emancipation, says he could prove a link between O'Connell's Catholic Association and illegal secret societies, and accuses the Catholic clergy of condoning, or at least tolerating, those societies.[20] In the cover letter to Sisson, Carleton once again offers to provide proof, and says: 'according to the present operation of Roman Catholic politics, the question of Emancipation is singularly mixed up with the immediate and personal interests of its most violent and outrageous supporters.' And later he comments:

---

17 Ibid., p. xi. **18** Leerssen, *Remembrance*, p. 196. **19** Ibid., p. 164. **20** See Robert Lee Wolff, *William Carleton, Irish peasant novelist: a preface to his fiction* (New York: Garland, 1980), p. 20.

> But the Priests are those whom I principally fear, not more from the habitual dissimulation of their character, than from my knowledge of the unforgiving fire which burns within them. Black, malignant, and designing, systemically treacherous and false, [they] are inherently inimical to Protestants, they brood over their purposes with a hope of revenge sharpened by the restraint which compels them to conceal it, and concentrated within their souls from want of expansion.

Carleton goes on to say that he would rather see his children dead than 'under the dreadful yoke of Romish influence'.[21] This was two years before he began writing for Caesar Otway's anti-Catholic *Christian Examiner*. Later in life, and after the debate over Catholics had died down in the wake of emancipation, Carleton seems to have moderated these views, though Barbara Hayley cautions us against exaggerating this change.[22] Carleton did expunge some particularly virulent passages from early anti-Catholic stories when he reprinted them,[23] wrote sympathetically of the plight of the Irish Catholic country people, and harshly criticized Protestant landlords. In his autobiography, begun when he was seventy-four and never completed, he recalled that in Co. Tyrone of his youth 'there was then no law against an Orangeman, and no law for a Papist', and he claimed 'although I conscientiously left the church, neither my heart nor my affections were ever estranged from the Catholic people, or even from the priesthood.'[24]

Not surprisingly, given these contradictory views, arguments about Carleton's role as a founder of modern Irish literature have always been troubled by the question of his relation to Catholicism. When Yeats edited *Stories from Carleton* for the Walter Scott publishing house in 1889,[25] his introduction took up the problem of Carleton and religion. Yeats acknowledged that Carleton had 'drifted' into Protestantism (though the Peel memorandum hardly suggests 'drift'), but claimed that 'his heart, anyway, soon returned to the religion of his fathers; and in him the Established Church proselytizers found their most fierce satirist.'[26] This did not stop the *Nation* from reviewing the book negatively on account of Carleton's apostasy. A small controversy ensued, in which Yeats tried to intervene by reviewing his own book in the *Scots Observer*, which, not surprisingly, did not really work. Yeats had the sense to print the review anonymously, but scholars agree that there is sufficient evidence that he wrote it. As Foster points out, Yeats 'steadfastly argued that Carleton remained

---

21 See David Krause, *William Carleton the novelist: his carnival and pastoral world of tragicomedy* (New York: UP of America, 2000), p. 69. **22** Hayley, *Anglo-Irish tradition*, p. xi. **23** Hayley points out, however, that he did not expunge them all, and that he even added some anti-Catholic passages to early stories for re-publication (Hayley, *Anglo-Irish tradition*, p. xi). **24** William Carleton, *The autobiography* (1986; Belfast: White Row Press, 1996), pp 37, 92. **25** The volume included 'The poor scholar', 'Tubber Derg', 'Wildgoose Lodge', 'Shane Fadh's wedding', and 'The hedge school'. **26** Foster, *Irish story*, p. 117.

essentially Catholic; and that this was somehow part of his essential authenticity,'[27] a view of the relationship between Irishness and Catholicism he would
later abandon. For Yeats, Carleton was above all an ethnographer and a social
historian – as part of this controversy, he wrote a letter to the editor of the
Nation called 'Carleton as an Irish historian.' Foster argues that Yeats's work in
the 1890s contained a surprising number of echoes from Carleton, and that
Yeats found in Carleton's work the 'clarity and lack of sentimentality' that he
was trying to establish in his own poetry. Yeats claimed that '[t]here is no wist-
fulness in the works of Carleton. I find there, especially in his longer novels, a
kind of clay-cold melancholy.'[28] In this way, Carleton was the imperfect precursor of Synge for Yeats: 'On one level, he might seem to come within Yeats's
imposed ban on stereotypical and unsubtle national image-making. In another
way, however, Carleton was capable of his own version of the uncompromis-
ingness, originality, rigour, "salt and savour" which Yeats missed in the Davis
school and found in Synge.'[29] In a later review of Carleton's autobiography Yeats
explicitly cast Carleton as a founding figure of Irish national literature, calling
him the 'creator of a new imaginative world, the demiurge of a new tradition.'[30]

Current scholarship on Carleton, somewhat surprisingly, often feels compelled to take up the question of Carleton, authenticity, the national tradition,
and religion in similar terms. This means that often critics treat Carleton as an
ethnographer and pose the question of religion in his works in terms of his criticisms of, or loyalty to, Catholicism. Robert Lee Wolff, for example, asserts that
Carleton's 'attacks on the faith and its clergy were by no means 'very little' or
even all 'early'[31] and emphasizes the Protestantism of the early works in particular. David Krause's recent book goes out of its way to refute such claims, arguing that Carleton 'paradoxically and emotionally remained loyal to his Catholic
heritage'.[32] And Krause criticizes scholars like Wolff who, he says, assess
Carleton's work in religious rather than fictional terms.[33] Critics have continued to debate the issue in these terms, I think, because what is at stake is
Carleton the ethnographer – his authenticity in terms of representing the peasantry, folk culture, and a foundation of the national tradition. If scholars conclude that Carlton is in some fundamental way an anti-Catholic writer, then his
portraits of the Catholic country people begin to look increasingly like condescending stereotypes. If, on the other hand, scholars argue that he remained loyal
to Catholicism on some essential level, a level usually characterized as emotional, unconscious, or paradoxical, it becomes possible to recuperate a kind of
anthropological accuracy in his works.

27 Ibid. p. 118. **28** Ibid., p. 119. **29** Ibid., p. 124. **30** John P. Frayne (ed.), *Uncollected prose by
W.B. Yeats* (London: Macmillan; New York: Columbia UP, 1970), i, p. 394. **31** Wolff, *Carleton*,
p. 5. **32** Krauss, *Carleton*, p. 77. **33** Ibid., p. 37; other examples include James H. Murphy,
who observes 'Carleton was not strongly religious, was never part of the establishment and
always retained a sense of Catholic grievance'; James H. Murphy, *Ireland: a social, cultural and
literary history 1791–1891* (Dublin: Four Courts, 2003), p. 83.

I want to propose a different set of terms for thinking about Carleton's representations of Catholicism and folk culture. These terms owe something to contemporary research into popular religion, and something to current thinking about popular literary genres. Rather than acceding to the opposition between the religious and the fictional proposed by Krause, I want to sketch some features of an imagination that is at once literary and religious. Both the novel in its classic form and efforts to chart the contours of Catholicism as a belief system emphasize interior states of mind. In contrast, the approach I will pursue is better suited to the relative lack of interiority or psychological complexity in Carleton's stories, a trait they share with much sentimental fiction and melodrama. It also treats popular religion as 'lived religion' rather than ideology, and focuses on externals like practice rather than interior states – on what people do, rather than what they 'believe'. It sees faith and materiality, the sacred and the profane, as intertwined rather than separate realms. This approach to a religio-literary imagination gives particular emphasis to two things that I will focus on: bodies and rituals.

I will examine bodies first, in relation to Carleton's most famously anti-Catholic text. 'The Lough Derg pilgrim' was Carleton's first publication; as is well known, it appeared in 1828 in Otway's *Christian Examiner*. Later, when Carleton reprinted it, he expunged some of the more offensive passages, but plenty remain. The story is a Protestant parable, full of the vocabularies and images that were standard in anti-Catholic discourses, narrated with irony and condescension by an older and wiser speaker looking back upon a period of youthful folly. One of Carleton's arguments is that the pilgrimage and Catholicism as a whole are hypocritical and fraudulent, that they are composed of a series of empty forms and bodily gestures that are devoid of meaningful content or true religious consciousness, and that conceal human weakness and immorality – like the dissimulating priests in the letter to Sisson. In his autobiography, Carleton recounts an incident when, temporary down and out in Dublin, he spent the night in a cellar inhabited by beggers: 'Crutches, wooden legs, artificial cancers, scrofulous necks, artificial wens, sore legs, and a vast variety of similar complaints, were hung up upon the walls of the cellars, and made me reflect upon the degree of perverted talent and ingenuity that must have been necessary to sustain such a mighty mass of imposture.'[34] For Carleton, the Catholic body is like the bodies of these beggars. It is a kind of prosthesis, a deceptive shell that performs ritual falsehoods.

In the story, Catholic bodies have an independent existence that reveals the impostures of the pilgrimage. Before he goes to Lough Derg, the narrator, who is, he says, 'completely ignorant' of religion,[35] acquires a reputation for piety by praying louder and fasting longer than his competitors. Once he begins the stations, bodily pain strips the ritual of genuine religious significance: 'I was

34 Carleton, *Autobiography*, p. 165.   35 Carleton, *Traits*, i, pp 240.

absolutely stupid and dizzy with the pain [...] I knew not what I was about, but went through the forms in the same mechanical spirit which pervaded all present.'[36] He occupies 'an inverted existence, in which the soul sleeps, and the body remains awake',[37] and his body produces involuntary groans and shrieks. We are also told that 'the language which a Roman Catholic of the lower class does not understand, is the one in which he is disposed to pray'.[38] By the time he confesses, he says he could not remember 'a tithe of my sins' and that 'the priest, poor man, had really so much to do, and was in such a hurry, that he had me clean absolved before I had got half through the preface, or knew what I was about.'[39] The narrator has also been impersonating a priest; his two traveling companions take him for one (or, rather, they pretend to), and he does not undeceive them. Catholicism is a religion of false exteriors, mechanical rites performed in ignorance of their meaning. The interior states it does foster are morbid manifestations of a gothic imagination worthy of Maturin's *Melmoth the wanderer*. Carleton knew Maturin's works, and even met him once in Dublin. During the vigil, the speaker has been told that pilgrims who fail to stay awake will be damned in the next world and go mad in this one, and his body prays while he sleeps: 'After all, I really slept the better half of the night; yet so indescribably powerful was the apprehension of derangement that my hypocritical tongue wagged aloud at the prayers, during these furtive naps.'[40]

In 'The Lough Derg pilgrim' the body functions as the site where the cruelty and emptiness of Catholic doctrine and Catholic rituals reveal themselves. The narrator comments, 'I verily think that if mortification of the body, without conversion of the life or heart – if penance and not repentance could save the soul, no wretch who performed a pilgrimage here could with a good grace be damned.'[41] But the body is also the site of unconscious resistance to those doctrines and rituals, and the foundation of a superior religion. The battle between the forces of Catholic superstition and Protestant rationality is fought out on the level of the body, between, for example, the body's natural and beneficial urge to sleep and the hypocritical tongue's mechanical delivery of prayers that mean nothing. As the speaker walks towards the lake, his body rebels against the unnaturally somber and morbid frame of mind he is forcing himself into with Catholic prayers:

> Despite of all the solemnity about me, my unmanageable eye would turn from the very blackest of the seven deadly offences, and the stoutest of the four cardinal virtues, to the beetling, abrupt, and precipitous rocks which hung over the lake as if ready to tumble into its waters [...] I was taken twice, despite of the most virtuous efforts to the contrary, from a Salve Regina, to watch a little skiff, which shone with its snowy sail

36 Ibid., pp 256–7. 37 Ibid., p. 261. 38 Ibid., p. 262. 39 Ibid., p. 263. 40 Ibid., p. 261. 41 Ibid., p. 257.

spread before the radiant evening sun, and glided over the waters, like an angel sent on some happy message. In fact, I found my heart on the point of corruption, by indulging in what I had set down in my vocabulary as the lust of the eye.[42]

This lust of the eye, and the obstinacy of the body generally, signifies an alternative religion, one that is in accordance with nature rather than violating it. In a common literary formulation, it is connected with the beauties of the natural world. Earlier in the walk, the speaker describes the beauties of the natural setting: 'The rapid martins twittered with peculiar glee, or, in the light caprice of their mirth, placed themselves for a moment upon the edge of a scaur, or earthy precipice, in which their nests were built, and then shot off to mingle with the careering and joyful flock that cut the air in every direction. Where is the heart which could not enjoy such a morning scene?' But the speaker's 'mistaken devotion' has rendered him immune to what he calls 'those sensations which the wisdom of God has given as a security in some degree against sin, by opening to the heart of man sources of pleasure, for which the soul is not compelled to barter away her innocence, as in those of a grosser nature.'[43] Ultimately, it is the speaker's body, and in these passages especially its pleasures, rather than his mind, that is naturally Protestant. While this aligns Protestantism with a natural world obedient to God's plan, it also threatens to open Protestantism to the treachery and falsehood of the Catholic body. Interestingly, Carleton's autobiography recalls that Sisson, to whom he sent the Peel memorandum, 'in consequence of some dreadful accident, lost the greater portion of one leg and thigh; but so admirably was this replaced, that to an ordinary eye he looked like a man afflicted only with slight lameness.'[44]

So bodies need to be read carefully; the ordinary eye might miss their true meaning. How does one distinguish between the beggar impostures in the cellar and the upstanding librarian? This issue is taken up in 'The Lough Derg pilgrim' in several scenes illustrating what is perhaps best thought of as the question of Catholic versus Protestant readership or spectatorship. To the discerning eye, the speaker's body and clothing indicate the ludicrous nature of his quest, his pretensions, and his religious imagination. It is an index to the kind of knowledge that the older narrator has and the younger self lacks; his body tells us what he does not yet know – that his quest is ridiculous. 'I […] cut an original figure, being six feet high, with a short grey cloak pinned tightly about me, my black cassimere small-clothes peeping below it – my long, yellow, polar legs, unencumbered with calves, quite naked; a good hat over the cloak – but with no shoes on my feet, marching gravely upon my pilgrimage.' Some people he passes smile or laugh at his appearance, and he concludes that these were 'Protestant grins',[45] while Catholics read his exterior differently, taking him for

---

42 Ibid., p. 251. **43** Ibid., p. 243. **44** Carleton, *Autobiography*, p. 189. **45** Carleton, *Traits*, i,

a priest and showing respect. The story contains an implied Protestant specta-
tor/reader, who coincides with the educated, older and wiser narrator. And the
narrator explicitly contrasts the reader's 'free, manly, cultivated understanding'
with the feelings of his younger self upon reaching the site. A related instance
of Catholic credulity leading to misreading of the body occurs in 'Phelim
O'Toole's courtship', in which Phelim's besotted parents are convinced that the
ravages of small pox have made his face more rather than less attractive.

In Carleton's religio-literary imagination, then, bodies figure in several ways:
as the deceptive exteriors of Catholicism, as the natural, God-given foundation
of rational Protestantism, and as objects that demand interpretation and therefore provide indexes that separate the discerning from the credulous viewer or
reader. Much of Carleton seeks to unmask their deceptive appearances, to point
to the fake wens and artificial legs hanging on the wall. But he also suffers from
the apprehension that appearances, bodies, and clothing, and perverse readings
of them, contain a slippery truth and power of their own. 'In such a world as
this, where outsides are so much looked to', he muses in his autobiography,
'What good was my intellect to me when in shabby apparel? What person
could discover it in a man with a seedy coat upon his back, when that man was
a stranger? We ought not to expect impossibilities.'[46] In 'Phelim O'Toole's
courtship', Phelim O'Toole is actually irresistible to the women he courts. He
becomes engaged to three of them; his parents' fond reading of his exterior is
correct in a sense.

Much previous criticism has treated Carleton's bodies (often more or less by
implication) in the context of a combination of the carnivalesque and the tragic.
They function as evidence of a living, vital, community and tradition, eating,
drinking, fighting, courting, while, in other moments, they register the maiming
of that community by poverty, famine, and ill-governance. John Wilson Foster,
for example, comments that '[f]or all the deprivation suffered by Carleton's
people, they are a rich and lively assortment, even in the throes of hunger and
sickness they have a feverish energy.'[47] I am arguing that if we attend more
specifically to Carleton's representations of religion on the one hand, and to their
relation to the literary (as opposed to the ethnographic) features of his writing
on the other hand, a related but somewhat different picture emerges. Carleton's
Catholic body is a sign of corruption, of a dying culture, but it is also the sign of
a culture that survives by imposing its appearances on reality in a wily and sometimes unsettling fashion. It reasserts itself, not in the religious realm, but in questions of readership and audience, and in plot structures that illustrate the power
of exteriors or the power of a Catholic reading of the body. Carleton embeds
that distinction embodied by his parents between folk culture as vital and folk
culture as fading in representations of the body, and the body is a source, not
simply of vitality or impoverishment, but of ambiguity.

p. 244. **46** Carleton, *Autobiography*, pp 177–8. **47** Cited in Krause, *Carleton*, pp 36–7.

Turning to ritual, I will argue that Carleton's religio-literary imagination combines a focus on the externals of appearances and lived religion with questions of literary form and readership. Carleton takes two important Catholic rituals – marriage and pilgrimage to a holy well – and evacuates their sacred meaning. But he does so only to recreate and re-figure these rituals, and their status as set apart from the profane world – as sacred – in other, cognate objects and occasions. And he invests them with this new kind of sacredness by using the tropes of melodrama and sentimental fiction.

Unlike 'The Lough Derg pilgrim', 'Shane Fadh's wedding' (first published in 1830), is narrated by one of the country people – Shane himself – rather than by an educated Protestant observer. Much of the interest of the story revolves around Carleton's comic, ethnographic exploration of Irish country wedding customs. But the story also displays an interest in marriage as a sacrament. Shane and Mary want to get married, but Mary's father opposes the match. So they decide to run away together in order to force his consent, a practice that, Carleton tells us, is common in the Irish countryside. And he bears this out by delineating the customs surrounding it in much the same humorous, ethnographic mode that he uses to describe the wedding itself. When the couple are about to go to Shane's uncle's house to spend the night, however, the tone shifts abruptly into a different register, and the following scene takes place:

> 'Well, Mary,' says I, 'a-cushla-machree, it's dark enough for us to go; and, in the name of God, let us be off.'
>
> The crathur looked into my face, and got pale – for she was very young then: 'Shane,' says she, and she thrimbled like an aspen lafe, 'I'm going to trust myself with you for ever – for ever, Shane, avourneen,' – and her sweet voice broke into purty murmurs as she spoke; 'whether for happiness or sorrow God he only knows. I can bear poverty and distress, sickness and want with you, but I can't bear to think that you should ever forget to love me as you do now; or that your heart should ever cool to me: but I'm sure,' says she, 'you'll never forget this night, and the solemn promises you made me, before God and the blessed skies above us.'
>
> We were sitting at the time under the shade of a rowan-tree, and I had only one answer to make – I pulled her to my breast, where she laid her head and cried like a child, with her cheek against mine. My own eyes weren't dry, although I felt no sorrow, but – but – I never forgot that night – and I never will.'[48]

This exchange constitutes the sacred aspect of the marriage, set apart from the profane festivities that surround it in situation, tone, and vocabulary. It solemnizes their union in much the same way a church wedding would. It echoes

---

48 Carleton, *Traits*, i, p. 56.

the ceremony fairly directly – 'in poverty and distress, sickness and want,' and it is here, not at the actual wedding ceremony, that we see Shane make a solemn promise to Mary before God. The scene connects their union to the sacred by using the language and imagery of sentimental fiction. Yeats may have found the later Carleton unsentimental, but this story combines Carleton's humorous, ethnographic mode with some of the classic tropes of sentimentality. Shane and Mary's hearts are so full that words are inadequate, as evidenced by Mary's inarticulate murmurs and Shane's wordless response. In sentimental fiction, the language of the body – turning pale, trembling, weeping – signifies deep emotion and moral worth, and the tableau of Mary with her head on Shane's breast, her cheek to his cheek, employs the kind of suggestive but controlled eroticism that characterizes many of the discourses of feeling.

By way of a brief comparison, I want to observe that all these characteristics are also found in Sydney Owenson's *The wild Irish girl*, but there is a difference between the two texts. In Owenson, Catholic ritual is picturesque and seductive but to be rejected, a beautiful set of exterior forms concealing interior corruption and danger. Horatio muses:

> What a religion is this! How finely does it harmonize with the weakness of our nature; how seducingly it speaks to the senses; how forcibly it works on the passions; how strongly it seizes on the imagination; how interesting its forms; how graceful its ceremonies, how awful its rites […] Who would not become its proselyte, were it not for the stern opposition of reason – the cold suggestions of philosophy.'[49]

On the other hand, the romance between Horatio and Glorvina is frequently cast in religious terms, and his romantic devotion is explicitly described as religious devotion. On May day, for example, Horatio and his 'lovely votarist'[50] participate in a kind of natural marriage ceremony, in which she gives him a rose and he pledges to her. He later refers to the occasion as a 'sacred covenant'.[51] A few pages after the ceremony, Horatio and Father John witness an old woman performing the pattern at a holy well, and Father John describes to Horatio Lough Derg and the 'votarists' who visit it.[52] The connection here between two kinds of devotion is explicit – and purely metaphorical. Owenson uses the vocabulary of religion to describe Horatio's romantic commitment and the transformation Glorvina causes in him, rescuing him from his corruption and ennui.

In contrast, Carleton uses the language of sentimental fiction in order to re-create the sacred aura that he has expunged from the actual wedding ceremony. He does not make religion a metaphor for romantic love. In many of his stories, he represents Catholic practices in a manner that we might think of as

49 Sydney Owenson (Lady Morgan), *The wild Irish girl* (Oxford: Oxford World's Classics, 1999), p. 50. **50** Ibid., p. 140. **51** Ibid., p. 154. **52** Ibid., p. 153.

revising Victor Turner's formulation of the 'liminal' – a rite or condition which is removed from everyday life and in which established social rules and hierarchies are temporarily suspended. Liminality produces what Turner calls communitas, an unmediated, egalitarian community among participants. Obviously there is a connection to a Bakhtinian carnivalesque here, too. Several scholars, including Diarmuid Ó Giolláin, have read patterns at Irish holy wells partly in these terms.[53] Carleton's popular festivals do display these features to some extent. But the actual religious rituals themselves are often stripped of their associations with the sacred. That is to say, they are stripped of their associations with whatever enables them to offer access to the liminal. Instead, they usually replicate the hierarchies and conflicts of the profane world. Another example is to be found in Carleton's story, 'The station,' which, in its original form in particular, gave Carleton the opportunity to denounce the practice of confession and to illustrate the myriad class and social distinctions in the rural community.

In 'Shane Fadh's wedding', when the narrative arrives at Shane and Mary's actual wedding ceremony, Carleton takes pains to include it, but to barely narrate it at all, and to completely overshadow it with Shane's anxiety to prevent the other men present from beating him to the first kiss. Shane recounts:

> While the priest was going over the business, I kept my eye about me, and, sure enough, there were seven or eight fellows all waiting to snap at her. When the ceremony drew near a close, I got up on one leg, so that I could bounce to my feet like lightening, and when it was finished, I got her in my arm, before you could say Jack Robinson, and swinging her behind the priest, gave her the husband's first kiss.[54]

The next man to get a kiss is the priest, who shoves back the other participants bodily to claim his privilege. The sacred element of the marriage has been transferred to the sentimental language of the scene under the rowan tree, so here the ceremony appears as 'going over the business,' and as part of the profane world. This transaction between the sacred and the profane, the ethnographic and the sentimental, is also evidenced by Carleton's revisions over time. Barbara Hayley shows that many of the sentimental passages were added or augmented as part of the revisionary process Carleton undertook as, over the years, he sought to moderate some of the anti-Catholic tenor of his work.[55] So adding sentiment and looking upon Catholic ritual more tolerantly advanced in his writings together.

We find a similar transfer of the energies of the sacred to the realm of domestic affections and family life in 'Tubber Derg; or, the Red Well.' We also

---

53 See Diarmuid Ó Giolláin, 'The pattern', in J.S. Donnelly, Jr, and Kerby Miller (eds), *Irish popular culture, 1650–1850* (Dublin: Irish Academic, 1999), pp 201–21. **54** Carleton, *Traits*, i, p. 65. **55** Hayley, *Anglo-Irish tradition*, p. 43.

find a similar substitution of a partially secularized ritual for an explicitly Catholic one. This story first appeared as 'Landlord and tenant in 1831' in the *National Magazine*. It is a story about bad landlords, tenant rights and the virtues of industriousness, faith, and charity. In the text, Tubber Derg is not, or not explicitly, a holy well where one would make a pattern. But I think it is clear that Carleton wants to suggest holy wells in 'Tubber Derg', and he gives an extended description of a pattern at a holy well in 'Phelim O'Toole's courtship'. Most holy wells in Ireland were named after saints, but not all of them were,[56] and Carleton's name – the Red Well – and the description of the water invoke the penitential aspects of the pattern as well as foreshadowing Owen McCarthy's trials and hardships: 'as the traveler ascended […] towards the house, he appeared to track his way in blood, for a chalybeate spa arose at its head, oozing out of the earth, and spread itself in a crimson stream over the path in every spot whereon a foot-mark could be made.'[57] A chalybeate stream contains iron, so the water turns red. This also provides an echo of Carleton's description in 'Phelim O'Toole's courtship', a large part of which is disapproving. That description includes the sight of 'men and women […] washing the blood off their knees, and dipping such parts of their body as were afflicted with local complaints into the stream.'[58]

But the well in 'Tubber Derg' is a different kind of sacred site – one that represents the prelapsarian domestic bliss in which Owen McCarthy and his family live when the story opens, and which is ruined by the economic collapse that occurred after 1814 and the by callousness of Owen's landlord and the landlord's agent. The story opens with an idealized description of the valley containing the well and Owen's house, and with the domestic tableau of a contented Owen surrounded by his family: 'a little chubby urchin at his knee, and another in his arms […] whilst Kathleen his wife, with her two maids, each crooning a low song, sat before the door, milking the cows.'[59] Then it documents the decline of the family's circumstances, a function of the 'national depression',[60] to the point where a desperate Owen decides to travel to Dublin to beg his absentee landlord for clemency in person. At the start of this secular pilgrimage, his favorite child runs after him and asks for another kiss. His quest is described in terms of a popular religious pilgrimage – 'He had done his duty – he had gone to the fountain-head, with a hope that his simple story of affliction might be heard',[61] and it even suggests the penitential nature of such pilgrimages because he is pushed down the stairs by the landlord's servant and gets a wound on his head. But it is not successful, and while he is away, his family is evicted and the child dies. He is haunted by her request for a last kiss, which he takes as a prophecy or foreshadowing of her death.[62]

56 Michael P. Carroll, *Irish pilgrimage: holy wells and popular Catholic devotion* (Baltimore: Johns Hopkins UP, 1999), p. 25.   57 William Carleton, *Traits and stories of the Irish peasantry*, 2 vols (Gerrards Cross: Colin Smythe, 1990), ii, p. 364.   58 Ibid., p. 194.   59 Ibid., p. 365.   60 Ibid., p. 372.   61 Ibid., p. 379.   62 Ibid., pp 381, 399.

Carleton spends a lot of time describing Owen's grief over the loss of his home and his child – and, because she is buried at Tubber Derg, they are metonyms for one another – and his continuing determination to find a moral, respectable, and financially secure life for his remaining family. The main point I want to make is not simply that Carleton employs the languages and tropes of sentimentality, which he does, but that they have a particular relation to religion here, signified by the fact that the story re-writes the holy well into an emblem of a sacred domestic space, and sends Owen on two journeys that are profane, but are also imbued with the religion of domesticity. This conjunction of the religious and the domestic is also indicated, for example, when his wife Kathleen wonders whether their luck has turned for the better because Alley, the dead child, is interceding for them in heaven, and the narrator comments: 'there was something beautiful in the superstition of Kathleen's affections; something that touched the heart and its dearest associations'.[63] The superstition of the affections is an apt phrase for this kind of re-writing of the sacred as the domestic. We might also call it a species of syncretism that is both religious and literary.

Owen's second pilgrimage takes him back to Tubber Derg, and to the girl's grave, where his neighbors, grateful for his charity and help in earlier days, have put up the grave stone that he could not afford when she was buried, turning a private burial site into a public sacred space. Owen asks at the grave for the dead child to 'pray for us before God, an' get him an' his blessed Mother to look on us wid favour an' compassion.'[64] This pilgrimage is successful. Immediately afterwards, Owen is given the chance to rent a farm nearby the well. He builds a new house on it that resembles 'that of Tubber Derg in its better days' as nearly as possible[65] and concludes his life happily, surrounded by his family, in a repetition of the original tableau: 'Kathleen and two servant maids were milking, and the whole family were assembled about the door.'[66] The moral of the story, according to him, is never to give up one's trust in God, and he is contrasted to 'many of his thoughtless countrymen' who should learn from his example.

I have been arguing that the religious ambiguity of bodies and the re-writing of Catholic ritual and the sacred in sentimental and domestic terms is characteristic of Carleton's religio-literary imagination. In sketching some of the features of this imagination, I hope to shift the ground of critical discussions of Carleton and religion, away from questions of authenticity and his loyalty (or lack thereof) to Catholicism. I think this shift can also help us account for some of the formal divisions and transitions that characterize Carleton's writing in *Traits and stories*, such as the combination of the carnivalesque and the sentimental, or Carleton's uncertainty about whether the culture he sought to document was fading away, or whether it was re-inventing itself in new forms and new practices. And it can help us understand why he

---

63 Ibid., p. 399. 64 Ibid., p. 409. 65 Ibid., p. 414. 66 Ibid.

was an important predecessor to the ethnographic modernism of Yeats and
Synge, while also working in the popular modes of religious and sentimental
sensibility. The difficult and obscure interior zones represented by Carleton's
views on religion or the question of his authenticity are still worthwhile subjects of study and debate. But I hope now scholars will also begin to examine
the fascinating exteriors, bodies, and rituals that preoccupied his religio-literary imagination.

Nationalism as blasphemy: negotiating belief and institutionality in the genre of Fenian recollections

AMY E. MARTIN

In his 1896 autobiographical account of the Fenian movement in Ireland, *Recollections of Fenians and Fenianism*, John O'Leary devotes much of the second volume of his text to describing the Fenian doctrine of 'no priests in politics'. His obvious imperative is to expose the ways that the British state and the Catholic Church operated in tandem to repress Fenian insurgency in Ireland.[1] According to O'Leary and other Fenians, the Church, in disciplining or even excommunicating those who subscribed to Fenian politics, operated through technologies of surveillance similar to those of the imperial state. O'Leary provides the following example:

> Miss – gets the *Irish People*. Father – heard it, and went to her house and told her that she committed a mortal sin every time she read that paper. She replied she believed she did not, and would continue to read it. 'Then,' says the priest, 'you are a Protestant, and you will not be allowed the sacraments.' The cry of the priests against their political opponents used to be that they were infidels. This priest preferred the less vague but more ridiculous charge of Protestantism, believing, or pretending to believe, that it was some sort of heresy to differ with him in a purely political matter.[2]

This brief anecdote serves several functions – for example, to demonstrate the everyday means by which the Catholic Church sought to repress the Fenian movement and the way that such surveillance intersects with sectarianism. The story of the unnamed woman also makes clear that Fenianism, or even sympathy for or interest in the movement, became subject to charges of heresy and blasphemy. As O'Leary's analysis makes apparent, such charges displayed a strange elasticity that unveils their purpose. He calls attention to the accusation's

---

1 See Donal MacCartney, 'The church and Fenianism', in Maurice Harmon (ed.), *Fenians and Fenianism: centenary essays* (Seattle: University of Washington Press, 1970), pp 13–27; Oliver P. Rafferty, *The church, the state, and the Fenian threat, 1861–75* (London: Macmillian Press, 1999). 2 John O'Leary, *Recollections of Fenians and Fenianism*, 2 vols (Shannon: Irish UP, 1969), ii, p. 118.

multiple, almost protean definitions when wielded by the unidentified priest. He first identifies reading the official newspaper of the Fenian movement as 'a mortal sin,' which quickly becomes equivalent with 'Protestantism', an anathematized identity in the context of sectarian politics. Finally, the recrimination is described more generally as 'heresy', a charge that conflates political dissent and religious disobedience into a single transgression.

O'Leary mocks the logic at work here, challenging the Church's authority to intervene in what he defines as 'purely political' matters. He makes clear that the charges of blasphemy and heresy provided a method for ecclesiastical interventions into secular affairs. This story stands as one of many examples that O'Leary provides in order to establish how Fenianism and its primary organization in Ireland, the IRB, were represented by the Church and also by constitutional nationalists as blasphemous and heretical. Yet, in the course of his *Recollections*, O'Leary does not simply reject these indictments. Rather, as do several other Catholic Fenian writers, he embraces the descriptives at the same time that he interrogates the Church's use of them. For example, by the end of O'Leary's text, he insists upon his text as an example of political and religious blasphemy.

This essay investigates what is at stake in this recurrent claim to blaspheme in Fenian recollections. Using O'Leary's text as my primary example, I ask why Fenians adopt the position of blasphemer, and how they rework what it means to be heretical and blasphemous. This strategic use of religious discourse provides the foundation for a critique of institutionality and an analysis of the problems that institutions pose for anti-colonial nationalisms in particular. By speaking from the position of blasphemer and heretic, Fenians articulate a nationalist politics that reckons with the problems of state formation, the sociopolitical role of the Catholic Church in Ireland, and the imbrication of Church and state in the 1860s, problems that were imminent and urgent as the process of decolonization approached at the end of the nineteenth century. Since blasphemy tests and hence reveals the limits of toleration within political and religious institutions, writing such as O'Leary's anticipates some of the problems that radical nationalism faced upon embracing the state form when imagining an independent Ireland. Would it be possible for Fenians to imagine an Irish state that did not reproduce the imperialist state? At the same time, the authority of the Church to accuse Fenians (some of whom were Protestants or atheists) of blasphemy could only be applied unevenly. Thus, the category of blasphemy reveals sectarian national identity and religious difference as problematic foundations for an anti-colonial politics; one can see a latent critique of identity politics as the basis of nationalist mobilization. At the same time, the charge of 'Protestantism' in the preceding anecdote suggests the tendency of institutions towards homogenization and discrimination rather than a full calculation of diversity. Fenian writers asked whether there might be some way to envision a more complex relation between self and nation than the subordination of the individual to the larger social unit through institutions and through a unitary identity. How might blasphemy and heresy provide some kind of answer to these thorny questions?

By reading the claim to blaspheme as an important feature of O'Leary's *Recollections*, I argue that the blasphemous stance provides Fenian nationalists with a way to occupy certain categories of identity and politics, while preserving a space for critique and for resisting the limits that such categories place on individual belief and speech. This complex position is mirrored in the way that Fenian recollections engage with the conventions of several familiar genres of writing. Recollections fulfill certain expectations of autobiography and nationalist history, but they simultaneously transgress and complicate them. A careful analysis of the structuring principles of blasphemy and heresy thus allows us to understand how Fenian writers offer eloquent articulations of the problems raised by the forms of nationalist writing and nationalism itself as well as impassioned attempts – not always successful – to envision a genre and a politics that transcend these limitations.

O'Leary's narrative and others like it exist as part of a larger archive of writing, what I am calling the genre of Fenian recollection. In Ireland, the United States, and England, the late nineteenth and early twentieth centuries marked the appearance of numerous books about Fenianism written by members of various Fenian organizations. Joseph Denieffe's *A Personal narrative of the Irish Republican Brotherhood* (1904), John Devoy's *Recollections of an Irish rebel* (1929), John O'Leary's *Recollections of Fenians and Fenianism* (1896), Richard Pigott's *Personal recollections of an Irish national journalist* (1882), Jeremiah O'Donovan Rossa's *My years in English jails* (1882), and Mark Ryan's *Fenian memories* (1949) – these volumes stand as the more popular of numerous publications which told the story of the first two or three decades of the Fenian movement, from the 1850s to the 1880s. As their titles reveal, these narratives without exception take the form of texts of personal remembering: 'personal narratives', 'recollections', 'reminiscences', and 'memories'. Unlike, for example, Charles Gavan Duffy's documentations of the Young Ireland movement,[3] these books complicate to varying degrees their status as objective forms of history-writing by signaling that the insurgent's memory counters official histories and state representations of Fenianism.

Fenian writers excavate their memories in order to produce written testimonies to history hitherto deemed irrelevant to or rendered silent before colonial law and the imperial record. They reinsert such episodes into a state history that presents itself as complete and closed to such interventions. These narratives set themselves up against 'misrepresentations' of the Fenian movement and of Fenian history, the 'prose of counter-insurgency'.[4] Alternative history finds

3 See Charles Gavan Duffy, *Young Ireland: a fragment of Irish history, 1840–1850* (New York: G. Munro, 1880), and *Four years of Irish history, 1845–1849* (New York: Cassell, Petter, Galpin, 1883).   **4** See Ranajit Guha, 'The prose of counter-insurgency', in Ranajit Guha and Gayatri Chakravorty Spivak (eds), *Selected subaltern studies* (New York: Oxford UP, 1988), pp 45–87.

substantiation in the truth-claim of witnessing and remembering, signalled by repeated phrases such as 'I have seen', 'I remember' or 'I shall never forget.' The individual nationalist's memory becomes the locus for the suppressed history of resistance to colonialism. The Fenian writer is metaphorized, as their 'larger historical participation [makes them each] a metaphor of the witness of the past.'[5] Fenian recollections promise that, by making public those memories, a new form of Irish national history will be born. Such memory-work allows these writers to communicate the politics and rationality of anti-colonial insurgency so often denied by counter-insurgent ideology.

This formula in which personal history is subsumed by the project of national history is intrinsic to nationalism. I call this the synecdochal logic of nationalism, for the writing subject becomes the synedoche of the nation. Indeed some recollections follow such a structure quite strictly, and others, which do not, as we will see, still make some synedochal claim. For example, in an assertion common to the genre, Mark Ryan subordinates the personal and subjective nature of his recollections to the overriding imperative to provide a particular version of national history. He writes, '[m]y sole desire is to do justice to the patriotic Irishmen with whom I had the privilege of being associated in a movement which unselfishly sought to bring about the independence of the Irish nation, and to vindicate their imperishable principles.'[6] All other desires, politics, all experience itself must be subsumed by the drive to produce nationalist counter-history. In some recollections, this claim is borne out by seamless shifts between the first person narrative mode of witnessing and the omniscient narration associated with traditional history writing.

However, in others, the synedochal gesture is complicated or undermined. Consider Richard Piggott's declaration that he can only access his memories unevenly: 'as "through a glass darkly," the dim shadows of previous events – some partly illuminated by the vivid light of perfect memory; others discernible through the haze of intervening years.'[7] In various texts, moments of forgetting or of refusal to speak destabilize the fluid relation between individual memory and the production of a new history. Amnesia and aphasia interfere with the writer's ability to produce a reliable or complete counter-history. At other times, writers reject the idea that a single Fenian can write the history of the movement; they offer instead episodic, circumscribed and partial memoir, one open to challenge or supplementation and unclassifiable in terms of genre.

These tensions between the promise to provide stable counter-history and the vicissitudes of doing so, are mirrored in the reception of Fenian recollections by critics, historians, and fellow nationalists upon their publication and even to the present. For the most part, these texts have been read as curiosities and failures in

5 Melvin Dixon, 'The black writer's use of memory', in Geneviève Fabre and Robert O'Meally (eds), *History and memory in African-American culture* (New York: Oxford UP, 1994), p. 22. 6 Mark Ryan, *Fenian memories* (Dublin: M.H. Gill, 1946), p. xxiii. 7 Richard Piggott, *Personal recollections of an Irish national journalist* (Cork: Tower Books, 1979), p. 1.

both literary and historical terms. They fail because they do not meet the expectations of the genres of autobiography or nationalist history. In their random, often limited nature, recollections have been unsatisfying to readers who looked for a definitive, official account of the elusive Fenian movement.

I want to use Jacqueline Rose's provocative definition of failure to present an alternative reading of this genre, however. Rose writes, '[f]ailure is [...] a measure of the impossibility of what is being required. Failure understood in this context is suggestive and provocative.'[8] Similarly, David Lloyd has suggested that '"episodic and fragmentary" history can be read as the sign of another *mode* of narrative, rather than an incomplete one, of another *principle* of organization, rather than one yet to be unified.'[9] Fenian recollections fail, I argue, for reasons that are theoretically and historically interesting. They grapple, often unwittingly and sometimes explicitly, with constitutive contradictions about the relation between the individual and the nation. These tensions become a structuring principle of the genre. A careful reading can recast Fenian recollections as radical theorizations of the problems faced by nationalists when writing history from memory and when trying to formulate any stable relationship between memory, history, the state, and Ireland.

There are several ways to contextualize these strange yet suggestive attributes of recollections. The ambivalences and tensions of the genre can in fact be found in the movement itself. In many ways, the IRB and other Fenian organizations had the characteristics of mainstream, statist nationalisms – the goal of an independent Irish state, a highly organized structure with visible leaders, and the use of apparatuses such as newspapers. In other ways, the movement resembled a decentered form of insurgency.[10] The IRB was a secret, oath-bound society that the British authorities found inchoate and nearly impenetrable. In an 1868 essay, 'How to deal with Fenianism,' George Sigerson describes the movement as 'hydra-headed' and then goes on to explain: 'Its mode of government is not from above downwards, but from beneath upwards. Its root cannot be severed at a single stroke, for it does not spring from one or two principal men, but arises by some thousands of inconspicuous rootlets.'[11] This grassroots, hydra-like form of organization meant that central leadership was often rendered irrelevant to local cells of the organization. This allowed them to maintain relations with diverse politics and movements – from the Brotherhood of St. Patrick to the First International – without subsuming them within a nationalist imperative. At the same time, Fenianism rejected constitutional politics and any engagement with

8 Jacqueline Rose, *States of fantasy* (Oxford: Clarendon, 1996), p. 89.   9 David Lloyd, *Anomalous states: Irish writing and the postcolonial moment* (Durham, NC: Duke UP, 1993) p. 127. 10 Luke Gibbons, 'Identity without a centre: allegory, history and Irish nationalism,' in *Transformations in Irish culture* (South Bend, IN: University of Notre Dame Press, 1996), pp 137–43; David Lloyd, 'Nationalisms against the state' in *Ireland after history* (South Bend, IN: University of Notre Dame Press, 1999), pp 19–36.   11 Seamus Deane (ed.), *The Field Day anthology of Irish literature*, 3 vols (Derry: Field Day, 1991), ii, pp 244–5.

the legal channels of the British state, relying instead on extra-constitutional struggle and 'physical force' when deemed necessary. In some respects, therefore, Fenianism conforms to David Lloyd's definition of a 'nationalism against the state' in that its politics and structure defied the forms of the imperial state and refused to reproduce them in its own organization.[12] Hence, when Fenian writers claim to write national history at the same time that they trouble their own authorial authority and imagine their histories as incomplete, these narrative contradictions reflect the co-existence within Fenianism of statist forms with radical forms of anti-colonial nationalism which critiqued the state.

As Sigerson's description suggests, the decentered structure of Fenianism made it difficult for the British authorities to repress it effectively, in particular when using the system of informers upon which it had relied in the past. The controversy over informers provides another lens through which to consider the contradictory impulses at work in the genre. Autobiographical nationalist history relies on a structure of individual witnessing. The idea that a single subject could tell the whole truth of the movement is central to the use of informers, the British state's primary form of the surveillance of Fenians. In a parallel literary history, mid-Victorian British and Irish popular culture was saturated with first-person narratives that promised to unveil the secrets of the movement to an anxious public. Thus, it is not surprising that Fenian recollections would work to avoid replicating autobiographical histories that relied on this formula.

Finally, it is worth considering the historical period during which the genre arose. Recollections began to appear in the 1880s and were published regularly throughout the first two decades of the twentieth century. During this time, Gladstonian home rule politics raised the real possibility of the end of the Act of Union, and the capture of the state seemed imminent. These developments provoked serious debates among nationalists about the form of an independent Irish state. Fenian writers wrote their counter-histories in the face of the demands inaugurated by the possibility that an Irish state would exist, to some degree, in the image of the British one. Recollections had to simultaneously resist imperial history and be intelligible to the state form coming into being; at the same time, they had to negotiate the critiques of state formation central to much Fenian politics.

In some sense these writers were caught between the British imperial State, the Irish state about to come into being, the increasingly influential home rule movement, and the Catholic Church. At the end of the nineteenth century, they faced the intensification and immediacy of certain fundamental questions. How would the desire of nationalism for the state be fulfilled, and what nation and what identity should be spoken and written into being? How could a seemingly imminent process of institutionalization provide a space for political and

---

12 Lloyd, 'Nationalisms against the state', pp 19–36. My reading of Fenian recollections is deeply indebted to Lloyd's work in this essay.

religious diversity yet avoid the structures of power typical of both Church and State? The genre of Fenian recollections attempts to respond to these seemingly impossible questions. Once we understand the genre of Fenian recollections in this way, the claim to blaspheme and to speak heretically appears to us in a different light.

The convergence of failure, contradiction and blasphemy is particularly apparent in John O'Leary's *Recollections of Fenians and Fenianism*. One of the early publications of its kind, O'Leary's narrative takes some of the tendencies of the genre and manifests them with such intensity that the text appears completely idiosyncratic. This makes O'Leary's text a most useful example; what is latent in other recollections becomes a more apparent structuring principle. It is anomalous but also paradigmatic.

The history of its anticipation, publication, and reception is symptomatic of the 'failures', in Rose's sense, of the genre. By the time that John O'Leary published *Recollections* in 1896, the book had been long awaited by an avid reading public in Ireland. He was one of the key figures in the early years of the Irish Republican Brotherhood, serving as the editor of the Fenian newspaper, the *Irish People*. He was convicted of treason-felony in 1865, serving the next six years in a British prison; he then spent fourteen years in exile in Europe. O'Leary eventually returned to Ireland from France, a triumphant and celebrated homecoming made possible by the Amnesty Act that pardoned numerous deported Fenians. Throughout the 1890s, news that O'Leary was writing his reminiscences generated excitement among Irish nationalists. Broadsheets and subscription lists circulated to facilitate advance purchase of the forth-coming work.

But, upon its publication, many responses to the narrative were perfunctory at best. On 4 January 1897, Douglas Hyde wrote, 'indeed every word you have written interested me, and me perhaps more than others.'[13] Such a lukewarm declaration of interest from the president of the National Literary Society is hardly the unequivocal assertion of literary and historical value anticipated by those who canvassed for advance subscriptions. In addition, William Butler Yeats, who had urged O'Leary to record his memories, viewed the book as disappointing. His review in *The Bookman* of February 1897 provides an account of O'Leary's political influence and importance rather than discussing the text in detail.[14]

Recent critics share such opinions of *Recollections of Fenians and Fenianism*. As O'Leary's biographer, Marcus Bourke, states, '[t]o the student of Fenianism, or of Irish affairs generally during the period covered by O'Leary's memoirs, they usually produce a feeling of disappointment.'[15] Bourke's assessment recapitulates common criticisms of O'Leary's text: that it does not reveal enough

---

13 Douglas Hyde to John O'Leary, 4 January 1897, Assorted letters to John O'Leary, National Library of Ireland, MS 5927. **14** Allan Wade (ed.), *Some letters from W.B. Yeats to John O'Leary and his sister: from originals in the Berg collection* (New York: New York Public Library, 1953), p. 77. **15** Marcus Bourke, *John O'Leary: a study in Irish separatism* (Tralee: Anvil, 1967), p. 212. **16** Bourke, *O'Leary*, p. 213.

secret information about the IRB, and that it is not a definitive, complete history of the movement. Bourke also describes O'Leary's book as unusually 'discursive'.[16] Echoing this criticism, Malcolm Brown has described O'Leary's writing as having an unsatisfactory prose style loaded 'with the rhetorical device the French call *expoliation*, the nervous mannerism that corrects all its assertions with a qualifying afterthought.'[17] Indeed, the text displays a general unwillingness to assert anything unequivocally and a repetitive insistence on its own limitations and fragmentary status. O'Leary sets the text up as the failure which readers later declare it. The following passage is typical:

> And here, perhaps, it may be no harm to impress on the reader's mind that, as I am not writing my autobiography, in any other than a very partial and imperfect sense, I am not writing a history of Fenianism in any sense at all. Not what Fenianism did for Ireland, or failed to do, is, properly speaking, my theme, but merely how Fenianism affected me and how I affected it. This seems a narrow and somewhat egotistic – it is certainly an egotistic – point of view; but it is the only one possible to me just now.[18]

For O'Leary, the personal nature of the narrative, writing as a direct participant, places a limit on the historical value of the text and offers access only to fragments of history. O'Leary rejects the synecdochal vision of some recollections as well as the informer logic that they unwittingly reproduce. His self-reflexive narrative, what he himself calls his 'incurable discursiveness',[19] is not simply a mannerism or a sign of failure. Instead, I contend that he attempts to work through the more radical possibilities of the genre.

Once we recast O'Leary's 'failure' in this way, we can see that he does something similar with the category of blasphemy. He devotes a surprising amount of attention to the doctrine of 'no priests in politics' and to the Catholic Church's condemnation of Fenianism in the 1850s and 60s. His second volume is in fact overtaken by the subject:

> I am afraid I have wearied my readers, and shall have to weary them still more, with details of our protracted controversy with the priests. But if I instruct someone, I am content, for the nonce at least, to amuse but slightly. Scarcely anyone in Ireland knows anything, save vaguely, of that not distant past of which I am writing [...] of the war we waged against the priests some thirty years ago, or, perhaps I should say, of the war the priests waged against us; a war the like of which is being fought over

17 Malcolm Brown, *The politics of Irish literature: from Thomas Davis to W.B. Yeats* (Seattle: University of Washington, 1972), p. 153.   18 O'Leary, *Recollections*, i, p. 67.   19 O'Leary, *Recollections*, ii, p. 132.

again before my eyes as I write, and which I fear will have to be fought over and over again before Irishmen can possess their souls in peace or their bodies in safety.[20]

What begins as an apology to the reader becomes a rationale for his obsessive representation of the 'war' between Fenianism and the Catholic Church. O'Leary positions the Fenian doctrine of 'no priests in politics' as part of a continuum, a protracted battle against the exercise of power by the Church in secular matters that continues into the 1890s.

Several historical processes have explanatory power when considering the continuum posited by O'Leary. First, he clearly wishes to offer an account of the specific period represented by his *Recollections*. He documents with great care the systematic denunciation of Fenianism by the Catholic Church in the 1850s and 1860s. He describes how Catholic Fenians were subject to religious penalties – denial of the sacraments, refusal of absolution, even excommunication – as were those who read, distributed or sold the *Irish People*.[21] Sunday services in many parishes included lengthy 'altar denunciations' of those in the community who sympathized with Fenians.[22] Such altar denunciations often named business people who sold the paper and demanded that all members of the parish boycott these vendors.[23] He includes newspaper narratives describing how newspaper readers lost their jobs within the Catholic education system or when a priest 'would go to their employers and deprive them of their employment.'[24]

Shifting his focus to Church leadership, he provides a chronicle of early condemnations by Church officials such as Cardinal Cullen. Fenian oaths required the use of God's name to swear allegiance to the IRB, 'inviolable secrecy regarding all the transactions of this secret society,'[25] and total commitment to the cause of Irish independence. Priests and bishops objected to the use of God's name in the oath-taking and to the clause of secrecy which prevented Fenians from making full confessions. When the oath was amended to remove the clause of secrecy, religious condemnation continued, focusing on the blasphemous utterance of God's name. Fenians pointed out that the Church had long supported other oath-taking movements only to find that new justifications for the denunciation appeared. Cardinal Cullen attacked the Fenian press as 'one of the most fatal and widely diffused means employed by the demon for the destruction of souls [...] which, whilst pretending to be the organs of the Irish people, seem to have no object but to vilify the Catholic Church, and to withdraw our people from its pale.'[26] Catholics were told that 'the only protection against the

20 O'Leary, *Recollections*, ii, pp 116–17.   **21** See John Newsinger, *Fenianism in Mid-Victorian Britain* (London: Pluto, 1994), pp 32–9.   **22** O'Leary, *Recollections*, ii, p. 66.   **23** Ibid., ii, p. 67.   **24** Ibid., ii, p. 118.   **25** The original oath of the Irish Revolutionary Brotherhood is reproduced in O'Leary, *Recollections*, i, p. 120.   **26** O'Leary, *Recollections*, ii, p. 49.

poison they contain, is to banish them from every house, and to destroy them when they fall into your hands.'[27] Cullen warned that Fenianism was driven by the 'revolutionary spirit' of continental revolutions and would lead to rabid attempts 'to abridge the rights and liberties of the Catholic Church' by the 'irreligious nationalists of Ireland'.[28] To demonstrate how Cullen's denunciation was put into practice, O'Leary includes accounts of the surveillance of Catholic Fenians by Catholic priests who 'play the detective in the service of England.'[29]

O'Leary suggests that that the basis for Church censure shifted over time; what began as an imputation of religious transgression had become a campaign to repress a politics deemed at odds with the institutional power of the church. Hence, blasphemy was transformed into a political accusation, an indictment in a struggle concerning secular power. The Church's exercise of power both mimicked and was coopted by state apparatuses of power. At the same time, the charge of blasphemy served as a mechanism of homogenization, attempting to reassert a Catholic national identity at the very moment at which the church claimed that Catholic hegemony was threatened.

O'Leary describes this historical episode as illustrative of a larger process by which the Church gained social and political power in mid-nineteenth-century Ireland. Emmet Larkin has documented the devotional revolution in Ireland that between 1850 and the 1870s transformed the fabric and culture of Irish life.[30] During this period, Catholicism infused Irish identity, producing a new union of religious and national forms. This revolution laid the groundwork for the institutional power and incursions into politics that so outraged O'Leary. Well after the days of Cullen's denunciation of Fenianism and the *Irish People*, the Church continued to play a complex and commanding role in numerous secular affairs, including eventually the Land League at the time when O'Leary was writing. Thus, the 'war' between the Church and the Fenians can, indeed, be located as part of the historical continuum that O'Leary describes.

O'Leary identified himself with an antisectarian, secular tradition of nationalism. He writes that, while many individual Fenians practiced Catholicism devoutly, the movement in most instances rejected all attempts 'to connect, directly or indirectly, Catholicity and Nationality.'[31] To him, the remedy to the expanding role of the Church in Ireland, its position as almost a second state apparatus of power, was a strict policy of 'no priests in politics'. He defines this doctrine as 'never, of course in the least den[ying] the absolute right of a priest [...] to hold any political opinion he liked but [...] wholly refus[ing] to consider that a political opinion gained any weight or force from being held by a priest.'[32] He makes clear that the invocation of sacred power and the use of the Church's moral and social authority could easily be channeled into forms of

---

27 Ibid., ii, p. 50. **28** Newsinger, *Fenians*, p. 38. **29** O'Leary, *Recollections*, ii, p. 123. **30** Emmet Larkin, 'The devotional revolution in Ireland, 1850–1875', *American Historical Review*, 77:3 (1972), 625–52. **31** O'Leary, *Recollections*, ii, p. 66. **32** Ibid., ii, p. 15.

control and coercion. According to O'Leary, the power of Catholicism in Ireland necessitated that its role in political matters be carefully circumscribed, whether that power is mobilized for or against nationalist causes. This might address what he saw as two seemingly antithetical but closely related dangers – Catholic nationalism and the Church's destruction of the more radical forms of anti-colonial nationalism.

Such elaborations of 'no priests in politics' remained blasphemous and heretical even in the 1890s. He states that

> this is as good a time as another to say a few words on our much-used and much-abused phrase – no priests in politics. Up to a short while ago, your orthodox agrarian person, with his P[arish] P[riest] as chairman of his society, and a C[atholic] C[urate] as secretary, was quite ready to hold that the doctrine of 'no priests in politics' was rank heresy. But agrarianists have fallen out, the shoe pinches again, and one section is quite Fenian now on this 'no priests in politics' question, while the other side, naturally, if not over wisely, thinks or pretends to think, that there is flat blasphemy in the phrase.[33]

Referring to the divisive and paradoxical role of the clergy in the Land League, this passage makes clear why the categories of blasphemy and heresy had continued analytic power for O'Leary. If the Church's claim to dictate political belief and practice was not curtailed, there was no hope that 'Irishmen [could] possess their souls in peace or their bodies in safety.' The growing institutional and secular power of the Catholic Church constituted a threat to freedom of mind and body in Ireland, much as the British state did.[34] Thus while O'Leary renders ironic the accusation that reading a Fenian newspaper is a blasphemous or heretical act, he professes that his text is blasphemous and heretical. Avowing blasphemy and heresy becomes a method of critique as well as a form of resistance to the exercises of power documented so thoroughly in the *Recollections*.

In her study of conversion, *Outside the Fold*, Gauri Viswanthan provides elegant definitions of blasphemy and heresy that can help us to understand O'Leary's investment in these categories. She writes:

> If blasphemers are defined as those who commit verbal offense in shocking, vile and crude language or imagery but without necessarily attacking points of doctrine, heretics on the other hand are those whose alternative interpretations of fundamental religious truths substantially undermine the stable foundation on which those truths stand, regardless

---

33 Ibid., ii, p. 180.   **34** O'Leary makes the material and analogical connection between Church and imperial state explicit numerous times through his *Recollections*. For example, he cites Charles Kickham's exclamation: 'The standard of the Church and the British flag! What a strange conjunction!' Ibid., ii, p. 69.

of whether the language they use is tasteless or not [...] A simple, yet unacknowledged, notion is that blasphemers may blaspheme without undermining the content or truth of any proposition because blasphemy's enemy is not a text or a creed but a community, along with the codes and rules it employs to sanction membership within it. Blasphemy shades into heresy when the text is subsumed so entirely within the identity of a community that the community *is* the text.[35]

I would add Joss Marsh's reminder that these terms are closely related to the categories of treason and sedition; all of them mark the boundary between that deemed permissible and that which is prohibited by an institution of power at a given time.[36] Thus, to be a blasphemer and a heretic is to operate within the parameters of an institution while challenging its boundaries through one's modes of speech as well as through radical critique. One defies the right of the institution to dictate not only belief but right action and expression. The heretical blasphemer occupies a position that redefines institutional limits by testing them and challenges the ideals of an institution, for example toleration or democracy, through provocation.

O'Leary understood the Church's power and influence on the hearts and minds of many Irish people and its central position within Irish culture. Similarly home rule signaled that the dismantling of the colonial state would be slow and that the new Irish state in its stead would be at least temporarily implicated with colonial power, mimicking its forms. Blasphemy and heresy, as Viswanathan and Marsh define them, provide a way for O'Leary to articulate a challenge from within, to resist a culture of consent and to dissent and to protest under the shadow of institutions that began to appear more and more ubiquitous and unassailable in Ireland.

As I have shown, it is no coincidence that Fenian recollections appeared during the late nineteenth century when some form of an independent Irish state began to be 'no longer in a future heaven', to use Franz Fanon's well-known phrase. The question of what home rule would mean and how the nation would be institutionalized led to obvious attempts to close down what had been a more open field of contestation under the broad category of Irish nationalism. Writers of Fenian recollections engage in a struggle that typifies this historical dilemma of the advent of the process of decolonization. Blasphemy provided a way to counter the fusion of nationalism with Catholicism as well as the Church's growing influence in secular affairs. But it also offered a way to imagine a nationalist politics that could not be fully coopted by the state form that had always so troubled Fenianism. In other words, some Fenian writers pro-

---

35 Gauri Viswanathan, *Outside the fold: conversion, modernity, and belief* (Princeton, NJ: Princeton UP, 1998), p. 242.   **36** Joss Marsh, *Word crimes: blasphemy, culture and literature in nineteenth-century England* (Chicago: University of Chicago, 1998), p. 7.

leptically envisioned the problems of fashioning the postcolonial state, of pressing radical anti-colonial nationalism into a form largely determined by imperial state formation. According to Kevin Whelan:

> The successor state sponsored a nationalistic project, constructed around the hegemonic bloc of the national bourgeoisie (agrarian and small business), and intertwining the state with the Church, eduction and media. Culturally, the new state lived within the paradigms created by the gifted generations of ideologues between 1880 and 1920 – notably Cusack, Hyde, Pearse, Yeats and Corkery – who created [...] a Catholic nationalist version of Irish history [...] the ossifying orthodoxy of the emergent nationalistic state which retains the institutional and ideological apparatus of the prior colonial state.[37]

In a sense, some Fenians provided an alternative politics that analyzed the process which Whelan describes. However, Fenians were not simply engaged in a critique of sectarianism, an advocation for the separation of Catholicism and the state, or anti-clericalism. Rather they present a radical critique of institutionality in the forms of both Church and state. By adopting the position of heretical blasphemers, these writers presented an implicit analysis of what can happen when powerful institutions curtail the right to express belief, religious or political. For when belief is codified into unquestionable doctrine or truth, it can lose its elasticity and its ability to challenge that which contains it. At stake in the assertion of heretical blasphemy is the continued right to speak the unspeakable whether seditious, offensive or blasphemous. At the same time, such provocations envision institutions as in a constant state of productive contestation.

Claiming a position as a heretical blasphemer allowed a writer like O'Leary to critique institutions and to maintain a critical relation to them even as the call to invest in them intensified. He reminds us that, as we imagine and engage with the institutions that govern us, there must always be a space that exists between the subject and the nation-state, between the individual and any institution to which he or she is subject. There must be a space for agency and resistance, a space for transgression and from which to blaspheme, from which to speak as a heretic.

---

37 Kevin Whelan, 'Between filiation and affiliation: the politics of postcolonial memory', in Clare Carroll and Patricia King (eds), *Ireland and postcolonial theory* (Cork: Cork UP, 2003), p. 94.

Religious ambivalence in May Laffan's *Hogan, M.P.*

JILL BRADY HAMPTON

The work of May Laffan (?1850–1916), who was known as Lady Hartley, is important to the body of nineteenth-century Irish fiction. It is valuable to scholars interested in both aesthetic quality and literature as insight to Ireland's nineteenth-century social and cultural environments.[1] Laffan's efforts, strongly in the genre of social realism, provide a novel approach, for her era, into both urban and rural Ireland. In *The cabinet of Irish literature*, published in 1883, the editors Charles Read and T.P. O'Connor acknowledge and applaud Laffan's originality in this field. They claim,

> Miss Laffan is to some extent the precursor of a new school in Irish fic-
> tion [...] she deserves the highest praise for the courage and remarkable
> skill with which she has exposed some of the shams and the narrowness
> that deface the society of Ireland as of every other country. Her writings
> in this respect mark unquestionably a new era in Irish literature.[2]

In Laffan's first novel *Hogan, M.P.* (1876), her depictions of both Catholic and Protestant characters as flawed human beings put individual faces on cultural and religious stereotypes, humanizing and dissolving accompanying assumptions. What is most striking about this novel is how she foregrounds her call for education reform, a policy she feels will best mediate cultural and religious dichotomies. She argues that the problem as well as the solution to Ireland's cultural and social problems resides within Ireland's secular and religious organizations, especially education.

As the product of what the nineteenth-century Irish defined as a 'mixed marriage', Laffan was particularly well suited to address the cultural complexity of her time. Her father was a Catholic, her mother a Protestant. To further complicate her allegiances, in 1882 May Laffan married Walter Noel Hartley, a Protestant. Although she continued writing through 1887, sometime after that year, she allegedly suffered a nervous breakdown, partially the result of Catholic negative reviews of her fiction.[3] Although raised a Catholic, Laffan's parents'

1 James H. Murphy, *Ireland: a social, cultural and literary history, 1791–1891* (Dublin: Four Courts, 2003), p. 160. 2 Charles A. Read and T.P. O'Connor, *The cabinet of Irish literature* (London: Blackie, 1883), p. 296. 3 For biographical information about May Laffan, I am indebted to Professor James H. Murphy.

mixed marriage could have explained her sometimes ambivalent attitudes towards both Catholics and Protestants, an ambivalence James H. Murphy notes can be particularly harsh: '[t]he novels of May Laffan […] constitute a sustained attack against Irish Catholic respectability.'⁴ While this is clearly evident in her writings, at the same time she also vigorously eviscerates Protestants. What she has little patience for in both communities is complacency concerning social and educational issues. That idea of social responsibility, linked to the education reformation, whether Catholic or Protestant, is key to all of Laffan's work.

The concept of social irresponsibility in both Catholic and Protestant worlds resonates throughout *Hogan, M.P.* At twenty-nine years of age, the protagonist of her novel, Hogan, is on the rise both socially and professionally. Although Catholic, he attended Trinity College, where he barely earned a degree, and has begun to aspire to the elitism and political power of the Protestant world. Hogan's mixing with the Protestant aristocracy is seen as such a sign of rising stature that even his uncle, a Catholic bishop, cannot help but take pride in it. The bishop, brother to Hogan's widowed mother, is the single most important early influence on Hogan's life. The narrator ironically describes the bishop as a 'very useful personage' who could charge higher prices for his religious and social efforts as 'a Bishop's spiritual services [were] naturally of greater value than those of the inferior clergy'.⁵

At first, despite his pride, the bishop advises Hogan against the venture into Ascendancy circles. He warns, 'you and the likes of you have nothing to do with that sort; far better keep to your own people.'⁶ However, the narrator quickly acknowledges, '[t]hough the Bishop spoke in this slighting way, he was secretly delighted, and his nephew saw it plainly.'⁷ On the other hand, later in the volume, in another conversation about current religious perspectives, one of Hogan's new friends exclaims,

> [t]he monstrous insolence of the English is at the bottom of all the trou-
> bles here. Talk of Infallibility and the Pope's assumptions, – God bless me!
> what is it, compared to the Anglo-Hibernian Protestantism […] every-
> where John Bull goes with his egotism and his Bible […] the story is
> identical; hatred and rebellion spring up at once.⁸

Even as Laffan denigrates the classism of the Catholics, she takes a swipe at Protestant arrogance.

Although Laffan is often didactic about Protestant and Catholic issues, she also uses place to intimate religious characters or situations. Perhaps nowhere does she express more clearly her ambivalent attitudes about religious conflicts than in *Hogan*

4 Murphy, *Catholic fiction and social reality in Ireland, 1873–1922* (Westport, CT: Greenwood, 1997), p. 29.   **5** May Laffan, *Hogan M.P.*, 3 vols (1876; New York: Garland, 1979), i, p. 18.   **6** Ibid., i, p. 50.   **7** Ibid., i, p. 50.   **8** Ibid., i, p. 154.

M.P. In a particularly descriptive passage before Hogan's immersion in the political
world, she emphasizes the comfort and warmth of the cozy Catholic world he is
forsaking. Hogan and the bishop, numbed slightly by 'excellent dry champagne',
have spent the day together strolling arm in arm along the sea at Howth.[9] They ride
in a snug first-class train compartment back to Dublin where they drive to St
Swithin's for benediction with the Lady Prioress, a close friend of both. The chapel
is described in images of security and domesticity as 'pretty', 'warm and comfortable' with 'a soft, rich light.'[10] Relaxed and warm, Hogan 'yawned to his heart's content'.[11] Afterwards, he sits beside 'a magnificent fire blazing; and Sister Veronica fuss-
ily light[ing] the gaselier'[12] while wine and cake are served. He and the Bishop
absentmindedly compliment the lay sister Veronica on the room's cleanliness and
coziness. She replies appropriately, '[d]irty corners is ve[n]ial sins.'[13]

Contrast these warm, cozy Catholic scenes with the dinner party scene at
Lord Brayhead's, a powerful member of the Ascendancy, who has invited Hogan
to his home as a candidate running for parliament. In Lord Brayhead's home, 'a
huge red-brick corner house', the rooms are heated by 'great stoves placed
beneath the staircase'.[14] Here, there is no welcoming fire to warm and mes-
merize but a hidden source of heat, modern and mechanical. Despite the fact
that it is the middle of winter, a conservatory is filled with spring flowers.
Narcissus and hyacinths are pointedly mentioned, both flowers recalling the
deaths of self-absorbed young men in ancient myth. Intoxicated with this display of upper-class affluence and power, appropriately self-absorbed Hogan does
not see the lethal risks in his ambitions and is caught unaware of the anti-
Catholicism beneath his host's social civility.

As guests arrive at the dinner party, some warned in advance to be polite to
the Romanist Hogan, a lack of intimacy among the Protestant Ascendancy is
underscored. The aging debutante Diana Bursford's 'cold, well-bred, smiling
manner' hides a 'torrent of disgust, contempt, and fierce self-upbraiding' because
she has failed to make a match yet. Diana's voice is cold, another woman's tone
'acid' and 'spiteful'.[15] The comparisons stretch to the servants. Lady Brayhead's
maid is 'grim' in contrast to voluble, nurturing Sister Veronica. Lady Brayhead,
despite the efficient stoves, has 'thin chilly fingers'[16] in contrast to the mother
superior in the earlier scene with whom '[t]he cold weather agreed [...] and
gave her a fine healthy colour'.[17] Furthering the comparison, the mother superior is tall, with 'a merry, cheerful face, with keen grey eyes [...] and large white
teeth gleaming in a wide mouth, which seemed always smiling'[18] while Lady
Brayhead is described as a little 'soured woman' 'with a perpetual red nose, and
pinched-up, wintry little face. In the hottest day of midsummer it was her pecu-
liarity to look cold'.[19] Her relationship with her husband is formal; she calls him

9 Ibid., i, p. 228.   10 Ibid., i, p. 234.   11 Ibid., i, p. 235.   12 Ibid., i, p. 236.   13 Ibid., i, p. 236.
14 Ibid., i, p. 262.   15 Ibid., i, p. 278.   16 Ibid., i, p. 263.   17 Ibid., i, p. 236.   18 Ibid., i, p. 237.
19 Ibid., i, p. 264.

'my lord' and is subservient to him. On the other hand, the mother superior only uses the words 'my lord' as an exclamation. When she is with the bishop and Hogan, she 'plump[s] down on her knees' beside the fire and addresses Hogan as 'John dear' and 'my dear child'.²⁰ The conversation among the three Catholics is as natural and lively as the one between the Protestant Lady and Lord Brayhead is stilted and formal.

Despite her obvious regard for the Catholic domestic scene, Laffan complains that they lack a large middle class, well-educated enough for self-government. Therefore the Protestants will control the home rule campaign. Because it is the first election following the 1872 Ballot Act, the one Hogan runs in promises to be interesting. The secret ballot offers Catholics an opportunity to improve their condition. The Irish middle class – newly wealthy whiskey merchants, businessmen, and some farmers whose sons were attending Trinity and whose daughters were being convent-educated – was quietly acquiring power. Consequently, the education of this rapidly emerging multi-layered group was central to the social and political concerns of the day. Although the political campaign is fundamental to the plot structure of *Hogan, M.P.*, the education theme is a continual subtext. Indeed, Stephen Brown's *Ireland in fiction* in its brief review claims that the novel is a '[p]icture of Dublin society, showing how Catholics are handicapped by their want of education and good breeding, due, in the Author's view, to a wholly wrong system of Catholic education.'²¹

From the novel's opening pages, Laffan focuses on the significance of education. It begins on a July morning at St Swithin's Convent school's 'closing-out' ceremony, with an epigraph by Francis Bacon on the usefulness of studies '"for delight, for ornaments and for ability."' Ironically, these young Catholic women's education serves primarily the needs of the marriage market, not their intellectual advancement or adaptability to a changing world. Citing her six years of personal experience as a student herself, Laffan writes about this subject with authority in her article 'Convent boarding-schools for young ladies', published in the June 1874 edition of *Fraser's Magazine*. Her chief concerns in the article are the uselessness and expense of the partial education the girls receive. Although she is careful to include ordinary Protestant as well as Catholic boarding schools in her denunciations, she claims that the defects at the Protestant schools are being corrected.²² Significantly, culture is developed in the homes and schools usually run by these convent-educated women so that their opinions and prejudices continually permeate the general social structure. Laffan's portraits of the various Irish and Anglo-Irish families and educational systems demonstrate how these elements affect, at the simplest level, social conversation, and at the most complex, political and power relationships.

20 Ibid., i, p. 237. **21** Stephen Brown, *Ireland in fiction: a guide to Irish novels, tales, romances, and folklore* (1919; New York: B. Franklin, 1970), p. 132. **22** May Laffan Hartley, 'Convent boarding-schools for young ladies', *Fraser's Magazine*, 9 (1874), 778–86.

Nellie Davoren, ultimately rejected by Hogan, is the novel's idealized woman. While Nellie does not attend a Catholic convent school, at the request of his uncle she is present and meets Hogan at the 'closing-out' ceremony at St Swithin's. Like Laffan, Nellie is the daughter of a mixed marriage; her father was a Protestant, her mother a Catholic. From the opening description, Nellie is set off as different from and thus superior to the other young ladies. Laffan focuses on dress in her comparisons between Nellie and the convent-school graduates. Both Hogan and the reverend mother notice and admire her, 'a slender girl of eighteen, quietly dressed in grey silk'.[23] In contrast to Nellie's grey old-fashioned gown, the young Rafferty girls, schooled at St Swithin's, are dressed in blue silk and yellow lace with panier and bouffawns. The reverend mother warns another young student, the heiress Mary Brangan, that '"[l]ove of dress [...] is a snare and a delusion; and it is degrading to every one; but it is especially revolting in a child who, like you, has had the benefit of years of training and religious education."'[24] Just what those years of training and religious education produce is obvious, according to Laffan.

Significantly, when Hogan approaches the bishop for campaign advice, the prelate urges him to consider an education platform.[25] But since he lacks the sophisticated, political education necessary to comprehend broader solutions to Ireland's problems, Hogan jumps on the home rule bandwagon where he sits useless and used in ignorance of the true motivations behind its power plays. Broken in finances and in faith, Hogan forsakes Nellie and marries the weary, older Protestant woman, Diana, who has campaigned for a husband as arduously as Hogan strove for parliament. Their 'mixed marriage' provides them with a miserable life.

Nevertheless, just when Laffan seems to shake her ambivalence and make a clearly partisan statement deriding one religious or another, the narrative shifts once again. Another mixed marriage endures happily. In Protestant Dermot Blake, Laffan seems to suggest that only an Irishman educated abroad and matured by personal experience in different cultures can escape Ireland's duplicity and social and political quagmires. Dermot, recently returned from travels to India, the Cape, and California, is an underdeveloped character, but his impact on the novel is, nonetheless, important. He meets the lovely Nellie through the kinship they share to her paternal, Protestant aunt, Dorothy O'Hegarty. His sincerity, genuineness, and common sense more than make up for his unsophisticated conversation. When Aunt Dorothy comments derogatively on the dress of some '"R.Cs"', he asks her what that means. She explain that '"R.Cs"' means a Roman Catholic, '"common people, – trade, you know"'[26] Dermot replies, '"Haw! Why, you know, ma'am, in Kerry, the best families round are that per-

---

23 Laffan, *Hogan*, i, p. 20. **24** Ibid., i, p. 40. **25** William Gladstone, whose first administration (1868–74) covers the time period of the novel, was introducing legislation for Catholic higher education, something Laffan must have been aware of. **26** Laffan, *Hogan*, iii, p. 174.

suasion. What dooced difference does it make?"[27] Indeed, Dermot and Nelly marry and live happily ever after.

Those words seem to speak for Laffan. Strict religious affiliation, she believed, made little difference in an Ireland where social and political worlds were rapidly changing, beginning to blur the boundaries between allegiances. In the end, Laffan was unable to bear the strong criticism of her work that came especially from Catholics. However, her recovered work and the voices of her characters are serving better and more effectively her original vision. Throughout her fiction, Laffan's examination of social and religious conflict is directed toward portraying a pluralistic rather than a dichotomous Irish culture and society desperately in need of increased social activism and educational reform. Her work mediates rather than perpetuates conflicts in late nineteenth-century Ireland.

27 Ibid., iii, p. 175.

Walter McDonald's window on Maynooth, 1870–1920

LOUISE FULLER

Key insights into Irish Catholicism in the late Victorian era and early twentieth century, can be found in the writings of a priest who was at St Patrick's College, Maynooth from 1870 until his death in 1920. After emancipation in 1829, Irish Catholics became increasingly confident and by the close of the century Catholicism had become the badge of Irish identity. Throughout the century the Catholic Church had successfully promoted a modernizing ethos both in organizational and devotional terms, which was to guarantee it a defining role in any future political shape that the country might take. As Emmet Larkin has written, it managed to build itself into the 'very vitals of the nation'.[1] The Catholic ethos that developed placed a heavy emphasis on discipline and could be characterized as authoritarian, legalistic and prescriptive. This has to be understood, of course, in the context of influences coming from Britain and the rest of western Europe in the nineteenth century. The Catholicism that evolved from that time was a peculiarly Irish hybrid of Tridentinism, folk religion and Victorian puritanism – what was often been referred to derisively as 'le catholicisme du type irlandais'.

Walter McDonald was born in June 1854 in Emil, in the parish of Mooncoin, Co. Kilkenny. His father was a tenant farmer and his mother also came from farmer stock. He went to the local national school in Carrick-on-Suir, from there to the diocesan seminary, St Kyran's in Kilkenny (later spelt St Kieran's) at the age of eleven in 1865, and from there as a student for the priesthood to Maynooth in 1870. Eleven years later he joined the staff of Maynooth as professor of theology and spent the rest of his life in teaching and administration at the college.

Maynooth was, at that time, the most important seminary in the English-speaking world and its intellectual character influenced English-speaking Catholicism internationally well into the next century. It played a very significant role in the forging of that Catholic culture in Ireland. By the second half of the nineteenth century, half of the priests of Ireland had been educated in Maynooth.[2] McDonald believed that the measure of a good university was the

1 Emmet Larkin, 'The devotional revolution in Ireland, 1850–1875', *American Historical Review*, 77:3 (1972), 644–5. 2 Patrick Corish, *The Irish Catholic experience* (Dublin: Gill and Macmillan, 1985), p. 162

original research and published work of its professors and lived up to this in his own academic life. By the standards of his day, he was exceptionally independent-minded. But sadly for him, his ideas were rather too original and thus risqué for the Catholic Church both at home and in Rome and most of his work was banned by the Church authorities.

His best-known works in chronological order are *Motion: its origin and conservation* (1898)[3] which was to cause his first clash with the ecclesiastical authorities, *Some ethical questions of peace and war* (1919)[4] and *Some ethical aspects of the social question* (1920).[5] Shortly before his death he appointed Professor Denis Gwynn his literary executor for works not requiring the ecclesiastical approval of an *imprimatur*.[6] He had been writing his reminiscences over a number of years and was particularly keen that they be published. His book *Reminiscences of a Maynooth professor* was published by Jonathan Cape posthumously in 1925.[7] The book deals with the conflicts and controversies he was involved in arising from his ideas and writing. It also provides a remarkable insight into seminary life and the formation of seminarians in Maynooth from the perspective of a student and later of a college professor.

His reflections on the intellectual culture of Maynooth, on the teaching staff and on Catholic theology are very critical, but his perspective is always that of a loyal churchman concerned with raising the intellectual standards of the Irish Catholicism of his day. What is remarkable is the extent to which he was ahead of his time highlighting and questioning all manner of problematic areas in the Church, many of which were not dealt with until the time of the Second Vatican Council.

He arrived in Maynooth at a time of transition. The Irish Church Act, which disestablished the Church of Ireland, came into force in January 1871. This had important repercussions for Maynooth, an institution which had been founded by act of parliament and was partly funded by the government and over whose administration the government had a formal influence. The running of the college was handed over to its episcopal trustees and the annual government grant ceased, leaving the college in very straitened financial circumstances. The picture McDonald gives of Maynooth in his day, is of an Irish Church very cut off from new and influential currents of thought in science and philosophy, which were presenting challenges to traditional Catholic teaching at that time,

---

3 Walter McDonald, *Motion, its origin and conservation* (Dublin: Browne and Nolan: London: Burns and Oates, 1898).   **4** Walter McDonald, *Some ethical questions of peace and war, with special reference to Ireland* (London: Burns, Oates and Washbourne, 1920; Dublin: University College Dublin Press, 1998).   **5** Walter McDonald, *Some ethical aspects of the social question: suggestions for priests* (London: Burns, Oates and Washbourne, 1920).   **6** National Archives, Dublin, last will and testament of Revd Walter McDonald.   **7** Denis Gwynn (ed.), *Reminiscences of a Maynooth professor* (London: Jonathan Cape, 1925, Cork: Mercier, 1967). Citations here are primarily from the later abridged edition. Citations from the earlier edition are indicated by publication date.

and which were set to undermine it more in the future, if not met head on. On
his arrival at Maynooth, McDonald was very critical of the lack of text books
and the poor library facilities. He was caustic about the approach to teaching,
which did not develop the critical faculty and the use of Latin, he felt, was a
further obstacle to students deriving full benefit from their seminary course. Of
Mr Hackett, the philosophy lecturer, he wrote:

> His one notion of teaching was to keep us to a dead grind of some old, tra-
> ditional statements of doctrine, proofs, and answers to objections [...] very
> unlike what one meets in the real world. Darwin was then revolutionizing
> thought; but we overturned him in two or three brief sentences.[8]

According to McDonald, 'we were educated in a fool's paradise as if we
were still in the eighteenth, or even the sixteenth, century.'[9] And he pointed out
that 'the whole College was run in that way.' He continued that 'Utilitarianism'
was not mentioned by Dr Walsh, nor when you read Crolly would you 'ever
suspect that the Social Revolution was at hand and that the principles on which
it is based had been already proclaimed in Germany'.[10] William Walsh was a
professor of theology. He was appointed president of the college in 1880, and
went on to become archbishop of Dublin in 1885. George Crolly was also a
professor of theology and both he and Walsh had published books on their subject. In McDonald's estimation, Maynooth produced 'good average men'[11] and
he was not alone in thinking this. The narrowness of the intellectual training
received in Maynooth was a constant theme of the priest novelist Canon
Sheehan, himself a student in Maynooth from 1869 to 1877[12] and thus a contemporary of McDonald's, as for example in *Luke Delmege*,[13] where Luke represents the Maynooth intellectual, whose narrow training causes him to adopt
a text-book approach to life. And the same ideas were echoed by Gerald
O'Donovan, a student in Maynooth from 1889 to 1895, in his autobiographical
novel, *Fr Ralph*.[14]

McDonald was also critical of the teaching of theology. The professor, he
pointed out, gave them 'dictates, wherein the doctrine, the arguments, and the
answers to objections were put more pithily, so that one could easily commit
them to memory and make a better show at the examinations'.[15] There was
little sense of theology as a science which needed to develop as other branches
of knowledge, nor was there any attempt to grapple with the arguments of the
Rationalists which were becoming a force in all Protestant and most Catholic
countries. He pointed out: 'we were behind our time; slaying foes that had been

8 Ibid., p. 66.   9 Ibid.   10 Ibid., pp 66–7.   11 Ibid., p. 131.   12 See Canon Sheehan, *The literary life and other essays* (Dublin: Phoenix, n.d.), pp 110–14.   13 P.A. Sheehan, *Luke Delmege*
(London: Longmans, 1919).   14 Gerald O'Donovan, *Fr Ralph* (1913; Dingle, Brandon, 1993).
15 McDonald, *Reminiscences*, p. 72.

disabled or killed long ago, and unaware of, or closing our eyes to, the new method of attack.'[16]

Before long McDonald had an opportunity to make his own contribution to the development of theology. The bishop of Ossory, Dr Patrick F. Moran (Cardinal Cullen's nephew and later to be Cardinal archbishop of Sydney) needed help in the diocesan seminary of St Kieran's in Kilkenny, and although McDonald was not yet ordained, he appointed him professor of philosophy and dean, with general charge of the whole college. The bishop applied to Rome for a dispensation and McDonald was ordained priest on 14 October 1876 when he was twenty-two years old. Some time later he was also given responsibility for dogmatic theology. By this time McDonald was beginning to experience fears and doubts about the foundations of his faith and he found that the conservative nature of his training in Maynooth left him ill-equipped to grapple with them. He remarked:

> the conservatism in which I was trained very nearly drove me out of the Church on many occasions, or into a mad-house [...] the good, easy men who, for the honour of God would in the interest of religion, insist on these traditional views – making dogmas of what are but school traditions – are tormenting souls and driving them out of the Church.[17]

At this point McDonald had no great ambitions for advancement in academic life – he expected to go on teaching at St Kieran's until such time as he was appointed to a parish as a curate and thereafter as parish priest. But Bishop Moran had other things in mind for him and in 1881 he was back in Maynooth as professor of theology against the background of the land war and the political ascendancy of Parnell. On the political issues of the day, the staff were divided. McDonald was one of five members of the college staff who forwarded a joint subscription over their names to the 'Parnell Testimonial Fund' in a letter which was published in the *Freeman's Journal*.[18] This was despite the fact that the Vatican had expressed its concerns in relation to the turn of political events in Ireland. Rome took a further step when a circular was dispatched to the Irish bishops on 11 May 1883 condemning 'such collections as are raised in order to inflame popular passions, and to be used as the means for leading men into rebellion against the laws.'[19] At the next meeting of the trustees of the college, a resolution was passed that members of college staff were to abstain from taking a side on public questions as to which the bishops were divided.[20]

16 Ibid., p. 74. 17 Ibid., p. 93. 18 Ibid., pp 107–8. 19 See *Freeman's Journal*, 16 May 1883, p. 5. For background to these events see Ambrose Macaulay, *Patrick Dorrian* (Dublin: Irish Academic, 1987), pp 355–9. 20 McDonald, *Reminiscences*, pp 107–8. McDonald explains that this resolution was not entered in the Minute Book, kept in the College for the use of the staff. An examination of the minutes for 1883 confirms this.

In 1888 McDonald was appointed prefect of the Dunboyne Institute, the graduate school of Maynooth seminary, and this allowed him to put into practice some of the ideas that he felt most strongly about. Essentially he encouraged in his students liberty of opinion, allowing them to defend their opinions and to criticize his. As time went by, he realized more and more that it was not a question of learning simply what had been taught traditionally; but of harmonizing it with new insights from the physical sciences. When a conflict occured this meant that there were aspects of the traditional philosophy and theology which he felt had to be rejected. In his *Reminiscences* he recalls that the two conflicts which caused him most turmoil were, firstly, those of the physical sciences with traditional and official teaching, and, secondly, those of historical criticism with the content of the deposit of faith, or to put it in another way, the question of error in the Bible.[21] Round about the time that he became prefect, the trustees ordered that the old practice of publicly defending certain theses should be revived, which meant that every year a body of theses had to be drawn up to be defended against all comers, professors and others. These theses were to be published in the college calendar.

Not surprisingly when McDonald's opinions were set down publicly, they aroused opposition from some of his colleagues. The first serious trouble came at the end of the academic year 1893–4, when his thesis on the theology of grace, *De Gratia,*[22] was printed and distributed to the professors and other members of the staff. The senior professor of dogmatic theology and the president of the college confronted McDonald. He was asked to withdraw certain passages in his thesis as contravening faith. McDonald refused to do so and set himself to write a series of papers, wherein he defended his position. The papers soon expanded into a substantial book, which he published in 1898, entitled *Motion, its origin and conservation*. In the book he examined the theology of grace in light of contemporary scientific ideas on motion, attempting to reconcile the Catholic world-view with the ideas of modern physics. In August 1897, some months before the book appeared he was invited to read a paper at the International Catholic Scientific Conference at Fribourg. In this paper, entitled 'The kinetic theory of activity', which was published in the proceedings of the Fribourg Congress, he proclaimed openly his disputed views. The paper was also published in the *Irish Ecclesiastical Record* of October 1897.[23] The bishops at their standing committee meeting decided that the matter should be referred to Rome.[24] The book was condemned by the Sacred Congregation of the Index on 15 December1898 and McDonald was ordered to 'withdraw from publication, as far as can be, all copies of his book, to renounce the opinions therein contained and to abstain in future from further teaching the same.'[25]

---

21 Ibid., p. 118. **22** *Maynooth College Calendar, 1892,* pp 193–213. **23** Walter McDonald, 'The kinetic theory of activity', *Irish Ecclesiastical Record* [hereafter *IER*], fourth series, 2 (1897), pp 289–308. **24** McDonald, *Reminiscences* [1925], pp 123–4. **25** Dublin Diocesan Archives

In his *Reminiscences* McDonald tells us that he was resolved to comply strictly with the demands of his ecclesiastical superiors, but that he 'was no less resolved to know precisely what I was to avoid, and to teach nothing but what I believed to be true.'[26] He wrote to Cardinal Ledochowski, who had issued the decree, an explanatory letter, containing twenty six of the disputed theses asking for directions.[27] After three months the cardinal wrote back saying that it was not customary for the Index to make schedules of erroneous propositions, however enclosing the animadversions of two consulters for his instruction. McDonald was gratified to see that these did not express any condemnation of his propositions as being directly opposed to revealed doctrines. In the meantime he found a number of books and essays by eminent authorities in France, which appeared to support his views and he wrote again to the cardinal calling his attention to them. The cardinal replied suggesting that he refer the matter back to the Irish bishops and let them decide whether the matter should be referred to Rome for fuller consideration. McDonald duly wrote to Cardinal Logue of Armagh, explaining that he was prepared to abide by the decision whatever it might be, but that he was anxious to know whether the objections to his theses were the private opinions of two theologians, whose knowledge of the particular question he was addressing might not be quite up to date, or whether it was, in fact, an authoritative decision against him.[28] Cardinal Logue referred the matter to the next bishops' meeting, whereupon their decision was to send the matter back to Rome to secure an authoritative doctrinal decision.[29]

While the reputation of Maynooth for orthodox teaching was obviously involved in any censure of one of its principal professors, the bishops at this time, McDonald pointed out, placed no obstacles in his way nor did they express any adverse opinions either on his teaching, or on his action in demanding an authoritative decision. The letter which he now prepared, showed that the views of the Roman consultors were in conflict with views that had been propounded by some of the foremost experts in philosophy and theology and ran to a pamphlet of forty-six pages. The document was duly dispatched to Rome in November 1899 and he heard nothing until May 1900. The letter that Logue got back was to the effect that McDonald should be admonished and removed from his chair, if it was felt that the doctrine which he was teaching in class was not in conformity with Catholic teaching. The letter was shown to McDonald by the vice-president of the college, Dr O'Dea, with an oral message from Logue that for the future he should confine himself to the official teaching of the Church when expounding these questions.[30] In the minutes of

[hereafter DDA], Walsh papers, 1885–1921, Roman Correspondence, S. Congregazione de Propaganda Fide [hereafter Propaganda] to Archbishop William Walsh from, 20 Jan. 1899. **26** McDonald, *Reminiscences* [1925], p. 132. **27** Ibid., pp 136–43. **28** Ibid., pp 152–3. **29** Ibid., pp 153–5. **30** Ibid., p. 156. See Armagh Diocesan Archives [hereafter ADA], Logue 13, publications: McDonald's book, folder 9, Propaganda to Michael Cardinal Logue 17 Apr. 1900 and Dr Thomas O'Dea to Logue, 19 May 1900.

the trustees of the college for 1900 and 1901 there are resolutions to this effect.[31] While he retained his chair, one book after another which he wrote during these years was refused an *imprimatur*, which caused him a great deal of frustration in his later years, particularly because he had long held that in the matter of appointments original publications were the surest test of a professor's value to his college.

Notwithstanding his personal difficulties McDonald continued to influence important developments in the college. In 1895 at the centenary celebrations of the college he proposed the idea of the Maynooth Union and gave the first paper, which was published in the *Irish Ecclesiastical Record*.[32] The idea of the union was that the college would keep in touch with former students, but also that it would be more open to the world outside.[33] An early development which came out of the union, was the procurement of a grant to buy more literary works for the library. From his early years as a student McDonald had been critical of the dearth of reading material in the college and now he went about securing a regular supply of the best reviews in theology and philosophy, but he was disappointed that there was so little demand for what he termed 'scientific' periodicals. He felt very strongly that priests should be trained to use newspapers during their seminary course and when he pressed for this without success, he wrote to prominent seminaries in England, America, France, Belgium and even Rome to enquire whether newspapers were permitted. The replies were such that he prepared a list for the trustees of the college who made a slight relaxation of the rule. They allowed the *Saturday Review* but not the *Tablet* or the weekly addition of the *Times*. They would not allow the *Freemans's Journal*, the oldest of Dublin's daily newspapers and the recognized organ of Irish Catholics.[34] The Catholic Record Society of Ireland was also set up after committee meetings in 1910 and 1911 of the Maynooth Union, for the purposes of collecting and publishing documents not published before, or if published, not generally available especially those having a bearing on ecclesiastical history,[35] and the journal *Archivium Hibernicum* appeared in 1912.

In his *Reminiscences* McDonald wrote that he 'had long felt the want, in our College, of a journal wholly devoted to theological science [...] in which the latest questions would be discussed'. He felt that 'in Maynooth we were somewhat out of touch with life' and that contacts with other journals would keep Maynooth's faculty of theology '*au courant* with what was being said and done in the schools of theology the world over.'[36] He broached the idea to his colleagues

31 Maynooth College Archives [hereafter MCA], B2/1/2, Minute of trustees, 20 June 1900, 26 June 1901 in *Journal of the trustees, minutes, 1881–1921*. 32 See 'A Maynooth union', paper read by Walter McDonald at the centenary celebration of Maynooth College, 27 June 1895, *IER*, third series, 16 (1895), pp 673–87. 33 John Paul II Library, NUI, Maynooth, *Records of the Maynooth union 1895–1959; 1961*. McDonald, *Reminiscences*, pp 143–6. 34 McDonald, *Reminiscences*, pp 143–6. 35 Patrick Corish, *Maynooth College, 1795–1995* (Dublin: Gill and Macmillan, 1995), p. 248. 36 McDonald, *Reminiscences*, p. 194.

who were interested. But he was very conscious, in light of his own experience, that the purpose of the review would be defeated, if the bishops did not allow it to be independent. From the outset he made it clear that the kind of ground that the review would cover should be different, 'higher than' what appeared in the *Irish Ecclesiastical Record*. In regard to that journal he pointed out:

> The *Record* was owned by Messrs. Browne and Nolan, whom a whisper from Cardinal Logue or the Archbishop of Dublin would frighten into refusal of any article or even dismissal of any editor, who must, therefore always take care to please – or not to displease – Ara Coeli and Drumcondra – no easy task, if one were, at the same time bent on developing theological science.[37]

McDonald wrote to William Walsh, archbishop of Dublin on behalf of those involved, setting out their plans for the project on 14 July 1905.[38] Walsh sent him a copy of the diocesan regulations with regard to censorship of books and other publications. An editorial committee was duly set up, but before long McDonald was embroiled in the censorship issue again. In a letter to Walsh on 1 August 1905, he pointed out that a review, edited by five professors empowered to examine for degrees in theology, should not require any further supervision before being passed for publication and gave several examples of serious reviews dealing with religion such as *Revue Biblique,* the *American Catholic Quarterly, Civilta Catholica*, and the *American Ecclesiastical Review* which were published without either *Nihil Obstat* or *Imprimatur*.[39] Walsh responded on 20 October that he could find no way round the censorship problem, but assured McDonald that he could count on him subscribing to the journal.[40] But five days later he wrote again to McDonald indicating that there was 'a difference of opinion amongst the Bishops' as to the wisdom of publishing the new quarterly and asked that his 'name [should] not appear in any list of subscribers.'[41] It would appear that Walsh had consulted Cardinal Logue in the interim, as he received a letter from Logue dated 24 October 1905, which began as follows:

> Considering Dr. MacDonalds (*sic*) articles in recent numbers of the 'Record', I should not like to give my name as subscriber to a periodical of which he is the leading director. I gave expression to this view quite freely and openly when I was at Maynooth. I believe that unless the periodical be kept under strict censorship, its publication will be a dangerous experiment.[42]

37 Ibid. Ara Coeli was the residence of the archbishop of Armagh and the archbishop of Dublin lived at Drumcondra. 38 D.D.A., Walsh Papers, 1905, Box 377 II, Walter McDonald to Archbishop William Walsh, 14 July 1905. 39 D.D.A., Walsh Papers, 1905, Box 377 II, Walter McDonald to Archbishop William Walsh, 1 Aug. 1905. 40 McDonald, *Reminiscences*, p. 201. 41 Ibid. 42 D.D.A., Walsh papers, 1905, Box 377/ I, Michael Cardinal Logue to

The bishops were wary of the review and indeed disapproved of the proposed review and there was no point in arguing further. Canon Dunne, the president of Holy Cross College, Clonliffe, was appointed censor and the first issue of the *Irish Theological Quarterly* appeared in 1906.[43]

However, within a month of the first issue of the review, being published, the president of the college Dr Mannix received a letter from the secretaries of the Bishops' standing committee, to the effect that at their recent meeting surprise was expressed that permission for the journal was not sought from the trustees of the college.[44] McDonald replied on behalf of the editorial committee.[45] He pointed out in the letter that the journal was not published by the Faculty of Theology *per se*, but by members of that faculty on their own responsibility, subject to the laws of the Sacred Congregation of the Index. Despite pressure, McDonald persisted in his refusal to seek the permission of the trustees for the journal and they 'continued to publish with the uncomfortable feeling that [they] were under suspicion and disliked'.[46]

Certain articles of his at the time, he felt made conservative people uneasy: articles such as 'The proof of infallibility',[47] 'Studies in idolatry',[48] and 'The ethical aspect of boycotting'.[49] Two other articles which showed his interest in social issues were 'About socialism' and 'The living wage'.[50] That said, the review was making headway. Circulation was increasing; it was being noticed by Protestant journals and it was making a profit. For his first year's work he recalled that he got a cheque for in excess of £97.[51] But then McDonald heard rumours that some of his recent writings were again being delated to the Holy See. He called on the president, Dr Daniel Mannix, to see if there was any truth in these rumours. Dr Mannix told him that the Irish bishops had been pressed by Rome, for about twelve months, to proceed against him. He read to him excerpts of a letter he had received from Logue to the effect that the bishops had put him and the other professors there to prepare students for the mission and not to investigate useless questions.[52]

When McDonald protested against such a narrow view of his duties, Dr Mannix drew his attention to a particular article published in 1908, which in his own view, was not appropriate to the times. The article 'The Hazel Switch' appeared in the *CYM* (*Catholic Young Men*), the journal of the Catholic Young Men's Society in January 1908.[53] In 'The Hazel Switch' McDonald was dealing with the question of how far one is justified in using pressure, moral or physical, to compel others to respect equitable rights. A legacy of the land agitation

Archbishop William Walsh 24 Oct. 1905. **43** McDonald, *Reminiscences*, p. 201. **44** Ibid., p. 202. **45** Walter McDonald to Archbishop Daniel Mannix, copy of letter 7 Apr. 1906 in Mannix's hand in MCA, 20/5/21. **46** McDonald, *Reminiscences*, p. 204. **47** McDonald, 'The proof of infallibility', *ITQ*, 2 (1907), 485–98. **48** McDonald, 'Studies in idolatry', *ITQ*, 1 (1906), pp 464–75. **49** McDonald, 'The ethical aspect of boycotting', *ITQ*, 1 (1906), pp 333–47. **50** McDonald, 'About socialism', *ITQ*, 1 (1906), pp 93–102 and 'The living wage', *ITQ*, 3 (1908), pp 73–82. **51** McDonald, *Reminiscences*, p. 205. **52** Ibid., pp 205–7. **53** Ibid., p. 210.

in Ireland was the policy known as the 'Hazel Switch', whereby landless men drove cattle off ranches using the hazel rod. In the article McDonald pointed out that despite the fact that Pope Leo XIII condemned boycotting, at the time of the Land League,[54] the clergy's dislike of the method was tempered by the fact that they themselves were of the tenant farmer class. The article essentially was a warning to the clergy, that they should be wary of condemning cattle driving or trade unions or the strike weapon in the battle against inequity, lest 'they should set themselves against the whole democratic movement, and thereby lose the people, as they have been lost in France and Italy.'[55]

While Maynooth may have been very cut off from currents of thought in European Catholicism, it is nonetheless important to place all of these matters in the context of developments outside of Ireland. The papacy felt increasingly threatened by all manner of social, political and scientific developments in the nineteenth century and reacted by strengthening its defences, becoming increasingly dogmatic and taking measures to centralize power in Rome. Matters came to a head towards the end of the century, when a number of Catholic scholars known as the modernist movement broke away from Scholastic philosophy and began to search for ways of expressing their faith that would make sense to the modern mind, as they saw it. In 1893 Pope Leo XIII issued an encylical *Providentissimus Deus*, in which he rebuked the modernists and urged Catholic scholars to take as their guides scholastic theology and the teaching of Thomas Aquinas. In 1907 Pope Pius X issued the decree *Lamentabili*, condemning sixty-five errors, which were listed and attributed to the modernists. This was followed by the encyclical *Pascendi* in September of the same year. In his *Reminiscences* McDonald denounces the modernists, and expresses the opinion that their project in the *Irish Theological Quarterly* suffered because they were seen as modernists. And, indeed, this is evidenced in a letter that Cardinal Logue received in 1908 from the Sacred Congregation for the Propagation of the Faith again registering concerns in relation to some theories of McDonald's, regarded as not in keeping with official Church teaching and specifically recommending that these matters should be dealt with in accordance with what was set down by the pope in the decree *Lamentabili* and the encyclical *Pascendi*.[56] Shortly after this time McDonald severed his connection with the *Irish Theological Quarterly*, feeling that it did not allow him the opportunity to develop the science of theology which was his idea in the first place. No articles appeared in McDonald's name in 1909. The *Irish Theological Quarterly* ceased publication in 1922 and did not resume until 1951.

McDonald became involved in another very public controversy after the passage of the Universities Act in 1908. Dr O'Hickey, the professor of Irish in

---

54 *Litterae Sanctissimi D.N. Leonis XIII ad Episcopis Hiberniae, 1888*, S. Congr. De Propaganda Fide, Romae, *Acta Sanctae Sedis*, 21 (1888), pp 3–5. 55 Mc Donald, *Reminiscences*, pp 207, 213. 56 A.D.A., Logue XIII publications: McDonald's book, Folder 9, Propaganda to Michael Cardinal Logue, 25 February 1908.

Maynooth, disagreed publicly with the bishops on the issue of whether Irish should be a compulsory matriculation subject in the new National University, the bishops having representatives on the university senate which was to decide the matter. The manner of O'Hickey's disagreement with the bishops was any-thing but discreet and led to his dismissal from his chair. On McDonald's advice, he took his case to Rome, lost, and came back a very disappointed man.[57] McDonald became controversial again with the publication of two further books written during the war years, and published when the war was over, *Some ethical questions of peace and war, with special reference to Ireland* and *Some ethical aspects of the social question; suggestions for priests*. Both books were published in London by Burns and Oates and received the *imprimatur* from the Westminster censor. In the former book, McDonald questioned the legitimacy of the Irish bishops' decision to resist, what he saw, as the British government's right to impose conscription on Ireland in 1918. Once again he was outspoken on a highly sensitive political issue, taking up a position that did not endear him to a constituency far wider than bishops and clergy at the time. He was highlight-ing what he saw as the opportunism of the bishops in following the popular mood, as opposed to taking a stand which would have demanded moral courage.[58] McDonald's ability to engage with contemporary issues and project into the future was apparent in *Some ethical aspects of the social question,* when he warned that when the war was over, unresolved issues between employers and labourers would re-emerge and that priests would 'soon have to take sides, with the workingman or against him.'[59]

What he had warned of in 'The Hazel Switch' had, in fact, happened. He pointed out that churchmen were happy to stand by the farmers in the land struggle, notwithstanding excesses, because they were of the same class, but that the same could not be said when 'Mr Larkin roused the workingmen of Dublin' in the labour struggle of 1913, because the priests could not identify with their cause in the same way.[60] He went on to point out that 'the future of religion depends largely on the side we take,' advising priests 'not to be fright-ened by such epithets as Revolution, Socialism, Syndicalism' and of the impor-tance of distinguishing 'between the main principle, or current, of [a] revolu-tion' and the attendant excesses which all good men deplore.[61]

So what kind of assessment does one make of McDonald? The fact is that apart from his writings, little is heard of him.[62] He was nobody's hero, too crit-ical to be revered by the clergy and not critical enough to be hailed as an anti-clerical intellectual by the literary intelligentsia. There was an uncompromising

57 For a fuller treatment of this issue see Leon O Broin, 'The Gaelic League and the chair of Irish in Maynooth', *Studies*, 52 (1963), pp 348–62. 58 McDonald, *Ethical questions of peace and war*, pp 3–9, 89–97. 59 McDonald, *Ethical aspects of the social question*, p. 2. 60 Ibid. 61 Ibid., pp 3–4. 62 In this respect the author wishes to express her gratitude to Mgr. Patrick J. Corish, Mgr. Denis O'Callaghan, Cronan Ó Doibhlin, Armagh Diocesan Archivist, and David Sheehy, Dublin Diocesan Archivist for their assistance.

harshness to his criticism of Maynooth, the bishops and his colleagues in the college. His stance on the O'Hickey affair was generally regarded as ill-advised by other priests. A very critical review of his book *Reminiscences* by Fr Peter Finlay S.J. in *Studies* in 1925 perhaps reflects how many clergy would have seen McDonald.[63] In the *Irish Ecclesiastical Record* in 1945, Cornelius Mulcahy, a fellow professor in Maynooth, was high in his praise of McDonald. He had witnessed McDonald's will, however, and related that when McDonald gave him his *Reminiscences* to read a few days before he died, he, Mulcahy had 'disapproved of and endeavoured to dissuade him from their publication'.[64] So, is one to see him as an intolerant crank, an arrogant academic who saw himself as intellectually superior to his colleagues, unkind in his references to them, disloyal to the institution where he had been educated and where he worked for almost forty years, or as a courageous clergyman not afraid to speak his mind, prophetic, questioning many aspects of institutional Catholicism as he experienced it and anxious to give voice to his concerns for the long-term good of that institution? The tragedy for McDonald, and perhaps for the Church of his day, was that because some of his ideas were seen as a threat to theological orthodoxy, and because he pursued them so doggedly, he came to be seen as somewhat of an eccentric genius, which meant that many of his ideas never received the hearing that they may have deserved. A hundred years on and in light of the Second Vatican Counil, many of his thoughts and observations can be seen as perceptive and far-seeing. Perhaps the best note to end on is that he was in many ways a man before his time.

---

63 Peter Finlay, 'Dr Walter McDonald and his *Reminiscences*', *Studies*, 14:56 (1925), pp 648–54.
64 Cornelius Mulcahy, '*Reminiscences*', *IER*, fifth series, 66 (1945), pp 162–3.

Tell this to the Indians: the religious basis of William Warren Baldwin's *Thoughts on the civilisation* of the aboriginal Canadians of Ontario, 1819

G.K. PEATLING

William Warren Baldwin is usually studied, if at all, as a member of a politically influential family in early nineteenth-century Upper Canada, and specifically in connection with their contributions to the growth of self-government in the province, after Baldwin's family emigrated to Canada from Cork, in 1799.[1] Baldwin's thoughts on the north American Indian question, formulated in 1819, which form the focus of this essay, have been barely analyzed at all however. Baldwin was a white settler in a landowning family, and his proposals for an Indian policy incorporated many of the limitations that one might expect of that position, but also some surprisingly radical and sympathetic features. The essay will examine Baldwin's ideas and discuss their relationship to his Irish background, education and religious faith, and suggest possible sources of these ideas.

In the early eighteenth century, the Baldwins appeared to be an Ascendancy family, and William's grandfather John had been lord mayor of Cork in 1737:[2] but the family experienced some financial difficulties and a loss of status thereafter. Baldwin's father Robert, John's second son, was a minor legal official, landowner, and political reformer, helping to edit a journal favourable to the Volunteer movement of the early 1780s. As political turmoil and the family's financial problems intensified, the family emigrated to York county in Upper Canada arriving in 1799. William, the fifth of sixteen children, travelled with his father as his eldest surviving son, and established a legal practice as his main source of income in York county, close to modern-day Toronto.[3] In Upper

* I would like to thank the staff of Toronto Reference Library for their assistance.

1 R.M. and J. Baldwin, *The Baldwins and the great experiment* (Don Mills, Ontario: Longmans, 1969); Gerald Marquis Craig, *Upper Canada; the formative years, 1784–1841* (Toronto: Mcclelland and Stewart, 1963), pp 115, 193–4, 202–3, 257; George Earl Wilson, *The life of Robert Baldwin: a study in the struggle for responsible government* (Toronto: Ryerson Press, 1933), pp 3–70. 2 Richard Caulfield (ed.), *The council book of the corporation of the city of Cork: from 1609 to 1643, and from 1690 to 1800* (Guildford: J. Billing, 1876), pp 569–79. 3 William Warren Baldwin papers (Toronto Reference Library), section 2: unpublished manuscript by William on his father Robert Baldwin; Wilson, *Robert Baldwin*, pp 2–7; Baldwin, *Baldwins*, pp 1–65. Protestant and Canadian dimensions of the history of the Irish diaspora in north America remain deplorably understudied in Irish studies: see most recently W. Jenkins, 'Between the

Canada, the Baldwins interested themselves in the causes of political reform and responsible government as they had done in Ireland. Biographers and historians, indeed, focus on this dimension of the Baldwins' activities. There is a common failure to notice or mention William Baldwin's interest in policy towards Canada's first nations. Even though it is one of few surviving pieces of Baldwin's writing, his *Thoughts on the civilisation* of Ontario Indians, written at the request of the Bible Society at York in 1819, has been particularly little considered.[4]

Baldwin's *Thoughts* were formulated with an overtly proselytizing purpose in view, Baldwin being part of a committee of the Bible Society charged with suggesting 'what may be the [...] practicable mode of civilizing the Indian tribes throughout this Province & of communicating to them religious knowledge and the blessings of the Christian Faith.' This project was in no way underwritten by assumptions of cultural relativism understood in modern terms, but then, of course, few at the time would have been motivated by such assumptions. Indeed, Baldwin supposed the Christianization of the Chippewa and Mississauga tribes to be feasible precisely because they were currently utterly without civilization, in 'the lowest state of barbarism': it is here that Baldwin's own lack of close scrutiny of the nations in question himself, and his deference to the opinion of those whom he described as acquainted with the Indians, most obviously affected his conclusions. 'The Indian mind' thus being 'a blank unencumbered with laws, customs or superstitions,' Baldwin felt that the impressing of Christian beliefs and customs upon this Indian mind along lines he suggested should not prove difficult, and in fact that the Indian would thus be acting according to '*the natural tendency of human nature*', and retracing the steps taken earlier by European peoples. With the Western customs into which the first nations were to be to be initiated would come not just Protestant Christianity, but Western education and individual property ownership. Baldwin, of course, envisaged a system of Indian settlements which would transcend the tribal system, not least because he had determined, from the outset of his analysis, that the pre-existing tribal organization could be ignored.

Baldwin's assumptions that the so-called 'civilisation' of the first nations on European terms was possible did, however, presuppose that aboriginal Canadians possessed an inherent capacity close to that of Europeans. Baldwin contended that prior to the Columbian exchange, and the devastating impact of European colonization, Amerindian peoples had been showing a tendency to civilization and advance. This American civilization 'would no doubt have

lodge and the meeting-house: mapping Irish Protestant identities and social worlds in late Victorian Toronto,' *Social and Cultural Geography*, 4:1 (2003), pp 75–98. 4 William Warren Baldwin papers, 'Thoughts on the civilisation of the tribes of Indians spread over this province, intended to be read before the Bible Society at York, as introductory to the discussion of such resolutions as may be suggested by their committee to whom this subject was referred at the last annual meeting', pp 18–19: quotations hereafter are from this unpublished manuscript unless otherwise indicated.

continued to advance and spread [throughout the continent …] had not the European discoveries cut that progress short.' Spanish avariciousness and greed led to military conquest and deceitful manipulation, while in British north American aboriginals had been mistreated in other more subtle ways, continually urged to move as Europeans acquired more land, even if by purchase. 'No sooner has the Indian ventured to put the plough into the soil than his white neighbour' wished to take the spot: even though such land was not taken by force, this pushed the native American into a new wilderness deprived of his footing in civilization. This was inimical to the settling of the native peoples on the land, which Baldwin believed the first condition of their civilization and learning the sanguine habits of thrift and steady regular industry. If more peaceful cultural influence had been attempted – a scenario Baldwin did not consider inherently unlikely – Baldwin believed that the native peoples would have been in a very much superior condition from that which was observed as he wrote, which would have been a much more desirable consummation.

It was again precisely because Baldwin thought the European lifestyle so obviously the superior that he believed no force, only persuasion and encouragement, were needed to draw the aboriginals into adopting it: the chief measures of coercion, Baldwin argued, were necessary to prohibit the sale of alcohol among the first nations, and he called for sympathetic treatment of those aboriginals who fell into difficulty with the law. Indeed, Baldwin's confidence in the inability of the Chippewa and Mississauga tribes to resist the so-called civilizing process is most obviously evident in the nature of the chief mechanism he proposed. This consisted in the Christian education of a small number of Indian children from a very young age. These children, Baldwin argued, should be encouraged to retain their Indian tongues and certainly not be discouraged from returning to their tribes when reaching an appropriate age (such as twelve or fourteen), since, Baldwin explained, they were to 'be intended as the keys by which to gain admittance to the hearts of these sullen wanderers of the forests.' It is perhaps the clearest indication of Baldwin's view as to the weakness of native American culture that he expected such returned Europeanized adolescents to resist pressures to assimilation, and rather instead to be capable of 'leading and carrying [their tribes] with them', a mechanism which would thus Europeanize the nations. Further, the Chippewa and Mississauga tribes would thus be turned from 'a declining perishing race, useless and burdensome fickle friends & uncertain allies, into a vigorous and strengthening population,' and, as 'faithful subjects', would exercise in turn a major influence for good (that is, for further Europeanization) throughout the interior of the continent. This was not a particularly realistic scheme, and Baldwin appeared unaware that even some white Europeans encountering native Americans had long been instead attracted or successfully assimilated to tribal life.[5]

5 Richard Van Der Beets (ed.), *Held captive by Indians: selected narratives, 1642–1836* (Knoxville:

Baldwin's ideas were thus condescending to aboriginal peoples, and dismissive of their cultures. There is a complete absence of engagement in any dialogue with the first nations, and consequentially and, in Freirean terms, predictably an ill-thought out attempt to ventriloquize their positions.[6] These assumptions were however hardly unexceptional at the time, even from acclaimed radical philosophical perspectives such as Rousseau's,[7] and some features of Baldwin's ideas were more sympathetic. He did not, as some commentators continue to, deny the detrimental effects of the European colonization of the American continent,[8] or argue that the British conquest of north America was justified by the superiority of British civilization, the end result, or the geopolitical necessity of resisting French influence.[9] Nor did he assume that genocidal racial conflict was inevitable in such contact zones.[10] Instead, he implied that the beneficial features of cultural contact could have been effected peacefully, that the entire enterprise could be regarded as having most regrettable features, or even wholly undesirable ones, unless it were supplemented by further efforts to better the condition of native Americans. Although Baldwin called for efforts to 'humanize' the Indian children, this was not an attempt to argue that native Americans were subhuman, which was or had been one response from Europeans in the contact zone,[11] and he argued that aboriginal Canadians had a potential not unlike that of white Europeans, which the hunter-gathering lifestyle and contact with these same white Europeans had prevented them to date from realizing. Baldwin was thus one of the sequence of white reformers and proselytizers who interested themselves in a condescending, if well-meaning way, in native affairs throughout nineteenth-century north America.[12] The remainder of this essay will endeavour to map the dimensions of his ideas on these subjects onto different influences from his upbringing, Irish family background, education and religious ideas.

Born in 1775, Baldwin was one of the generation of Irish Protestant gentry youths sent to be educated in Scotland, in his case Edinburgh University, in the

University of Tennessee Press, 1994); Linda Colley, *Captives: Britain, empire and the world, 1600–1850* (London: J. Cape, 2002), pp 137–67.   **6** Paulo Freire, *Pedagogy of the oppressed* (1972; London: Pelican, 1985).   **7** Jean-Jacques Rousseau, 'The second discourse: discourse on the origin and foundations of inequality among mankind,' in Susan Dunn (ed.), *Jean-Jacques Rousseau, The social contract and the first and second discourses* (1753; New Haven: Yale UP, 2002), pp 69–148, especially pp 87–113.   **8** As in the common American nationalist myth of the winning and civilization of 'the wilderness'. For a recent example of a work laced with such assumptions, see Dinesh D'Souza, *What's so great about America* (New York: Penguin, 2003).   **9** See Niall Ferguson, *Empire: how Britain made the modern world* (New York: Basic Books, 2003).   **10** This is the attitude taken in Jared M. Diamond, *Guns, germs, and steel: the fates of human societies* (New York: W.W. Norton, 1997), a book, nonetheless, ironically criticized for its 'political correctness'.   **11** See the discussion in Ania Loomba, *Colonialism-postcolonialism* (London: Routledge, 1998), pp 57–68.   **12** Helen Maria Hunt Jackson, *A century of dishonor: a sketch of the United States government's dealings with some of the Indian tribes* (1888; Boston: Roberts, St Clair Shores, Mich., Scholarly Press, 1972).

1790s. It is a certainty that Baldwin was there exposed to the ideas of the Scottish Enlightenment.[13] A range of academic debates have been joined about the nature of the political influence of this enlightenment project on both sides of the Atlantic. It is generally accepted that Enlightenment thought had an influence upon the radical politics of groups such as the United Irishmen.[14] More optimistic scholars such as Kevin Whelan and Luke Gibbons argue that the Irish radicals evinced a political philosophy peculiarly free of the sectarian and other inegalitarian elements evident elsewhere in Enlightenment thought, an understanding which in some cases carries the politically charged implication that the sectarian dynamic evident in the violence of 1798 must have been sown by another agent, most plausibly British policy.[15] Other scholars are not so sure: Nancy Curtin argues, conversely, that the Enlightenment project itself contained a potentially gender-neutral dynamic, which was overridden instead by those who applied it in particular situations,[16] and Elaine MacFarland suggests that the bisectarianism of 1790s radicals was often superficial, or ineffective.[17] Whelan himself has argued that other stadial dimensions of Enlightenment thought associated with Hume and Smith carried deeply divisive implications for Irish politics, implicitly justifying British intervention in the country as a necessary influence in carrying Ireland to the higher state of society associated with commerce and the privatization of land and communal resources.[18] The case of the Baldwin family supports less optimistic interpretations of the impact of Enlightenment thought on Irish political life. The Baldwins involved themselves in reforming politics at the time of the Volunteer movement and of the recovery of the Irish parliament's legislative independence, but much of this involvement took place when the prime issue concerned the rights of a Protestant-dominated parliament vis-à-vis the British ministry and executive.[19] The Baldwins' attitude to the Catholic question was at least less firmly stated. It is significant that William's own biographical account

---

13 Baldwin, *The Baldwins*, pp 35–6.   **14** Marianne Elliott, *Partners in revolution: the United Irishmen and France* (New Haven: Yale UP, 1982), p. 20; E.W. McFarland, *Ireland and Scotland in the age of revolution: planting the green bough* (Edinburgh: Edinburgh UP, 1994), pp 9–23.   **15** Kevin Whelan, *The tree of liberty: radicalism, Catholicism, and the construction of Irish identity, 1760–1830* (University of Notre Dame Press, 1996), pp 98–130; Luke Gibbons, 'Towards a postcolonial enlightenment,' in Clare Carroll and Patricia King (eds), *Ireland and postcolonial theory* (University of Notre Dame Press, 2003), pp 71–81.   **16** Nancy J. Curtin, '"A nation of abortive men," gendered citizenship and early Irish republicanism', in Marilyn Cohen and Nancy J. Curtin (eds), *Reclaiming gender: transgressive identities in modern Ireland* (New York: St. Martin's, 1999), pp 33–52.   **17** McFarland, *Ireland and Scotland*, pp 53, 56–7, 72, 135–6; Nancy J. Curtin, *The United Irishmen: popular politics in Ulster and Dublin, 1791–1798* (Oxford: Clarendon, 1994), pp 47–51, 276–7, 284–5; Jim Smyth, 'Introduction: the 1798 rebellion in its eighteenth-century contexts,' in Jim Smyth (ed.), *Revolution, counter-revolution and union: Ireland in the 1790s* (Cambridge: Cambridge UP, 2000), pp 1–20.   **18** Kevin Whelan, 'Writing Ireland: reading England,' in Leon Litvack and Glenn Hooper (eds), *Ireland in the nineteenth century: regional identity* (Dublin: Four Courts, 2000), pp 185–98.   **19** Baldwin, *The Baldwins*, pp 17–33.

of his father's life, including recollections of their departure for north America, makes relatively little reference to the political situation in Ireland at the time, including the 1798 rebellion, William hinting instead at the larger role played by family indebtedness,[20] a suggestion with which some surviving documentation appears to concur.[21] As an official of a manorial court and a landowner in western Ireland, William's father Robert would have been happy with ideas of private property in land and used to regarding agrarian protestors such as the Whiteboys, with their notions of 'moral economy', as a nuisance or worse.[22] Echoes of this assumption, and of the Enlightenment stadial model of society, are found throughout Baldwin's *Thoughts* on the Indian question in his notion that European civilization and agriculture, 'silently' making way against the hunter-gathering lifestyle, would be the agent of civilizing the Indians and moving them to a higher state of society. As befitting the reification of commercial society, Baldwin's commentary on native peoples also echoes common contemporary patronizing views of the poor and their division into deserving and undeserving categories:[23] he depicted the current standard of behaviour among Indians as 'drunken, filthy, idle', though 'the more deserving of those poor people' were certainly more susceptible of improvement. 'At times it may happen that an opportunity would offer of dropping into the Indian ear some kind of suggestion of improvement in his condition, or some religious truth simple in its meaning but applicable to the man.'

The political influence of the Scottish Enlightenment on the history of north America is also a subject of keen debate about which very varied conclusions are drawn. Perhaps most discussed has been the influence of the Enlightenment on the founding of the United States, with a linked debate which traces this especially to Scottish and Scotch-Irish 'contributions' to the origins of the United States,[24] a nexus of Scottish and Irish connections to north America which has an obvious resonance with Baldwin's personal history. But the nature of this Scottish and Scotch-Irish influence was ambiguous. Some commentators have suggested that Enlightenment thinkers such as Francis Hutcheson helped to nurture the ideas of democracy and inalienable human rights embodied in the constitution of the United States.[25] On the other hand there is a long tradition,

---

20 William Warren Baldwin papers (Toronto Reference Library), section 2: unpublished manuscript by William on his father Robert Baldwin.   **21** National Library of Ireland, MS 13065, on the Baldwin family of Cork.   **22** M.J. Bric, 'Priests, parsons and politics: the Rightboy protest in County Cork, 1785–88,' *Past & Present*, 100 (1983), pp 100–22, 121; Oliver MacDonagh, *States of mind: a study of Anglo-Irish conflict, 1780–1980* (London: Allen & Unwin, 1983), pp 34–51.   **23** Boyd Hilton, *The age of atonement: the influence of evangelicalism on social and economic thought, 1795–1865* (Oxford: Clarendon, 1988).   **24** William Christian Lehmann, *Scottish and Scotch-Irish contributions to early American life and culture* (Port Washington, N.Y.: National University Publications, 1978).   **25** Ian McBride, 'The school of virtue: Francis Hutcheson, Irish Presbyterians and the Scottish Enlightenment', in D. George Boyce, Robert Eccleshall, and Vincent Geoghan (eds), *Political thought in Ireland since the seventeenth century*

especially in manifestations of Scotch-Irish identity, of extolling the military as much as the intellectual influence of the Scotch-Irish in the construction of the United States, a military role which encompassed the Indian wars as well as the war of American independence.[26] As Patrick Griffin has argued, the Hutchesonian notions of the moral worth of all human beings made less sense to Scotch-Irish populations exposed on white America's frontiers, where military superiority against native peoples assumed to be lesser beings could seem a more fundamental condition of liberty and of a higher civilization.[27]

Baldwin's work evinces aspects of these more chilling intonations of Enlightenment thought for native American peoples. His stadial conception that the permanent settlement of aboriginal Canadians on the land was the key to advancing them to a higher state of civilization recalled the Lockean valorization of the 'pursuit of property',[28] defined in western terms, forgone in the Jeffersonian wording of the United States constitution but close to the spirit of both north American states. Although constitutional history in the state in which the Baldwins settled, Canada, took a different trajectory from that in the United States, lacking such a revolutionary founding moment, Baldwin's thought was similarly underpinned by assumptions about the nature of freedom which privileged certain lifestyles. In the words of the chroniclers (and descendants) of the Baldwin family: '[a]s a young man, he had seen in Ireland the attempts of the Volunteers to achieve parliamentary reform blocked by the […] arbitrary methods of the Lord Lieutenant, the Castle group, and the Government placeman [sic] in the Irish Parliament. To William […] the same situation [was] being played out all over again in Canada.'[29] This may be indicative of the influence which William's Irish background exerted over his political activity in Canada, but it also indicates the limits of most historians' conceptions, and Baldwin's own conception in both national contexts, of the political nation. The Baldwins regarded it as a sufficient conception of political liberty to fight for responsible government in political contexts still dominated by a Protestant elite in Ireland and which almost totally excluded the first nations in Upper Canada. Notions of a historically based sympathy or elective affinity between the nationalist, Catholic or native Irish and native Americans have been posited by Luke Gibbons[30] and recently critiqued by

(London: Routledge, 1993), pp 73–99.   **26** G.K. Peatling, 'The "Irish", the "Scots-Irish", and the United States of America in the twentieth century: some patterns of exchange,' *Études Irlandaises*, 28:2 (2003), pp 81–98.   **27** Patrick Griffin, 'Frances Hutcheson and the Scots Irish: reconsidering the ideological origins of the American revolution', paper presented at the conference, 'Tracing the Enlightenment: the Ulster-Scots in Ireland and America', Trinity College Dublin, 28 Feb. 2004.   **28** Peter Laslett (ed.), *John Locke, Two treatises of government* (Cambridge: Cambridge UP, 1988).   **29** Baldwin, *The Baldwins*, p. 97.   **30** Luke Gibbons, *Transformations in Irish culture* (Cork: Cork UP, 1996), pp 3–7, 150–4; Luke Gibbons, 'Race against time: racial discourse and Irish history', *Oxford Literary Review*, 13:1–2 (1991), pp 95–117. There is also the linked debate on the 'whiteness' of the Irish in north America: see M.P. Guterl, 'The new race consciousness: race, nation and empire in American culture,

Joy Porter,[31] but these debates do little to advance our understanding of Baldwin's position, his family background of Irish nationalism in the form of late eighteenth-century Irish 'patriot politics' contributing little in the way of sympathy to Canada's first nations. In Canada at any rate, Baldwin also seemed at times to profess a British identity.[32]

Thus it seems clear that the most positive and sympathetic aspects of Baldwin's *Thoughts* on Indian policy emanated not from his exposure to the Enlightenment, nor from any formative political experience in Ireland, but from Baldwin's evangelical religious beliefs.[33] This is evident particularly in two dynamics of Baldwin's ideas. Firstly, it surfaces in his argument that 'native Americans' were capable, given the removal of inauspicious circumstances and of the retrograde influence of European policy, of a standard of civilization proximate to or as high as that of white Europeans. Baldwin's view that such attainment of equivalent standards was the natural tendency of the human mind was rooted in his biblicist interpretation of human origins. Scripture assured us, Baldwin argued, that all humans had common parents, 'Indian as well as white man', and it was the spread of humanity after the fall throughout the globe that led them to adopt varied customs. Baldwin felt there was evidence that inhabitants of the American continent, though separated from those of Europe and Asia, had exhibited a similar tendency to improvement, 'in Peru, Mexico and other smaller states [in] arts and civil polity, and it may be added [in] religion also, for though their religion was a system of idolatrous rites shocking to humanity, yet [it was] a system of religion of some sort', as well suited to these proponents and as rational as was the religion of the 'polished Greeks and Romans'. There is a stark insensitivity here about the value of native American as well as Aztec and Inca spirituality, but also assumptions that could have radical meanings in terms of racial equality. These meanings were not fully developed in Baldwin's own work, but were a couple of decades later in the writings of James Mursell Phillippo, a Baptist missionary working pre- and post-emancipation in Jamaica. As part of an argument, not unlike Baldwin's, for humane treatment and Christian missionary work amongst post-emancipation Jamaicans, Phillippo suggested in 1843 that evidence for the ability of peoples of African descent to respond to such cultural and intellectual stimuli could be deduced from the likely African influence upon critical building blocks of European civilization:[34] a strik-

---

1910–1925', *Journal of World History*, 10:2 (1999), pp 307–52.   **31** Joy Porter, 'The north American Indians and the Irish', *Irish Studies Review*, 11:3 (2003), pp 263–71. On these debates see Elizabeth Cullingford, *Ireland's others: ethnicity and gender in Irish literature and popular culture* (University of Notre Dame Press, 2001), pp 132–90; G.K. Peatling, 'The whiteness of Ireland under and after the union', *Journal of British Studies*, 44:1 (2005) forthcoming.   **32** Baldwin papers, 'Thoughts on the civilisation of the tribes of Indians'.   **33** For a discussion of definitions of evangelicalism in relation to this period, see Mark A. Noll, *America's God: from Jonathan Edwards to Abraham Lincoln* (Oxford: Oxford UP, 2002), p. 5.   **34** James Mursell Phillippo, *Jamaica: its past and present state* (London: John Snow, 1843). I am grateful to Mr

ing anticipation of aspects of the controversial work of Martin Bernal, during the phase when Bernal suggests that evidence for such influence was being system- atically written out of the western canon by racist thinkers,[35] and at a time when other writers have suggested that racial thinking was starting to be underpinned by a new set of pseudo-scientific assumptions.[36]

A second and cognate beneficial aspect of Baldwin's *Thoughts* comprises his perception of Christian duty and guilt. Omission of 'the faithful and honest dis- charge' of the 'religious duty to endeavour all in our power to communicate in Christian Charity the knowledge of God [... and of] the Gospel,' Baldwin sug- gested, 'it is to be feared, may have already involved us [Europeans in north America] in guilt.' Baldwin had second thoughts about a passage in which he sug- gested both Canadian aboriginals and Europeans would be punished for native vices such as 'drunkenness, adultery, murder, cursing, and various others', the Europeans since 'we introduce the means and temptations to these vices amongst the Indians, and make no exertion to correct them, to amend their morals or to awaken in them a sense of Religion;' but his initial suggestion may be significant, and it certainly would appear that Baldwin's acute sense of duty cohered with an appreciation of past errors in Europeans' actions towards native Americans.

So, in conclusion, what does Baldwin's example mean in the context of the study of religious belief, particularly in an Irish context? A considerable caveat should firstly be entered: in these exchanges Christian faith was not an influ- ence with unmitigated benefits. It, indeed, intensified Baldwin's scant acknowl- edgment for the sophistication of native spiritualities, cultures and lifestyles. We may not wish to condemn Baldwin personally for non-accordance with modern standards on this issue. But it is possible and necessary to make tran- shistorical judgements in these matters about the demerits and merits of belief systems. There is a tendency, by no means new but acquiring recent prominent rearticulation, including in relation to Irish history,[37] to conceive of a number of global conflict situations, past and present, as essentially religious or sectarian and in the nature of clashes of fundamentalisms.[38] This is an interpretation which of course has both a glib popular and some academic currency, and its acceptability at both levels has doubtless been facilitated by the decline of orga- nized religion in much of western Europe.[39] This present analysis of William

Franklin E. Smith for this point.   **35** Martin Bernal, *Black Athena: the Afroasiatic roots of classi- cal civilization* (New Brunswick: Rutgers UP, 1987); David Chioni Moore (ed.), *Martin Bernal, Black Athena writes back: Martin Bernal responds to his critics* (Durham, N.C.: Duke UP, 2001).   **36** Nancy Stepan, *The idea of race in science: Great Britain, 1800–1960* (Hamden, Conn.: Archon, 1982); Anne McClintock, *Imperial leather: race, gender and sexuality in the colonial contest* (New York: Routledge, 1995).   **37** John McGarry and Brendan O'Leary, *Explaining Northern Ireland: broken images* (Oxford: Blackwell, 1995), pp 171–213.   **38** Tariq Ali, *The clash of fundamentalisms: crusades, jihads and modernity* (London: Verso, 2002).   **39** Hugh McCloud and Werner Ustorf (eds), *The decline of Christendom in western Europe, 1750–2000* (Cambridge: Cambridge UP, 2003); Callum G. Brown, *The death of Christian Britain: understanding secularization,*

Warren Baldwin's thought questions these assumptions. Even though the Baldwins contribution to bi-sectarian amity in Ireland was, as has been discussed, limited, broadly it is true that evangelical religious impulses did the most to underpin the more humane dimensions of William Baldwin's thought, and ironically more so than the influences upon him of the secular humanism of the Enlightenment. As the basis of Baldwin's views can be seen as a form of what might anachronistically be called Protestant biblical fundamentalism, Steve Bruce's argument that Protestant forms of fundamentalism have a larger potential to be pacifistic than other forms, and especially than Islamic fundamentalism, may seem relevant to an explanation of the workings of these influences upon Baldwin.[40] But there are logical and historical problems with this argument, since fundamental commitments have proved possible to elements of either or any such creed which preach either patience under provocation or the necessity of purification, and what the semitic monotheistic creeds (Christianity, Judaism and Islam) have in common seems in analyzing Baldwin's case, as in many cases, more important than what separates them.[41] Elements of Baldwin's beliefs which seem to have been productive in his *Thoughts* on Indian policy seem illustrative of two principles. Firstly, the forms of moral discipline and duty provided by such a creed can outweigh impulses to retaliatory violence in a conflict situation.[42] Secondly, evangelical, proselytizing impulses characteristic of a monotheistic creed can be potentially disturbing to other forms of belief (as Baldwin's case certainly shows), but also have at their heart an impulse to reclaim a lost people because they are perceived as God's children as much as those of the missionary's own culture, and thus have an equal admissibility to cultural, civilizational, spiritual and other forms of progression. In other words, evangelical or even 'fundamentalist' religion can yield a perception of universal human rights at least as powerful as that of secular liberals. Secular scientific worldviews have inspired atrocities as much as have religious animosities over the last five centuries of human history. Study of Baldwin's case of course does not qualify us to determine the relative merits of spiritual and secular world views. But in fact historical study of such particular cases is valuable precisely

---

1800–2000 (London: Routledge, 2001); Alan D. Gilbert, *The making of post-Christian Britain: a history of the secularization of modern society* (London: Longman, 1980). **40** Steve Bruce, 'Fundamentalism and political violence: the case of Paisley and Ulster evangelicals,' *Religion*, 31:4 (2001), pp 387–405; Steve Bruce, *Politics and religion* (Cambridge: Polity Press, 2003), pp 142–60, 205–54. **41** Bruce B. Lawrence, *Shattering the myth: Islam beyond violence* (Princeton, NJ: Princeton UP, 1998); Karen Armstrong, *Islam: a short history* (London: Phoenix, 2001); Aziz Al_Azmeh, *Islams and modernities* (London: Verso, 1993); Edward W. Said, *Covering Islam: how the media and the experts determine how we see the rest of the world* (New York: Pantheon, 1981). **42** Adrian Guelke, 'Limits to conflict and accommodation', in Adrian Guelke (ed.), *New perspectives on the Northern Ireland conflict* (Aldershot: Avebury, 1994), pp 190–206, especially p. 202; Frank Wright, *Two lands on one soil: Ulster politics before home rule* (New York: St Martin's, 1996), pp 256–7, 523.

because it emphasizes the need for an understanding of historical contexts, as well as philosophical and transhistorical processes of evaluation often precipitately invoked in making such judgments.

Meanwhile in relation specifically to late eighteenth- and early nineteenth-century Ireland itself, there has been historiographical debate about change within Irish Protestantism and the role that evangelicalism, among other developments, played in shifts in a conservative political and social direction.[43] Baldwin's thought, however, offers aspects of a response to circumstances of cross-cultural contact – in both Ireland and Canada – that were conservative and sectarian, and aspects that were more pluralistic and open. The case of Baldwin thus accords with research which again suggests the ambivalence and textured nature of existing political and doctrinal positions, irrespective of the major shifts in the structures of Protestant beliefs and communities that some scholars have tried to identify.

43 S.J. Connolly, 'Ulster Presbyterians: religion, culture, and politics, 1660–1850', in H. Tyler Blethen and Curtis W. Wood, Jr (eds), *Ulster and north America: transatlantic perspectives on the Scotch-Irish* (Tuscaloosa: University of Alabama Press, 1997), pp 24–40; David W. Miller, 'Irish Christianity and revolution', in Smyth (ed.), *Revolution, counter-revolution and union,* pp 195–210; Louis M. Cullen, 'The politics of crisis and rebellion, 1792–1798', in Smyth, *Revolution, counter-revolution and union,* pp 21–38; Kerby Miller, 'Belfast's first bomb, 28 February 1816: class conflict and the origins of Ulster Unionist hegemony', *Éire-Ireland,* 39:2 (2004), pp 262–80.

Father Boyce, Lady Morgan and Sir Walter Scott: a study in intertextuality and Catholic polemics[1]

PATRICK MAUME

Fr John Boyce (1810–64) is known to students of Irish-American literature as the most intellectually sophisticated novelist of the 'famine exile' generation. His three novels, and his dispute with the didactic Catholic apologeticist Orestes Brownson, have attracted significant attention, notably from Donna Merwick[2] and Charles Fanning.[3] Their analyses, however, neglect important aspects of Boyce's worldview, while Merwick's polemic against intellectualist Catholic apologetics and the ultramontanism of later Boston Catholic clergy produces serious misreadings, adopted by Fanning.

This brief account of Boyce's life and his three novels stresses three keypoints. First, the principal target of his defence of the role of emotion and sentiment in religious faith is bibliocentric evangelical Protestantism, particularly the 'second reformation', the early nineteenth-century attempt to convert Irish Catholics to evangelicalism. Boyce shows some sympathy for religious tolerance, especially in his last novel *Mary Lee: or the Yankee in Ireland* (1859), but is significantly more anti-Protestant than previous accounts suggest. Secondly, Boyce's novels include collages of borrowings from other writers and recycled material from his own earlier works. The most significant borrowings are from Sir Walter Scott and Lady Morgan, whom one obituarist calls Boyce's favourite writer, possibly because of the Fanad setting of her novel *O'Donnell*. Thirdly, this essay discusses the portrayal of women in Boyce's novels, with particular reference to Queen Elizabeth I, in his historical novel, *The Spaewife* and the Madonna-like Mary Lee.

Boyce was born in Donegal town, son of Jerome Boyce, a Catholic hotelier and 'moderate upholder of the English administration' who owned the older part of the town and became a magistrate in later life. His brother James inherited their father's property: James's descendants remained prominent in Donegal clerical and political life.

1 Thanks to James McGuire and Breandan MacSuibhne, neither of whom are responsible for my interpretation. **2** Donna Merwick, *Boston priests 1848–1910: a study of social and intellectual change* (Cambridge, MA: Harvard UP, 1973) pp 40–59. **3** Charles Fanning, *The Irish voice in America: Irish-American fiction from the 1790s to the 1980s* (Lexington, KY: UP of Kentucky, 1990) pp 97–113; Charles Fanning. (ed.), *The exiles of Erin: nineteenth-century Irish-American fiction* (1987; Chester Springs, PA: Dufour, 1997), pp 97–100, 137–44.

The youthful John was well-known as an athlete; nostalgic descriptions of peasant cabins and a station mass in his first novel *Shandy Maguire* (1848) reflect youthful wanderings. The 1822 famine shaped his political outlook.[4] Boyce attributed the post-Napoleonic economic depression to the union; he believed that had the Irish parliament survived to encourage trade and commerce, alternative employment would have been available to those displaced from agriculture. *Shandy Maguire* figuratively describes how the cow Drimeendhu who supplied the family with milk (the Irish parliament) was stolen and dismembered; her guardians (the MPs) were blinded by a 'plasther' (bribes).[5] Boyce wrote verse from the age of ten; his first publication (aged seventeen) was a verse satire on an unpopular official. He studied classics locally before preparatory studies for the priesthood at St Finian's Catholic Academy, Navan, Co. Meath. He was an outstanding student at Maynooth.

Boyce was ordained in 1834 and served as curate in Glenties (1834–6), and Fanad (1836–45). In 1841 Boyce represented his parishioners in opposing construction of a constabulary barracks at Doaghbeg in north-eastern Fanad.[6] *Shandy Maguire* criticizes official attempts to suppress illegal whiskey distilling which was a major Donegal industry in the pre-famine era.[7] Boyce claims police ignored the complicity of magistrates and even legal distillers, who bought illegal spirits for resale, and that the force existed to provide jobs for Protestants and repress Catholics. One comic scene depicts a police officer receiving orders – forged by the trickster Shandy Maguire – to raid the house of a clerical magistrate for illegal spirits. His discoveries are hushed up by the authorities to keep this supporter of Protestant Ascendancy on the bench.[8] *The Spaewife* humorously attributes the English reformation to beer, contrasted with Irish loyalty to Catholicism and whiskey;[9] *Mary Lee* ridicules temperance societies as Yankee mean-mindedness and penny-pinching.[10] Boyce had a drink problem in later life; his fatal liver disease was possibly alcohol-related.

Boyce was an occasional contributor to the *Nation*; his novels contain appeals for Catholics and Protestants to work together for Ireland, usually implying that patriotism would also lead Protestants to Catholicism. *Shandy Maguire* denounces lay and clerical O'Connellites for opposing rebellion even when faced with the famine.[11]

Boyce's political views may have speeded his emigration in 1845, but he also realized famine emigrants needed priests. After a year in Eastport, Maine, Boyce

---

4 John Boyce, *Shandy Maguire* (1848; Boston: Patrick Donahoe, 1853), p. 99.   **5** Ibid., pp 33–5.
6 Hugh Dorian, *The outer edge of Ulster: a memoir of social life in nineteenth-century Donegal*, ed. Breandan Mac Suibhne & David Dickson (Dublin: Lilliput, 2000), pp 15, 47.   **7** David Dickson, 'Derry's backyard: the barony of Inishowen, 1650–1800', in William Nolan, Liam Ronayne and Mairead Dunlevy (eds), *Donegal: history and society* (Dublin: Geography, 1995), pp 425–9.   **8** Boyce, *Shandy Maguire*, pp 165–83, 190–3.   **9** John Boyce, *The Spaewife* (Boston, MA: Noonan, n.d. [1868]), pp 610–12.   **10** John Boyce, *Mary Lee* (1859; Baltimore: Kelly, Hedian & Piet, 1860), pp 68, 155–8, 255–65.   **11** Boyce, *Shandy Maguire*, pp 247–8.

moved to Worcester, Massachussetts, remaining parish priest of St John's church until his death and traversing central Massachusetts on missionary work. *Shandy Maguire, or, Tricks on Travellers* (1848) began as a short story in the *Boston Pilot*; the bishop of Boston commanded Boyce to extend it to novel length. It was extensively reviewed by British journals and translated into German. An 1851 stage adaptation by James Pilgrim was popular in America, where Shandy was played by the comedian Barney Williams, and in Europe, where Tyrone Power took the part. Boyce's literary fame was a source of pride to New England Catholics; his biographer claims he corresponded with writers including Dickens, Lever, Thackeray and Eugene Sue. This is unproven; Boyce destroyed his papers before his death. Boyce became a popular preacher and lecturer for charitable Irish and Catholic causes.

The book was, however, criticized by the influential New England Catholic convert publicist and literary 'gatekeeper' Orestes Brownson (1803–76), who accused Irish-American Catholics of subordinating Catholicism to Irishness, criticized Young Ireland, and argued that the Irish should work for reform through Westminster. Boyce's 1851 lecture 'The satisfying influence of Catholicity on the intellect and senses' defends devotional Catholicism against Brownson's emphasis on logic, stressing its multifarious appeals to different levels of understanding and its accessibility to the poor and illiterate. He had made this point, too, in *Shandy Maguire*. This view implies intellectual pursuits are reserved for an elite; Boyce believed in a hierarchical society and was disturbed by American social fluidity.

The Spaewife appeared in 1853 to mixed reviews; Boyce never completed a proposed sequel. During the 1850s Boyce found life increasingly difficult. His parish provided only a small income; he quarreled with his curate. His literary earnings were spent on charity; his finances were in disorder at his death. He also had to defend his parishioners against nativist mobs. In *Mary Lee* an emigrant's letter declares Irish Orangemen 'decent' compared with Yankee nativists, since they make no hypocritical pretensions about treating all religions equally.

Fr John Boyce died on the night of 1–2 January 1864. He is buried in the communal grave of the Jesuit community of Holy Cross College, Worcester; his biographer was a younger Donegal-born, Holy Cross Jesuit who knew him in later life.[12]

---

12 The memoir, principal source for Boyce's life, is prefixed to an 1868 reprint of *The Spaewife*. In 1941 Boyce's grand-nephew, Fr Charles Boyce (PP Termon and Gartan) anonymously published a 'new and revised edition', omitting a few embarrassing details but giving additional information on the Boyce family and extracts from the novels. See Charles Boyce, *Biographical sketch of Rev. John Boyce, D.D. (1810–64)* (Dublin, Juverna, 1941). G.M. McNamara, 'Rev. Dr John Boyce – "Paul Peppergrass" – 1810–64', *Donegal Annual*, 6: 2 (1965), pp 141–9 combines the nineteenth-century memoir and the critical writings of the early twentieth-century Boston Jesuit, Fr Michael Earls. Merwick, *Boston priests*, has information on Boyce's pastorate in America not available elsewhere.

Shandy Maguire is set in Donegal Town in 1828–9 during the final struggle over Catholic emancipation. It begins as Ribbon documents are planted on the young tenant farmer Frank Devlin by an agent provocateur instigated by land agent Archy Cantwell. Cantwell has caused the death of one girl, Mary Curran, and wishes to seduce Frank's fiancée Mary Connor by threatening her family with eviction. Boyce's idealized view of Irish womanhood cannot admit Mary Curran might actually have yielded; she dies of shame because Cantwell falsely boasted of seducing her. Cantwell is foiled by the Ribbon leader Shandy Maguire, a master of disguise who subjects local oppressors, including Cantwell's father, the significantly-named Reverend Baxter Cantwell, and the evangelical landlord Colonel Templeton to humiliating practical jokes.

Shandy's exploits interact with a second plot, drawing on Morgan's novels *O'Donnell* and *The O'Briens and the O'Flaherties*. Ellen, last descendant of the O'Donnell dynasty, whose painter father brought her up in Italy, like the heroine of *O'Donnell*, has returned to the ruins of her ancestral glories. She is supervized by the Spanish-educated parish priest, Fr Dominick, unbeknownst to her, her paternal uncle. Ellen, 'the Irishwoman as she ought to be', broods over the ruins of her ancestral castle and sings to her own harp accompaniment, like Glorvina in Morgan's *Wild Irish Girl*: 'the red spot on her neck, the "Baldearag" of the O'Donnells, glowed and smarted as if conscious of the indignant thoughts that burned within.'[13] Ellen loves Captain O'Brien, a Protestant officer of Irish descent, and prays for his reversion to faith and fatherland. O'Brien, disgusted with the oppression he witnesses, exposes Archy Cantwell's machinations and the Government's use of agents provocateurs. After Fr Dominick's house and chapel are destroyed by an Orange mob O'Brien renounces his commission and embarks for Spain with Ellen and Fr Dominick, now also converted to physical force.

Morgan's typical marriage plot symbolizes reconciliation of native and settler through Whig politics and enlightenment principles. Boyce celebrates reversion to Gaelic and Catholic roots. The name O'Brien derives from William Smith O'Brien but also from Morgan's *The O'Briens and the O'Flaherties*, where a young liberal Protestant of Gaelic descent discovers his senile father's involvement in a bizarre conspiracy to restore the High Kingship, spearheaded by a Jesuit uncle returned from Spain. The priest–uncle in *The O'Briens and the O'Flaherties* is a shadowy figure whose fanaticism destroys his brother and himself. In Boyce he is saintly and self-sacrificing, based on fond memories of Boyce's old parish priest. Merwick claims he is also inspired by the Spanish-educated Archbishop Daniel Murray of Dublin, who saw his house and chapel destroyed in 1798. Morgan's O'Brien escapes from demented ancestral traditions and government oppression to become a Napoleonic general; Boyce's O'Brien expects speedy return as a messianic deliverer. Ellen's birthmark refers to the widespread millenarian belief

13 Boyce, *Shandy Maguire*, p. 104.

that Ireland would be freed by an O'Donnell with the Balldearg; Boyce wrote while the Young Ireland revolt hung in the balance.

Boyce emphasizes the poverty, hunger and nakedness of the peasants and passionately denounces landlordism. He catalogues the vices of identifiable Donegal landlord families, such as Marchioness Conyngham's career as mistress to George IV, and the origins of union titles. Catholic middlemen are conspicuously absent, though symbolically presented as heirs to the old Gaelic aristocracy, just as Fr Dominick possesses artworks by Michelangelo and Rubens to link Irish Catholicism with continental civilization.[14] Boyce's views were not necessarily palatable to his own class; his father criticized *Shandy Maguire* as too anti-landlord.

The arrogance and pretensions of the landlords are encapsulated by the second reformation, which was underpinned by the view that landlords ruled tenants as a father rules his children, and were entitled – nay, obliged – to dictate their religion.[15] The Revd Baxter Cantwell acquires three permanent converts, all expelled from the Catholic Church for immorality; others revert to Catholicism, taunting the rector as they attend mass in new clothing supplied by him. Even his termagant English wife, portrayed as a conclusive argument for clerical celibacy, despises convert priests, including the Orange intellectual, the Revd Mortimer O'Sullivan.[16] Archy Cantwell mocks his father, declaring the Catholic faith so deeply intertwined with the lives of the peasantry they will never accept 'the bare Bible'; the only solution is extermination.[17]

The solemn dress and formal language of the Bible-reader Ebenezer Goodsoul are unsparingly satirized. Bible-readers were travelling evangelists – usually converts, employed to preach in a more popular style than patrician clerics and often in the Irish language. Merwick and Fanning treat Goodsoul as a sincere eccentric, overlooking Boyce's explicit statements that he was expelled from the Catholic Church for immorality, acts as pandar to Archy Cantwell, and uses evangelizing visits to seduce vulnerable women. His claim to Cantwell that his supposedly numerous converts attend Methodist meetings because their clothes are too shabby for the Church of Ireland reflects Catholic accusations that Bible-readers fabricated conversions to encourage donations.[18]

The landlord Colonel Templeton, based on E.M. Connolly who held a large estate in the Rossnowlagh and Ballyshannon areas, and served as Conservative MP for Donegal, 1831–49,[19] also receives excessive sympathy from Fanning and Merwick. Templeton is indeed more sincere than his underlings, 'an honest and upright magistrate' who never evicts a tenant 'without some legal cause – trifling, perhaps, it might often be'. This is faint praise, as is Boyce's remark that

14 Ibid., p. 244. 15 Patrick Maume (ed.), Charlotte Elizabeth Tonna, *Irish recollections* (Dublin: University College Dublin Press, 2004). 16 Boyce, *Shandy Maguire*, pp 291–3. 17 Ibid., pp 59–61. 18 Ibid., pp 53–64, 229, 302–3, 331. 19 James Anderson, 'Rundale, rural economy and agrarian revolution: Tirhugh 1715–1855', in Nolan, *Donegal*, pp 447–70.

Templeton, unlike 'charlatan' evangelists, realizes that Irish Catholicism is not produced by priestly coercion but represents genuine popular commitment – hence, we are told, the colonel relied on 'his power to bribe the pliant and persecute the stubborn'.[20]

Boyce's mockery of the second reformation extends beyond portraying its practitioners as heartless hypocrites. He ridicules its cerebral and bibliocentric approach to poor and ignorant people, and its insistence that those not saved according to evangelical formulae have no Christian faith whatsoever. Colonel Templeton evangelizes a woman with five children in a roadside hut. She has been evicted from his estate; her husband is dying in Lifford jail after attacking a tithe-proctor who seized the blankets from the bed where she lay in advanced pregnancy. Boyce claims '[w]e state the facts as given in evidence before the court'. After discoursing elaborately on the valuable gift he is giving her, he presents a Bible. She explains she cannot read, except for the crucifix on the wall:

> 'And what benefit, my good woman, do you derive from *reading* the cross, as you term it?'
>
> 'Why, when we luk at him there, we see our blissed Saviour, stripped a'most naked lake ourselves; whin we luck at the crown i' thorns on the head we see the Jews mockin' him, jist the same as – some people mock ourselves for our religion; whin we luck at his eyes, we see they wor niver dry, like our own; whin we luck at the wound in his side, why we think less av our own wounds an' bruises, we get 'ithin an' 'ithout, every day av our lives […]'
>
> 'Unfortunate woman […] you do not believe on Christ […] You don't depend sufficiently on the merits of the great atonement. You want faith to *regenerate* you […] Do you know what *spiritual regeneration* is? […] Do you understand what is meant by *justification by faith?*'[21]

Satisfied he has done his best, Templeton decides to demolish her hut as an eyesore.

Boyce points to the sexual vices of many aristocratic defenders of the Protestant constitution and claims the doctrine of justification by faith alone produces oppression, immorality and hypocrisy. He calls London more immoral than any Catholic city. He admits Paris approaches it in vice, but attributes this to proximity to London.[22]

If *Shandy Maguire* rewrites Morgan, *The Spaewife* draws on Scott. Like Scott, Boyce attributes his story to a persona who contributes an editorial introduction. In an 'Apology for a Preface' 'Peter Peppergrass' describes a quarrel with his uncle Tobias Drippindale, a 'stoop-shouldered, snarling old bookworm' who affects superiority because 'he sends me the reviews second-hand, and pays two-and-six-

---

20 Boyce, *Shandy Maguire*, p. 187. 21 Ibid., pp 224–5. 22 Ibid., pp 121–3.

pence a week for the attic', where Peppergrass lives. Drippindale sneers at the new novel, declaring Peppergrass barely equal to 'an olla podrida [mixed stew] such as *Shandy Maguire*'. Peppergrass shows Drippindale his manuscript preface; Drippindale destroys it contemptuously and Peppergrass cannot write another.[23]

The setting is England in 1561 after the return to Scotland of Mary Queen of Scots. Queen Elizabeth is persecuting English Catholics, dividing the Catholic powers by insincere marriage-negotiations, trying to prevent the marriage of Mary, whom she fears as rightful heir to the English throne, and plotting with Scottish rebels. Her position is complicated by her attachment to the earl of Leicester.

This echoes Scott's *Kenilworth* – Boyce frequently mentions Amy Robsart – but goes far beyond Scott. Citing a suggestion by the English Catholic historian Lingard, Boyce claims Elizabeth's lasting attachment to 'the man who often treated her with scorn, and repeatedly flouted her favours […] even when old age came to bring its wrinkles and gray hairs, and her favorite, once so handsome, became the bald and palsied libertine' suggests Leicester had a secret hold over her.[24]

In Boyce's telling, Elizabeth has a child by Leicester. Elizabeth seeks its death, but Leicester arranges its preservation. He carelessly entrusts it to the Spaewife, an old Scotswoman and reputed witch called Nell (Eleanor) Gower living in the woods near Wimbledon. Her principal Scottean original is Meg Merrilees from *Guy Mannering*. Boyce apparently intended her as a 'demented prophetess' found in several Scott novels, insane from oppression and thirsting for revenge. Nell's husband and sons were killed by Protestants in Scotland; Elizabeth hanged her brother. However, Nell's role as resourceful resistance leader makes her an overwhelmingly sympathetic figure; Boyce can only gesture towards the darker view – and incidentally explain her failure to expose Elizabeth – by having her confessor declare God commands her not to harm another's reputation by divulging a secret entrusted to her, however unworthy the beneficiary; he withholds absolution when she refuses. Boyce is thus forced to assert that a promise to a murderous tyrant outweighs thousands of lives and millions of souls.

Meanwhile Sir Thomas Plimpton, one of Elizabeth's confidential servants, seeks the estate of the recusant Sir Geoffrey Wentworth and the hand of Wentworth's daughter Alice. Plimpton physically resembles a conventional stage-puritan; close-cropped, ungainly, and a parvenu – his father hung for piracy. Elizabeth, initially reluctant, assents when Plimpton hints that Leicester is interested in Alice. Sir Geoffrey Wentworth is a pathetic pedant who immerses himself in the Church fathers and entomological studies as his co-religionists are persecuted and his steward plunders the estate. The innocent Alice, incidentally given a long reflecton on the emotional and aesthetic power

23 Boyce, *Spaewife*, pp 1–6. 24 Ibid., p. 14.

of Catholic sacramentalism which rehashes Boyce's own rejoinder to Brownson,[25] naively decides that the queen, as a woman, will not tolerate such injustice. She goes to London to plead with her, like Jeanie Deans in *The Heart of Midlothian*. 'Elizabeth would have granted her prayer, had she still retained a single sympathy for human kind.'[26] Despite the endeavours of his clever and faithful Irish servant Reddy Conner, from Tubbernasiggart in Donegal (mentioned in *Shandy Maguire*), Sir Geoffrey is dispossessed; Reddy and Sir Geoffrey go to London seeking Alice. Alice is assisted by Nell and Rodger O'Brien, sent by Mary to offer refuge in Scotland. O'Brien, born in Ireland but brought up in France, speaks Wardour Street English rather than Reddy's Hiberno-Irish dialect. After various intrigues the characters appear before Elizabeth in open court. Sir Geoffrey dies making a brave and futile plea to Elizabeth; he joins the hands of Alice and Rodger O'Brien. The child of Elizabeth and Leicester is smuggled to Spain by Nell Gower, who forces the queen to allow her and her friends to leave for Scotland. Plimpton, who guessed Elizabeth's secret and foolishly tried to blackmail her, goes to the Tower.

Sir Geoffrey is regarded by some commentators as a critique of Brownson's intellectualized version of Catholicism. Merwick and Fanning even call Sir Geoffrey the real villain and suggest Elizabeth's vices are those of the heart. This is ridiculous. Sir Geoffrey is not a portrait of Brownson but a literary descendant of Baron Bradwardine in *Waverley*, whose pedantic antiquarianism leads to his Jacobitism and dispossession. Scott implies that such religious and political loyalties themselves reflect dangerous detachment from the world, hardly Boyce's intention. Sir Geoffrey is not a heartless calculating machine; his loyalties are reinforced by pride in the traditions of his family, founders of a ruined abbey where he takes refuge, and memories of his dead wife and her faith. These are the attachments Boyce praises in Irish-Americans and Brownson derides as irrelevant to true faith.[27] He brings his house to financial ruin trusting a dishonest steward; this is done partly from selfish obsession with his studies, but also from misplaced trust and generosity to the poor. He does neglect and even spite his friends – notably his daughter and the faithful Reddy Connor – but he also displays and attracts genuine love and loyalty, and dies asking forgiveness.

Elizabeth receives all the anger and venom lavished on the Protestant Ascendancy in *Shandy Maguire*. Her vices are inborn. 'Bastard offspring of perjury and lust,' she inherits 'the vilest passions of Henry, her father, and the levity of her unfortunate mother, Anne Boleyn.'[28] Boyce repeatedly asserts that as a bastard Elizabeth has no right to the throne. The sympathetic characters publicly disown the temporal as well as spiritual authority of Elizabeth.[29] Her usurpation unsettles the whole moral order; one of Plimpton's followers calls

---

25 Ibid., pp 147–9. **26** Ibid., p. 117. **27** Ibid., p. 251. **28** Ibid., p. 57. **29** Ibid., pp 474, 702–4.

marriage 'a device of the cozening monks and priests to grow rich [...] what hath wedlock now to do with the rights of sovereigns and princes?'[30] Without the supervision of Catholic clerics, Protestant belief in justification produces moral chaos. Sir Geoffrey's English servants loot his house before deserting him, proclaiming:

> [t]hey're only Protestant sins [...] mere trifles [...] Shoulst thou rob a church, or kill thy neighbour, or burn a house, or steal thy master's gold, why, thou'rt only to wait patiently for the grace of repentance, and give thyself no concern for thy soul's welfare, since thou canst not [...] do any good work of thyself [...] compare that with the old religion [...] nothing but penance, and prayers, and fastings, and alms, and pilgrimages, and contritions, and restitutions.[31]

Boyce emphasizes Elizabeth's *politique* religious compromises and her command of public relations to present her as a hypocrite cultivating popularity to gain power:[32] her intrigues destroy the good name, and ultimately the life, of the naively honest and straightforward Mary:[33]

> She was so far Protestant as to love its freedom from religious restraint; it gave her an independence, a peculiar reliance on self, that accorded well with her natural disposition [...] had Elizabeth then been placed in any inferior position in life, she would have endeavoured to reason herself into infidelity.[34]

Elizabeth is driven less by political expediency than personal jealousy of Mary.[35] She is 'as cunning as a serpent, and as revengeful as a tigress [...] with the heart of a Jezebel, and the vulgarity of a courtesan' bound by sheer animal lust to a man whom she hates, who is blackmailing her. 'Elizabeth was enamoured of the person of the earl, and the earl enamoured of the throne of the queen.'[36] Boyce insinuates that the favourites and ministers who lavished her with praise were her lovers in every sense of the term. Elizabeth rages over her relationship with Leicester to her only confidante:

> I surrendered my whole being to him. I sacrificed what the world calls honor to appease his godship, and which was dear to me in life, because in losing it I knew I should lose his respect [...] now am I debased and degraded at his feet [...] a woman in whom no drop of tame blood ever ran; whose passions, wild as her father's, have never once been bridled but to deceive those pious fools who surround my throne and call me

---

30 Ibid., p. 332. **31** Ibid., pp 424–5. **32** Ibid., pp 54–5, 264, 684. **33** Ibid., pp 16–17. **34** Ibid., pp 62, 64–5. **35** Ibid., pp 10, 264. **36** Ibid., p. 398.

virgin [...] I laugh at the thought [...] I'm a woman, and greedy of men's homage as of their love. I would draw all that could minister to my passions around me [...] let the highest of them betray but a sem-blance of indifference to my favours, and I cut off his head as I would a poppy, or send him to feed rats in the Tower dungeons.[37]

When Elizabeth sees Rodger O'Brien she lusts after him; Boyce declares him-self ashamed 'that there ever raged in the female bosom so gross and fierce an element.'[38] The ranting nymphomaniac portrayed by Boyce would have lost power in six weeks; but he revels in prurient delight at heaping humiliations on a Protestant icon.

A subtext implies that the apostasy of England reflects racial unworthiness. Reddy Conner denounces

the lazy, beef-eatin', beer-drinkin' Sassenaghs [...] The smell av mate afther two days' fastin' id make [them] forswear the pope, if they wur sure of bein' hung two hours afther they got their bellies full [...] mate ivery day in the week's a mighty strong argument against Popery in this country [...] give me ould Ireland still [...that] niver sould her faith to fill her belly [...] it's too deep rooted down in her sowl to barter it for beef, beer, and Bibles.[39]

Catholic Ireland is presented as sole heir to pre-reformation England as well as to pre-reformation Ireland; this is symbolized by the union of Alice and Rodger. Nell Gower employs Irish labourers as muscle in streetfights. Several scenes echo Irish Catholic iconography of the penal days. Catholics worship-ping in a cavern are attacked by royal forces, who shoot a priest at the altar; another priest proclaims 'resistance is no longer a crime, but a duty.'[40] The ruined abbey reflects Boyce's memories of Donegal Abbey.

Boyce promised readers a never-completed sequel set in Edinburgh. *The Spaewife* prefigures elements of this sequel. Elizabeth orchestrates the forgery of letters attributed to Mary. Boyce thus implies that the casket letters, which sup-posedly proved Mary's adultery with Bothwell and complicity in the murder of her husband Darnley and whose authenticity is widely questioned, were also forged by Elizabeth. Darnley's jealousy of Rizzio is kindled by Elizabeth and her Scotch protégé the earl of Murray, whose soliloquies echo Macbeth. John Knox appears as a demented fanatic, loudly denouncing Elizabeth and Murray when they most require secrecy.[41] Nell Gower prophesies that she herself will live to see the death of Elizabeth, and the queen's bastard child will come between its mother and the angel of mercy on her deathbed.[42] Presumably

---

37 Ibid., pp 555–6. **38** Ibid., pp 727–8. **39** Ibid., pp 442–3. **40** Ibid., p. 413. **41** Ibid., pp 516–23, 525–50. **42** Ibid., pp 377–9.

Elizabeth would have killed it. The novel fails because Boyce cannot come to terms with the triumph of Elizabeth over Mary.

Mary Lee is noticeably better-written than its predecessors. A Scottean preface attributes it to Peppergrass's old schoolfriend Peter Pinkie, based on Peter Pattieson of the Waverley novels. Pinkie is a spoiled priest expelled from Louvain after throwing a volume at the philosophy lecturer to save himself from dying of boredom; he dies of rheumatic fever in St Louis, receiving the last rites from a cousin of Fr Prout. A letter entrusts his manuscript to Peppergrass and pleads unsuccessfully for his body to be shipped to Buncrana. Where the preface to *The Spaewife* is simply a disconnected defence of the book, this echoes the novel's wider theme of devotion versus intellectualism and Boyce's awareness that he would die and be buried in exile.

The novel is set in the Fanad of Boyce's early pastorate; Boyce lingers lovingly on the scenery and on the parlour where 'Fr John' relaxes.[43] The central plot concerns the 'matrimonial speculation' of Ephraim Weeks, Yankee cousin of the evangelical landlord Robert Hardwrinkle. Having discovered that Mary Lee, a locally-brought-up survivor of the shipwreck of the *Saldanha*,[44] is the missing daughter and heiress of a wealthy Virginia planter, Weeks decides to marry her before she uncovers her true identity. Foolishly confident of his ability to outsmart the despised Irish, he employs the wisewoman Else Curley as a go-between. Else, an effective rewrite of Nell Gower as Scottean 'demented prophetess' sees Weeks as a pawn to secure vengeance on Hardwrinkle, who evicted her. Hardwrinkle's father seduced her sister – it is noteworthy that the sister was indeed seduced – and sent her brother to die in Lifford jail.[45] The Hardwrinkles are Presbyterians rather than Anglicans, allowing Boyce to denounce Calvin as the 'subtle betrayer of the human conscience […] dark plotter of treason against the human soul.'[46] Else has abandoned her religious duties for thirty years to avoid being diverted from revenge; only fondness for her foster-child Mary Lee restrains and redeems her. Mary loves the fugitive Young Irelander Randall James Barry, based on Thomas D'Arcy McGee, hidden by Boyce's brother during his 1848 escape, and is defended by Lanty Hanlon, another version of Shandy Maguire, given the rabbit-skin cap of Carleton's Phelim O'Toole – Patrick Magill's 1922 novel *Lanty Hanlon* may echo Boyce. Weeks suffers some of the same humiliations as the Orangeman Dumpy Dowser in *Shandy Maguire* at the hands of peasants, aware of the treatment their compatriots received in New England, who acknowledge American help during the famine but complain that Yankees take all the good out of it by 'boastin' an' puffin' […] like an auctioneer sellin caligoes at a fair'.[47] Barry is eventually freed, and Hardwrinkle acci-

---

43 Boyce, *Mary Lee*, pp 319–20.   **44** The action takes place *c.*1850 and Mary is eighteen; the real-life *Saldanha* was wrecked in 1811!   **45** Boyce, *Mary Lee*, pp 129–30.   **46** Ibid., p. 206.   **47** Ibid., pp 106, 150, 154.

dentally killed, in a courtroom riot where Else plays the same role as Nell Gower, waving a dagger and proclaiming resistance no longer a crime but a duty. After vengeance is accomplished by providence, Else is reconciled to the Church. Even the celebrated passage where Boyce describes a graveyard and pours scorn on those who believe Irish-Americans should blot out such hallowed memories and assimilate to a land which persecutes them is expanded from *Shandy Maguire*.[48]

Like *The Spaewife*, the novel centres on the repeated humiliations of its villain. Weeks gazes on Mary Lee's mementoes of Ireland's past with 'a cold, prying curiosity', and glimpses her rosary with 'a contemptuous smile' over cross and crucified.[49] He reads Paine's *Age of reason* and ignores classical and modern literature.[50] When a servant is compared to Caleb Balderstone, the faithful retainer in Scott's *Bride of Lammermoor*, Weeks asks if this is one of the Balderstones of Skowhegan, to be told '[h]e was born of a wizard, and shall live as long as the world lasts'.[51] Weeks was once a Methodist class-leader but sees Unitariansim as the most sensible religion. 'It don't suit men in trade to spend whole hours at prayer, and neglect their business [...] business is a sacred thing and must be attended to.'[52] His experience of Protestant sects convinced him that those who profess religion are mostly hypocrites. Hardwrinkle protests, but his own miserliness and oppression illustrate Weeks's thesis. Catholicism, on the other hand, places too much restraint on business practices; Weeks thinks the gospel should be watered down to avoid injuring trade.[53] He is so flexible, it transpires, that even his name is not his own. Boyce emphasises that Weeks does not represent all Protestant New Englanders, but only the commercial class; women, labourers, and farmers are more religiously observant.

Weeks's frankly avowed amoralism and generous acceptance that others are just as much entitled to cheat him as he is to cheat them make him more sympathetic than the canting Hardwrinkles, but commentators exaggerate Boyce's tolerance by seeing the book too exclusively in an American context. In Weeks's departure to denounce the Irish in American newspapers, Boyce expresses the hope that the Catholic Donegal of his memories will be preserved from the Yankee commercialism and irreligion which surround him.

Mary Lee is mellower than *Shandy Maguire*, partly because Boyce's hopes for millennial deliverance have been replaced by patient trust in the eventual triumph of moral force. One striking difference is the presence of unequivocally sympathetic Protestant characters, the benevolent Leveresque paternalist landlord Captain Petersham, who denounces game-laws, sympathizes with rebels, and loves a good drink,[54] and his high-spirited sister Kate. Brownson is satirized as Dr Henshaw, a converted Scottish writer for the *Edinburgh Review* – notoriously associated with arrogant philistine rationalism – who thinks the best way

---

48 Ibid., pp 223–5. **49** Ibid., p. 45. **50** Ibid., pp 57–8. **51** Ibid., pp 66–7. **52** Ibid., p. 201.
53 Ibid., pp 268–9. **54** Ibid., pp 275–6.

to convert Protestants is to tell them all non-Catholics will be damned, then bully them with logic. When Henshaw discovers that Kate reads Swift he denounces him while she praises Swift's patriotism, wit and humour. Commentators rightly point out that this acceptance that literature has non-didactic functions makes Boyce unique among Irish-American literary polemicists of his generation. His admiration for Swift, however, is not unrestrained; he specifies that Kate dips into Swift's works rather than reading straight through.[55] Henshaw is rebuked by Fr John, who accuses him of egotism and tells him the intellect cannot be converted without the heart. The devotional writer Fr Faber does more than Henshaw/Brownson because he writes for the millions and seeks their salvation rather than intellectual vainglory.[56]

Boyce's devotional Catholicism is encapsulated in the heroine Mary Lee, compared to the Madonna in Raphael's *Espousals of the Virgin* and to the central figure of Richard Dalton Williams' poem 'A Sister of Charity'.[57] While nursing a shipwrecked cabin-boy, confident that the Virgin Mary will protect her from typhus, she explains Marian doctrine to Kate, who tells Mary she has just encountered the best book of apologetics, namely Mary herself.[58] Kate is converted by the example of Mary and of 'Uncle Jerry' Guirkie, an eccentric Dickensian philanthropist inspired by the charitable spirit of Catholicism. Merwick bizarrely presents the dispute between Henshaw and Fr John over the best means of conversion as Boyce displaying pluralism by 'defending Kate's Protestantism'. Henshaw remains unimpressed.

Although not Catholic, Randall is attracted by the image of the Virgin; Else predicts marriage to Mary Lee will convert him. Captain Petersham remains Protestant, but accepts his sister's conversion to 'a decent religion'; he despises 'the hypocritical twaddle' of evangelicals and would sooner see Kate peddle eggs than turn Methodist.[59]

A shipwrecked 'negro' plays a significant though minor role in the plot, which displays disturbing ambivalence on slavery. Jerry Guirkie feels particular sympathy for blacks; Boyce frequently compares the plight of the Irish peasantry to that of slaves, and we are told 'Sambo' was repeatedly flogged, yet he appears a stereotypical faithful slave with no desire for permanent escape. Boyce, apparently, denounces the treatment of the Irish as blacks because the Irish were not blacks. Weeks' remark that New England abolitionists who persecute Irish Catholics display 'a half sentimental, half benevolent kinder squeamishness, with a slight dash of the religious in it for seasoning' towards blacks while secretly despising them reflects the speaker's moral deformity – he has been overseer on a plantation – and contains a painful degree of accuracy.[60] It is, nonetheless, a disquieting reflection of the Irish-American alliance with the antebellum Democrats that the novel, published in the slave state of Maryland, ends with

---

55 Ibid., pp 162–8, 175–6. **56** Ibid., pp 325–7. **57** Ibid, pp 81, 361. **58** Ibid., pp 191–9. **59** Ibid., p. 186. **60** Ibid., p. 233.

the departure of the idealized Mary Lee, her rebel lover and Lanty Hanlon to share her fortune as heiress to a slave plantation.

Boyce was not a great novelist, but remains interesting. Constrained by discrimination and witness to famine, he became an exile seeking wholeness in memories, devotions, and alcohol and patching together texts to find expression for his experiences. His insistence that the lived faith of the Irish people represented an argument for Catholicism more formidable than any intellectual treatise prefigures later priest-novelists, such as Canon Sheehan, who blended devotional Catholicism with nostalgic images of a pious rural Ireland for emigré audiences and worried about the role of the priest amid the breakdown of older social hierarchies.

A Victorian atheist encounters Roman-Catholic Ireland

WALTER L. ARNSTEIN

As of the year 1880, no newspaper reader in either Great Britain or Ireland would have been unfamiliar with the name of Charles Bradlaugh (1833–91), that notorious advocate of atheism, republicanism, and birth control. Born in metropolitan London in 1833 and baptized a member of the Church of England, he had quarreled as a youth with the parish vicar and had been expelled from his religious duties, his job, and his family. While earning a living as a solicitor's clerk, Bradlaugh during the 1850s became a charismatic free-thought speaker and pamphleteer who soon graduated from the open-air soap-box to lecture halls to which he could attract as many as 4,000 listeners. Under the pseudonym 'Iconoclast', he declaimed on topics such as 'The existence of God' and debated Anglican clerics and Roman Catholic priests.

In the course of his life, Bradlaugh was called many names: free-thinker, infidel, secularist, materialist, atheist. He never hesitated to employ the word 'atheist', which, in accordance with its Greek origin, he defined as 'without God.' He did not deny there was 'a God', declared Bradlaugh in 1859, 'because to deny that which was unknown was as absurd as to affirm it. As an atheist he denied the God of the Bible, of the Koran, of the Vedas.' He dismissed the 'agnosticism' professed by Thomas Henry Huxley, George Eliot, and Leslie Stephen as 'a mere society form of Atheism'.[1]

In the course of the 1860s, Bradlaugh became the editor of a weekly periodical, the *National Reformer*, and the president of the National Secular Society, a free-thought organization that by 1880 could claim some 6,000 members in more than 60 branches. In its organization, rituals, and activities, admittedly, the giant London branch of the society resembled a nonconformist chapel.[2]

---

1 See Walter L. Arnstein, *The Bradlaugh case: atheism, sex, and politics among the late Victorians* (Columbia: University of Missouri Press, 1983), pp 8–11. [The book is a republication, together with a new chapter, 'Postscript: the Bradlaugh case revisited', of *The Bradlaugh case: A study in late Victorian opinion and politics* (Oxford: Clarendon, 1965).] Huxley coined the word 'agnostic'. See Cyril Bibby, *T.H. Huxley: scientist, humanist and educator* (London: Watts, 1959), p. 60. 2 Arnstein, *Bradlaugh case*, pp 12–14. The organization sponsored dances, choral singing, baby naming, and lectures that resembled sermons. One clergyman in 1880 called attention to 'the apostolic zeal, the vehement impatience with false doctrine, [and] the abiding faith in great principles' that characterized Bradlaugh's platform manner and that resembled those of a Puritan minister. See *Northern Echo*, 26 May 1880, quoted in Arnstein, *Bradlaugh case*, pp 13–14.

Bradlaugh was not merely an atheist, however. He was also a republican, a highly controversial appellation in the United Kingdom of Queen Victoria. Bradlaugh sympathized with movements to transform the German, Italian, Spanish, and French monarchies into republics, and he was a great admirer of the post-Civil War United States – which he visited on three occasions. Although an undercurrent of republicanism could be found in England as well as Ireland throughout the nineteenth century,[3] in England it reached its apex in 1870–1 in the context of the reclusiveness of the widowed Queen Victoria and the foundation of the Third Republic in France. Bradlaugh helped organize a network of English republican clubs, and he denounced the dynasty that had reigned since 1714 as 'remarkable neither for virtue, intelligence, decision of character, nor devotion to national interests', and as a pivot of social class privilege.[4] Bradlaugh's vitriolic *Impeachment of the House of Brunswick* (1871) became a best-seller.[5] The movement ebbed, but the transformation of Britain into a republic with the abdication or the death of Queen Victoria remained Bradlaugh's long-term goal.

The most notorious of the movements that Bradlaugh championed was Neo-Malthusianism, the belief that the most significant long-term solution to the poverty of the labouring classes was to limit the size of their families. As Bradlaugh wrote in 1876, 'we think it more moral to prevent the conception of children, than, after they are born, to murder them with want of food, air, and clothing'.[6] In 1876, in collaboration with his new associate, the dynamic Annie Besant, he deliberately republished a forty-year old pamphlet by an American physician, *The fruits of philosophy; or the private companion of young married couples.* The result was one of the most dramatic trials of the century. Bradlaugh and Besant were heard, found guilty of obscenity, and saved from prison only by a legal technicality. The astonishing furor that the case aroused can be explained by the conviction of Bradlaugh's critics that teaching methods of contraception would destroy rather than cement the marriage bond. It would promote premarital indulgence, encourage adultery, and endorse prostitution. The trial made Bradlaugh more than ever a symbol of public notoriety.[7] No wonder that in 1880 Queen Victoria could write that it was 'not only his known atheism but [...] his other horrible principles which make him a disgrace'.[8]

Now what did this notorious Victorian have to do with Ireland? The answer is: a great deal, if only because by 1868 Bradlaugh had set himself an additional

3 For England, see Richard Williams, *The contentious crown: public discussion of the British monarchy in the reign of Queen Victoria* (Aldershot: Ashgate, 1997). **4** Quoted in David Tribe, *President Charles Bradlaugh, M.P.* (London: Archon, 1971), p. 122. See also Fergus D'Arcy, 'Charles Bradlaugh and the English republican movement,' *Historical Journal* 25 (1982), pp 367–83. **5** Quoted in Tribe, *Bradlaugh*, p. 131. **6** Quoted in his introduction to the reprint of *The fruits of philosophy* in Sripati Chandrasekhar, *'A dirty, filthy book'* (Berkeley: University of California Press, 1981), p. 91. **7** The fullest account may be found in Roger Manvell, *The trial of Annie Besant and Charles Bradlaugh* (New York: Horizon, 1976). **8** Philip Guedalla, *The queen and Mr Gladstone*, 2 vols (London, 1933), ii, p. 96.

goal – as an adherent of the most radical wing of the Liberal Party, to represent the borough of Northampton as a Member of Parliament.[9] Like other advanced Liberals of his day, he often expressed strong sympathies for the subject nationalities of Europe, such as Italians and Hungarians rebelling against Austrian rule and Poles rebelling against Russian rule. Unlike a great many fellow Englishmen, however, he fully recognized the reality of the spirit of nationality in mid-nineteenth-century Ireland. As he remarked in 1873, 'I am one of those who can see no difference between Poland and Ireland, between Hungary and Erin's green land [...] I confess that I cannot believe that [...] that which is patriotism in Warsaw becomes treason in Dublin streets.'[10]

Bradlaugh differed from fellow English radicals in another respect. For almost three years – between the ages of seventeen and twenty – he had actually lived in Ireland as a British soldier, as a private stationed near Cork. It was in Ireland that he learned how to fence and how to ride. It was in Ireland also that he developed a keen sense of sympathy for the often grim life led by Irish peasants. On one occasion, persuaded that the law was on the side of the local tenants, he pulled down a gate by which a landlord had blocked a traditional right-of-way. On another occasion, he and his fellow soldiers were compelled to enforce a legal order to evict a peasant family and destroy the cottage in which the family lived. The wife pleaded eloquently that her ailing husband be left to die in peace in the house, but Bradlaugh's captain felt compelled to obey orders. The house was pulled down, the husband died, and three days later the maddened widow, clutching a dead baby, appeared at the barrack gates. It was an episode that Bradlaugh never forgot. Indeed, as a Member of Parliament, he was to recount it to the House of Commons thirty-five years later.[11] In his eyes, such incidents justified a deep Irish sense of grievance against landlords and arbitrary laws.

In the year 1867, Fenian leaders in London, two of whom had consulted Bradlaugh, had boldly proclaimed the establishment of an Irish Republic with the words: 'We have suffered centuries of outrage, enforced poverty, and bitter misery.'[12] Bradlaugh strongly sympathized with the Fenian demand for 'absolute liberty of conscience and the complete separation of Church and State' in their

9 Bradlaugh's election address of 1868 is reprinted in *Champion of liberty: Charles Bradlaugh* (London: C.A. Watts & Co., 1933), pp 165–7. He advocated compulsory national education, land law reform, the equal treatment of labour before the law, and a complete separation of church and state. **10** Speech on Ireland (1873) quoted in *Champion of liberty*, pp 240, 243. Two complementary articles deal with the subject in detail: Nigel H. Sinnott, 'Charles Bradlaugh and Ireland,' *Journal of the Cork Historical and Archeological Society* 77 (1972), pp 1–24; Fergus D'Arcy, 'Charles Bradlaugh and the Irish Question: a study in the nature and limits of British radicalism, 1853–91,' in Art Cosgrove and Donal McCartney (eds), *Studies in Irish History presented to R. Dudley Edwards* (Dublin: University College, 1979), pp 228–56. **11** Quoted in Sinnott, 'Bradlaugh', p. 20. See also Hypatia Bradlaugh Bonner, *Charles Bradlaugh*, 2 vols (London: T. Fisher Unwin, 1895), i, pp 25–40. **12** Bonner, *Charles Bradlaugh*, i, pp 252–4.

projected Irish republic, but recent scholars have rightly noted that Bradlaugh opposed an armed rebellion at that time because he felt certain that it would cost thousands of lives and fail all the same. The Fenian rebellion of 1867 was indeed readily suppressed by a combination of bad weather and government spies and soldiers.[13]

Anglo-Irish relations were embittered anew by that insurrection and by its aftermath which included both the execution of the 'Manchester martyrs' and the explosion at Clerkenwell prison in which twelve died and 120 were injured. Bradlaugh had pleaded against the executions but felt compelled to condemn the explosion as 'this fearfully mad crime',[14] one that might well plunge the British and the Irish 'into a fratricidal struggle'.[15] Yet early in 1868 he lectured in Dublin, and the Reform League of Ireland thanked him for 'his truly phil-anthropic and patriotic exertions and sentiments on behalf of poor Ireland'.[16]

The Fenian insurrection inspired William Ewart Gladstone, on being named Liberal prime minister, to proclaim a 'mission to pacify Ireland' that in 1869 and 1870 led to the disestablishment of the Protestant Church of Ireland and to a land reform act. Eventually it would also inspire Gladstone's conversion to 'Home Rule', to the conviction that Ireland should once again possess its own legisla-ture. Charles Bradlaugh had become a convert to home rule thirteen years ear-lier – at the very time that Isaac Butt first led a party of Irish home rule MPs in the House of Commons. If the states of New York and Massachusetts could have their own legislatures in the American union, if Hungary could have its own par-liament in the Austro-Hungarian Empire, then why could not Ireland have its own parliament in the United Kingdom? So argued Bradlaugh from 1873 on.[17]

In the course of the later 1870s the economic situation in Ireland deterio-rated because of bad harvests and of American agricultural competition. Beginning in 1879, the militant Irish Land League campaigned against tenant evictions in an at times violent manner, while Charles Stewart Parnell began to coordinate 'the land war' with the work of the Irish home rule party at Westminster. In 1880 he took over its leadership.

The state of the British economy and Irish unrest contributed that year to the triumphant return, after six years of Conservative rule, of William Ewart Gladstone and the Liberal Party. The most remarkable of the newly-elected members that helped make up the Liberal majority was Charles Bradlaugh. He decided to add icing to his victory cake by claiming to 'affirm' rather than to 'swear' the required parliamentary oath of allegiance – thereby confirming for freethinkers in parliament an option, a badge of respectability, that he had ear-

13 Ibid., i, pp 254–55; Sinnott, 'Bradlaugh', pp 12–13. Fergus D'Arcy argues persuasively that the Fenian leaders must have sought Bradlaugh's skills not as a draftsman of their proclama-tion but as a potential English ally. See D'Arcy, 'Bradlaugh and the Irish question', pp 234–5.
14 Bonner, *Charles Bradlaugh*, i, pp 256–7.   15 *National Reformer*, 16 Feb. 1868, quoted in D'Arcy, 'Bradlaugh and the Irish question', p. 237.   16 Quoted in Sinnott, 'Bradlaugh', p. 16.
17 Quoted in *Champion of liberty*, pp 245–6.

lier helped extend to freethinkers in law court proceedings. By a vote of nine
to eight, however, a select committee denied him that option. Bradlaugh there-
upon publicly announced that, although the words of the oath 'are to me
sounds conveying no clear and definite meaning', he would speak them in the
spirit of the affirmation that had been denied him and thereby comply 'with the
forms of the House'. Bradlaugh's subsequent attempt to take the required oath
was met by a storm of protest, however, and a second select committee, by a
vote of eleven to ten, foreclosed the option of the oath also. Eventually
Gladstone persuaded the House to give Bradlaugh the opportunity to affirm
after all, subject only 'to any liability by statute'.[18]

Bradlaugh did therefore serve as a Member of Parliament between July 1880
and March 1881 – that dramatic autumn and winter during which the Irish
land war reached fever pitch. Although he questioned the Irish home rule
policy of unlimited parliamentary obstruction, Bradlaugh proved to be one of
but eight Liberals willing to support the Irish in opposing a new coercion act
that suspended the right of habeas corpus in Ireland.[19] The Roman Catholic
Tablet took note of Bradlaugh's 'ostentatious defence of Irish interests in
Parliament'.[20] Bradlaugh's brief parliamentary career ended when a court found
his claim to affirm invalid and vacated his seat. Despite numerous legal and legislative maneuvers, despite two reelections for his Northampton seat, despite
fiery speeches and militant protest movements, Bradlaugh was to be kept out of
the House of Commons throughout the remainder of the 1880–85 parliament.

What is of primary interest here is the manner in which Bradlaugh's long
struggle to enter Parliament intersected the multi-faceted 'Irish Question'. Many
home rule party members were well acquainted with members of the radical
wing of the Liberal Party and with Bradlaugh in particular as fellow advocates of
causes such as land reform. Parnell and Bradlaugh were indeed fellow vice-pres-
idents of the Democratic League of Great Britain and Ireland.[21] When Parnell
spoke briefly on behalf of Bradlaugh's admission in May 1880, he conceded, however, that he could recall no time when 'he was less confident in the belief that
the mass of the Irish people were behind him [...] Catholic members for Ireland
had felt very strongly on this question – very strongly indeed.'[22]

So they had felt, and so they were to feel – during the next five years.
Parnell's stand was immediately criticized by a Catholic priest in the leading
Dublin paper. We Irish, he declared,

> may be hot-headed and impulsive, but we [...] have no sympathy with
> Atheism, blasphemy, and the fruits of a foul philosophy. We recognize no

18 Quoted in Arnstein, *Bradlaugh case*, p. 80.   **19** Quoted in ibid., p. 87.   **20** *Tablet*, 26 Feb.
1881, p. 328.   **21** See Arnstein, *Bradlaugh case*, p. 207 and Alan O'Day, 'The Parnellites and
British radicalism', in *The English face of Irish nationalism: Parnellite involvement in British politics, 1880–86* (Dublin: Gill and Macmillan, 1977), pp 79–92.   **22** *Hansard's parliamentary debates*,
3rd series, 253 (1880), col. 657, quoted in Arnstein, *Bradlaugh case*, p. 205.

freedom of opinion there [...] For my part, I should rather see the foreign rule of England, bad as it is, replaced by the iron despotism of Russia, and Ireland turned into a waste like Siberia, than look for freedom through a political alliance with Bradlaugh and his 100,000 Atheists.[23]

In 1881 the Irish home rule party voted henceforth to oppose every legislative step that might admit Bradlaugh to Parliament. That policy proved most influential in May 1883, when Gladstone made one of the most eloquent speeches of his life in favour of the so-called Affirmation Bill – as a measure to advance the cause of religion, of religious liberty, and of the right of the electors of Northampton to have their votes respected. The measure went down to defeat by a margin of 292 to 289. Most of its opponents were Conservatives, but home rulers dominated the final days of the debate, when James Charlie McCoan assured the House that '[a]ll Ireland, from Cape Clear to the Giant's Causeway is against it.'[24]

'Bradlaugh Bowled Out by the Irish Vote,' boasted *United Ireland*, the most radical of the nationalist weeklies,[25] and London's chief Liberal paper, the *Daily News*, agreed. The fiery young home rule MP, T.P. O'Connor, had no doubt that 'it was the Irish vote which was the real, the influential, the potent factor in the whole struggle.'[26] Tactical political considerations may well have played a role in that vote, but so did a very genuine concern with both religion and respectability. When discussing the nineteenth century, it is easy to speak of 'Roman Catholic Ireland'. Yet it is useful to keep in mind that until the general election of 1880 a majority of Ireland's 105 representatives in the Westminster Parliament had always been Protestants and that the nationalist tradition represented by the Young Irelanders of 1848, the Irish Republican Brotherhood of the 1860s, and Isaac Butt's home rule party during the 1870s had been either secular or, at the very least, ecumenical, in religious affiliation. According to the Religious Census of 1881, Roman Catholics numbered 76 per cent of the Irish population. For the very first time, they also made up a majority, 53 per cent (56 out of 105) of all Irish MPs. Only four of the Parnellite MPs in the 1880 5 Parliament were non-Catholic; Parnell himself was one of those four.[27]

At a time that at most one Roman Catholic could be found among 493 English and Welsh MPs, it is not surprising that Henry Edward Manning, the convert cardinal who headed the hierarchy in England – should come to see the Roman Catholic Irish home rule MPs as part of his personal flock. He had long been frustrated by the tendency of many English people to continue to look on Roman Catholicism as an alien force. Now, with the help of the Irish

---

23 *Freeman's Journal*, 26 June 1880, p. 5, quoted in Arnstein, *Bradlaugh case*, p. 208. **24** *Parliamentary debates*, 3rd series, 278 (1883), cols 1479–80, quoted in Arnstein, *Bradlaugh Case*, p. 212. **25** Quoted in Arnstein, *Bradlaugh case*, p. 213. **26** *Daily News*, 5 May 1883; T.P. O'Connor, *Gladstone's House of Commons* (London, Ward and Downey, 1885), p. 335. **27** O'Day, *English face*, p. 16.

MPs, he could oppose Bradlaugh and lead a politically popular but fundamentally conservative campaign to promote public morality in the form of sermons, newspaper articles, correspondence with political leaders, public petition drives, and the lobbying of MPs within the corridors of the house of commons.[28] When the Affirmation Bill was defeated, his weekly mouthpiece, the *Tablet*, could exult:

> [I]t is the Irish members to whom the laurels are due, and English Catholics may well be gratefully mindful that it was Irish voices and Irish votes which chiefly prevented atheism from having a share in English law-giving […] In whatever else divided, in the face of aggressive atheism Ireland is true to herself, and her members are as one.[29]

When the other English convert Cardinal, John Henry Newman, was asked his opinion, he responded that

> [I]t little concerns Religion whether Mr. Bradlaugh swears by no God with the Government, or swears by an Impersonal, or Material, or Abstract and Ideal Something or other, which is all that is secured to us by the Opposition […] Looking at the [Affirmation] Bill on its merits, I think nothing is lost to Religion by its passing, and nothing gained by its being rejected.[30]

Manning was privately outraged. Did the octogenarian Roman Catholic sage truly have to pour cold water upon the fire of ecumenical national religious revival that Manning had so eagerly kindled?

In the meantime, Parnell was proving so successful in balancing the revolutionaries and the constitutionalists as well as the religionists and the anti-clericals among his supporters that he emerged from the general election of November 1885 with a disciplined body of eighty-six Irish home rule party supporters.[31] Three months later, a party that had allied itself unofficially with the Conservatives on matters such as the Affirmation Bill of 1883 and government subsidies for Roman Catholic elementary schools in England and Ireland, found itself allied anew with the Liberal Party, for Gladstone had become a convert to Irish home rule.

---

28 See, Arnstein, *Bradlaugh case*, pp 174–85. **29** *Tablet*, 12 May 1883, p. 721, quoted in Arnstein, *Bradlaugh case*, p. 224. **30** Quoted in Arnstein, *Bradlaugh case*, p. 230. **31** C.J. Woods, 'Parnell and the Catholic Church', in D. George Boyce and Alan O'Day (eds), *Parnell in perspective* (London: Routledge, 1991), pp 9–37 deals persuasively with the creation of the clerical/nationalist alliance. In *The Roman Catholic Church and the Plan of Campaign in Ireland, 1886–88* (Cork: Cork UP, 1978), p. 318, Emmet Larkin goes so far as to describe 'the concluding of the clerical-nationalist alliance of 1884' as 'the fundamental turning point' in the process of transforming the Roman Catholic Church into the state church of the independent Ireland that emerged in the 1920s.

Liberals such as Bradlaugh were faced with a choice. Should they follow the chief political radical of the day, Joseph Chamberlain, in his 'Liberal Unionist' opposition to Gladstone's scheme, or should they align themselves with Gladstone, Liberalism's 'Grand Old Man'? Bradlaugh hesitated scarcely at all. Opponents of the measure admittedly insisted that 'Home Rule means Rome Rule', and Bradlaugh had once pointed out that 'the Rome of the Vatican fears every shadow the light of freedom throws across its rule'.[32] Yet at a large meeting in London's St James's Hall and in a several masterful orations in the House of Commons, Bradlaugh defended home rule. '[T]he true remedy for Ireland,' he insisted, 'was for Ireland to redress her own grievances in her own Parliament by Members elected by her own people.'[33]

Liberal division spelled defeat for Gladstone's first home rule measure by a vote of 343 to 313, and the general election that followed led to six years of Conservative rule. By the time Gladstone received in 1893 a second opportunity to introduce a home rule bill, both Parnell and Bradlaugh were dead. But during the five years left to him before his death in January 1891, Bradlaugh remained the most stalwart champion of Irish causes among British MPs.[34]

In 1888 he also carried through Parliament an affirmation bill. Manning still protested, but in the house of commons, the Irish members 'now sat silent and acquiescent'.[35] Indeed, by a ratio of 30 to one, they voted in favour of the measure. As one Irish nationalist MP confided to Charles Bradlaugh in the house of commons lobby, 'Mr Bradlaugh, you have been the best Christian of us all.'[36]

It is appropriate to approach much of human history in a spirit of irony. Such a spirit is peculiarly appropriate when we remember what occurred when a notorious Victorian atheist encountered Roman Catholic Ireland.

---

32 Quoted in Sinnott, 'Bradlaugh,' p. 19. **33** Quoted in D'Arcy, 'Bradlaugh and the Irish question,' p. 252. **34** See D'Arcy, 'Bradlaugh and the Irish question,' pp 252–5. **35** *Tablet*, 21 Apr. 1888, p. 638; *Times*, 15 Mar. 1888, p. 9, quoted in Arnstein, *Bradlaugh case*, pp 315–16. **36** Quoted in Bonner, *Charles Bradlaugh*, ii, p. 196.

Frances Power Cobbe and the patriarchs

MAUREEN O'CONNOR

Frances Power Cobbe (1822–1904), progressive reformer, iconoclastic theologian, lecturer, abolitionist, woman's advocate, and defender of animals, was born in 1822 at Newbridge House, Donabate, Co. Dublin, into a prominent Anglo-Irish family, distinguished by its service to the British military and the Anglican Church, having produced five archbishops. While virtually forgotten today, she was at the centre of the social, literary, and intellectual circles of note in late-Victorian England. She could count among her friends and acquaintances Matthew Arnold, Charles Darwin, Charles Lyell, Fanny Kemble, the Brownings, Lord Tennyson, Mary Somerville, J.S. Mill, Rosa Bonheur, Thomas Carlyle, Elizabeth Gaskell, and Lord Shaftesbury. In fact, the only eminent figures of the day she expressed regret at never meeting were George Eliot and Harriet Martineau.[1] She was not only famous, but also enormously influential as an activist and a thinker, having, for instance, been instrumental in the passage of the Matrimonial Causes Act of 1878.[2] According to Barbara Caine, '[i]n her recognition of the connection between the many forms of female oppression evident within the family, the Church, and the intellectual and professional worlds, Cobbe came closer to propounding a theory of patriarchy than did any other Victorian feminist.'[3] She is beginning to emerge from her undeserved obscurity, as the last few years have seen renewed interest in her. However, even though Cobbe lived in Ireland for the first thirty-six years of her life before relocating to England, what little that has appeared about her so far takes minimal account, if any, of the impact on her work of her Ascendancy background, its gender implications, particularly.[4] This is what Ann Owens Weekes refers to as the 'emotional, psychological, social, and economic deprivations of the status-less woman in the man's world of Anglo-Ireland'.[5] Recent critical assessments

1 Frances Power Cobbe, *Life of Frances Power Cobbe: by herself*, 2 vols (Boston, New York: Houghton Mifflin, 1895), ii, p. 520. 2 Deirdre Raftery, 'Frances Power Cobbe (1822–1904)', in Mary Cullen and Maria Luddy (eds), *Women, power and consciousness in nineteenth-century Ireland* (Dublin: Attic Press, 1995), p. 108. 3 Barbara Caine, *Victorian feminists* (Oxford: Oxford UP, 1992), p. 104. 4 Raftery, 'Cobbe', p. 192. See also Moira Ferguson, *Animal advocacy and Englishwomen, 1780–1900: patriots, nation, and empire* (Ann Arbor: University of Michigan Press, 1998), p. 129; Janet L. Larson, 'Where is the woman in this text? Frances Power Cobbe's voices in *Broken Lights*', *Victorian Literature and Culture* 31:1 (2003), passim; Sandra J. Peacock, *The theological and ethical writings of Frances Power Cobbe, 1822–1904* (Lewiston: Edwin Mellon, 2002), pp 160–8. 5 Ann Owens Weekes, *Irish women writers: an uncharted tradition* (Lexington: University of Kentucky Press, 1990), p. 61.

suggest that Cobbe's near-total historical disappearance is due to the difficulties she presents to ready categorization, and her often frustrating ideological inconsistencies and idiosyncracies. It is my contention that Cobbe's various modes of patriarchal resistance are at once stimulated and undermined by her experience as an Anglo-Irish woman, including a strain of unregenerate Protestant conservatism, which often erupts in inconvenient contradictions.

An indefatigable advocate for the oppressed and subjugated, including black slaves, animals, and women of all classes, especially working-class girls, her rhetoric in defence of the defenceless was nevertheless diffused through a complex of competing beliefs and allegiances. The discriminatory class and race affinities typical of a Victorian suffragist were complicated for Cobbe by a consciousness of belonging to an especially besieged class in late nineteenth-century Ireland, one marked by racialized sectarian difference. In her study of nineteenth-century Englishwomen active in the cause of animal protection, Moira Ferguson observes that in a 'revised vocabulary of rights the discourses against cruelty to animals, abuse of women, and enslavement overlapped and elided with one another, contributing at the same time to an updated definition of what constituted Englishness.'[6] The 'Englishness' under construction in Ferguson's examination of the rhetorical imbrications among emancipatory causes is a national identity forming and reforming in reaction to imperial expansion. Ferguson contends that the depredations attendant on colonialism, which potentially allied the colonized in the peripheries with other powerless, marginalized communities, constituted a source of anxiety and ambivalence for the white, middle-class, English, Protestant activists in London who were championing women, animals, and slaves at home. However, Cobbe, though she took pride in being unidentifiable as 'Irish', lived in the colonial periphery for over a third of her life and was not English, nor was she middle class, but the daughter of a landlord of a sizeable estate with close family ties to British aristocracy. She was brought up by a beloved Irish nurse, taught native Irish children in her role as big-house daughter, lived through the famine, and in 1848 inadvertently contributed funds to the local 'Cutthroat Club', which was threatening violent insurgence, targeting the Cobbe family.

And so, in the critique of domination that Cobbe pursued over several decades, the points of intersection among her uneasy alliances with both the exploiters and the exploited are uniquely unstable. Thus it is that the strident and impassioned opponent of slavery, who was especially exercised about what she considered England's appallingly misplaced sympathies with slaveholders during the American civil war, could, in an emancipation tract of 1863, speak pleadingly of negroes 'displaying the peculiarly Christian virtues of placability and patience, in a matter hardly to be paralleled in the annals of the Caucasian race,'[7] and could also, in an anti-vivisection article written in 1895, assert that 'a Fuegian who eats

6 Ferguson, *Animal advocacy,* p. 42.   7 Frances Power Cobbe, *The red flag in John Bull's eyes,*

his mother and can't count his fingers cannot be pigeon-holed a "Person.'"[8] This often self-cancelling impulse to pigeon-hole leads to frequent lapses in reasoning, despite Cobbe's vaunted rationalist ethos. Her position on the rights of animals, for instance, vacillates from essay to essay in her many works denouncing vivisection: on the one hand she charges with base hypocrisy an English public that pampers and admires its pets but allows other animals to be tortured on the dissector's table, yet on the other hand, she avails herself of a hierarchical 'diminishing scale of sensibility' when she wants to distinguish between the justified killing of animals for sport and the inhuman practices of science.[9] Similarly, she draws distinctions between the rights lower-class Italian women were entitled to and those that should be extended to lower-class English women, whose superior Saxon 'race' could potentially overcome the biological determinism Cobbe associated with class, criminality and, indeed, religion.[10]

Even when not blinkered by class or race prejudice, Cobbe's notions of gender could be conservative, if not quite conventionally essentialist. 'If my sex has a "mission" of any kind,' she says in response to being summarily dismissed as a harmless 'good lady' by the Jesuit George Tyrell, 'it is surely to soften this hard old world, such as men (priests included) have left us.'[11] In her autobiography Cobbe declares women to be the 'equivalents' rather than the 'equals of men,' and, looking back on her long and vigorous struggle on behalf of her sex, she concludes, 'I would far rather that women should remain without political rights to the end of time than that they should lose those qualities which we comprise in the word "womanliness"'. This startling assertion is followed by an almost equally disorienting discussion of women's superior rationality to men, whose excessive emotionalism leads them to loss of self control and violence. Unlike belligerent men, female revolutionaries, she tells us, will 'accomplish our emancipation by persuasion and reason'.[12] In her 1863 demythologizing attack on conventional Christianity, in which she proposes her own religion of the future, *Broken lights: an inquiry into the present condition and future prospects of religious faith*, Cobbe writes admiringly of a certain quality of 'manliness' lacking among contemporary moral authorities, especially among so-called 'muscular' Christians, in whom she detects a debilitating 'effeminacy', demonstrating through her own intellectual performance that the more desirably gendered trait is likely to be found in strong-minded women like herself now and in the future. It is Cobbe's lifelong struggle with spirituality that follows from *Broken*

tract number one (London: Ladies' London Emancipation Society, 1863), p. 4. **8** Frances Power Cobbe, 'The ethics of zoophily', *Contemporary Review* 68 (1895), p. 504. **9** Ibid., p. 503; see also Frances Power Cobbe, 'Zoophily', *Cornhill Magazine* 45 (1882), p. 287; Frances Power Cobbe, 'The rights of man and the claims of brutes', *Fraser's Magazine* 68 (1863), p. 596. **10** Compare the representations of lower-class women in Frances Power Cobbe 'Women in Italy in 1862', *Macmillan's Magazine* 6 (1862), p. 368, and 'Wife-torture in England', *Contemporary Review* 32 (1878), pp 67–9. **11** Cobbe, 'Ethics of zoophily', p. 497. **12** Cobbe, *Life*, ii, p. 533.

lights, and her traditionalist, perhaps atavistically evangelical, despair at what she regarded as an increasingly soulless age, which finally estranged her from younger feminists towards the end of her career, most significantly Annie Besant, who reacted to Cobbe's denunciation of atheism, in the 1884 essay, 'A faithless world', as a betrayal, in Besant's words, by 'a woman who has done so much to degrade the Bible from [its] unique position.'[13]

While Cobbe strenuously distanced herself from Christianity's formal institutions, she was unable to sever her ties with basic inherited beliefs or the Christian god, and her abiding conviction in the superiority of the Protestant faith never slackened. What Besant saw as Cobbe closing ranks with the 'tyrannical Establishment', marks one of a series of 'conversions' Cobbe underwent in her life, often arising from specifically religious crises, as she moved from evangelicalism to agnosticism to theism, with occasionally side-trips to Unitarianism. Always a fervently religious child, at the age of seventeen she experienced her first 'conversion', an especially intense, though private, renewal of commitment to her family's faith, and dedicated herself to studying the bible and the writings of the Church fathers, with the unexpected result that she found herself thrown increasingly into doubt, particularly as regards biblical accounts of miracles. By the age of twenty, in her own words, her 'efforts to believe in orthodox Christianity ceased', she became an 'Agnostic'.[14] She recounts this time as one of lonely wanderings through the Irish countryside, in the course of which her romantic and deeply spiritual sensibilities reasserted themselves; the 'storm of youth over', as she describes it, she began to pray once more, and never again lost faith in God, though she had lost faith in Christianity's holy book and even in its saviour. During this period she had read *A discourse of matters pertaining to religion,* by the controversial American abolitionist and theologian, Theodore Parker, who rejected Calvinism's oppressive paternalism as 'cruel and unreasonable' and who renounced the miraculous authority of both scripture and Jesus Christ. His vision of a personally authorized religion and of a rational yet loving deity that was both 'Father and Mother of the World'[15] comforted and inspired Cobbe, who corresponded with Parker for the rest of his life and edited his fourteen-volume collected works after his death.

She kept secret her rejection of the faith of her fathers until the death of her mother, a weak and timid but loving woman to whom Cobbe was devoted.

---

13 Annie Besant, *A world without God: a reply to Miss Frances Power Cobbe* (London: Freethought, 1885), p. 12. **14** Cobbe, *Life,* ii, p. 81. **15** Larson, 'Where is the woman?', p. 127, fn 5, quotes Cobbe in her preface to Theodore Parker's *Collected works* (i, p. xviii), 'All the power and care and forethought and inexorable loving which we attribute to the Fatherly character is fulfilled in Him. And all the inexhaustible forgiving love and tenderness which a mother's heart reveals is His, too [...]. Too long has the Catholic Church separated off this *Mother Side* of Deity into another object of worship; and more fatal still has been the error of the Reformed Churches, who in rejecting the Madonna have rejected all that she imaged forth of the Divine mansuetude and tenderness.'

Then, in an aggressively anti-patriarchal gesture, she declared her theism, scandalizing her father, remembered by Cobbe as having a 'fiery temper and despotic will', who turned her out of the house, exiling her to her brother's farm in Donegal, where she spent a year before she was allowed to return home, and only then in order to resume her housekeeping duties.[16] The lone sister to five brothers whose preference and privilege she resented, Cobbe returned from her brother's farm even more indignantly conscious of the absurd inequities of her helpless position as daughter. Sandra J. Peacock argues that as a result of her mother's invalidism and despite the many responsibilities she enthusiastically and ably assumed from a young age, '[f]ulfilling her duties [...] conferred upon her no corresponding rights or privileges, and Cobbe soon learned the limits of her position in the family.'[17] When her father died and left the estate to his eldest son, bequeathing Frances only as much money per year as she had been receiving as pocket money, thereby implicitly consigning her to a life of dependence on her brother and sister-in-law, Cobbe left Newbridge for good. In her study of Anglo-Irish women's autobiographies (a survey that does not include Cobbe's two-volume work), Elizabeth Grubgeld notes that the theme of the big-house functions ambivalently in women writers' treatment of it: 'If the house is conventionally presumed to act as an extension of the self in Anglo-Irish literature, in the writings of many women it acts as a metaphor of that which threatens a self whose pivotal awakening is to its freedom from place.'[18] While Cobbe suggests that her own escape was a lucky one, made possible, significantly, through her father's death, at the same time she never ceased to mourn leaving Newbridge, an event she calls 'the worst wrench of my life'.[19]

This wrench was followed by a tour of Europe and the Middle East, which included Jerusalem, Cairo, Alexandria, Athens, and Rome and from which emerged a collection of essays in 1864, *The cities of the past,* essays that, according to Peacock 'reveal the complexity of her views of religion, race, and British world hegemony'.[20] Certainly her inveterate Anglo-Saxonism, jingoistic support of empire, and belief in Christianity's ascendancy over any other system of belief suffered no diminution as a result of her travels. In the 1868 essay, 'The religions of the world,' she phlegmatically observes that '[n]o-one disputes the superiority of Christianity, *such as we have it*, to Islam,' and that the 'Chinese religion has long been the despair of Theologians'.[21] However, she directs her most thunderous broadsides against Catholicism, 'the great moral plague',[22] and not against a non-Christian faith. 'Cobbe judged "races" primarily by their religious beliefs, further refining her hierarchy of racial categories', according to Peacock,

16 Cobbe, *Life*, i, pp 71–94. 17 Peacock, *Theological and ethical writings*, p. 31. 18 Elizabeth Grubgeld, 'Gender, class, and the forms of narrative: the autobiographies of Anglo-Irish women', in Susan Shaw Sailor (ed.), *Representing Ireland: gender, class, nationality* (Gainesville: UP of Florida, 1997), p. 142. 19 Cobbe, *Life*, i, p. 194. 20 Peacock, *Theological and ethical writings*, p. 139. 21 Frances Power Cobbe, 'Bunsen's life and last book', *Fraser's Magazine* 77 (1868), pp 790, 794 (italics in the original). 22 Cobbe, 'Women in Italy', p. 369.

who describes this ranking as one that 'placed Muslims and Christian Arabs much higher than Indian followers of Hinduism, Africans, and Irish, all of whom she viewed as childlike polytheists'.[23] There is an abundance of evidence for Cobbe's anti-Irish sentiments and repulsion towards Catholicism, no doubt deeply ingrained by the anti-papist siege mentality that was her cultural inheritance, reinforced by sometimes traumatic personal experience, but she writes in an 1877 essay, 'The Celt of Wales and the Celt of Ireland,' 'happy is the child who has an Irish nurse',[24] and her autobiography portrays touching affection between herself and her Irish nurse, or 'Nanno,' Mary Malone, who called Frances her 'darlint'. These recollections also reveal that Cobbe and her brothers found nursery tales of the 1798 rebellion thrilling, and that they 'played at rebellion as children'.[25] Peacock contends that the 'Irish were the target of her most vituperative racist rhetoric',[26] but Cobbe's anti-papist vitriol was more steadily concentrated in another direction: she does derogate the Catholic Irish frequently, but never with the ferocious intensity or, more significantly, the consistency that distinguishes her rants against Catholic France. Her anti-Irish statements are rarely so blunt as, 'I intensely dislike France',[27] or '[a]bove all, we distrust French ideas, French phrases, French turns of thought, the pitiless logic, the unattackable dialectics, the sentimental hyperboles of the French writer.'[28] It is France, and to a lesser degree Italy, that Cobbe blames for the importation into England of 'foreign atrocities', the scientific practices Cobbe represents as the torture of women and animals. Among her list of French perpetrators she names Charcot and Pasteur, though Cobbe also pilloried and actively petitioned Italian scientists.[29] Her most famous anti-vivisection tract, 'The rights of man and the claims of brutes', begins with a mock fairy tale describing dissolute, Mariolatrous France with its 'luxurious delights' and 'gilded temples', some of which screen from public scrutiny an assembly of 'many learned men [...] adorned with tokens of favour of the great prince, and with the ensigns of the noble order called that of Honour,' who conduct unspeakable experiments on the truly 'noble', the 'tame and inoffensive', 'sensitive animals'.[30]

In contrast, while Cobbe makes frequent recourse to many racist clichés about the Irish – that they are dirty, indolent, barbaric and child-like, 'cannot a abide a law',[31] are 'utterly unable to comprehend the nature of veracity',[32] improvident and impulsive, as well as boastful and vulgar, dreamy and clamorous – she defies other stereotypes, especially, and significantly, in regards to the two

23 Peacock, *Theological and ethical writings*, pp 130–1. **24** Frances Power Cobbe, 'The Celt of Wales and the Celt of Ireland', *Cornhill Magazine* 36 (1877), p. 670. **25** Cobbe, *Life*, i, p. 141. **26** Peacock, *Theological and ethical writings*, p. 160. **27** Cobbe, *Life*, ii, p. 331. **28** Frances Power Cobbe, 'A French theist', *Theological Review*, 2 (1865), reprinted in Frances Power Cobbe, *Darwinism in morals and other essays* (London: Williams and Norgate, 1872), p. 130. **29** See, for instance, the list of offenders Cobbe draws up in 'Vivisection, its two-faced advocates', *Contemporary Review* 41 (1882). **30** Cobbe, 'Rights of man', pp 588–9. **31** Cobbe, 'Celt of Wales', p. 676. **32** Cobbe, 'Women in Italy', p. 373.

issues most urgently important to her: she maintains that Irishmen (at least as long as they remain on native soil), 'of all classes are proverbially kind and even chivalrous to their women' and that they are 'more kind to animals generally than the English peasantry'.[33] She boasts of the fact that not a single license for vivisection has been applied for in her native country. It is also clear that her experience in teaching underprivileged children in Bristol, her first job after leaving Ireland, compared unfavourably to teaching Irish children, who were much quicker to understand a joke, a disappointment to the witty Cobbe, however earnest her compensatory claims for the English child's superior retention of knowledge.[34] However, she sees this same kindly, vibrant people as displaying 'a predisposition towards occasional outbursts of insane violence, fanaticism and treachery', as she observes in 'The Fenians of Ballybogmucky', an essay that also compares the Irish to the 'Hindoo and the Negro', who is 'treacherous and ferocious for his brief hour of frenzy beyond, perhaps, what a Saxon well may be'.[35] As undeniably offensive as these passages are, it is important to note the qualifier 'occasional', the fact that frenzy is 'brief', at the same time though, while this 'predisposition' is one found in a population 'habitually mild, warm-hearted, docile, religious' – and she does commend the warm humanity and generosity of the Irish in other texts, even if she feels such qualities are squandered[36] – both good and bad qualities are finally assigned to racial factors.

In her writings concerned most centrally with Ireland, however, including the early sections of her autobiography, Cobbe never fails to acknowledge that Ireland has been wronged by England, that those wrongs are 'without excuse', and that the country's problems stem from this fact.[37] One of her most startling articulations of this appeared in an 1866 essay, 'The Fenian "Idea"': 'Irishmen lay under disabilities, political, social, and ecclesiastical, so severe and numerous that it really seems to have been a question what they were expected to do except to break some of these arbitrary laws, and so incur some cruel penalty.'[38]

---

33 Cobbe, 'Wife-torture', pp 58–9; Cobbe, 'Celt of Wales', pp 671–2; Cobbe, *Life*, i, p. 163. **34** Cobbe, *Life,* i, p. 146; on the wit of Irish children versus the English student's more 'durable' intelligence; Cobbe, 'Celt of Wales,' p. 666, judges the 'Irish mental machinery better oiled than English', and compares the English mind to the Celt's, even more unflatteringly, though less explicitly, through the use of 'beef' as an adjective, when she says, '[t]he Celt may be silly but never beef-witted'. **35** Frances Power Cobbe, 'The Fenians of Ballybogmucky', *Argosy* (1865), reprinted in Frances Power Cobbe, *Hours of work and play* (London: Trübner, 1867), pp 257–8. **36** See Cobbe, *Life*, i, pp 33, 138; Cobbe, 'Celt of Wales', pp 668, 672–3; Cobbe, 'Wife-torture', pp 58–9. **37** See Cobbe, 'Celt of Wales', p. 665, in which she states that Ireland's problems are the result of wrongs committed by England, specifically in this case the deracination of native culture; see also Frances Power Cobbe, 'The Fenian "Idea"', *Atlantic Monthly* 17 (1866), reprinted in Cobbe, *Hours*, p. 118, in which she admits that 'the real wrongs inflicted by England upon Ireland are probably as bad as ever disgraced the history of a conquest, in itself without excuse'; Cobbe, *Life*, i, p. 5, in which she recalls with pride her eighteenth-century ancestor, Archbishop Cobbe, who 'contended vigorously against the penal laws'. **38** Cobbe, 'Fenian "Idea"', p. 119.

Though she angrily condemns Irish ingratitude for improving efforts made by
sympathetic landlords, like her father, Cobbe's essays on Fenianism are distinguished more by dismay and regret than anger, and she sees the Irish falling into
the same kind of error that has led traditional Christianity astray, that is, an over-
reliance on the fragile human construct of history for central articles of faith, a
disabling belief in myths and stories, in the illusions of memory. In the case of
the Irish, this meant that they inhabit

> a world of […] unreal splendours regretted in the past and utterly unreal
> and impossible future hopes. They neither see where England has actu-
> ally wronged Ireland heretofore, nor how her Constitution opens to
> them now […] the lawful means of obtaining all just redress […] they
> can desire. Instead of this, they are still talking of Tara and Kincora, of
> Ollamh Fodhla and Brien Boiromhe.[39]

In the words of Sandra Peacock, 'for Cobbe, history was a feeble prop for both
Christian pretensions and Irish delusions.'[40]

The Irish peasant's regrettable flaws, then, are the same that afflict the faith
of Cobbe's childhood, from which she never fully withdrew her deepest emotional and even intellectual allegiances.[41] Like imperfectly healed scars, the com-
missures joining the affective and the ideological thicken and warp when the
two causes to which Cobbe devoted her adult life, women and animals, are
metaleptically transformed into the 'wronged' Celt, as happens occasionally in
other texts. For instance, in her autobiography, Cobbe takes issue with the case
against granting women equal rights that typically proceeds by asking why there
has never been a female Shakespeare. She dismisses the question by arguing that
a 'Celt claiming equal representation with a Saxon, *or any representation at all,*
might just as fairly be challenged to explain why there has never been a Celtic
Shakespeare or a Celtic Tennyson.'[42] In an essay written in the same year on
behalf of animal rights, the 'despised animal' is compared to the persecuted Irish,
a comparison that follows one of Cobbe's curious justifications of fox hunting.[43]
It is moments such as these that reveal the cause of animal protection, the final
campaign claiming her considerable rhetorical energies, to be the most deeply
riven, most compromised by contradictions, the most revealing, perhaps, of the
sympathies at war for Cobbe since the days of her privileged yet powerless
daughterhood.[44] The powerlessness to intervene in violence and the resultant

---

39 Ibid., p. 123. **40** Peacock, *Theological and ethical writings,* p. 167. **41** Ibid., p. 254, speaking
of Cobbe's late career, suggests that an '[e]vangelical palimpsest has clearly re-emerged';
Larson, 'Where is the woman?', p. 124, detects, from as early as *Broken lights,* 'superlative
moments in her discourse' when 'Bibliolatry and Christolatry, scourged but not destroyed,
sneak back into Cobbe's temple in disguise.' **42** Cobbe, *Life,* ii, p. 526 (italics in the original). **43** Cobbe, 'Ethics of zoophily', p. 506. **44** See Margot Gayle Backus, *The gothic family
romance: heterosexuality, child sacrifice, and the Anglo-Irish colonial order* (Durham: Duke UP, 1999),

traumatic splintering of young Frances's identificatory impulses emerge most poignantly in her autobiography, written towards the end of her life. Hard upon a brusque dismissal 'of any comparison between the cruelty of field sports and the deliberate chamber sport of vivisection,' she admits that 'of course I disliked then, and always, hunting, coursing, and shooting; but as a woman, I was not expected to join in such pursuits, and I did not take it on myself to blame those who followed them,' a strikingly uncharacteristic retreat into 'feminine', child-like passivity. She says that though she gave up fishing herself, 'angling scarcely comes under the head of cruelty at all and is perfectly right and justifiable when the fish are wanted for food and are killed quickly'. Yet when watching the 'bright creatures,' she 'say[s] in [her] heart a little thanksgiving on their behalf instead of trying to catch them,' perhaps seeing in the contingency of their free-dom a reflection of her own.[45]

Marian Scholtmeijer has suggested that 'if the object of feminism is to defeat androcentric culture, then animals offer an ideational model for ontological defiance'.[46] The complex and multiple ontologies Cobbe at once inhabited and defied may account for her anxiously overdetermined vivisector, who figures as, simultaneously, and somewhat confusedly, the brutal wife-beater, the heartless slave-owner, the Caliban-like savage familiar from imperial typology, the slick, arriviste professional, as well as the wicked priest of the Spanish Inquisition, and is associated with republicanism and the fall of the Second Empire.[47] Cobbe's anti-physician discourse was rooted not only in an abhorrence of the rising pro-fessional middle class, associated with scientific progress, but also in her inerad-icable religious convictions: a Christian distaste for scientific materialism, the privileging of the body over the soul, as well as a racialized animus against Catholicism. Even her impassioned rhetoric on behalf of the most helpless vic-tims of unchecked materialism is potentially undone by a version of the doc-trine of election. Not every animal is saved. Cattle are denied the sympathy and protection extended most urgently to dogs and horses; Cobbe accords those

---

for the complexities of identity the Anglo-Irish child negotiates, p. 76.   **45** Cobbe, *Life*, ii, pp 561, 560.   **46** Marian Scholtmeijer, 'The power of otherness: animals in women's fiction', in Carol J. Adams and Josephine Donovan (eds), *Animals and women* (Durham: Duke UP, 1995), p. 232.   **47** The frequency of such analogies prevents a full account here, but for some exam-ples of comparisons between vivisector and wife-beater, see Cobbe, 'Criminals, idiots, women, and minors', *Fraser's Magazine* 78 (1868), pp 783, 793, fn; and Cobbe, 'Wife-torture', pp 64, 72; slave owner: Cobbe, 'Zoophily', p. 280; and Cobbe, *Red flag*, p. 4; savage and 'mon-ster': Cobbe, 'Wife-torture', p. 65; Cobbe, 'Rights of man', p. 597; and Cobbe, *Life*, ii, p. 606; middle-class professional: Cobbe, 'Rights of man', pp 588–9; Cobbe, 'Zoophily', p. 283; and Cobbe, *Life*, ii, p. 607; priest of the Spanish Inquisition: Frances Power Cobbe, 'Mr Lowe and the Vivisection Act', *Contemporary Review* 29 (1877), p. 340; and Cobbe, 'Zoophily', p. 288. One scientist whose irredeemably evil nature is explained by Cobbe identifying him as a red Italian is Dr Schiff of Tuscany; see Cobbe, *Life*, ii, pp 563–4. Significantly, she refers to vivi-section in this same text as 'hydra-headed', a pejorative conventionally used to describe the restless mob, p. 632.

metonyms of the Anglo-Irish world special status. Disapproving of 'vegetarian error', she believes, '[w]e may slay cattle for food,'[48] but extols those 'creatures we love and who return our affection,' specifically the 'noble horse and friendly dog,' those creatures to be counted foremost among 'the orders of animals [to whom] we are in a much nearer relation, for these are the servants given us expressly by God, and fitted with powers and instincts precisely suiting them to meet our wants,'[49] a placing of animals in divinely-ordered service to humanity that would seem to be giving succour to the enemy. She insists that 'till a man has learned to feel for all his sentient fellow-creatures, whether inhuman or in brutal form, of his own class and sex and country, or of another, he has not yet ascended the first step towards civilization,'[50] yet sees no inconsistency in constructing her own elaborate 'scale of sensibility' to determine levels of obligations to people and animals alike. Even as she inveighs against the latitude granted male doctors to gleefully torture women and animals, hunting and other masculinist field sports identified with the Ascendancy are spared her criticism, are, in fact, defended, if somewhat unconvincingly. She claims it would be 'absurd and Quixotic to interfere with the vivisector if he never did anything worse to animals than the sportsman or farmer do every day,' that it is illogical to compare 'fox hunting, rabbit guns and Strasbourg geese' to 'the cutting up of living dogs and cats in a laboratory',[51] and that 'fox hunting and coursing and duck-shooting' may be excused on the basis that 'the sympathy of the sportsman is with his hounds and horse, or his grey-hound or retriever'.[52] In a discussion of another pair of actively suffragist, animal-loving, Anglo-Irish women, the novelists Somerville and Ross, Bi-ling Chen sees their representations of the fox hunt as 'expos[ing] the fatal power the privileged have over the underprivileged'.[53] What, then, does it mean for Cobbe to deny the fox redemption?

48 Cobbe, 'Rights of man', p. 598; this assertion follows a story of her father's from the Mahratta wars, when he witnessed 'various revolting scenes of famine, wherein the sacred cows of the Hindoo temples were standing gorged to repletion [...] while the starving population lay dying and dead of hunger all around', p. 592. It is worth remembering that Cobbe was a witness to the Irish famine.   49 Cobbe, 'Mr Lowe', p. 343; Cobbe, 'Ethics of zoophily', p. 503; Cobbe, 'Rights of man', p. 601; this last essay refers to horses as those 'noblest and most sensitive of creatures', p. 588, and devotes several paragraphs to the unparalleled virtues of the dog, which Cobbe pronounces 'peculiarly beneficent', 'endowed with a capacity for [...] devotion whose parallel we must seek only in the records of the purest human friendship', endowed with 'wondrous instincts', and 'evidence of the Creator's goodness', pp 601–2.   50 Frances Power Cobbe, 'Dogs whom I have met', *Cornhill Magazine* 26 (1872), p. 977.   51 Cobbe 'Mr Lowe', pp 345, 342.   52 Cobbe, 'Zoophily', p. 287.   53 Bi-ling Chen, 'De-mystifying the family romance: a feminist reading of Somerville and Ross's *The big house of Inver*', *Notes on Modern Irish Literature* 10 (1998), p. 17.

From Templeglantine to the Golden Temple: religion, empire, and Max Arthur Macauliffe

TADHG FOLEY

This essay addresses aspects of the role of religion in colonial situations, especially some of the problems raised by religious conversion in such a context. It will focus on the extraordinary example of Max Arthur Macauliffe, a native of Limerick, who became a judge in the Indian Civil Service, converted to the Sikh religion, and did the classic translation of the *Granth*, the sacred book of the Sikhs, into English.

In the discourse of colonization (to be distinguished from that of colonialism) in the nineteenth century, the enterprise was frequently conceived of in missionary terms. Indeed, religious missionaries were seen, and saw themselves, as being, unproblematically, adjuncts to secular colonization. Imperial attitudes to indigenous religions varied generally from outright hostility to grudging toleration. From the foundation of the National Colonization Society in 1830, which propagated the ideas of Edward Gibbon Wakefield, colonization was theorized and justified totally in economic terms. Though there was occasional semantic slippage, a 'colony' was primarily a people rather than a place. A colony was a group of, say, British people who abandoned their 'home' for, in effect, 'a home away from home.' It was the economic, political, social, and cultural destiny of this colony that was almost the only focus of the discourse of colonization. The cultural fate of indigenous peoples was of little or no analytical, or indeed any other, importance. They were seen variously as natural hazards, impediments to the march of empire, or as potential 'labour' when rescued from their 'savagery' or 'barbarity'.

The National Colonization Society engaged in two related activities: the promotion of 'systematic colonization' rather than sporadic and random emigration, and the theorization of colonization by means of the new 'science' of political economy. The Society complained that colonization was once a noble, even heroic, activity engaged in by the highest in the land; now the colonies were used, in the words of Charles Buller, for 'shovelling out paupers' or as dumping grounds for criminals. The idea of colonization was to 'plant' new English nations abroad ('plantation' was an earlier name for colonization), so the colony had to be its exact 'representative', a child of the 'Mother Country', complete with family resemblances. But with the emigration of, overwhelmingly, members of the lower classes and with convict colonization (planting with 'nettle-seed', as Archbishop Richard Whately of Dublin, a member of the

Society, picturesquely put it in 1832),[1] the new 'English' nations would scarcely be clones of the original stock but rather a 'monstrous family'.[2] What the Society advocated, as against this horizontal segment of plebeian British society, was a vertical cross-section, ideally including representatives of all classes.

The original function of missionaries was to service the colony, that is, the settlers. John Elliot Cairnes stated that the 'grand object' of the governments of England in its early period of colonization or 'plantation' [1492–1776] was to 'enforce uniformity' of religion at home.[3] But a variety of religions was exported to the colonies, such as puritanism to New England, Quakerism to Pennsylvania, and Roman Catholicism to Maryland, while in Virginia and Carolina, the Church of England was established by law. The religious belief prevailing in a colony was reflected in its legislative assembly and embodied in its laws.[4] However, according to Herman Merivale, 'With unity of religious belief at home, such questions need not be debated; but in the present condition of the British community they become of most pressing and practical interest.'[5] In the latter part of the nineteenth century, with the predicted domination of the doctrine of free trade and the apparently irreversible movement towards colonial self-government, the economic and political bonds which had 'unified' the empire had, in the view of many, to be replaced by cultural bonds. In the words of Cairnes, 'Instead of a great political, we shall be a great moral, unity; bound together no longer indeed by Imperial ligaments supplied from the Colonial Office, but by the stronger bonds of blood, language, and religion.'[6] According to Merivale and others, the imperial and colonial governments also had a duty of promoting the 'civilization' of native tribes in the colonies. He claimed that in history 'no instance can be shown of the reclaiming of savages by any other influence than that of religion.'[7] This view was generally accepted by the colonizers; the only debate centred on whether the natives should be civilized before being Christianized or vice versa. The spectre of conversion in the other direction was rarely, if ever, broached in these texts.

In Britain, enthusiasts for *laissez-faire* often neglected to apply their doctrine to the relationship between religion and the state. It is sometimes difficult to distinguish between a principled liberal distaste for church establishment and a calculated pragmatism fearful of its possible consequences. State support for churches, ranging from full establishment to aid of various kinds, did not neces-

1 Quoted in John Elliot Cairnes, 'Colonization and colonial government,' in Tom Boylan and Tadhg Foley (eds), John Elliot Cairnes, *Collected works,* 6 vols (London and New York: Routledge, 2004), iii, *Political essays,* p. 29. I am extremely grateful to Dr Maureen O'Connor for the unstinting help she has given me with this essay. **2** Ibid., p. 25, quoting Samuel Hinds, bishop of Norwich. **3** Cairnes, 'Colonization and colonial government', p. 19. **4** Ibid., pp 18–19. **5** Herman Merivale, *Lectures on colonization and colonies, delivered before the University of Oxford in 1839, 1840, and 1841* (London: Longman, Green, Longman, and Roberts, 1861), p. 599. **6** Cairnes, 'Colonization and colonial government', p. 58. **7** Merivale, *Colonization and colonies,* p. 294.

sarily have the same consequences at 'home' and in the colonies. Writing before the disestablishment of the Church of Ireland, Merivale observed that endowment would make other churches more tenacious of their own faith and could provide a 'bond of union to innumerable sects, which have no natural motive for seeking each other's alliance, to combine civil with ecclesiastical opposition [...] to unite all the scattered force of the majority against the governing body.'[8] While there was much truth in this in 'old' (that is colonizing) countries, 'every part of it applies with tenfold force to the circumstances of new ones,' while, 'dissent itself is materially changed in its character by transplantation. Sects acquire in a more marked degree the external character of churches.'[9] 'It would,' concluded Merivale, 'be extremely difficult, and of very doubtful policy, to establish and endow a branch of the national Church, under such circumstances, even in colonies not possessing a free government.'[10] By 1860, he noted that state aid had been 'almost wholly withdrawn from the service of religion in the colonies.'[11]

In 1869, in conformity with the notion of 'governing Ireland according to Irish ideas,' Gladstone disestablished the Church of Ireland. In Britain, Newman and some of his colleagues from the Oxford Movement, as converts to Catholicism were, not surprisingly, opposed to the control of religion by the state. But in the context of Sikhism and India, Macauliffe strongly defended the doctrine of Erastianism. Rejecting religious *laissez-faire*, he described Sikhism as a 'comparatively young religion',[12] and so, in terms of Mill's 'infant industry' argument, in need of state protection. Opposing the civil policy of 'religious neutrality',[13] he believed that priests and religious leaders should be 'kept in proper subordination to civil authority,' though for him this meant that the state had a reciprocal duty of protection.[14] According to Macauliffe some religions 'make for loyalty and others for what we may call independence. Some religions appear to require state support, while others have sufficient vitality to dispense with it.'[15] He claimed that just as Buddhism without state support had 'completely lost its hold in India, so it is apprehended that without State support Sikhism will also be lost in the great chaos of Indian religious systems.'[16] Popular Hinduism seemed so diverse, complicated, and contradictory that it almost defied analysis. As Tony Ballantyne puts it, '[l]ike the jungle it was so often compared to, Hinduism seemed wild, exuberant and threatening to nineteenth-century observers.'[17]

8 Ibid., p. 601.   9 Ibid.   10 Ibid., p. 602.   11 Ibid., p. 607, footnote.   12 Max Arthur Macauliffe, 'The Sikh religion under Banda and its present condition', *Calcutta Review*, 73 (1881), pp 155–68, reprinted in Darshan Singh (ed.), *Western image of the Sikh religion: a source book* (New Delhi: National Book Organisation, 1999), pp 269–84; p. 283, and reproduced in Max Arthur Macauliffe, *The Sikh religion: its gurus, sacred writings and authors*, 6 vols (1909; Delhi: Low Price Publications, 1998), 'Introduction', i, p. lvii.   13 Macauliffe, *Sikh religion*, 'Preface,' i, p. xxv.   14 Macauliffe, 'Sikh religion under Banda', p. 271.   15 Macauliffe, *Sikh religion*, 'Preface', i, p. lv.   16 Ibid., i, p. lvi.   17 Tony Ballantyne, *Orientalism and race: Aryanism in the British empire* (Basingstoke and New York: Palgrave, 2002), p. 101. I am very grateful to Dr Ballantyne for his expert advice and encouragement when he taught at NUI, Galway.

Max Arthur Macauliffe is a name unknown in the west. It does not appear in the *Dictionary of national biography* and, though he died in England, he is not mentioned in *Who was who?* In his 1999 'source book', *Western image of the Sikh religion*, an anthology of writings on Sikhism by western writers from the eighteenth to the twentieth centuries, out of twenty essays, the editor, Darshan Singh, reprinted no fewer than seven by Macauliffe.[18] A contemporary authority, W.H. McLeod, speaks with surprise of the 'paucity of scholarly studies of Macauliffe's contribution,' though he was a prominent reformer of nineteenth-century Sikhism and he produced the classic translation of the *Guru Granth Sahib*, the holy book of the Sikhs. This translation was contained in what McLeod described as Macauliffe's 'famous and enduring work', *The Sikh religion: its gurus, sacred writings and authors*, published in six volumes in 1909 by the Clarendon Press, Oxford, and running to almost 2,500 pages.[19] Apparently it has never gone out of print. Harbans Singh, one of the few scholars who have written on Macauliffe, described him as 'a young English [*sic*] civilian' whose translation was the result of a 'sustained and monumental labour of love,' a 'work of recognized excellence and dignity' which, over the years, had been 'a beacon in the Sikh literary world.' According to Singh, Macauliffe's translation of the Sikh scriptures and his lives of the Gurus still remained 'unsurpassed':

> For as long as there is anyone wanting to explore this faith through the medium of the English language, Max Arthur Macauliffe's name will live […]. He is today remembered in the Punjab with much affection and reverence as an example of a civilian who […] devoted himself to research and learning for the restoration or interpretation of some aspect of the Eastern culture.[20]

His work made the Sikh religion 'more extensively known and created among its votaries a new intellectual ferment. The publication in 1909 of *The Sikh religion* laid the foundation of Sikh literature in English.'[21]

Macauliffe's embrace of 'Indian ideas' was such that he converted to the Sikh religion and was a leading member of Tat Khalsa, the western-influenced radical section of the Singh Sabha reform movement, founded in Amritsar in 1873. Though his translation was undoubtedly uncritical, according to McLeod, 'its influence has been profound. No other work has so effectively instructed western readers about Sikhism, with the result that the Tat Khalsa interpretation of the Sikh faith and community has been firmly fixed in the western understanding.'[22]

---

18 Singh (ed.), *Western image, passim*. 19 W.H. McLeod, 'II. Religious studies in the UK: Profile (9): Max Arthur Macauliffe (September 29, 1837–March 15, 1913),' *Occasional papers: British association for the study of religions*, 78 (1996), pp 6–12. 20 Harbans Singh, 'English translation of the Sikh scriptures – an arduous mission of a Punjab civilian,' in K.S. Bedi and S.S. Bal (eds), *Essays on history, literature, art and culture: presented to Dr M.S. Randhawa on his sixtieth birthday by his friends and admirers* (New Delhi: Atma Ram, 1970), p. 139. 21 Ibid., p. 144. 22 McLeod, 'Macauliffe',

All commentators on Macauliffe are mistaken about the date and exact place of his birth, and none of them is aware that the original version of his name was Michael McAuliffe. He was born in Glenmore, Monagea, Co. Limerick, on 11 September 1838. He was educated at Glenmore and Templeglantine schools (his father taught at both schools, becoming headmaster at the latter), at Springfield College, Ennis, Co. Clare, and at Queen's College Galway, where he graduated in languages in 1860. In 1862 he joined the Indian Civil Service and was posted to the Punjab, where he eventually became a judge. Based in Amritsar, he began translating the *Granth* into English; in 1893 he resigned from his official position to engage full-time in this great enterprise. Harbans Lal states that, as well as this *magnum opus*, Macauliffe published widely over almost forty years and spoke before gatherings of scholars in India, Italy, France, and England.[23] He died in London on 15 March 1913.

An almost exclusively culturalist postcolonial theory finds it difficult to deal with a colonial regime that can celebrate an indigenous system of belief in the interest of its own political and economic ambitions. In the case of the Sikhs, not only was subaltern speech allowed, it was in many cases manifestly encouraged. It is understandable that one might be suspicious of an imperial trajectory that begins with the denigration and ends with the glorification of the 'other'. This was a divide-and-conquer strategy, a 'killing with kindness', which was linked to the incorporation of Sikh military prowess as guardians of the Raj. In his valuable book, *Orientalism and race: Aryanism in the British empire*, Tony Ballantyne's project is to decentre the empire, seeing it as a complex network, a web instead of a spoked wheel. He plays down the dominance of the centre over the peripheries and emphasizes the agency of the colonies especially in the construction of knowledge. According to Ballantyne, '[l]ate eighteenth-century Orientalists imbued by cosmopolitanism and convinced by the unity of humanity, found many affinities between Hindu and Christian belief.'[24] This is doubtlessly true. But surely the purpose of this homage to Hinduism is the political and economic subjugation of Hindus. Though Ballantyne's targets are Edward Said and Gauri Viswanathan, his own perspective is basically culturalist, not acknowledging that the celebration of, indeed the complete identification with, a culture (as in Macauliffe's case) is not incompatible with, indeed may well be one of the best modes of achieving, political domination. As in the oriental art of judo, the opponents' own strength and weight are used to defeat them.

In language that recalls Sir Henry Maine's reiterations of the trope of the 'timeless East', with its 'darkness', its 'night', its 'torpor', its 'sleep', and its doubtless dogmatic 'slumber' – a vision of India as a stagnant and unchanging society communicated to thousands of young men entering the Indian Civil Service[25]

p. 10. **23** Harbans Lal, 'The western gateway to Sikhism: the life and works of Max Arthur Macauliffe', in Kerry Brown (ed.), *Sikh art and literature* (London and New York: Routledge, 1999), pp 129–30. **24** Ballantyne, *Orientalism and race*, p. 117. **25** Ibid., p. 52.

– Macauliffe concluded his essay, 'How the Sikhs became a militant people', with these words regarding the Sikh Gurus:

> In them the East shook off the torpor of ages, and unburdened itself of the heavy weight of ultra-conservatism which has paralysed the genius and intelligence of its people. Only those who know India by actual experience, can adequately appreciate the difficulties the Gurus encountered in their efforts to reform and awaken the sleeping nation [...] I am not without hope that when enlightened nations become acquainted with the merits of the Sikh religion, they will not willingly let it perish in the great abyss in which so many creeds have been engulfed.[26]

Macauliffe saw the Sikhs as India's indigenous 'English'. He summed up 'some of the moral and political merits' of the Sikh religion as follows:

> It prohibits idolatry, hypocrisy, caste exclusiveness, the concremation of widows, the immurement of women, the use of wine and other intoxicants, tobacco-smoking, infanticide, slander, pilgrimages to sacred rivers and tanks of the Hindus; and it inculcates loyalty, gratitude for all favours received, philanthropy, justice, impartiality, truth, honesty, and all the moral and domestic virtues known to the holiest citizens of any country.[27]

Central to Macauliffe's later thinking was the view that Sikhism was independent of Hinduism, in western terms, a 'reformation' of it, indeed, the Anglicanism of the Orient.[28] He wrote, however, in 1881 that '[n]otwithstanding the exertions of the gurus, the Sikhs of the Punjab have now completely relapsed into idolatry, and [...] their worship in all respects resembles that of the Hindus.' But, he claimed, the Hindu corruptions of the religion of Nanak and Gobind were now 'bitterly deplored by all educated and intelligent Sikhs'.[29] He saw 'a wonderful analogy between the spiritual condition of Europe and Asia' in the middle ages:

> In Europe and Asia all learning was in the hands of the priesthood, and this admittedly led to serious abuses in both continents. But when things are at their worst they often mend. During the very period that Wycliffe and Luther and Calvin in Europe were warning men of the errors that had crept into Christianity, men like Kabir and Guru Nanak were denouncing priestcraft and idolatry in India, and with very considerable success. Most of the medieval saints who led the crusade against super-

26 Max Arthur Macauliffe, *How the Sikhs became a militant people* (1905), in Singh (ed.), *Western image*, pp 357–79; pp 378–9. This passage is reproduced almost word-for-word in Macauliffe, *Sikh religion*, 'Introduction', i, pp lxxxvii–iii.   **27** Macauliffe, *Sikh religion*, 'Preface', i, p. xxiii. **28** Max Arthur Macauliffe, *The holy writings of the Sikhs*, in Singh (ed.), *Western image*, pp 285–326; p. 286.   **29** Macauliffe, 'Sikh religion under Banda', p. 277.

stition founded sects which still survive, but the most numerous [and] powerful of all is the great Sikh sect founded by Baba Nanak.[30]

For Macauliffe Sikhism emphasized inner individual formation before outward rituals, structures, professions of faith. He quoted Milton, without naming him: God preferred '[b]efore all temples the upright heart and pure'.[31] He rejected the approaches of the Scribes who idolized the letter of the law as against its spirit and of the Pharisees who stood on ceremony and outward show and whose related belief in 'impurity and defilement' made them, like the Hindus, 'a sect apart'. Macauliffe then quoted Christ's statement that '[t]here is nothing from without a man that entering him can defile him, but the things which come out of him, these are the things which defile a man.' By this statement Christ 'emancipated his followers for ever from the thraldom of caste, and opened the portals of progress and enlightenment to his fellow creatures.'[32] Sikhs 'rejected the idolatry and superstitions of the Hindus, [and] taught that God was one alone.'[33] Sikhism rejected the excessive ritualism of the Hindus, on the one hand, and their excessive penances and austerities, on the other. 'Contrary to the practice of the ancient Indian ascetics,' Macauliffe wrote, 'the Gurus held that man might obtain eternal happiness without forsaking his ordinary worldly duties.'[34] Guru Nanak taught that 'a man who married, attended to his secular avocations, and neglected not at the same time the duties of his religion, was as surely pursuing the noble path as the cenobite and the anchorite.'[35]

While the majority of Sikhs in the 1870s would have seen Sikhism as derived from Hinduism,[36] Macauliffe spoke of Hinduism as being related to Sikhism as Roman Catholicism was to Protestantism. He saw Hinduism as

> like the boa-constrictor of the Indian forests. When a petty enemy appears to worry it, it winds round its opponent, crushes it in its folds, and finally causes it to disappear in its capacious interior [...] Hinduism has embraced Sikhism in its folds; the still comparatively young religion is making a vigorous struggle for life, but its ultimate destruction and assimilation in the body of the huge and resistless leviathan is inevitable. Notwithstanding the Sikh Guru's virulent denunciation of Brahmins, secular Sikhs, as we have seen, now rarely do anything without their assistance. Brahmins help them to be born, help them to wed, help them to die, and help their souls after death to obtain a state of bliss. And

30 Macauliffe, *Writings of the Sikhs*, p. 287. 31 Ibid., p. 289, quoting *Paradise lost*, i, l. 18. 32 Macauliffe, 'The Sikh religion', in Singh (ed.), *Western image*, pp 327–55; p. 337. Christ's statement is from Mark 7:15. 33 Macauliffe, *Holy writings*, p. 294. 34 Macauliffe, *Sikh religion*, 'Introduction', i, p. lxiv. 35 Max Arthur Macauliffe, 'The Diwali at Amritsar: the religion of the Sikhs', in Singh (ed.), *Western image*, pp 229–46; p. 237. 36 N.G. Barrier, 'Trumpp and Macauliffe: western students of Sikh history and religion', in Fauja Singh (ed.), *Historians and historiography of the Sikhs* (New Delhi: Oriental Publishers and Distributors, 1978), pp 166–85; pp 172–3.

Brahmins, with all the deftness of Roman Catholic missionaries in
Protestant countries, have partially succeeded in persuading the Sikhs to
restore to their niches the images of Devi, the Queen of Heaven, and of
the saints and gods of the ancient faith.[37]

Pace Isaiah, it would appear that the only circumstances in which the lion could
lie down with the lamb was when the lamb was securely lodged in the belly of
the lion.

The distinction between sacred and profane languages and the controversies
between Catholics and Protestants in the west about vernacular versions of the
sacred scripture had their analogues in the east. According to Macauliffe, the
'great Pandits and Brahmans of Hinduism communicated their instructions in
Sanskrit, which they deemed the language of the gods. The Gurus thought it
would be of more general advantage to present their messages in the dialects of
their age,'[38] to be taught to all people, castes, and classes. A Brahman, however,
had urged '[t]hat religious instruction ought not to be communicated to every
one, it being forbidden to instruct Sudars and women in the sacred lore.'[39] The
greatest religious reforms, in Macauliffe's view, had 'been effected by the laity.'
The clergy, 'apart from their vested interests', were 'too wedded to ancient systems, and dare not impugn their utility or authority.'[40]

The India Office had commissioned a German missionary, Dr Ernest
Trumpp, to translate the *Granth* into English but the partial translation, which
appeared in 1877, was unacceptable, indeed offensive, to many Sikhs. Macauliffe
undertook a new translation as an act of reparation to the Sikh people. It soon
became obvious that he could not combine this work with his official duties.
He received financial support from various Sikh sources that enabled him to
resign from the Indian Civil Service in 1893. He was bitterly disappointed when
his requests for patronage from the Punjab government were either rejected
outright or were responded to parsimoniously. He incurred extra expense by
employing *gyanis* (professional interpreters of the Sikh scriptures) to help him
with his great task, reputedly spending two lakhs [200,000] of rupees out of his
own pocket. For Macauliffe, writing and translation were collaborative acts and
the frontispiece to his *Sikh religion* consists of portraits of Macauliffe and of four
of his Sikh assistants. He worked closely with Sikh scholars, sending them every
line of his translations and revising his drafts in response to their recommenda-
tions. This, he believed, was an entirely novel plan, for not even the most eminent oriental scholars in the west submitted their translations to native scrutiny
nor were their works accepted by indigenous scholars. Clearly Macauliffe had
in mind here the most eminent of all western scholars of the orient, the
German-born professor of comparative philology at Oxford, Max Müller,

---

37 Macauliffe, 'The Sikh religion under Banda', p. 283.   **38** Macauliffe, *Sikh religion*,
'Introduction', i, p. l.   **39** Ibid. 'Sudars' or Sudras: lowest of four great Hindu castes.   **40** Ibid.,
i, p. liv.

whose translations of the Hindu scriptures had brought honour and glory to that religion in the west. Müller never visited India and presumably he never acquired the services of native scholars. When his work was completed, Macauliffe asked that it be scrutinized by a committee of Sikh scriptural scholars who suggested various emendations and gave it their seal of approval, both linguistic and theological. As well as translating the *Granth*, he decided to include biographies of the ten Gurus of Sikhism and of the Bhagats, the Sant poets whose works also appear in the *Granth*. It was the first published exegetical work on the Sikh scriptures as previous expositions had come down by word of mouth through, for instance, hereditary *gyanis*.

Trumpp's translation had been commissioned by the Secretary of State for India, but not so Macauliffe's. His *Lecture on the Sikh religion and its advantages to the state* dealt specifically with this question. According to N.G. Barrier:

> Sikh loyalty to the *raj* had been mentioned briefly in other essays, but the lecture especially underscored this dimension of recent Sikh experience. A 'bulwark of British power in the land', the Sikhs would continue to remain friendly allies. The only danger, said Macauliffe, was the erosion of Sikh power through inadequate education and a decline in population. The British consequently should take immediate steps to provide the Sikhs with more patronage. Implicit throughout the lecture was a message that such support also should be extended to Macauliffe.[41]

Though Maculiffe saw his labours as serving the political interests of the Sikhs, he by no means saw them as anti-imperial. Indeed, his public lecture, 'How the Sikhs became a militant people', was presided over by no less a figure than Lord Kitchener of Khartoum. In the introduction to *The Sikh religion,* he enumerated some of the 'advantages of the Sikh religion to the State'.[42] He stated that according to Guru Gobind Singh, the English would come and be joined by the Khalsa [initiated Sikhs], rule in the east as well as in the west:

> The combined armies of the English and the Sikhs shall be very powerful, as long as they rule with united councils. The empire of the British shall vastly increase, and they shall in every way obtain prosperity [...] Then in every house shall be wealth, in every house religion, in every house learning, and in every house happiness.[43]

It was, continued Macauliffe, 'such prophecies as these, combined with the monotheism, the absence of superstition and restraint in the matter of food,

---

41 Barrier, 'Trumpp and Macauliffe', p. 179. **42** Macauliffe, *Sikh religion,* 'Preface', i, p. xviii. **43** Ibid., i, p. xix. In other versions of this text Macauliffe has instead of 'in every house happiness', substituted 'in every house a woman'. There was, it seems, no woman in Macauliffe's house; certainly there is no indication that he ever married.

which have made the Sikhs among the bravest, the most loyal and devoted subjects of the British Crown.'[44] In a further passage he stated that

> It is admitted that a knowledge of the religions of the people of India is
> a desideratum for the British officials who administer its affairs and indi-
> rectly for the people who are governed by them so that mutual sympa-
> thy may be produced. It seems, at any rate, politic to place before the
> Sikh soldiery their Guru's prophecies in favour of the English and the
> texts of their sacred writings which foster their loyalty.[45]

Speaking of the Sikh religion and 'its prophecies in favour of the English',[46]
he said that recognition of Punjabi as an official or optional official language of
the Punjab, 'instead of the alien Urdu, would be a most powerful means of preserving the Sikh religion.'[47] A main function of his translation was to promote
'a knowledge throughout the world of the excellence of their religion' which
'would enhance even the present regard with which [Sikhs] are entertained, and
that thus my work would be at least of political advantage to them.'[48]

Ireland had an anomalous position in the nineteenth century as, after the Act
of Union of 1800, it was constitutionally a 'sister kingdom' and an intrinsic part
of the United Kingdom. Though officially a part of the apparatus of empire, in
most other respects Ireland was a colony in all but name. Both India and Ireland
were submitted to a secular, briskly modernizing dose of political economy,
securely underpinned by the doctrine of utilitarianism, to awaken them from
the torpor of indigenous, superstitious religious beliefs. Later in the century, the
universalist pretensions of these imperial schemes were impugned and seen as
'English ideas'; there was a renewed valorization of indigenous institutions,
practices, and values. In the popular idiom of the time, India and Ireland were
to be governed by, respectively, 'Indian' and 'Irish ideas'.

In the sixteenth century, Spenser saw the Irish as irredeemably other, suitable only for subjection; in the nineteenth century, Whately saw them as merely
historically backward rather than as ontologically inferior. They could be assimilated, especially through education, to proper English civilization, though this
involved the task of changing Irish character. The Irish national character he saw
as feminine and as such unsuited to modernity and Whately's project was nothing less than a re-gendering of Ireland. In the 1860s, Arnold delighted many a
Celt by not only accepting but celebrating their difference. His Celticism celebrated Ireland's femininity, but in the interest not of autonomy but of union, the
ideal marriage partner for the solid, rational, if prosaic, John Bull.[49]

---

44 Ibid., i, p. xix.   **45** Ibid., i, p. xxii.   **46** Ibid., i, p. xxiii.   **47** Ibid., i, p. xxiv.   **48** Ibid., i, p.
vii.   **49** See Timothy P. Foley, 'Public sphere and domestic circle: gender and political econ-
omy in nineteenth-century Ireland', in Margaret Kelleher and James H. Murphy (eds), *Gender
perspectives in nineteenth-century Ireland: public and private spheres* (Dublin: Irish Academic Press,
1997), pp 21–4.

Cairnes, in a series of articles in the *Economist* in 1865 found 'English theory' at variance with 'Irish ideas' about landed property and insufficient to explain Irish 'fact'.[50] In his review of James Anthony Froude's *The English in Ireland in the eighteenth century*, Cairnes wrote of the 'marked deference' Anglo-Indian rule

> has invariably shown towards the laws, institutions, and traditions of the people of India. Every custom, not positively criminal, has been respected; the native religions have not only been tolerated, but in many instances endowed; the Hindoo and Mohammedan codes have been incorporated into the jurisprudence administered in our courts; the land settlements are elaborate attempts made, with whatever success, certainly in good faith, to give effect to the ancient traditions and practices of the country. If this method of government has been found efficacious in India, why should it not have been attended with equal benefit to Ireland?[51]

Cairnes contrasted Froude's views unfavourably with those of Sir George Campbell: 'Mr. Froude says that no regard should be paid to Irish ideas and practices. Sir George Campbell tells us, on the contrary, to take Irish ideas and practices as the basis of our land legislation.'[52] In his 1868 pamphlet, *Ireland and England*, Mill declared that Ireland should be governed by Irish ideas. India, he wrote, was now governed 'with a full perception and recognition of its differences from England. What has been done for India has now to be done for Ireland.'[53] Justin McCarthy, in his *History of our own times*, has a chapter entitled 'Irish ideas'. The parliament, he wrote, 'which was called together in the close of 1868 was known to have before it this great task of endeavouring to govern Ireland according to Irish ideas.'[54] With Gladstone, the doctrine of governing Ireland according to Irish ideas had become official wisdom, especially as enshrined in the 1881 Irish Land Act.

The best known cultural version of this approach is Arnold's Celticism. While *Punch* and other organs, in the wake of Darwin's *The origin of species* (1859), were simianizing the Irish, Arnold, in his lectures published in 1867, when Fenianism was at its height, flattered Celts by finding them imaginative and sensitive. This love-bombing of the Celts, instead of the cold, legalistic Act of Union, called for a 'union of hearts', hegemony was to replace coercion, carrots were to replace sticks. This is the genesis of the doctrine of 'constructive Unionism'. When home

---

50 John Elliot Cairnes, 'Ireland in transition', in Boylan and Foley (eds), Cairnes, *Collected works*, vi, pp 208–50; p. 231. See also Thomas A. Boylan and Timothy P. Foley, *Political economy and colonial Ireland: the propagation and ideological function of economic discourse in the nineteenth century* (London and New York: Routledge, 1992), chapter 6. 51 John Elliot Cairnes, 'Froude's *English in Ireland*', in Boylan and Foley (eds), Cairnes, *Collected works*, vi, pp 324–44; pp 337–8. 52 Ibid., vi, p. 338. Campbell was an Indian civil servant whose book, *The Irish land act* (London: Trubner, 1869), greatly influenced Gladstone's 1870 Irish Land Act. 53 J.S. Mill, *Ireland and England* (1868), in John Stuart Mill, *Collected works*, 33 vols (Toronto: Toronto UP and London: Routledge & Kegan Paul, 1982), vi, pp 507–32; p. 519. 54 Justin McCarthy, *A history of our own times*, 4 vols (London: Chatto and Windus, 1881), iv, p. 257.

rule was later to be 'killed with kindness', the 'kindness' and not the 'killing' was emphasized. It should be noted that while Arnold was delivering these lectures at Oxford which popularized the gender-based distinction between rational, masculine Saxons and sensitive, feminine Celts, his colleague at Oxford, the celebrated oriental scholar, Max Müller, was deploying exactly the same set of categories with reference to India, distinguishing between the Aryan north, masculine, tall, militaristic, meat-eating, monotheistic, and the Dravidian south, effeminate, short, lazy, vegetarian, polytheistic. The Punjab, situated in the north, was the first home of the Aryans in India.[55] Macauliffe wrote that under the early Gurus the Sikh religion was 'a system of quietism' but that Guru Har Gobind was the first who gave 'a martial direction to the religion'. It was, however, 'in the person of Guru Gobind Singh that the Sikh religion acquired its highest martial character – a character which is still impressed on it, and which has rendered the Sikhs some of the finest soldiers of the East.'[56] He had written in one of his first essays that the 'meekness and passive submission of the religion of Nanak were changed under Har Gobind into independence and heroic activity.'[57] The indigenous peoples of colonized countries were almost invariably feminized by the imperial and colonial powers. However, in the case of the Sikhs, Macauliffe was anxious to emphasize their vigorous masculinity, indeed their military prowess and the corresponding muscularity of their religion; they were physically and spiritually worthy of being collaborators with the British in ruling India.

Like Matthew Arnold's flattering representations of the Irish, Macauliffe's magnificent contribution to Sikhism was also, and ultimately, in the interests of empire. Embracing Sikhism could be seen as ruling India by Indian ideas, though, of course, actual Indians would have had little involvement in the enterprise. But Macauliffe had it both ways. Seeing Sikhism as an oriental version of Protestantism, he could also claim to be ruling India by *English* ideas. Embracing the other, as in Oscar Wilde's prose poem on the subject of Narcissus, 'The Disciple', Macauliffe had the very great pleasure of embracing himself. The romance of empire was at once auto-erotic and homo-erotic. His fellow Irish, James and Margaret Cousins, converts to theosophy, who had emigrated to India, took a different position on empire. As Gauri Viswanathan puts it in her book, *Outside the fold: conversion, modernity, and belief,* James Cousins 'found himself drawn to the larger project of establishing the common foundations of Irish-Indian culture as the first step toward the overthrow of colonial rule in both countries.'[58] As the Sikhs got more interested in Indian nationalism, the British, for some reason, tended to lose interest in them and in their religion.

---

55 This north-south stereotype also came to be applied to Ireland: northern people were held to be industrious, with an eye for the main chance, and emotionally and linguistically reserved while southern people were seen as lazy, improvident, loose-lipped, and emotionally incontinent. **56** Macauliffe, *Holy writings*, p. 310. **57** Macauliffe, 'The rise of Amritsar and the alterations of the Sikh religion', in Singh (ed.), *Western image*, pp 247–68; p. 253. **58** Gauri Viswanathan, *Outside the fold: conversion, modernity, and belief* (Princeton: Princeton UP, 1998), p. 205.

Irish evangelicals and the British evangelical community, 1820s–1870s[1]

JANICE HOLMES

In the nineteenth century, the only schism to affect the Church of England was started in the 1830s by a group of Irish Anglican clergy and laity in the Wicklow mountains south of Dublin. The most spectacular display of religious fervour to occur within nineteenth-century British Protestantism originated in the hills of north Antrim. One of the leading evangelical conferences was run by an Irish clergyman and his wife. In 1874 the most famous American evangelists of the time, D.L. Moody and I.D. Sankey, spent over two months of their British campaign in Belfast and Dublin.

What links these events together is their association with evangelicalism, a movement of religious ideas that emerged in the opening decades of the eighteenth century and exercised a transformative influence on Protestantism in western Europe and America. This movement placed particular stress on a personal experience of God through 'conversion', the sole authority of the Bible and the atoning power of Christ's death on the cross. Convinced that believers were going to heaven, evangelicals were imbued with a powerful sense of assurance about their souls' future and, as a result, were driven by the desire to tell others about this 'good news'. The rise of evangelicalism in the eighteenth and nineteenth centuries, therefore, was accompanied by a massive increase in evangelistic activity and the proliferation of social and philanthropic endeavour.[2]

The spread of evangelicalism to Ireland was complicated by its demographic circumstances. Unlike England and north America, the majority of the Irish population was Catholic. The Church of Ireland was hampered by its at times excessively close relationship with the British state and the Presbyterians were preoccupied with internal wrangling over 'new light' theology. It was not until the 1780s that evangelicalism began to expand and by the middle of the nineteenth century, Irish Protestants, to a greater or lesser extent, had adopted an evangelical outlook.[3]

As a theological system, evangelicalism demanded a full commitment. Those who adhered to it were earnest and hard-working, deeply committed to pur-

1 I would like to acknowledge the support of the British Academy in the preparation of this chapter. 2 For a basic description of evangelical theology see David Bebbington, *Evangelicalism in modern Britain: a history from the 1730s to the 1980s* (London: Unwin Hyman, 1989), pp 1–10. 3 For the origins of evangelicalism in Ireland see David Hempton and Myrtle Hill, *Evangelical Protestantism in Ulster society, 1740–1890* (London: Routledge, 1992).

suing what they felt to be God's will. Their lives were governed by a strict routine of personal devotions, public worship and 'good works'. Thoughts, feelings and motives were monitored through a constant process of self-regulation and self-criticism. Such an intense spiritual commitment created a bond of allegiance with others who had had a similar experience. Evangelicals soon formed themselves into tightly-knit, cohesive communities, linked by the bonds of family, friendship and aspiration. These communities frequently superceded the geographical boundaries and denominational barriers that separated their members. Like-minded individuals throughout Britain, Ireland and America were sustained by letters and publications, by societies, conferences and meetings and by the work of a vast army of itinerant preachers.[4] These networks served to support and encourage, to disseminate information and to co-ordinate activity within the evangelical community itself. Other networks revolved around the fundamental evangelical belief in the necessity of conversion for those outside the evangelical frame. All were in agreement that 'lost sheep' needed to be 'found' and that it was their religious duty (as commanded by scripture) to bring them back into the fold. In Ireland, however, this conversionist impulse had controversial consequences. Because the majority of the Irish population was Catholic, not Protestant, by extension, any outwardly evangelistic activity was bound to involve Catholics, even if they were not deliberately targeted, which they quite often were. Accusations of proselytism and sectarian riots had serious implications for community relations and political stability and many historians have commented upon the critical role evangelicalism played in the polarization of Protestant and Catholic in the nineteenth century.

In Ireland, these two types of evangelical networks – the 'co-ordinative' and the 'conversionist' operated quited differently. Within 'co-ordinative' networks, the 'Irishness' of Ireland's evangelical community was largely disregarded. Shared religious values and theological emphasis superceded issues of national identity and sense of place. What mattered here was not one's secular but one's spiritual citizenship. Within 'conversionist' networks, however, Ireland's geographic distinctiveness and the presence of a large body of Irish Catholics meant that the relationship to British evangelicalism would always be a self-conscious one. British evangelicals could be massively ignorant about the religious situation in Ireland and veer widely off course in their ethnic and religious assumptions. For their part, Irish evangelicals could never quite hide their sense of religious isolation in what was so self-evidently a Catholic nation.

Irish Protestantism was not just linked to Britain through evangelical networks. Each of the main denominations owed its existence, in one way or another, to the expansion of British power in Ireland and, since the reformation

---

4 Although the evangelical community in the nineteenth century included North America and parts of continental Europe, for the purposes of this paper, I am confining its definition to Britain and Ireland.

of the sixteenth century, its association with the Protestant faith. All of them had, in varying degrees, both formal and cultural links to their British counterparts and saw themselves as operating within a denominational environment that spanned the Irish sea.

The Church of Ireland had the most formal connection to Britain. As the established church it was supported by the British state through an extensive system of endowments and tithes. This relationship was strengthened by the Act of Union in 1801 which united the Irish and English Churches into 'one Protestant Episcopal Church' and declared that its 'continuance and preservation [...] shall be deemed and taken to be an essential and fundamental part of the Union.'[5] Even before this legislative union, the Church of Ireland's doctrines, worship and discipline had mirrored those of the Church of England. It adhered to the Thirty-Nine Articles and used the Book of Common Prayer. After the union it was influenced by the Oxford movement and by the trend towards gothic architecture. Even though most of its manpower was largely Irish by the nineteenth century, many of its clergy felt more at home in England than in their Irish dioceses. When Richard Chenevix Trench was appointed archbishop of Dublin in 1856 he accepted the position as 'a matter of duty'. 'England is my world,' he said, 'the land of all my friends. The English church seems to me to feel full of life and hope and vigour, of which I see little in Ireland.'[6] Other members of the Church establishment also saw themselves as part of a wider Anglican community. In 1900, about 45 per cent of Irish divinity graduates could be found in English and overseas parishes.[7]

Given the strength of these links to England, the Church of Ireland maintained a reasonably separate identity. Despite the Articles of Union, it kept its own court of final appeal and its own Convocation. Most of its bishops and clergy were Irish born and educated. In the 1860s, only 10 per cent of Irish clergy had been educated outside Ireland.[8] Some of these men were keen to promote the idea, originating in the seventeenth century, that the Church of Ireland was a direct descendant of the early Irish church and not just a branch of the English body. In certain circles, the Church of Ireland as the church of St Patrick was thought a credible theory.[9]

Disestablishment, unsurprisingly, contributed to this feeling of institutional distinctiveness. According to R.B. McDowell, many 'never quite forgave

---

5 Alan O'Day and John Stevenson (eds), *Irish historical documents since 1800* (Dublin: Gill and Macmillan, 1992), p. 8. **6** Quoted in R.B. McDowell, *The Church of Ireland, 1869–1969* (London: Routledge Kegan Paul, 1975), p. 8. **7** Ibid., p. 85. **8** Ibid., p. 1. **9** Alan Ford, '"Standing one's ground": religion, polemic and Irish history since the reformation', in Alan Ford, James McGuire and Kenneth Milne (eds), *As by law established: the Church of Ireland since the reformation* (Dublin: Lilliput, 1995), pp 39–50; Fergal Grannell, 'Early Irish ecclesiastical studies', in Michael Hurley (ed.), *Irish Anglicanism, 1869–1969* (Dublin: Allen Figgis, 1970), pp 39–50; Desmond Bowen, *The Protestant crusade in Ireland, 1800–70* (Dublin: Gill and Macmillan, 1978), pp 50–3.

England' and the relationship between the two Churches in the 1870s has been described as 'tentative and spasmodic'.[10] The Irish Church then embarked on its own path, implementing revisions to the Book of Common Prayer that reflected its theological concerns, even if they did not alter its basic Anglican ethos. For the Church of Ireland, the weakness of its formal links to the Church of England and a sense of its Irish origins were not enough to overcome a shared religious culture, liturgical environment and clerical mobility. Not even disestablishment could shake its basic Anglicanism.

The Presbyterian Church in Ireland is frequently described as the 'eldest daughter' of the 'Old Kirk in Scotland'.[11] In 1642 Church of Scotland chaplains and elders attached to Munroe's army encountered Scottish migrants with Presbyterian leanings who had settled in Ulster with the plantation. They constituted the first Synod of Ulster to care for their religious needs.[12] Throughout the seventeenth and eighteenth centuries, Irish Presbyterianism relied heavily on 'the old mother' for ministerial provision, forms of worship and most importantly, theological creeds. Irish congregations followed the Westminster Confession of Faith and the Church of Scotland's Code of Discipline. Divisions that surfaced around the content and use of these forms, although rarely having any relevance in Ireland, were often replicated there. Changing theological fashions, like the growth of 'new light' ideas, also spread from Scotland to Ireland, primarily through the large number of Irish seminarians who attended Scottish universities. Most went to Glasgow where, in the mid eighteenth century, roughly one-third of the student body was Irish.[13]

In the nineteenth century, the Irish church developed into a fully-fledged denomination. This was demonstrated in 1840 when two of the largest branches of Irish Presbyterianism united to form a General Assembly. In 1853 it established its own theological training college and from then on, the majority of Irish ministerial candidates were educated at home. Between 1840 and 1870 of the 435 clergy ordained into the Irish church who had degrees, 306 had received them from Irish universities. Of the 674 ministers ordained during this period, 73 per cent served their entire careers in Ireland, only 14 went to Scotland and 20 to England; the rest went overseas.[14]

---

10 McDowell, *Church of Ireland*, p. 50; Gabriel Daly, 'Church renewal, 1869–1877', in Hurley (ed.), *Irish Anglicanism*, p. 35.   11 John Barkley, *A short history of the Presbyterian Church in Ireland* (Belfast: Publications Committee, Presbyterian Church in Ireland [1959]), p. 1; J.L. Porter, *Life and times of Henry Cooke, D.D., LL.D.* (Belfast: William Mullan, 1875), p. 274.   12 R.F.G. Holmes, *Our Irish Presbyterian heritage* (Belfast: Publications Committee, Presbyterian Church in Ireland, 1985), pp 26–8.   13 McBride, *Scripture politics: Ulster Presbyterians and Irish radicalism in the eighteenth century* (Oxford: Clarendon, 1998); Ian Hezlett, 'Students at Glasgow university, 1747–68', in W. Donald Patton (ed.), *Ebb and flow: essays in church history in honour of R.F.G. Holmes* (Belfast: Presbyterian Historical Society, 2002).   14 John M. Barkley, *Fasti of the General Assembly of the Presbyterian Church in Ireland, 1840–1870 (Part I)* (Belfast: Presbyterian Historical Society, 1986), pp 80–1; Ken Brown, 'Life after death? A preliminary survey of the

Even though its manpower and training was almost exclusively Irish, Irish Presbyterians actively cultivated their social and cultural links to the Scottish church. In 1836 the Church of Scotland readmitted Irish ministers, excluded since 1799, into 'ministerial communion'. In giving the official thanks of the Presbyterian Church in Ireland to the Scottish General Assembly, the Revd Henry Cooke extolled the historic link between the two bodies and testified to their shared resources and forms of worship. 'Though in different lands, and in different outward circumstances, we form, in spirit and communion, one Presbyterian Church.'[15] Within seven years, this alliance had shifted to the newly-formed Free Church of Scotland, but the pulpit exchanges, guest lectures and fund-raising tours continued unabated.

As the nineteenth century progressed, small cracks began to appear in this harmonious relationship. In the 1880s Scottish Presbyterians gave their support to Gladstone's home rule bill. For Irish Presbyterians, this was a shocking betrayal. In a letter to 'a friend in Scotland', the Revd Hugh Hanna enquired:

> Is it in reality so that when half a million Irish Presbyterians declare their solemn conviction that Mr Gladstone's policy would imperil Irish Protestantism, would be fatal to the best interests of Ireland, that any section of Scotch Presbyterians should support that policy, and array itself in antagonism to their kinsmen in Ireland? Is it possible that political partisanship can dominate all the considerations of a common lineage and a common faith, and that any part of Scotland would forsake its own flesh and blood to promote the policy and restore the power of a fallen leader, proposing the most dangerous projects to recruit his political fortunes?[16]

The pressure of political circumstances may have tempered, but they did not sever, the links between Irish and Scottish Presbyterians.

Irish Methodism also had strong links to Britain. Although drawing its original adherents from existing pietist groups in eighteenth-century Ireland, like the Huguenots, Palatines, Baptists and Quakers, they were soon incorporated into the wider Methodist community which had its origins in England with John Wesley. The early preachers and organizational meetings were overwhelmingly English in tone. Of the nine itinerant evangelists present at the first Irish 'Conference' in 1752, only one was Irish.[17] Wesley stationed his preachers with no regard for their ethnic origin, so it was in England that early Irish Methodists made their deepest impression.[18]

Irish Presbyterian clergy in the nineteenth century', *Irish Economic and Social History*, 22 (1995), p. 54. **15** Quoted in Porter, *Henry Cooke*, p. 273. **16** Quoted in Graham Walker, *Intimate Strangers* (Edinburgh: John Donald, 1995), p. 12. **17** Dudley L. Cooney, *The Methodists in Ireland* (Blackrock: Columba, 2001), pp 124–5. **18** Robert Gallagher, *Pioneer preachers of Irish Methodism* (Belfast: n.p., 1965), pp 150–64.

By the 1780s Irish Methodism had established itself as a separate entity. It was holding its own annual conference and the majority of its preachers were Irish born. By the nineteenth century it was responsible for making all its own strategic and financial decisions. Even so, Irish Methodists, like their Presbyterian counterparts, operated in a denominational environment where England (or Scotland) was the dominant partner. Even though the Irish conference was fully independent, until 1868, in order for its decisions to be legally binding, they had to be approved by the 'Delegate', the designated representative from the English conference. Although largely a ceremonial position, he was given the title of 'President' and presided over the Irish proceedings. Irish Methodists were eager to have their contributions to the wider Methodist community properly recognized. In his introduction to the *Life and letters of the Rev. William Smiley*, an Irish Methodist minister who never served outside Ireland, the Reverend Thomas McCullagh was at pains to point out to his potential English readership how extensive this contribution had been.

> Before the Act of Union had constituted the two islands the United Kingdom, the Methodism of Dublin and Cork was one with that of London and Bristol. By Wesley's *Deed of Declaration* provision is made for the perpetuated connection of the Methodism of Ireland with that of England. One of the most remarkable, in some respects extraordinary, of the early Methodist preachers was Thomas Walsh; one of the most distinguished scholars called to the work last century was Adam Clarke; one of the most honoured by Wesley of his assistants was Henry Moore; and the first President of the Conference after the death of Wesley was William Thompson. All these were born and born again in Ireland. Irish Methodism has co-operated with that of Great Britain from the earliest in the work of gospel propagandism beyond the sea [...] In 1769 Methodism was introduced into America by Irish emigrants, and ever since, by a continuous flow of emigration, the Methodism of Ireland has helped to enrich that of the United States and Canada.[19]

McCullagh's concern that British Methodism might lose interest in its Irish branch was clearly driven by the circumstances of the time, given he was writing in 1888. The desire for ongoing inclusion in a wider Methodist polity was, however, more than just a knee-jerk reaction to political circumstances. It was part of their denominational identity.

The last Protestant group, although technically not a denomination, also cultivated an institutional network that relied heavily on their British co-religionists. The Brethren (or Plymouth Brethren) emerged in Dublin among a group of

---

19 Mary H.H. Smiley, *The life and letters of the Rev. William Smiley* (London: T. Woolmer, 1888), pp xiv–xv.

Trinity College students and young Irish Anglican clergy. Anthony Groves, J.G. Bellett, John Nelson Darby and their friends began meeting together for prayer and Bible study in 1825. By 1827 they were 'breaking bread', drawn together by their ideas of Christian unity. All were unhappy with the divisions within British Protestantism and felt that the liturgical forms and membership restrictions within existing denominations were damaging to the spread of the gospel. They wanted to return to the style of worship practiced in the early Christian church and to this end eschewed an ordained clergy and a set form of service and practiced adult baptism. Similar ideas had emerged among individuals in Bristol, Plymouth and Barnstaple and by virtue of complex webs of personal contacts, these disparate groups were put in touch with each other and soon formed themselves into a loose collection of independent 'assemblies' or 'meetings'.[20]

By 1848, this coalition had split into two distinct groups: the Open, or Independent, Brethren, who followed Groves, and the Exclusives, who followed Darby. Exclusives had adopted a form of central authority whereby discipline was administered through a 'central meeting'. The Opens had no such structure. Each assembly was autonomous and responsible for its own preaching and discipline. Without any substantial denominational structures to hold them together, the Brethren relied heavily on informal networks to spread information and provide mutual encouragement, such as periodical publications and annual conferences. They also relied on a large body of lay evangelists who itinerated around the country to provide teaching, and to seek conversions. Even though the number of Brethren assemblies remained relatively small (in 1851 there were only 132 assemblies in England, 75 in Scotland and 48 in Ireland),[21] it, and the leaders associated with it, played a central role in the British evangelical scene far greater that their size would have warranted.

Irish Protestantism and its denominations were rooted in Britain and based on British models. As members of these denominations, Irish Protestants were shaped by the 'Britishness' of their denominational allegiances. Although each of the four denominational groups developed a greater structural identity as distinct religious institutions over the course of the nineteenth century, they all shared a subordinate relationship with their British co-religionists. For the most part they saw themselves, not as members of distinctly 'Irish' churches, but as members of a wider denominational network, one that incorporated family, friends and churches from other regions of the British isles, and at times, overseas, and one that shared common liturgical forms and denominational customs that were British in origin.

In the nineteenth century, the growth of evangelicalism as a movement of religious ideas began to cut across these denominational networks. Evangelica-

20 F. Roy Coad, *A history of the Brethren movement* (Exeter: Paternoster, 1976); Robert Baylis, *My people: the history of those Christians sometimes called Plymouth Brethren* (Wheaton, IL: Harold Shaw, 1997). 21 Baylis, *My people*, p. 29.

lism's theological emphases and its activist ethos began to bring like-minded individuals, regardless of denominational affiliation, together. Evangelicals were fundamentally pragmatic when it came to the work of conversion; they were prepared to work outside denominational structures in order to achieve results. As a result, an evangelical community that encompassed both Britain and Ireland began to emerge.

Within the co-ordinative networks of personal faith and community support, the distinctiveness of Irish evangelicals was rarely recognized. For all evangelicals, a personal experience of conversion was an essential part of their faith. Once saved, they were then expected to exhibit the 'fruits' of conversion in their daily lives, such as regular Bible reading and private devotions. In this respect, Irish evangelicals were no different than their English and Scottish counterparts. For example, James Morgan, one of the leading Irish Presbyterian ministers, described his and his brother John's conversion in classic evangelical terms. John, for unknown reasons had been

> brought under deep religious convictions [...] his spirit was sore vexed [... b]ut the day of deliverance came. God the Spirit who showed him his sins revealed the Saviour also, and he became a holy, happy Christian. When his own peace was established, he burned with zeal and anxiety for my salvation. I loved him exceedingly, and soon became awakened, enlightened, and quickened. I had no bitter or deep exercises, but was at once constrained by the love of Jesus.[22]

Anne Jocelyn and Theodosia Wingfield, aristocratic cousins and members of the Church of Ireland, exhibited, in their diaries and letters, the constant self-regulation that the evangelical life required. Anne's accusations of pride – 'at breakfast very proud towards one in heart' – vanity – 'my dress has been a great snare to me' – and sloth – 'I was too long at the garden today. I was unprofitable.' – reflected standard evangelical concerns to avoid 'worldliness' and use time to its best advantage.[23] Theodosia berated herself for the grief she felt at the death of her husband. 'I do not suppose,' she wrote a friend,

> there could be a stronger lesson of the vanity of every thing earthly, than to look at me, last year, and this. The prospects of happiness I seemed to set out with! And now, where are they? A living monument that man in his best estate is altogether vanity – and see how my heart, without my knowing it, was on earth [...] But I shall say no more, for these complaints only grieve my God, and annoy you.[24]

22 James Morgan, *Recollections of my life and times: an autobiography* (Belfast: William Mullan, 1874), p. 7. 23 Diary of Lady Anne Jocelyn, National Library of Ireland, 18,430. 24 Robert Daly (ed.), *Letters and papers by the late Theodosia A., Viscountess Powerscourt* (Dublin: J.S. Folds,

Such expressions of unworthiness, and a continual striving to do better, were feelings that evangelicals throughout Britain would have recognized and understood.

Co-ordinative networks operated most visibly to sustain the British evangelical community and to provide for its spiritual and structural needs. They had nothing to do with Ireland or Irish concerns and 'Irishness' was not a factor in the way Irish evangelicals were perceived by the evangelical community as a whole. For example, William Pennefather was born in Dublin in 1816 to a wealthy Anglican family with substantial political connections. He was educated in England but graduated from Trinity College in 1841. While a student he attended Dublin's centre of evangelical Anglicanism, Bethesda Chapel. He also got involved in efforts to promote the Protestant cause in Connemara and came into contact with the Revd Alexander Dallas and the Society for Irish Church Missions, a polemical group committed to the conversion of Irish Catholics.[25] However, Pennefather's career lay, not in carrying out the work of the second reformation, but in providing a service for the wider evangelical community. Appointed to Aylesbury in 1847, he soon transferred to Barnet and then to St Jude's in north London. Here he founded the Barnet (later renamed Mildmay) Conference, an annual gathering to promote co-operation between evangelicals of differing denominations, and a training home for deaconesses.[26] When Pennefather left Ireland, he left his 'Irishness', and any concern he may have had for Irish Protestantism, behind. His ministry was a supportive one, and within that context, his Irish origins were not important.

A similar disregard for Ireland's distinctiveness can be seen even when the co-ordinative work is located in Ireland. Even though most Brethren assemblies were located in England, one of the most important networking events in the evangelical calendar was the annual Dublin Believers' Meetings held in June. Established by two Quakers, William Fry, a solicitor, and Henry Bewley, a coffee merchant, this week-long series of meetings was held in Merrion Hall and designed to support full-time evangelical workers from across Britain. By the 1890s these meetings were hugely popular and had been attended by the leading names in the evangelical community including Reginald Radcliffe, a gentleman preacher, and Richard Weaver, the 'converted collier'.[27] Merrion Hall was itself a focal point for evangelical activity in Ireland in general and was visited throughout the second half of the nineteenth century by a stream of famous evangelicals.[28] The Dublin meetings were co-ordinative in their content and purpose; they were designed to encourage full-time evangelists. Their geographic location was a function of the enthusiasm of its founders (and of their status within the British evangelical community), not an outcome of their conversionist intent.

1839), p. 8. **25** Bowen, *Protestant Crusade*, pp 208–56. **26** Revd Robert Braithwaite (ed.), *The life and letters of the Rev. William Pennefather, B.A.* (London: John Shaw, [1878]). **27** *The Christian*, 11 June 1891, p. 21. **28** Merrion Hall Dublin. *Centenary: one hundred years of witness, 1863–1963* ([Dublin]: n.p., [1963]); *Jubliee Year. Brief history of Merrion Hall, Dublin, 1863–1913* (Dublin: n.p., [1913]).

In the nineteenth century it was possible for Irish evangelicals to operate within the British evangelical community without regard for their nationality or ethnic background. Their accounts of conversion and their efforts to live godly lives conformed to norms that were accepted and understood within the evangelical community as a whole. For Irish evangelicals who chose to exercise their talents in Britain, their place of birth was almost entirely disregarded. They were absorbed into the British networks and their Irishness, if indeed they had ever had any, was left entirely behind. Much of the reason for this was because these networks were meant to serve the evangelical community itself. Conversion experiences were private affairs and the conventions surrounding them were 'learned' through biographies and personal testimonies that were generated for internal consumption. Conferences were intended for those already within the evangelical fold, where secular citizenship simply did not matter.

While British and Irish evangelicals clearly operated within a world of shared theological values and social support, there were times when the relationship between the two could be fraught with tension and misunderstanding, if not downright racism. The crucial determinant was the role conversion played in the evangelical mindset. Their belief in the utter necessity of a transformative experience, combined with an unwavering dedication to bringing it about in others was often perceived as aggressive and invasive by the societies in which they operated. In England, evangelical activity directed towards the working classes often provoked a violent response,[29] as the experience of the Salvation Army clearly demonstrates. In Ireland, however, efforts to evangelize the 'unsaved' were given a sectarian twist because approximately 80 per cent of the population happened to be Catholic.

Evangelicals throughout Britain and Ireland were undeterred by their, at times, hostile reception. In order to pursue their conversionist objectives they developed a wide range of strategies and methods that they employed with monotonous predictability. Open air and itinerant preaching by laymen was the most common. Gospel services, or 'revival missions', would be held in civic buildings and continue for a week or more. Bible and tract distribution and district visiting were also popular and a range of societies and practical aids were developed to support them. Together, these activities became known as 'home mission' efforts and they proliferated throughout Britain and Ireland in the nineteenth century. Some were linked to specific denominations; others were interdenominational and attracted evangelicals from a range of church backgrounds.

When these conversionist networks came to operate in Ireland, only then did that country and its evangelical inhabitants' distinctive place within the British evangelical community become apparent. The network that has attracted

29 David Hempton, 'Evangelicalism in English and Irish society, 1780–1840', in Mark A. Noll, David W. Bebbington and George A. Rawlyk (eds), *Evangelicalism: comparative studies of popular Protestantism in north America, the British Isles, and beyond, 1700–1990* (Oxford: Oxford UP, 1994), pp 154–71.

the most scholarly attention has been the one behind the 'second reformation', the aggressive campaign to convert Irish Catholics in the early and mid nine-teenth century. The efforts of the Reverend Edward Nangle on Achill and the work of the Revd Alexander Dallas and the Society for Irish Church Missions have been extensively analyzed elsewhere.[30] The conclusions that have emerged all suggest that the conversionist impulse was based on a strong dose of anti-Catholic feeling and that, even though it comprehensively failed in the long run to convert more than a few Irish Catholics, it had a massively destructive impact on Protestant-Catholic relations. It also placed severe pressure on the relation-ship between British and Irish evangelicals. As Desmond Bowen makes clear, Irish evangelicals may have been willing to accept Dallas as a 'zealous and hon-oured Evangelist', but they increasingly disapproved of his methods, and, more to the point, the negative impact they were having on small Protestant com-munities in the south and west.[31]

The negative attitudes of Dallas and his Irish Church Missions colleagues towards Irish Catholics and the state of religion in the country were reflected in the English evangelical community as a whole. The Irish were seen as dom-inated by a superstitious religion which had contributed to the backward eco-nomic and social condition of the country. Some were aware of a Protestant minority in the northern part of the island, but felt that for the most part, these communities were religiously lethargic and practiced only a formal, dead reli-gion. For example, many of the English and Scottish lay evangelists who were part of the nineteenth-century conversionist network visited Ireland on their regular preaching 'tours'. In their published accounts they all demonstrate a low-grade intolerance of Catholicism as a belief system and a patronizing approach to individual Catholics. When Richard Weaver went to Limerick, he saw a Catholic woman struggling on her knees, rosary beads in hand, towards a roadside shrine. To him, such actions were excessive and unnecessary and 'I prayed to God to open the poor woman's eyes'.[32] Given that no evangelist's memoirs were complete without the conversion of a Catholic, Weaver was pleased to report, before the end of the week, this woman's salvation. As open-air preachers, a primary concern was the potential disruption of their meetings. Irish Catholics featured largely in this role. In the 1890s, when two women from the Scottish-based Faith Mission preached in Blackrock, their meetings, as their founder later recounted, were 'noisy – what else could you expect in a Roman Catholic community.'[33] Gipsy Smith, when concluding a service in

30 Bowen, *Protestant crusade*, pp 195–258; Irene Whelan, 'Evangelical religion and the polar-ization of Protestant-Catholic relations in Ireland, 1780–1840' (PhD, University of Wisconsin-Madison, 1994); Stewart J. Brown, 'The new reformation movement in the Church of Ireland, 1801–29', in Stewart J. Brown and David W. Miller (eds), *Piety and power in Ireland, 1760–1960: essays in honour of Emmet Larkin* (Belfast: Institute of Irish Studies, 2000), pp 180–208. 31 Bowen, *Protestant Crusade*, p. 254. 32 Revd James Paterson (ed.), *Richard Weaver's life story* (London: Morgan and Scott, n.d.), p. 147. 33 I.R.Govan, *Spirit of revival: the*

Bolton, found a hostile element in the crowd 'set up one of those wild Irish Catholic yells and closed in upon us.'[34] When the conversionist activity of British evangelists intersected with Ireland, it was a picture of a violent and priest-ridden people that emerged.

Ireland's religious demography, as many evangelicals recognized, was much more complex. During the Ulster revival of 1859, many British evangelicals found their ethnological assumptions about Irish Protestants and Catholics challenged. In 1859 British evangelicals tried to ascribe the physical manifestations of religious conviction, the falling, shaking and ecstatic visions that had so dominated the press reports of the revival, to the Irish character. According to one Methodist minister, such manifestations 'had been considered as somewhat peculiar to the Celtic race ... [and] ... to the Irish character'.[35] The 'warm-hearted, enthusiastic temperament' of the Irish was perceived to be particularly susceptible to such emotional phenomena.[36] In reality, the majority of physical manifestations were experienced by Protestants in the north of the country, but for those British evangelicals who recognized the distinction, their descriptions were equally stereotypical. According to the Revd Alexander Dallas, manifestations had occurred most in the north of Ireland 'where the temperament of the people, who were partly of Scotch extraction, was much colder than that of the south'. For him, this proved the revival was of divine origin, and not the result of human weakness.[37] Other commentators portrayed the 'Ulster Scots' as 'a cool, shrewd, practical set, in love with argumentative preaching and quiet, intellectual religionism', and as 'notoriously cool, practical, money-making and fond of disputation'.[38] However, for others these racial distinctions were irrelevant. Ireland was not the 'Isle of Saints' for nothing; 'the natives always had a stock of religious, or at least theological fervour, stronger in all its manifestations than that bestowed on the cooler-headed and less easily moved Saxons'.[39] For British evangelicals, revival excitement was a product of Ireland's distinctly sectarian religious landscape.

The flip side of British evangelical attitudes towards Ireland was its perception of its own religious superiority. When news of the Ulster revival began to spread, British evangelicals were astonished that it had broken out in a country they considered so far removed from their notions of 'true' religion. England was 'a far more fit receptacle for Divine influence, and far more likely to experience a revival which shall preclude the latter day glory, than Ireland with its poverty and Popery, with its suffering and sin'.[40] This fact caused some evangelicals to see the revival as a check to their national pride. 'Is it not a bold reproof for our sec-

story of J. G. Govan and the Faith Mission (4th ed., Edinburgh: Faith Mission, 1978), pp 99–100. **34** Gipsy Smith, *Gipsy Smith: his life and work* (London: National Council of Evangelical Free Churches, 1905), p. 102.   **35** *Wesleyan Times*, 27 June 1859, p. 419.   **36** *Record*, 21 Dec. 1859, p. 3.   **37** Ibid., 16 Jan. 1860, p. 4.   **38** *Times*, 16 Sept. 1859, p. 7; *Revival*, 17 Sept. 1859, p. 58. **39** *Times*, 16 Sept. 1859, p. 7.   **40** 'The great revival', in *Methodist New Connexion Magazine* 62 (1859), pp 597–8.

ularity and unbelief, that we, as a professedly Christian nation, should now be dry and parched, while showers of blessing descend upon other nations whom we have been accustomed to regard with shame and pity?'[41] This racial snobbery, combined with a mixture of envy and fear, highlighted the 'Irish' dimension of the Ulster revival and clearly delineated the racial and cultural gap between British evangelicals and their Irish co-religionists.

When D.L. Moody and I.D. Sankey, the leading evangelists within the trans-Atlantic evangelical community, arrived in Dublin in October 1874, for the first time they conducted their services in a city where Protestants were in the minority. Their visit also highlights the distinctiveness of Irish evangelicals within the wider British evangelical community. Despite the bonds of denomination and a shared religious culture, Irish Protestants occupied a relatively precarious position in Ireland. They were extremely conscious of their minority status, particularly in the southern part of the island, and were keen to preserve a harmonious relationship with their Catholic neighbours. Moody and Sankey's meetings operated as a focal point of renewal and encouragement for those living in small, isolated Protestant communities. Making a 'pilgrimage' to an area of Protestant strength and attending massive meetings acted to reaffirm their Protestant identity and encouraged them to return to their localities secure in the knowledge that they were members of a vibrant religious community. The members of Dublin's Anglican hierarchy were able to use these meetings to reassert themselves in the wake of disestablishment and to demonstrate their ability to adjust to the difficult changes which their new voluntary position had thrust upon them.

The boost Moody and Sankey's visit gave to southern Protestants must, however, be balanced against the threat it posed to denominational coherence, and by extension, Irish Protestantism in general. Moody's emphasis on denominational co-operation and personal dealing with souls made him open to the criticism that he was trying to divide Irish Protestants and led to the charge that he was trying to promote Brethrenism. True, Moody's earliest Dublin contacts were leading member of the Brethren movement, and many of his methods smacked of its rejection of ordination and proper liturgical forms. In a letter to a local paper, 'Zenas' argued that individuals converted at Moody's meetings would join neither a dissenting chapel nor the Church of Ireland, but would become part of 'the inchoate masses of religionists (the weakness of Protestantism in Ireland) whose highest boast is that they belong to no Church on earth,' a direct swipe at local Brethrenism.[42] In Ireland, dismantled denominations and unordained preachers represented a grave threat to the future of Protestantism on the island. The challenge which Moody's preaching posed to denominational structures in general was, in the Irish context, translated into an assault on one of the fundamental pillars of Irish Protestant strength.

---

41 Ibid.   **42** *Dublin Evening Mail*, 22 Oct. 1874.

Evangelical religion in England and Ireland was, as one of its leading historians has suggested, 'fruit of the same tree'. It had 'a shared theology, similar organizational structures, an overlapping leadership, and a common commitment to evangelism and the reformation of manners'. However, the social consequences of the movement were fundamentally different in the two countries. Evangelicalism in England created class tension while in Ireland the fracture points were sectarian.[43] That said, Irish evangelicals functioned within a wider British evangelical community. The denominations they belonged to were, despite long-established national structures, British in origin and consistently subordinate to British hierarchies. Irish evangelicals clearly drew comfort from this relationship. The imperial benefits of this alliance were not lost on them and when it was politically threatened, as it was in 1870 and 1886, they responded with appeals to their British co-religionists not to abandon them.

The religious culture that accompanied the growth of British and Irish evangelical life sought to supercede these denominational barriers and unite believers through a common theology and set of spiritual goals. In an environment where denominational differences did not matter, Irish evangelicals found that their national distinctiveness went equally unnoticed. Their conversion experiences and their participation in co-ordinative networks showed that they could participate in the wider evangelical community as spiritual equals. In essence, evangelicalism gave its adherents a new kind of citizenship.

Once outside this comfortable environment, Irish evangelicals found their geographical origins, and the fact that they were surrounded by Catholics, problematic for their reception within British evangelicalism. When British evangelicals engaged in home mission activity in Ireland, or commented on the Ulster revival, they revealed their fundamental misunderstandings about Irish Protestants and their position within the country. For their part, Irish evangelicals, although they found it relatively easy to integrate into a wider evangelicalism, were consistently reminded of their minority status within Ireland's religious demography and approached the conversionist activity of their British brethren with, at times, ambivalence. Irish evangelicals may have wanted to eschew their ethnic and geographic origins, but the evangelical emphasis on conversion meant that they were never entirely successful in doing so.

---

43 Hempton, 'Evangelicalism', p. 171.

Religion, community relations and constructive unionism: the Arklow disturbances of 1890–92

MARTIN DOHERTY

This essay explores the relationship between street-based evangelicalism, sectarianism and politics in late nineteenth-century southern Ireland. Throughout the century, Ireland had experienced periodic outbursts of Protestant evangelical fervour, taking their most spectacular form in the great 'Ulster Revival' of 1859. Large-scale attempts at the mass conversion of Irish Catholics from the 1820s had been informed by talk of a 'second reformation', and although it failed to deliver, it did have its well-publicized, localized successes. Moreover, the differences between Anglicans and non-Anglicans had been substantially lessened by evangelicalism, and evangelicals had more or less taken over the Church of Ireland by the late 1860s.

The effects of the second reformation had been to heighten sectarian tensions in many areas and since anti-Catholicism was the most common unifying feature of evangelical Protestantism,[1] it was practically inevitable that attempts to 'share the faith of the Gospel', would lead to trouble. To the evangelical mind, Catholicism was 'a system of idolatry and superstition; calculated to train the population in principles of perjury, obscenity, intolerance, persecution, and sedition [...] the instrument of war, the handmaid of hatred, the sower of sedition, the prompter of perjury, the mediator of murder, the parent of every cruelty, and the nurse of every crime.'[2] For evangelicals, it was Catholicism which kept the south and west of Ireland backward and in a permanent state of distress and rebellion. So while references to 'the miserable Roman Catholics of Ireland' were scarcely likely to win friends amongst Catholics,[3] religion and politics were interwoven into the very fabric of this profoundly divided society. Evangelicalism and conversionism could not be merely religious matters as the home rule campaign became more and more identified as a demonstration of Catholic power, while resistance to it was almost exclusively Protestant.[4] As Marcus Tanner points out, for a Catholic to join a Protestant church meant

1 David Hempton and Myrtle Hill, *Evangelical Protestantism in Ulster society, 1740–1890* (London: Harper-Collins, 1991), p. 165. 2 R.J. McGhee, *Letter to the Queen and to her representative the lord lieutenant of Ireland* (London: Protestant Evangelical Mission, 1869), p. 15. 3 Ibid., p. 28. 4 R.V. Comerford, 'The Parnell era, 1883–1891', in W.E. Vaughan (ed.), *A new history of Ireland*, VI: *Ireland under the union, 1870–1921* (Oxford: Clarendon, 1996), p. 71.

more than abandoning transubstantiation. 'It implied joining the world of the magistrate, the landlord and the big house.'[5]

Moreover, the new, aggressive self-assertion of Roman Catholicism from the 1860s, also stoked the fires of Protestant evangelical fervour. It has been argued that Irish Catholicism had adopted 'a militancy [which] English as well as Irish Protestants perceived as symptomatic of a revived counter-Reformation.'[6] As new Catholic churches and cathedrals sprang up around the country, the first, let alone the second reformation, seemed to be in danger. In short, as the home rule crisis built a head of steam, and the Plan of Campaign re-inflamed agrarian tensions, the combination of reinvigorated Catholicism and politicized evangelicalism was both an engine and an indictor of the gradual worsening of sectarian relationships in many parts of the island.

These tensions burst into open conflict with astonishing speed in Arklow, Co. Wicklow, in the spring of 1890. Generally, landlord-tenant relationships in Wicklow had been good, and the Plan of Campaign phase of the land war had recently fallen flat in the area.[7] The town itself was overwhelmingly Catholic but had a small and vigorous Protestant population, and by all accounts, intercommunal relationships had traditionally been smooth. The immediate occasion for the outbreak of sectarian hostilities was the launching of a series of street services by the local Church of Ireland clergyman, Revd Richard Hallowes in April 1890. On Easter Sunday, Hallowes and his curate John Harrison and two other clergymen, accompanied by a few assistants and brass instruments, appeared in the street and began preaching the Gospel. They then issued a circular, stating that they did so because of the existence of sectarian differences between Protestants and Roman Catholics and their desire to induce all sects of Christians in Ireland to meet together and get rid of the bitter feelings which kept them so widely apart. No attempt was made to approach the Roman Catholic clergy and, as an official report into the subsequent disturbances noted, the evangelicals 'deliberately proceeded to initiate a series of public meetings [...] which they perfectly well knew would be bitterly opposed by the priests of the congregation to whom their addresses were directed.'[8] Revealingly, the police quickly expressed the fear that the services would lead to riot and disturbance, a view reinforced by memories of an episode in 1881, when local Catholics had attacked an open-air evangelical mission, held in a tent outside the town.[9] The police quietly approached the clergymen with a request to desist, and the Protestant Archbishop of Dublin was

5 Marcus Tanner, *Ireland's holy wars. The struggle for a nation's soul, 1500–2000* (London: Yale UP, 2003), p. 211.   **6** Catherine B. Shannon, *Arthur J. Balfour and Ireland, 1874–1922* (Washington: Catholic University of American Press, 1988), p. 78.   **7** R.F. Foster, *Charles Stewart Parnell: the man and his family* (Atlantic Highlands, NJ: Harvester, 1976), p. 172.   **8** National Archives, London [henceforth NA] CO 904/182, f.282, *Memorandum giving facts as to the street preaching in Arklow*, 1892.   **9** For an account of this episode, see P.J. Power, 'The Arklow question: sectarian disturbances in the late nineteenth century' (MA, NUI, Maynooth, 1995), pp 8–9.

seen by an officer of the Royal Irish Constabulary. The Solicitor General's office was approached for a ruling on whether or not the preaching could be banned. It could not, but those taking part might be prosecuted if an obstruction were caused or a breach of the peace provoked. The police were directed to caution the clergymen to this effect, which they duly did.[10]

This early intervention by the police seems to have been counter-productive, for rather than inducing the ministers to give up, it provoked them to write an angry letter to the local and national newspapers. What is striking about this early communication, is the overtly political note struck at the very beginning, in a letter ostensibly about religious matters:

> Sir – Will you kindly permit me to call the attention of your readers to a case of religious intolerance in this town of Arklow, which well illustrates what Protestants in Ireland may expect at the hands of the Roman Catholic country-men, should the Home Rulers have their way? I, with the other Protestant clergymen here, went out into the streets of Arklow on Easter Sunday and preached the Gospel. I need hardly say not one word was said by us which could in any wise offend; yet the authorities have warned us that if we attempt to preach again the people of the town will even resort to riot, and use every means to insult and injure us personally.[11]

However, the fears of the police were realized, when on Sunday 25 May the clergymen tried to hold an open-air service in the part of the town known as the Fishery. The evangelists were soon surrounded by a hooting, jeering, can-rattling band of local Catholics, who thus succeeded in drowning out their words and hymns. It was only with difficulty that the preachers were extracted by the police. According to the unionist *Wicklow News-letter* the ministers had visited the area, desirous of giving offence to none and actuated by the best of motives:

> They were cursed, stoned, and hooted by a howling mob, and narrowly escaped personal injury […] a more disgraceful and uncalled for attack was never perpetrated upon men who were exercising a right recognized in all Christian communities [… T]he spirit of Bedlam seemed to have broken loose; the women became almost frantic, and yelled, and cursed, and blasphemed with appalling energy, while their male friends assisted with a heartiness that was only equalled by their cowardice […] The Rev Mr Hallowes and Rev Mr Harrison calmly addressed some kindly words to their assailants, but without avail and when, after singing three hymns and reading portions of Scripture, they were obliged to give up their service, they were followed through the streets by the mob, the members of which conducted themselves in the most ruffianly manner.[12]

10 NA CO 904/182, f.282, *Memorandum.*   **11** *Irish Churchman and Protestant Review*, 23 May 1890.   **12** *Wicklow News-letter*, 31 May 1890.

Private approaches by the Archbishop failed to dissuade Revd Hallowes, who determined to continue his services in the face of the mounting opposition of the mob.[13] His next several services ended in disorder and as the summer wore on, the weekly scenes became increasingly alarming. Soon, the deleterious effects of the disturbances on community relations were being widely commented upon. A local Catholic doctor wrote to the press that whatever Hallowes's intentions, his actions had been interpreted by certain of the Roman Catholics as an aspersion on their own clergy and doctrines and an insult to their religion. While both preachers and protesters were unrepresentative of the majorities of both communities, it was a dangerous thing to unfurl the banner of sectarianism:

> [I]t is a short step from turbulence and disorder, to violence and bloodshed [...] the curse of sectarian hatred has manifested itself widely and deeply. In a town which can ill afford any commercial depression, business has been injured, even thus early, to an alarming extent. People who have lived hitherto in peace and harmony now view one another with distrust. Rancour is in many hearts. In the newspapers we have had mutual recrimination. In the streets we have had violence and bloodshed. These are the results of the street preaching in Arklow.[14]

The *Wicklow News-letter* saw the root of the problem in the 'poisonous rancour with which the minds of too many of the [Catholic] flock in Arklow are unhappily filled.'[15] Tempers worsened in August, when the local magnate, the earl of Carysfort, denounced the Catholics from the Arklow bench. His Lordship declared that the scenes of riot and turbulence might lead to bloodshed, 'but we will have such a force brought into the town as will put a stop to such conduct, even if the whole of the population turns out to oppose us.'[16] Tactlessly, he referred repeatedly to the 'disgrace' which the 'Roman Catholics' were bringing upon themselves and their town. Fr Dunphy, the parish priest, who happened to be a well-known nationalist and Land Leaguer, heard the outburst and replied in court with a defiant speech of his own:

> The faith of the Irish Catholics is so strongly planted in their breasts, no matter how poor they may be, that they would prefer to die or suffer any amount of coercion rather than have that faith subjected to insult. The Catholics of Arklow had been called ignorant, unlettered, rude, etc., and epithets of the worst description had been heaped upon them by the preachers and those associated with them. They had been followed to the vicinity of their houses, and annoyed day after day and week after week. Hymns which they did not want to hear had been dinned into their

---

13 NA CO 904/182, f.283, *Memorandum.*   14 *Wicklow News-letter*, 16 Aug. 1890.   15 *Wicklow News-letter*, 9 Aug. 1890.   16 *Wicklow News-letter*, 9 Aug. 1890.

ears; they had been ridiculed for their poverty; and both their clergy and their doctrine had been insulted and scoffed at. His Lordship had talked about bloodshed, but he (Father Dunphy) for one would not coerce his people to remain in their houses or to shut their doors. They ought to have the liberty at least of every other British subject to enjoy the freedom of the streets and their honest recreation. These people valued their little homesteads and premises, and the approaches to them just as much as his Lordship did his lawns, and the roads that lead to his castle. His Lordship made a great mistake if he thought the people would stand this interference with their liberty, and he (Father Dunphy) would tell him that they cannot nor won't stand it.[17]

As relations worsened, many of the Protestant traders of the town began to complain of a system of 'exclusive dealing' which was being adopted by local Catholics, and a variety of more or less open calls to boycotting of Protestant businesses appeared in the local nationalist press.[18] As the disturbances continued into the autumn, 180 extra police and soldiers were required every Sunday to maintain order, which they managed to do with considerable difficulty. Saturday and Sunday evenings would often see disturbances in the town and the police would break up hostile crowds with drawn batons, necessitating the dressing of several broken heads by local doctors.[19]

What needs to be explained here is the ferocious hostility of local Catholics to street preaching by small bands of evangelicals who, in Arklow, were well-known members of the local community. Some were quick to scent a political conspiracy. The nationalist *Wicklow People* regarded talk of 'freedom of speech' as a ridiculous pretence:

> They want to make a point for [Irish chief secretary, A.J.] Balfour. Forsooth, if they are not allowed to preach at Papists, willing or unwilling, it's an argument against Home Rule! Well, let us suppose their plan were taken up. How would it work? The Catholic priests might not meddle in the melee at all. We have, thank God, a goodly number of Protestant Home Rulers, although the vast majority, to their shame, grab all the benefits which, despite their bigoted votes, the party of the people win. When one of these preachers commenced to address the Papists, just let some truthful Protestant historian give him a history of Cromwell, of the Battle of the Diamond, or the martyrdom of Father Delany, of Arklow, in 1649, or of Father Murphy in '98, or an account of the present un-Christian crusade carried on by the class with whom Protestant bishops and the Representative Church Body are identified against the toil-earned property of the Irish farmers.[20]

17 *Wicklow People*, 9 Aug. 1890. **18** *Wicklow People*, 27 Sept. 1890. **19** *Wicklow People*, 16 Aug. 1890. **20** *Wicklow People*, 31 May 1890.

Elsewhere in the same issue, the *Wicklow People* denounced 'the unprece-dented action of the four clergymen who have attempt to literally CRAM THE BIBLE DOWN THE THROATS OF THE POOR, uneducated people of the fish-eries.' However, what is striking about the paper's stance is not its religious, or rather the theological aspect, but the undisguised contempt for 'Protestants' and the historical and present grievances of which 'Protestants' were guilty. Frequently there were complaints in nationalist papers about 'insults' offered by the preachers to Catholics, their clergy and their religion, but it seems more likely that Arklow's Catholics were rejecting, not the message, but the messen-gers. Indeed, an arresting feature of local nationalist press coverage of the Arklow events, is the naked sectarianism often on display. But this sectarianism was concerned not with religion as such, but rather uses religious affiliation as the vehicle for the articulation of traditional political and socio-economic grievances. For example, an issue of the *Wicklow People* of June 1890 declared with respect to the land struggle that:

> [i]t is even yet a nauseating spectacle to see the way the bulk of non-Catholic farmers hold aloof from the struggle in which they should be as much interested as anyone. They grab at all the legal advantages won by the sacrifices of Catholics, and slyly grab, where they can sneak into the dirty work, the farms sacrificed by the same plucky papists. But while this meanness, alas! (we reluctantly write it) attaches to the bulk of the Protestants, there are noble exceptions.[21]

The most noble of the exceptions of course was Parnell himself, and it seems that really serious disorder in Arklow was avoided only by his personal intervention. On 13 August, Parnell had written to the chief secretary and sug-gested that all open-air meetings be prohibited in Arklow. Balfour replied that this could not legally be done, and that the preaching itself was legal, so long as it did not lead to obstruction of the highway. Then, on Sunday 24, August, the authorities noted a complete change in the behaviour of the local Catholics, when they did not appear at Hallowes' service at all, and instead attended a counter-meeting organized by Fr Farrelly at the Sandhills about a quarter of a mile away. Apparently, the action of the priests in leading the crowd away had been instigated at the request of Parnell, on the understanding that if the police prevented the obstruction caused by the preachers, the crowd would stay away. If the police were withdrawn, the mob would return.[22]

Fr Farrelly was also a well-known nationalist and had been heavily involved in land agitation which had earned him a brief spell of imprisonment.[23] And again, like the *Wicklow People*, the priest emphasized the political, above the reli-gious aspects of the affair:

21 *Wicklow People*, 28 June 1890. **22** NA CO 904/182, f.283–4, *Memorandum*. **23** Power, 'Arklow', pp 11–12.

Were the open-air meetings carried on in the town directed for the promotion of religion? ('No, no'.) Did they think that Mr Hallowes or the
other three clergymen had the slightest idea of converting the people of
Arklow? ('No'). They had no hope or idea of converting the people, but
they had an intention of insulting them, and by the insults to excite them
to outrage, and from the outrage to raise a cry against home rule (cheers)
[…] The slightest outrage committed by the people of Arklow would be
entered down against them, and at the next general election would be
magnified into a monstrous outrage […] the Catholics of Arklow had
shown that they were worthy to be treated with their own government
(cheers). It was better always to look forward – never to look back; better
to look forward with hope than to look to revenge; better to look to the
bright star that was leading them on to victory, Mr Parnell (cheers), than
to give way to their own natural feelings on an occasion like the present,
and, by any act of theirs, to provide an argument for their enemies against
the concession of their just rights (cheers).[24]

Thus, for many of the Arklow Catholics, Hallowes' services were insulting intru-
sions, offensive reminders of the contempt held for them by their erstwhile mas-
ters, to whom, in a changed political climate, they would no longer even listen.

For the Tory politicians who had promised resolute government to Ireland
after the trauma of the Land War, the Arklow affair was particularly unwelcome.
The chief secretary, Arthur Balfour, was scarcely the 'bloody' tyrant portrayed in
nationalist propaganda, and was probably sincere when he wrote that 'I am
merely doing my best to prevent them picking each other's pockets and cutting
each other's throats.'[25] Almost equally contemptuous of all sides in the Arklow
case, he described Hallowes as 'a mad attorney turned parson – a horrible combination,' and regarded the clergyman as a dangerous proselytizer, intent on pro-
voking the Catholic population. Hallowes, he reported, was now in the habit of
parading through the streets singing hymns, and coming to a stand at a point
carefully chosen so as to command the Catholic chapel, and the houses of the
Catholic priest and curate. The authorities had no wish violently to disperse the
crowd and thus enflame nationalist opinion; nor could they simply suppress the
services and be seen to give in to mob rule. But what worked in England,
would not work in Ireland:

In the opinion of lawyers on this side of the Channel, a man may be
guilty of the offence of taking part in an unlawful assembly if he does
anything which may reasonably be expected to have the result of inducing somebody else to tear him to pieces. In truth, I do not know how
Belfast would be governed upon any other principle […] The thing may

---

24 *Wicklow News-letter*, 30 Aug. 1890. **25** quoted in Shannon, *Balfour*, p. 284.

any day get beyond a joke. Yesterday, as I learn from the Magistrate in charge, the police had at one point to fix bayonets.[26]

And if thwarted in legally preventing Hallowes' activities, Balfour was not shy about letting his opinion of them be known in public. Hallowes had written to him in January 1891 to complain about certain remarks made from the bench in an unsuccessful private prosecution that month, and unwisely perhaps had sent a copy of his letter to the *Daily Express*. Balfour sent him a contemptuous reply, making sure that copies appeared in the *Times*, the *Daily Express* and most of the Irish papers:

> You state in your letter that you only demand the privileges accorded by English law to English clergymen in England [… b]ut I must remind you how different are the circumstances of the two countries. In Ireland, the divisions between different sections of the community, caused by differences of creed, are so deep and so far-reaching, religious convictions are so closely interwoven with political passions, that a course which would be innocent, and even praiseworthy, on one side of St George's Channel, may be morally, if not legally, indefensible on the other. That this is so must be a matter of the deepest regret, but it is a fact which cannot be ignored; and though it affords not a shadow of excuse for the violence of a mob, it may possibly afford sufficient grounds for criticizing the action of those by whom that violence is knowingly provoked.[27]

Significantly, the *Irish Catholic* called Balfour's letter 'eminently sensible'.[28] In April 1891, the Chief Secretary took advantage of another opportunity to lambaste Hallowes in print:

> I cannot express approval of conduct which, if deliberately imitated by all sects and in all places in Ireland, would set the whole country in a blaze of sectarian fury. It is because I am an earnest supporter of the rights of free religious discussion and of free religious worship that I regret to see those rights abused, even with the best intentions; and it is because I am a Protestant that I regret that those who abuse them should belong to my own communion.[29]

In March 1891, Hallowes and Harrison were successfully prosecuted by a local man for obstruction. Fines were imposed, which the clergymen refused to pay, with the result that they were sentenced to two weeks' imprisonment. 'Both gentlemen were removed to prison in evident glee […] Mr Hallowes crying

---

26 NA CAB 37/29/8, *Memorandum submitted to the Lord Chancellor of England by the Chief Secretary for Ireland*, 2 Feb. 1891. 27 *Times*, 23 Feb. 1891. 28 *Irish Catholic*, 27 Feb. 1891. 29 *Daily Express*, 9 Apr. 1891.

out, "Hallelujah, hallelujah", and Mr. Harrison, "Praise God, praise God".[30] Now that it had been proven in court that the clergymen were responsible for obstruction caused by the mob which came to abuse them, it was henceforth possible for the police legally to force them to 'move on' once they stopped to preach on the public highway. Events would be played out as follows: after church service, Hallowes and Harrison would appear in the street, supported by up to two hundred men, women and children. Having read some passages of Scripture, the group would set off down the Main-street, signing hymns, with fifty police bringing up the rear. All the doors in the street remained tightly shut, a consequence of an instruction from the priests to the Catholics to stay indoors and make no disturbance. Instead, they beat their doors as the procession passed, so as not to be able to hear the preaching or the singing. On arrival at the schoolhouse, the procession turned around and walked back up the Main-street for 200 yards and then back down again. Back at the school, Hallowes would stop and begin preaching. Since he insisted on stopping about fifteen yards in front of the school, he was told by the police to 'move on'. Hallowes would refuse to do so, raising his arms and shouting 'I will not move on. Why don't you arrest me?' The police then advanced upon him slowly, obliging him to move on, whereupon Hallowes would try to dart round behind them, or hop up on the wall of his school, where the police could not molest him. According to a visiting lay preacher, Hallowes gave whatever violent, physical, and personal resistance he was able, but would be pushed slowly up the street by the police, followed by his band of supporters. This would continue for an hour or so, until Hallowes led the group to the parade ground, opposite the Roman Catholic Church. Since the ground was already occupied by a large force of military to prevent a service taking place, Hallowes would perch on the doorstep of a private house abutting the parade ground, and preach for half an hour.[31]

This performance was repeated, week after week, from March 1891 until April 1892. There were repeated violent confrontations between the evangelists and the police, although the local Catholics continued to stay away. The potential for trouble was still very real and when in July 1891, it was suggested that the police might be removed, the divisional commissioner advised against, stating that if they did not control the preaching, the people would take the law into their own hands, disorder would ensue, and 'the police would be obliged to interfere, and baton and perhaps fire upon the people.'[32] All the while however, Hallowes seemed more and more determined to infuriate the police. On one occasion in November 1891, he repeatedly dropped his bible as the constabulary attempted to move him on, apparently in the hope that the officers should trample it in the mud. He then proceeded to rub the mud-besmirched book in the faces of the constables as they passed him. He began singling out

30 *The Times*, 7 Mar. 1891. **31** *Freeman's Journal*, 1 Apr. 1891. **32** NA CO 904/182, f.299, *Memorandum*.

individual constables for vitriolic, personal abuse, and shortly afterwards, punched two full in the face with a clenched fist, while lashing out with his boots. At the service on 24 January 1892, Hallowes assaulted Constable Cooke by striking him in the face with his hands, and also assaulted the head constable. Harrison attempted to wrestle one constable to the ground, and several constables had their helmets knocked off and their uniforms torn. By this stage, the town's Catholics had abandoned the habit of staying indoors, and were now enjoying the services as amused spectators: about 1,000 people turned out to watch the bizarre proceedings on 31 January.

Certainly, the tolerance allowed him at Arklow was striking, as Hallowes himself was well aware. In the midst of one push-and-shove session in February 1892, he shouted that 'if the police were down in Tipperary, instead of slow march they would draw their batons and break the heads of the Nationalists, but they were afraid to touch *them*'.[33] This was fair comment, and in spite of his provocations, the authorities declined to take action against Hallowes, or indeed anyone else. Indeed, the police had been told by the authorities that should any *lay* supporters of the clergymen obstruct the police with violence, they should be arrested and prosecuted.[34] So, by implication, Hallowes and Harrison were not to be arrested, irrespective of the violence of their behaviour towards the police. A memorandum prepared at the time of the later Cork disturbances reported on the Arklow case that 'no prosecutions either against the preachers or the crowd which opposed them were instituted by the Government of the day, presumably being of the opinion that such prosecutions might tend to prolong and embitter the hostile feelings already excited and that the matter would probably die a natural death.'[35]

In the end, the initiative for ending the Arklow stand-off came from the local magistrates, four of whom secretly visited the under secretary, Sir West Ridgeway in February 1892. The group said that if Hallowes were allowed to preach from a position a yard or two outside his school gates, then the clergyman might be satisfied.[36] At the same time, the authorities were worried that the self-respect and morale of the police was being sacrificed at Arklow to 'political exigencies'. West Ridgeway recognized also that it was 'too bad that the Roman Catholic population should see that a Protestant clergyman is allowed to indulge with impunity in misconduct which would be promptly and severely punished if committed by one of themselves'.[37] So, from February Hallowes was allowed to preach in the street outside his school, and his confrontations with the police came to an end. Moreover, the local Catholics now more or less ignored him. Trouble at the services became less and less frequent, so that by 1895, the authorities could report

---

33 NA CO 904/182, f.302, *Memorandum.*   34 NA CO 904/182, f.301, *Memorandum.*   35 NA CO 904/182, f.273–4, *Arklow street preaching*, nd, probably 1894.   36 NA CO 903/1/89739, *Deputation of local magistrates with under secretary – notes of interview*, 5 Feb. 1892.   37 NA CO 903/1/80739, *Under Secretary to Chief Secretary*, 12 Feb. 1892.

that preaching now took place in several places in Arklow on Sundays and on fair days, and that no police protection was necessary. 'The Roman Catholics keep aloof from it.'[38] The point seems to be, however, that by acting so determinedly against Hallowes, from March 1891 until April 1892, the authorities had drawn the sting of the affair, so that when Hallowes was allowed again to take to the streets, the Catholics were no longer interested in him. The ending of his confrontations with the police meant the end of his entertainment value, which was not now replaced by a desire to lynch him.

The street preaching saga did not finish here, however. The indignation and interest of Arklow's Catholics having been exhausted, Hallowes and Harrison joined with gusto in the activities of the Open Air Mission for Ireland, which had been inspired by their 'great victory' in the Wicklow town.[39] Violent disturbances associated with street preaching continued for a number of years in several towns across the south and west. The disturbances at Arklow had lasted from April 1890, for just over two years: those at Cork, from November 1893 to November 1894; at Athlone, from August 1894 to November 1895; at Galway, from August 1894 to the spring of 1895; at Howth, from June to November 1895; and at Sligo, from August 1895 to the end of 1896. Most of these episodes were handled without excessive violence, the law having by then being clarified that although street preaching was legal, it might be prevented, if its prevention was necessary for the preservation of the peace. This often meant that preachers would be forced back into their hotels or lodgings, until hostile crowds had been dispersed.[40] Often, as at Howth, scenes similar to those at Arklow would be played out, with several hundred men, women and children surrounding a small band of evangelists, and ringing bells, sounding fog-horns, beating tin trays, blowing whistles, groaning, hooting, yelling and singing.[41] Hallowes and Harrison were both involved in preaching in Cork, Galway and Athlone, which was accompanied by trouble instantly upon their arrival. The scenes at Athlone in 1894 were among the most violent, with really vicious attempts to do serious harm to the preachers. On more than one occasion, the police came close to losing control of the situation and used batons on the very large and aggressive crowds. Following a riot in Athlone in September 1894, the Divisional Commissioner condemned Hallowes' behaviour as 'really outrageous, and it was with the greatest difficulty that the Police saved him from the violence of the mob, which he did everything in his power to aggravate.'[42] Harrison's participation in street services at Sligo in 1895, re-inflamed opposition to them, which had been on the way to dying out; an effigy of him was burned in the town in the midst of one disturbance.[43] The services generated

---

38 NA CO 904/182, *Street preaching, Arklow*, Dec. 1895. 39 *Daily Express*, 15 Feb. 1894. 40 NA CO 904/182, f.344, *Instructions issued by government to Royal Irish Constabulary*, 27 Aug. 1894. 41 NA CO 904/182, f.364b, *Howth, 22 June 1895*. 42 NA CO 904/182, f.354b, *Preaching on Sunday, 16 September, 1894*. 43 NA CO 904/182, f.368b, *Attack on Rev. Mr Harrison, 6 October 1895*.

considerable ill-feeling in Sligo, resulting in a number of ugly sectarian riots and attacks on the police. In Galway, in disturbances again involving Hallowes and Harrison, crowds of two or three thousand shouted and sang to drown out the words of the street preachers, and pelted them with mud, eggs, fish and stones, as well as launching violent physical assaults upon them. Again, police had to draw batons to save the preachers from serious injury or worse.[44] Plans for a campaign in Limerick, again involving Hallowes and George Williams of the Open Air Mission, were only abandoned after a hostile mob of 4,000 surrounded Williams' hotel.[45]

So, what may be said of the street preaching disturbances at Arklow and elsewhere which troubled the peace of unlikely little Irish towns for much of the 1890s? It should be stressed of course, that evangelistic street preachers like Hallowes, Harrison and Williams were not typical of the communities from which they sprang, and, indeed, many of their co-religionists regarded them as extremists and trouble-makers. Nevertheless, these episodes ought to be included in any wider discussion of Irish cultural and political movements of the last decades of the nineteenth century.

Neither side regarded the matter as entirely religious, and both were clear and open as to the political issues at stake.

The hostility of Roman Catholics to street preaching is best regarded as a demonstration of Catholic self-assertion, aggression and obstreperousness, after decades of intertwined religious, political and socio-economic animosity. For the British, street preaching was a potentially explosive issue, to be handled with the utmost sensitivity. By the 1890s, Irish Catholicism was imbued with too much self-confidence to be proselytized, and 'Bloody Balfour' too wary of its power not to try to appease it.

44 NA CO 904/182, f.359, *Preaching on 26 August, 1894.*   **45** NA CO 904/182, f.361, *Hostility to the preachers.*

Darwin at church:
John Tyndall's Belfast address

MATTHEW BROWN

When the Irish physicist and scientific naturalist John Tyndall (1820–93), a friend of Charles Darwin and fierce proponent of evolution, delivered his Belfast address in 1874, he did so amidst a particularly vituperative controversy between religion and science on the subject of human change. Since the publication of *The origin of species* in 1859, evolution, characterized by gradual change over long periods of time, became the predominant model of human ontogeny in the latter half of the nineteenth century. One of the last ideological challenges to the hegemony posed by the Darwinian or gradualist model was the narrative of instantaneous religious conversion. In its most traditional theological sense, the conversion experience represented that sudden transformation in individual psychology, ostensibly facilitated by divine intervention, from a state of non-belief to utter piety, an event late nineteenth-century psychologist and religious scholar William James famously describes in lecture ten of *The varieties of religious experience: a study in human nature* (1902), as 'striking instantaneous instances [... when] amid tremendous emotional excitement or perturbation of the senses, a complete division is established in the twinkling of an eye between the old life and the new.'[1] From the 1870s on, a torrent of books and articles was devoted to the study of instantaneous conversion (especially its theological and political import for evangelical Protestantism), of which Edwin Diller Starbuck's *Psychology of religion: an empirical study of the growth of religious consciousness* (1901) was one of the most influential. Furthermore, within the political register, conversion as a 'catastrophist' model of human ontogeny gathered wider significance as servant to or spoiler of British nationalism. As Gauri Viswanathan argues when studying cases of voluntary or forced conversion in nineteenth-century India, Ireland, and England, 'conversion ranks among the most destabilizing activities in modern society, altering not only demographic patterns but also the characterization of belief as communally sanctioned assent to religious ideology'.[2] In a Darwinian age of social, political, and scientific gradualism, conversion was often viewed as not only a 'spiritual but also a political activity' as well.[3]

1 William James, *The varieties of religious experience* (New York: Penguin, 1986), p. 217. 2 Gauri Viswanathan, *Outside the fold: conversion, modernity, and belief* (Princeton: Princeton UP, 1998), p. xvi. 3 Ibid., p. xvii.

In light of Viswanathan's study that masterfully historicizes conversion as a potent religio-political force in nineteenth-century Britain and Ireland, I want to focus more explicitly on John Tyndall's promotion of evolution – and his corresponding negative review of change by instantaneous conversion – in the Belfast address as an implicitly political gesture to deploy scientific naturalism as a means to ameliorate religious and cultural divisions in Ireland. Moreover, by attending to Tyndall's unique accommodation of spirituality to Darwinism, I also want to explicate how his work influenced the narrative structure of spontaneous conversion within the wide domains of religion, psychology, and Irish nationalism and poetry in the late nineteenth and early twentieth centuries. While Tyndall and his successors, like the psychologist William James, promoted possible configurations between conversion and evolutionist paradigms to the eventual endorsement of the latter as a model for psychological or political transformation, W.B. Yeats vehemently reacted against Tyndall's evolutionist sympathies, and gradualism more generally, in the 1890s by summoning a return to social and political change via conversion narratives. This contest between conversion and evolution, all but resolved in the scientific world by the turn-of-the-century, continued with renewed vigour in Irish literary life as writers like Yeats and James Joyce attempted to forge out of Ireland's various religious inheritances – ancient Celticism for Yeats, the Roman Catholic Church for Joyce – an aesthetic vision of colony.

One might say that Tyndall's support for Darwinian evolution matched to his careful critique of 'spontaneous generation' in the Belfast address was part of a much wider secular reaction to conversion as a scientific, religious and political force in the latter half of the nineteenth century. Expressions against conversion in British political life is perhaps best exemplified by W.E. Gladstone's pamphlet *The Vatican decrees in their bearing on civil allegiance: a political expostulation* (1874), in which Gladstone gives voice to the anxieties in Britain over a series of Catholic conversions. In his frothy invective against Rome, Gladstone insists that the English national formation, in both its political and theological instantiations, trumps the authority vested in the Catholic Church, an institution that he characterizes as corrosively atavistic, that had 'refurbished and paraded anew every rusty tool she was fondly thought to have disused [...and had] repudiated modern thought.'[4] Since Irish nationalism's increasing identification with Catholicism after Daniel O'Connell, Gladstone's apprehension about the potential rifts within Britain on questions of religion and national allegiance might also be deigned a thinly veiled censure of Irish Catholicism as a competing national formation. 'The response of nineteenth century Anglican England to a spate of Catholic conversions,'

4 W.E. Gladstone, 'The Vatican decrees in their bearing on civil allegiance: a political expostulation', in E.R. Norman (ed.), *Anti-Catholicism in Victorian England* (New York: Barnes and Noble, 1968), p. 216.

writes Viswanathan on the subject of Gladstone's secular anxiety, was 'interpreted as almost certain confirmation of the imperial reach of Rome as well as of the inexorable onslaught of Irish immigration' into England.[5] Thus, within the wider debates between science, politics, and religion in Britain and Ireland in the closing decades of the nineteenth century, the points of contact between nation and conversion were some of most theologically and politically volatile.

Within this contest over the political location of the Catholic in Britain, John Tyndall delivered his famous Belfast address in August 1874, the same year that Gladstone published his pamphlet decrying the influence of Rome over British national life and that J.H. Newman replied in the affirmative to Gladstone's query if Catholics can be trustworthy subjects of the state with the measured reply, 'I see no inconsistency in my being at once a good Catholic and a good Englishman'.[6] Tyndall, with his pertinacious evolutionism, was likewise interested in such matters of faith and self-determination that so inflamed Gladstone and Newman, and he deliberately entered the fray with the intent, as he wrote to friend and colleague T.H. Huxley, to 'be true to himself' and to forward his career commitment to scientific naturalism, Darwinism, and a materialist worldview that argued evolution's 'general harmony with scientific thought'.[7]

His agenda in the Belfast address, however, was very different from either Gladstone's political angling or Newman's theological defence. Tyndall firmly believed that scientific thought based on evolution and materialism would modernize Ireland and pry scientific learning from the grip of the Irish Catholic hierarchy. His *Apology for the Belfast address* (1874), published shortly after his lecture in Belfast, in no uncertain terms admits as much. In this short essay that re-states the central points of the address itself, Tyndall comments on the intellectual oppression waged in Ireland by 'Pope, Cardinal, Archbishops, and Bishops'; to accentuate this point, he cites a memorial penned in November 1873 by seventy students and ex-students of the Catholic University of Ireland and addressed to the Episcopal Board of their university. The epistle written nine months before the Belfast address interests Tyndall mainly because the students criticize the lack of training in the physical and natural sciences at the Catholic University and end by threatening that 'if scientific training be unattainable at our University, [we] will seek it at Trinity or at the Queen's Colleges, in not one of which is there a Catholic Professor of Science'.[8] Thus, both before he delivered his Belfast address and in its tem-

5 Viswanathan, *Outside the fold*, p. xi.   **6** J.H. Newman, 'A letter addressed to his grace the Duke of Norfolk on the occasion of Mr Gladstone's recent expostulation', in E.R. Norman (ed.), *Anti-Catholicism in Victorian England* (New York: Barnes and Noble, 1968), p. 223.   **7** John Tyndall, *Address delivered before the British Association assembled at Belfast, with additions* (London: Longmans, Green, 1874), p. 58.   **8** John Tyndall, 'Apology for the Belfast address', in John Tyndall (ed.), *Fragments of science: a series of detached essays, addresses, and reviews* (New York: D. Apppleton, 1898), p. 212.

pestuous aftermath, Tyndall saw a need to defend and promote science against theology for the betterment of scientific learning in Ireland. This discontent with the Irish Catholic hierarchy manifest in the student memorial also sig- nalled for Tyndall a much greater and imminent cultural change in Ireland that he illustrates in the *Apology*: 'Though moulded for centuries to an obedience unparalleled in any other country [...] the Irish intellect is beginning to show signs of independence; demanding a diet more suited to its years than the pabulum of the Middle Ages.'[9] Here, what is most obvious in Tyndall's remarks on Ireland is his strong bias for science as the overarching palliative for cultural and religious debates.

Significantly, the most controversial claims within the Belfast address aimed explicitly at fostering this separation of 'the Irish intellect' from the Catholic Church had been evolving throughout Tyndall's early career. Tyndall was born in Leighlinbridge, Co. Carlow circa 1820, trained in mathematics, surveying, and bookkeeping as a young man, and worked for the English Ordnance Survey before leaving to study physics, chemistry, and mathematics at Marburg University in Germany, where he received his PhD in 1851. His time in Germany, so Ruth Barton suggests, inculcated within Tyndall a life-long ado- ration of romanticism and idealism, especially as they found expression in the work of Kant and Fichte, intellectual influences he would later incorporate into his scientific studies. In 1853, Tyndall was appointed to the chair of the natural philosophy at the Royal Institution of Great Britain and, in the fol- lowing decades, conducted experiments and published papers on radiation, meteorology, glaciology research, and infrared analysis, all too wide interna- tional acclaim. During the 1860s, Tyndall was a member with Huxley and Herbert Spencer of the 'X Club', a group dedicated to 'developing naturalis- tic conceptions of man, nature, and society that were consonant with the find- ings of contemporary science [... and] were opposed to any external control of science, whether by political or theological authorities.'[10] In the Belfast address, ideological textures of scientific naturalism – what might be called the advance of scientific conceptions of nature and society against religious or national orthodoxy – are plentiful, especially in Tyndall's prominent desire in the opening paragraphs to connect natural phenomena to their physical prin- ciples and his oft quoted conclusion that '[a]ll religious theories, schemes and systems, which embrace notions of cosmogony, or which otherwise reach into the domain of science, must, *in so far as they do this*, submit to the control of science, and relinquish all thought of controlling it'.[11] Not surprisingly, Tyndall's knack for such declarative statements on evolution led many critics of the X-Club to misinterpret or simply overlook the group's core spiritual- ity. On this subject, one recent commentator about the X-Club writes that

---

9 Ibid., p. 214.   **10** Ruth Barton, 'John Tyndall, pantheist: a rereading of the Belfast address', *Osiris*, 2:3 (1987), 114.   **11** Tyndall, *Address*, p. 61 (emphasis in the original).

the 'essential religiosity of the dissident intellectuals [the X-Club] can scarcely be over-stressed'.[12] In fact, one of the main reasons the X-Club invested such a high value in evolution was that, unlike traditional theology, it held out the possibility of human improvement, a quality of evolutionary theory that Tyndall intuited in Darwin's work and accentuated in his nearly two hour lecture.[13] So, Belfast offered Tyndall a definitive and culminating moment to express his scientific and his spiritual sympathies, what Barton calls his 'natural supernaturalism' or 'pantheism' inherited from Thomas Carlyle and German romantic idealism.[14]

Tyndall had in previous lectures discussed the relation of religion to science, the former ideologically and structurally subservient to the latter. Strikingly, these earlier lectures saw no inherent dilemma over the compatibility of Darwinian evolution with Christian theology, two discourses that Tyndall believed could implicitly co-exist, albeit in a qualified relationship that, as we will shortly see, he pinpoints in the Belfast address. In a lecture to the British Association for the Advancement of Science at Liverpool in 1870, he quite plainly related to his audience: 'Trust me, [evolution's] existence as a hypothesis is quite compatible with the simultaneous existence of all those virtues to which the term Christian has been applied.'[15] If Tyndall qualified the essential religiosity of his scientific thought in Liverpool in 1870, why did the Belfast address delivered four years later elicit such a strong reaction from religious and lay authorities? As Tyndall would later write about this reaction, 'there must have been something in my particular mode of crossing it [experimental evidence] which provoked this tremendous "chorus of dissent".'[16] So, as Tyndall speculated, the reasons behind this dissent must have resided somewhere in the combination of the religious atmosphere of Belfast in the 1870s, the particular structure of religious and scientific faith explicated in the address, and the critique of conversion, both the political and theological varieties, within the lecture's closing paragraphs.

By the time of Tyndall's lecture, Belfast was already well heeled by religious debate caused by the politics of conversion. Since the 'second reformation' of the 1820s, organizations like the Hibernian Bible Society carried the evangelical word through Ulster and attempted to win Catholics to Protestantism. As historian Gerald Parsons notes when discussing the consequences of the evangelical bid to convert, the 'numerical returns for such Protestant efforts were small and short term,' while the 'damage done to Catholic-Protestant relation-

12 James R. Moore, 'Theodicy and society: the crisis of the intelligentsia', in Richard J. Helmstadter and Bernard Lightman (eds), *Victorian faith in crisis* (Stanford: Stanford UP, 1990), p. 173. 13 Tyndall sent a draft of the Belfast address to Charles Darwin on 5 August 1874, and Darwin responded with enthusiastic praise on 12 August. See: Charles Darwin, *A calendar of the correspondence of Charles Darwin* (Cambridge: Cambridge UP, 1994), pp 412–15. 14 For a masterful study on Tyndall's pantheism, see: Barton, 'John Tyndall', pp 111–34. 15 Tyndall quoted in Moore, 'Theodicy and society', p. 174. 16 Tyndall, 'Apology', p. 209.

ships on the other hand was enormous'.[17] Furthermore, the popularity of the evangelical faith, indexed by the evangelical revival in Ulster in 1859, in combination with the disestablishment of the Church of Ireland in 1869 (effective May 1871), resulted in traditional Presbyterianism in Belfast taking on the texture of evangelical Protestantism by the time Tyndall stood at the pulpit. Relying upon conversion as a political weapon, evangelicalism in Belfast in the 1870s gave 'coherence and legitimacy to Unionist intransigence, and it also – through links with co-religionists on the mainland – heightened a sense that Irish Protestants would find security through the association of a "British" identity' because of its pronounced streak of anti-Catholicism that was even more divisive than the call for 'No Popery' amongst other nonconformists.[18] Belfast evangelicalism thus went hand in hand with a stronger identification with British political identity. When Tyndall offered evolutionary science as a potential curative for religious and social sectarianism, it is little wonder that he could quite accurately report days after his lecture, '[e]very pulpit in Belfast thundered of me'.[19] And indeed, many pulpits did. The Irish Catholic Church was singularly cantankerous, especially the Bishop's pastoral of 1875 that declared, 'under the name of Science, [Tyndall] obtruded blasphemy upon the Catholic nation.'[20]

Much was at stake for Tyndall. When he addressed the Belfast congregation in August 1874, he did so not simply as a scientist voicing his evolutionist views, or even as a materialist testing religious faith (he had already done so in previous lectures). Tyndall spoke as an Irish scientist who had spent most of his professional life in England, as a lapsed Presbyterian turned pantheist, as a thinker committed to the social betterment inherent in science, and as president of the British Association in a city that had been for the previous twenty years a hotbed of conversion enthusiasm and religious dissent. The general scope of the lecture alone was probably enough to win the ire of Irish Catholics and union Protestants alike. The inflammatory thematic lines within the address itself consist of an analysis of matter through a fastidious and self-serving chronology of the atomic theory, a demand for scientific freedom from theological, political, or social restraints, an argument for the continuity of nature, and, finally, an admission that there are motivating forces beyond observable phenomenon unattached to traditional theology.[21] Critical to this address are the rhetorical moves executed by Tyndall that promote evolution.

There is no doubt that Tyndall baldly fawns over Darwin. So much is the Belfast address saturated with evolutionist figures that the address itself under-

17 Gerald Parsons, 'Irish disestablishment', in Gerald Parsons (ed.), *Religion in Victorian Britain: volume II, controversies* (Manchester: Manchester UP, 1988), p. 138.   **18** John Wolffe, *God and Greater Britain: religion and national life in Britain and Ireland, 1843–1945* (London: Routledge, 1994), pp 147–8.   **19** Tyndall quoted in Barton, 'John Tyndall', p. 116.   **20** Quoted in Richard Kearney, *Postnational Ireland: politics, culture, philosophy* (London: Routledge, 1997), p. 176.   **21** See Barton, 'John Tyndall', pp 117–19.

goes an evolution. It is not through mere oracular habit that Tyndall begins in evolutionist flair: 'An impulse inherent in primeval man turned his thoughts and questionings betimes towards the sources of natural phenomena'.[22] This trajectory originating in humanity's first cognitive spark narrates the struggle between scientific and religious thought to the ultimate endorsement of scientific naturalism. And peppered throughout this discussion is the omnipresent figure of Darwin. Discussing 'love and hate among atoms' in Empedocles, Tyndall claims that the doctrine of the survival of the fittest had been partly enunciated; he also sees proof for this doctrine on the atomic level when reading in Lucretius about competition between atoms. Tyndall writes that 'the fit ones persisted, while the unfit ones disappeared'.[23] Locating evolutionist schemes within the work of the ancients serves as prelude, of course, to crowning Darwin as the scientist who naturalizes evolution and gradualist models of change into modern science.

Complementing this support of Darwinian gradualism is the simultaneous negation of instantaneous conversion. In the address, Tyndall uses conversion to describe natural as well as theological phenomena. When discussing the conservation of energy, for example, he stresses the incompatibility of instantaneous change with scientific observation of the natural world. He reports that 'the vegetable world was proved incompetent to generate anew either matter or force [...] The animal world was proved to be equally uncreative.'[24] In context, Tyndall's critique of conversion occurred within the wider debates in the scientific community about 'spontaneous generation', a narrative of individual change that Tyndall takes up and vehemently refutes in the concluding sections of the Belfast address. Spontaneous generation – the idea that living things can suddenly originate from nonliving materials, that the inorganic can in an instant be converted into life – had been fiercely debated since 1860, and posed a problem for evolutionists and theologians alike. The idea that life could originate spontaneously obviously threatened the idea of a creator God. It also posed a problem for evolutionists and their profound philosophical assumption about the continuity of nature, the belief that 'there were no sudden unbridgeable gaps between similar living forms, which would require supernatural intervention.'[25] Because it was counter to his evolutionist faith in the continuity of the natural world, Tyndall came out against the pathologist Henry Bastian, the primary supporter for spontaneous generation within the scientific community, and, by the 1870s, his fierce campaign against spontaneous generation convinced many that the theory was incompatible with Darwinism.

For Tyndall, generation in nature does not spontaneously occur. As the thesis on the continuity of life (a cornerstone of evolutionist theory) suggests, change

22 Tyndall, *Address*, p. 1. 23 Ibid., p. 8. 24 Ibid., pp 45–46. 25 James E. Strick, *Sparks of life: Darwinism and the Victorian debates over spontaneous generation* (Cambridge, MA: Harvard UP, 2000), p. 2.

happens only where there is demonstrable antecedent life. Interestingly, his refutation of spontaneous generation occurs within a particularly anxious moment in the Belfast address when Tyndall hits the empirical limits of materiality through observation. About this limitation, Tyndall writes:

> Believing as I do in the continuity of Nature, I cannot stop abruptly where our microscopes cease to be of use. Here the vision of mind authoritatively supplements the vision of the eye. By an intellectual necessity I cross the boundary of the experimental evidence, and discern in that Matter which we, in our ignorance of its latent powers, and notwithstanding our professed reverence for its Creator, have hitherto covered with opprobrium, the promise and potency of all terrestrial Life.[26]

The intellect extends beyond the range of the senses, and Tyndall must accordingly convert his argument from an empirical to a faith-based approach, one that acts as if the laws of materiality remain intact beyond observable phenomena. Tyndall's quick answer is that they do, although the scientific questions posed by the mystery of unobservable phenomena, in which he still discerns the potent operations of materialism, precipitates a still greater question, one that Darwin encounters in the concluding moments of *The origin of species*; namely, what is the relationship between scientific materialism and the world beyond or before the senses, in the deep inner-workings of consciousness?[27] It is a question that the final sections of the lecture attempt to address.

Even though Tyndall claims that the individual cannot know the real nature of the external world, he believes that one can be assured of its existence and renders this argument through Mill, Kant, and Fichte. Despite his better attempts, what might be called the origin of things – the nature of life, matter, and consciousness – is, for Tyndall, 'the operation of an insoluble mystery'. Consequently, he identifies two alternative paradigms, with which we are by now familiar, to illuminate this mystery. The first model deployed to explicate the 'insoluble mystery' is conversion or creation through spontaneous generation, a scheme that Tyndall rejects because it is, in its fundamental operations, 'fashioned after the human model, and [acts] by broken efforts as man is seen to act'.[28] In this dazzling analogy, Tyndall argues that conversion is an artificial and manufactured narrative, modelled off the impulse to anthropomorphize the natural world. Conversion as herky-jerky anthropomorphism is then compared to evolution, which, as Tyndall emphasizes, describes how the natural world changes and continues *according to its own laws*. Here, Tyndall implies that if evolution proves the material basis for all observable phenom-

---

26 Tyndall, *Address*, p. 55. **27** Charles Darwin, *The origin of species* (New York: W.W. Norton, 1970), p. 199. **28** Tyndall, *Address*, p. 58.

ena, it will eventually prove the material foundations for unobservable phenomena as well. So, on the macro and micro level, Tyndall theorizes change as
the continuous interaction between species and environment, a self-assured
gradualist paradigm that refutes the anthropomorphisms of change through
spontaneous generation or instantaneous conversion, an argument he expands
upon in his 1878 essay *Spontaneous generation*. This is the most explicit show-
down between conversion and evolution within the whole of the Belfast
address and, in Tyndall's view, Darwin gains enormous relative strength from
the comparison.

At the end of his lecture, Tyndall restages the confrontation between conversion as subjective experience and evolution as objective science within the
individual psyche and imagines their interface in a slightly different way. Giving
predominant weight to science, he divides the mind between objective knowledge (science, understanding, reason) and feeling (poetry, emotion, creativity,
faith). These two sides of the human mind are necessary and moderately inter-
dependent with the stipulation that, just as the Church should not muscle into
scientific matters, feeling should not dominate intellect or objective knowledge. Tyndall somewhat accommodates religion to science by suggesting that,
because objective knowledge satisfies only human understanding, feeling is
necessary to motivate and vivify the understanding; objective knowledge alone
is insufficient as a totalizing model of human consciousness. Thus, if conversion
with its attendant emotional effects remains tethered to feeling and outside the
fold of scientific belief, then it has a limited function in individual psychology
that can, and to his mind should, accent objective knowledge. About this separation of scientific and aesthetic knowledge, Tyndall more pithily writes in his
Apology for the Belfast address: 'The Book of Genesis has no voice in scientific
questions [...] It is a poem, not a scientific treatise. In the former aspect it is for
ever beautiful: in the latter aspect it has been, and it will continue to be, purely
obstructive and hurtful.'[29]

Confining religion to the domain of feeling might also be called, in its
Irish contexts, a thinly veiled allegory for transcending religious and political
strife through the scientific method. The final paragraphs of his lecture, abundant with idealist claims to human improvement, testify to this end as the
author figures universal betterment to be one of the more general, positive
effects of science. For Tyndall, the 'lifting of the life is the essential point; and
as long as dogmatism, fanaticism, and intolerance are kept out, various modes
of leverage may be employed to raise life to a higher level.'[30] While the Belfast
address itself might strike one as vague on its national location or intended
national audience, Tyndall's subsequent *Apology for the Belfast address* is not.
Here, Tyndall explicitly names Ireland and the Irish Catholic Church as the
particular targets of his lecture. The true goal of his speech, so the final

29 Tyndall, 'Apology', p. 210.   30 Tyndall, *Address*, p. 62.

moments of the lecture claim, has been to forecast a 'religious vitalization of the latest and deepest scientific truth', a strategic line which attempts to knead, for this Irish audience anyway, religious enthusiasm into the larger structure of scientific learning.

What began as a defence for the compatibility of materialism and evolution ends by offering a model of human psychology that compactly structures scientific thought and religious feeling into the channels of the individual psyche. Of such import was Tyndall's work, both in the Belfast address and in his other essays more exclusively devoted to science and the constitution of the individual mind (for example, *On the scientific use of the imagination*, published in 1870), that theories on human ontogeny in the closing decades of the nineteenth century necessarily had to grapple with Tyndall.

I want to conclude by suggesting that spontaneous conversion as an atavistic social formation that troubles narratives of nation based on Darwinism (endorsed by, among others, Gladstone and Matthew Arnold in British political life, Tyndall in the domain of science, and William James within the fields of religion and psychology) gains significant momentum as a catalyst for political self-description and change in the Irish Revival in the 1890s, particularly in the early work of W.B. Yeats.

As a revivalist committed to discovering some ideal form of Irishness, Yeats in the 1880s and 1890s began assiduously to choreograph science and religion to the rhythm of 'Celticism' as proof for Irish exceptionality. In his youth Yeats read Darwin, Huxley, and Tyndall and prided himself on his refutation of traditional theology with passages lifted from the scientific naturalists. During the 1880s, however, he began to grow 'homesick for a spiritual experience'.[31] A disillusioned evolutionist, he turned to the study of world religions to help assuage his spiritual confusion, and the connections he forged between his theological and political efforts are evident in his 1897 essay 'The Celtic element in literature'. Written during a period when the poet wanted to forge Irish nationalism on the backbone of a Celtic race theory that was numinous without the divisive turns of Catholic or Anglo-Protestant theology, Yeats cast his intellectual nets across a wide variety of scholarship and attempted to craft out of this heterogeneity a master design drafting religion and science into the service of the Irish nation. Yeats ultimately settled on a final version in the 1920s with his oblique *A Vision* (1926). But in the 1890s, he was just beginning to show his paces.

What Yeats extracts from Celtic literature is what Matthew Arnold and Ernest Renan, two previous theorists on Celticism, similarly unearth: a repository of pre-Christian, pre-modern structures of belief that react against 'the

31 Stephen Coote, *W.B. Yeats: a life* (London: Hodder and Stoughton, 1997), p. 37.   **32** W.B. Yeats, 'The Celtic element in literature', in *Essays and introductions* (New York: Collier Books, 1961), p. 187.

rationalism of the eighteenth century [… and] the materialism of the nineteenth century.'[32] Yeats finds in Celticism, with its high degree of mysticism and pantheism, a profound narrative emphasis on instantaneous change. For the young revivalist fascinated by models of personal and political transformation, the characters active in Celtic literature enthral because they 'lived in a world where anything might flow and change, and become any other thing […] unbounded and immortal'.[33] Evident in Yeats's praise of metamorphosis in Celtic literature, characterized both by its political (in its unboundedness) and spiritual (in its immortality) content, is a deep-seated nostalgia for the conversion experience as a model for human change. For Yeats, studying these ancient sources promised to enliven the modern world and summon 'the vivifying spirit of excess' present in Celtic literature into the arts of modern Europe; to this end, he used ancient Irish sources centred on narratives of conversion to signal the means through which Europe may evolve towards adapting the symbolic movement, 'the only movement', as he wrote at the end of his essay, 'that is saying new things'.[34] His poetry at the time was similarly enamoured with the conversion experience. 'Fergus and the Druid', from *The rose* collection (1893), stages this process of conversion as a condition of an ancient and privileged spirituality. The poem begins with Fergus speaking to the Druid, 'This whole day have I followed in the rocks, / And you have changed and flowed from shape to shape, /[…]/And now you wear a human shape, / A thin grey man half lost in gathering night', to which the Druid responds as if to summon a conversion within Fergus himself, 'What would you, Fergus?'[35] In the Druid's presence, Fergus envisions conversion as politically and spiritually ennobling, however overwhelming such boundless change appears to be by the poem's end: 'I see my life go drifting like a river / From change to change; I have been many things /[…]/ And all these things were wonderful and great'.[36] Excommunicated from science in the dying years of the nineteenth century, conversion finds new life as a wonderfully contumacious literary device in Yeats who reminds us that, despite the near hegemony of gradualism, the desire for instantaneous change through radical psychological or political conversion was no less intense.

And perhaps this is why many of his modernist successors would, in narratives that gradually plot a character's psycho-social development, punctuate or cap this evolutionary course with an intense psychological conversion, otherwise know as an epiphany. Not all renderings of the conversion experience, however, are as sanguinary as Yeats. James Joyce's use of epiphany in *Dubliners* famously works in relative opposition to Yeats's Celtic conversion narratives. For example, the adolescent's morose realization at the end of 'Araby' is more qualified by how politically disabling it is: 'Gazing up into the darkness I saw myself as a creature driven

33 Ibid., p. 178.   **34** Ibid., p. 187.   **35** W.B. Yeats, *Collected poems* (London: Vintage, 1992), pp 27–8.   **36** Ibid., pp 28–9.

and derided by vanity; and my eyes burned with anguish and anger.'[37] As explicated in *Stephen hero*, that sudden spiritual transformation from one state to
another is, for Joyce, an *epiphany*. But unlike Yeats's dynamic conversions, Joyce's
epiphanies reveal the character's profound isolation in a given time and place, a
socio-political history that the epiphany realizes rather than transcends and that
confirms the character's unfortunate and unwavering paralysis.

37 James Joyce, *Dubliners* (New York: Penguin, 1993), p. 28.

Index